The Science of Leadership

THE SCIENCE OF LEADERSHIP

Lessons from Research for Organizational Leaders

Julian Barling

OXFORD
UNIVERSITY PRESS

OXFORD
UNIVERSITY PRESS

Oxford University Press is a department of the University of Oxford.
It furthers the University's objective of excellence in research, scholarship,
and education by publishing worldwide.

Oxford   New York
Auckland   Cape Town   Dar es Salaam   Hong Kong   Karachi
Kuala Lumpur   Madrid   Melbourne   Mexico City   Nairobi
New Delhi   Shanghai   Taipei   Toronto

With offices in
Argentina   Austria   Brazil   Chile   Czech Republic   France   Greece
Guatemala   Hungary   Italy   Japan   Poland   Portugal   Singapore
South Korea   Switzerland   Thailand   Turkey   Ukraine   Vietnam

Oxford is a registered trademark of Oxford University Press
in the UK and certain other countries.

Published in the United States of America by
Oxford University Press
198 Madison Avenue, New York, NY 10016

Library of Congress Cataloging-in-Publication Data
Barling, Julian.
The science of leadership : lessons from research for organizational leaders / Julian Barling.
    pages cm
Includes bibliographical references and index.
ISBN 978–0–19–975701–5 (alk. paper)
1. Leadership—Psychological aspects.   I. Title.
HD57.7.B36637 2014
658.4′092—dc23
2013036210

9 8 7 6 5 4 3 2 1
Printed in the United States of America
on acid-free paper

CONTENTS

Preface   *vii*
Acknowledgments   *xiii*

1. Organizational Leadership   *1*
2. Do Leaders Matter?   *31*
3. How Does Leadership Work?   *63*
4. The Typical Leadership Study: How Do We Know What We Know?   *97*
5. Are Leaders Born or Made?   *123*
6. Can Leadership Be Taught? Leadership Interventions in
   Organizations   *147*
7. Leadership in Different Contexts   *175*
8. Gender and Leadership   *203*
9. When Leadership Goes Awry   *237*
10. Enough about Leadership: Let's Talk about Followership!   *269*
11. Leading into the Future   *299*

Index   *313*

PREFACE

If you are reading this, my guess is that you have read other leadership books before this. So why read (or write) yet another leadership book? A brief look at the available leadership books, which fall into different categories, will help to answer this question.

On the one hand, there are innumerable "academic" books. Some of these books are written primarily for university classes. The best examples within this category could be Peter Northouse[1] and Gary Yukl's[2] very successful books, both of which cover all the major theories and controversies, but with a level of detail and written in a way that is unlikely to capture the attention of the general public or practicing managers. A second type of academic book is written by scholars who have been intimately involved in the initial development and subsequent research of a particular theory. The best example of this type is Bernard Bass and Ronald Riggio's *Transformational Leadership*.[3] While surely the most credible book on its topic, its interest to and utility for anything but a very specialized audience are limited. A third type of academic book would be the least useful of all for practicing managers or the general public. This type consists of colossal handbooks such as *The Bass Handbook of Leadership: Theory, Research and Managerial Applications*,[4] which are almost exclusively addressed to the needs of researchers and academic scholars.

On the other hand, there are leadership books written by a broad range of authors—consultants, former CEOs, professional sports coaches, former mayors, astronauts—offering their own ideas on organizational leadership with no credible research to support the central ideas proposed. Major authors identified with books of this nature include Steven Covey[5] and Rudy Giuliani.[6] Included in this genre are "how-to" leadership books, which achieve their popularity by offering linear solutions to complex problems in a way that is interesting to all. The problem is that even the specific lessons offered in acclaimed books developed without the benefits of scientific rigor, for example, Jim Collins' *Good to Great*,[7] do not necessarily hold up to more systematic scrutiny, thus we may end up drawing the wrong lessons from the wrong companies for the wrong reasons.[8] Regardless of whether they have received scientific support or not, the sheer abundance and popularity of books in this second category confirms the insatiable appetite for knowledge about leadership by those whose daily responsibilities require that they enact the best of leadership for the good of their organizations and the people who work in them.

How different, then, are academic and trade books on organizational leadership? So different, that they are most frequently written by different authors, read by different audiences, and sold in different types of stores in different locations (university campus bookstores vs. major booksellers).

So what is missing from this broad landscape? Personal experience gained through two decades of leadership development initiatives has taught me that there is a very large group of leaders in private, public-sector, and not-for-profit organizations who are intent on learning what is known about the best (and worst) of organizational leadership, but who are frustrated by the type of material available to them. Academic books are written using a style that leaves them largely inaccessible except to a small in-group of fellow scholars, researchers, and students. In contrast, while trade books are routinely reader-friendly and often offer compelling personal stories, the ideas that they convey have invariably not been subjected to any kind of scientific scrutiny, and implementing the ideas should come with the warning: Caveat Emptor!

ORGANIZATIONAL LEADERSHIP: TOWARD AN "EVIDENCED-BASED" APPROACH

Most people visiting their family doctor probably assume that everything their doctor does—what tests are conducted, the diagnoses derived, and the treatments prescribed—are based on the best and most current available knowledge. Most people in this situation would also be appalled to discover that this usually is not the case. Indeed, estimates suggest that only 15% of medical decisions attain this basic standard.[9] In response to this situation, David Sackett and his colleagues at McMaster University in Canada developed what they called "evidenced-based medicine," which they define as "the conscientious, explicit, and judicious use of current best evidence in making decisions about the care of individual patients."[10] Since then, there has been a concerted effort to implement evidenced-based medicine. For example, the journal *Evidenced-Based Medicine for Primary Care and Clinical Medicine* was established in 1996, and organizations such as the Cochrane Collaboration[11] (an initiative reaching over 28,000 people in more than 100 different countries) and the Center for Review and Dissemination,[12] both located in the United Kingdom, were created to make available to health care professionals reviews of the most recent and relevant scientific findings.

The field of management has performed no better, with estimates suggesting that human resource managers consciously access research-based knowledge to guide no more than 1% of their everyday workplace decisions.[13] The reasons for this sad state are many.[14] For example, the facts that academic researchers tend to focus on topics (e.g., motivation) that are of less interest to practitioners, that researchers are less interested in some topics (e.g., compensation) that are of considerable importance to practitioners,[15] and that academic research takes place in industry settings (e.g., education, manufacturing) that are of relatively little importance to the overall economy[16] all limit the extent to which practitioners turn to organizational research. The consequences for organizational functioning are potentially disastrous. For example, organizations continue to use forced ranking systems in performance management, base their motivational strategies on incentive systems and compensation,[17] and benchmark against other organizations—despite considerable evidence showing that such techniques are ineffective at best and harmful in more situations than we might care to acknowledge.

What does this mean for the understanding and practice of organizational leadership? Estimates of the extent to which leadership practices within organizations are guided by the best available knowledge do not even exist. But the abundance and popularity of leadership books whose content is in no way influenced by the most current and best available research-based knowledge leaves ample room for concern. Thus, the goal of this book is to bridge the gap between academic and trade books, with a book on organizational leadership that is based on findings from the enormous body of scientifically driven leadership research, but written in a way that is accessible to those who want to use this knowledge to guide their everyday behaviors, and those who hope to be in the position to do so in the future. Paraphrasing Sackett and colleagues' definition of evidenced-based medicine, the goal is that this book will bring evidenced-based leadership, "the conscientious, explicit, and judicious use of current best evidence in making decisions about leadership behaviors in the workplace," one step closer. In doing so, this is not another "how-to" leadership book offering easy and prescriptive linear solutions to complex problems. Instead, the essence of an evidence-based leadership approach is to acknowledge and respect the intelligence, experience, integrity, ingenuity, and flexibility of organizational leaders who are motivated to navigate their way through their daily maze.

While the book adopts an evidenced-based approach, a word of caution is in order here. Our society's obsession with the most recent scientific research should not be allowed to obscure decades-old "classics" containing valuable lessons that remain as relevant today as they were when the studies were conducted. Providing something of a needed balance, throughout the book I will draw attention wherever appropriate to these earlier "gems" in the development of our understanding of leadership.

CONTENTS OF THE BOOK

Two aspects that contribute to this book warrant mention. First, an evidenced-based approach to investigating organizational leadership is dependent on the reliable and valid assessment of different forms of leadership. To learn how researchers accomplish this, questionnaires assessing transformational leadership, ethical leadership, and abusive supervision are presented in full in the book. To gain more of a personal appreciation of these questionnaires, you will be invited (at the end of Chapter 4) to go online and complete these three questionnaires yourself with respect to your own leaders. This will show you personally how leadership is measured.

The second aspect is that organizational leadership has intrigued scholars from very different disciplines, resulting in separate literatures with anthropological, economic, sociological, psychological, historical, and political foundations. Instead of trying to afford equal coverage to each of these literatures in this book, which would either result in an inadequate coverage of each area or a book so large that it would be too daunting to read, the primary basis for this book is high-quality, psychological and behavioral research on organizational leadership.

STRUCTURE OF THE BOOK

Guided by an evidenced-based approach and paying primary attention to psychological and behavioral research, the goal of this book is to inform practicing, curious leaders of what is currently known about the nature, antecedents, and consequences of organizational leadership, and how this knowledge might apply to their everyday leadership behaviors. To accomplish this, the first three chapters discuss modern leadership theories (Chapter 1), whether leadership matters (Chapter 2), and how leadership works (Chapter 3). Given that an evidenced-based approach means that most of the material on whether leadership matters and how it works is based on research using techniques and methods that might not be familiar, Chapter 4 describes the basics of how leadership research is conducted. This is important, as understanding how we know what we know makes it more likely that we will accept the lessons from research.

The next two chapters focus on how leadership is learned, which first includes a consideration of the ever-controversial question of whether leadership is "born or made" (Chapter 5), and then whether formal organizational interventions to enhance leadership are effective (Chapter 6).

Reflecting on the research conducted to this point, much of what is known about organizational leadership derives from traditional, profit-oriented organizations. Issues raised and lessons to be learned from leadership in different organizational contexts (e.g., labor unions, military, the political sphere, schools, and sports) are discussed in Chapter 7. Gender and leadership remains a major organizational and social issue and is considered in Chapter 8. Unfortunately, as anyone who has spent any time in organizations will confirm, leadership is not always of the highest quality, and the nature and consequences of destructive and poor leadership are dealt with in Chapter 9.

No book on organizational leadership could be complete without a focus on the people being led; the role of followers in the leadership process is the topic of Chapter 10. The final chapter then looks to the future and raises issues that transcend specific topics dealt with throughout the book and that will be of much importance to the practice of leadership in the future. The book ends with some thoughts on what all of the material presented here means for everyday leadership behaviors.

NOTES

1. Northouse, P. G. (2013). *Leadership: Theory and practice* (6th ed). Thousand Oaks, CA: SAGE Publications.
2. Yukl, G. (2009). *Leadership in organizations* (7th ed). New York: Prentice Hall.
3. Bass, B. M., & Riggio, R. (2007). *Transformational leadership* (2nd ed). Mahwah, NJ: Lawrence Erlbaum.
4. Bass, B. M. (2008). *The Bass handbook of leadership: Theory, research and managerial applications*. New York: Free Press.
5. Covey, S. R. (1991) *Principle-centered leadership*. New York: Fireside.
6. Giuliano, R. W. (2005). *Leadership*. New York: Little, Brown.
7. Collins, J. (2001). *Good to great*. New York: Harper Collins.
8. Niendorf, B., & Beck, K. (2008). *Good to great, or just good? Academy of Management Perspectives, 22*(4), 13–20.
9. Pfeffer, J., & Sutton, R. I. (2006). Evidence-based management. *Harvard Business Review*, January, 62–73.
10. Sackett, D. L., Rosenberg, W. M. C., Gray, J. A. M., Haynes, R. B., & Richardson, W. C. (1996). Evidence-based medicine: What it is and what it isn't. *British Medical Journal, 312*, 71–72.
11. The Cochrane Collaboration. (n.d.) Working together to provide the best evidence for health care. Retrieved from http://www.cochrane.org/
12. Centers for Review and Dissemination. The University of York. http://www.york.ac.uk/inst/crd/
13. Rousseau, D. M. (2006). Is there such a thing as "evidenced-based management"? *Academy of Management Journal, 31*, 256–269.
14. Pfeffer, J., & Sutton, R. I. (2006). *Hard facts, dangerous half-truths and total nonsense: Profiting from evidenced-based management*. Boston, MA: Harvard Business School Press; Pfeffer, J., & Sutton, R. I. (2006). Evidence-based management. *Harvard Business Review*, January, 62–73.
15. Deadrick, D. L., & Gibson, P. A. (2007). An examination of the research–practice gap in HR: Comparing topics of interest to HR academic and HR professionals. *Human Resource Management Review, 17*, 131–139.

16. O'Leary, M. B., & Almond, B. A. (2009). The industry settings of leading organizational research: The role of economic and non-economic factors. *Journal of Organizational Behavior, 30,* 497–524.
17. Pfeffer, J. (1998). Six dangerous myths about pay. *Harvard Business Review,* May-June, 109–119.

ACKNOWLEDGMENTS

Writing a book like this yields many wonderful lessons for the writer. For one thing, I know more about organizational leadership now than I did when I started on this project several years ago. But that is by no means the only lesson learned. Writing this book has also served as a vivid reminder to me of what psychological research in the workplace has shown for more than three decades, namely that the support we receive from those around us—our supervisors, coworkers and peers, and our friends and family—enables us to accomplish more than we could ever do alone. One unrecognized benefit of writing a book of this nature is the opportunity to openly express my gratitude to those who deserve it.

A long, long time ago, I was heading down a path that was leading me anywhere but to where I am today, and I was privileged to have had three teachers who helped to turn me around and made their mark on my life. "Hughie" Wilson, my high school Latin teacher, was the first to show me what fun learning could be, how much there was to be learned, and how the effort required to do so was all worthwhile. Alma Hannon mentored me throughout my unforgettable years as a student and then faculty member (1971–1984) in the Department of Psychology at the University of the Witwatersrand (WITS) in Johannesburg. Alma showed us all that challenging conformity—whether intellectually or behaviorally—made for better people and a better society. Alma modeled so much for me by encouraging and allowing me to go beyond her own ideological boundaries. Jack ("Prof") Mann, the long-time head of the Department of Psychology at WITS, supervised my doctoral thesis and taught me the importance of thinking, speaking, and writing clearly and logically, and the need to continually expose all our ideas to alternative, rival hypotheses.

I am also blessed by having worked with people I am proud to call my colleagues and friends, all of whom have expanded my horizons in so many ways.[i]

---

i. The Gallup Organization in the United States conducted a multiyear research project aimed at identifying the elements of a great workplace. One of the 12 elements making up a great workplace is expressed in the statement "I have a best friend at work." How lucky I am to have had more than one!

For more than 30 years, Dan O'Leary has been a wonderful friend, and despite our being in different disciplines in psychology, or perhaps because of it, Dan has been a terrific source of fun and an amazing sounding board on issues both personal and professional. Kevin Kelloway has been around in different ways since the 1980s, first as a graduate student and then as a close friend and colleague. Together we have delved into more topics either of us could have imagined working on alone.

I was also fortunate to meet some very special people in the 1990s. Aside from the wonderful times Nick Turner and I had sitting around and sharing stories and research ideas (and drinking more than our fair share of coffee), Nick showed his friendship by volunteering to read the entire manuscript for this book, and then as usual, provided incredibly insightful comments. I first met Kate Dupré when she asked if I would supervise her Honours thesis almost 20 years ago, and our friendship and collaborative research has blossomed since then. I met Peter Bamberger and Mike Frone in the same fortuitous way: We were all independently engaged in similar research, and since then, still look for excuses to get together to share more discussions (whether about research, family, or whatever). Starting in the late 1990s, I spent 14 years as Chair of the Doctoral and Masters program in the Queen's School of Business. During that entire period, I was fortunate to work with Annette Lilly, who conspired to make work fun, interesting, and worthwhile. Last, I have had the privilege of working with Amy Christie for over a decade. Amy has that uncanny ability to leave you feeling better about yourself and knowing more than you did before you started the meeting.

Rick Iverson was both a close friend and colleague for almost to 20 years. Rick passed away much too soon in 2012, when he had his whole life ahead of him.

Not yet acknowledged is that I am so fortunate to be able to work with the most remarkable group of graduate students who enrich every moment of my working life.[ii] My current students, Amy Bergenwall, Alyson Byrne, Erica Carleton, Angela Dionisi, Jennifer Robertson, Kelsey Tulloch, Melissa Trivisonno, and Julie Weatherhead, indulgently watched me hide from them when writing this book, made comments on the drafts of chapters when I asked them to, and taught me what "leading up" really means. Former students Kara Arnold, Mark Beauchamp, Stacie Byrne, Jennifer Carson, Julie Comtois, Heather Dezan, Cecelia Elving, Sandy Hershcovis, Kristy Holmes, Colette Hoption, Michelle Innes, Rebecca Lys, Morrie Mendelson, Erin Reid, Niro Sivanathan, and Anthea Zacharatos also worked with me on topics relating to leadership and have gone on to wonderful careers and families of their

---

ii. Psychological researchers really ought to extend their focus to the support we receive from our "subordinates"; until they do so, the full story of how we manage to navigate our work lives and achieve our successes will always be incomplete!

own. I just hope that you all know how much your input, support, and questions have meant to me and have helped in my own involvement in leadership research and leadership development.

Without a doubt, this book would not have been started or completed without the support, advice, and understanding of Abby Gross at Oxford University Press. Abby was encouraging when I first pitched the idea of this book to her. When the inevitable obstacles emerged in writing this book, Abby showed more patience than I deserved, a perspective from which I learned so much, and a persistence that helped the book finally come to fruition. Suzanne Walker stepped in whenever necessary, removing whatever obstacle or burden stood in the way.

The fact that I have been able to spend the last two decades directly engaged in leadership research would not have been possible without the financial support from the Social Sciences and Humanities Research Council of Canada, Queen's School of Business, and, most recently, the Borden Chair in Leadership.[iii]

Through the Queen's School of Business' Executive Development Program and the Executive MBA Programs, I have had opportunities to be engaged in innumerable leadership development initiatives and learn from wonderful leaders who have shaped my ideas and research.

Many other people with whom I have worked have helped me in ways that they may not even know, including Catherine Bell, Glen Cavanagh, Olga Epitropaki, Milena Guberinic, Jane Helleur, Gail Hepburn, Peter Jensen, Ilona Kryl, Manon LeBlanc, Catherine Loughlin, Amy Marshall, Katie Morton, Mike O'Leary, Lisa Rodrigues, Judith Russell, Sheldene Simola, Frank Slater, Sean Tucker, Teresa Touchette, Rudy Trimpop, Tom Weber, Jeff Wylie, and Alysha Williams.

The wonderful young staff at Coffee and Co. in downtown Kingston provided the perfect place in which I could hide away and think and write.

As much as I have appreciated all these wonderful people, I have been privileged to learn from some other wonderful teachers. My wife Janice and children Seth, Monique, and Steven have all gone beyond any call of familial duty by commenting on draft chapters and collecting data for this book, and listening to my stories. Much more than that, however, they continue to teach me that there is a lot more to life than work. Each one of them, in their professional roles as teachers and as community volunteers, inspire me in the quiet way in which they spend their days dedicated to the well-being and advancement of others. Thank you!

---

iii. Another of the 12 Gallup elements for a great workplace: "I have the materials and equipment I need to do my work right."

CHAPTER 1

Organizational Leadership

What is leadership? At first glance, it might seem as if the answer to this question should be easy. After all, ideas about the nature of leadership have been around since time immemorial. They permeated the narratives of the great religions (Christianity, Islam, Judaism) and captivated classical Greek and Roman philosophers (e.g., Caesar, Cicero, Plato, and Plutarch), who in turn influenced Renaissance thinkers such as Machiavelli.[1] Today, there is no shortage of books describing and explaining modern organizational leadership. To appreciate this, searching for the term "leadership theory" on amazon.com resulted in 1,438 suggested books![2] Despite this, or perhaps even because of this, we have almost as many definitions of organizational leadership as people who have written on the topic.[3] A simple, clear-cut definition evades us for several reasons.

One reason for this this is that most writers and researchers are passionately attached to their own views and definitions of leadership; as a result, inconsistency abounds across definitions. Add to this the fact that beliefs about the nature of leadership change over time: Joseph Rost observed that control and centralization of power dominated definitions of leadership in the first 30 years of the 20th century, then traits and personality emerged in the 1930s and the group approach in the 1940s.[4] The 1950s saw leadership definitions emphasizing groups, relationships, and leadership behaviors, with the literature in the 1960s emphasizing the importance of working toward common goals. Complexity was a hallmark of leadership definitions in the 1970s, exemplified by eminent leadership scholar, James McGregor Burns, who defined leadership as "the reciprocal process of mobilizing by persons with certain motives and values, various economic, political and other resources, in a context of competition and conflict, in order to realize goals independently or mutually held by both leaders and followers" (1978, p. 436).[5] Recognition of the complexity of leadership accelerated in the 1980s, and instead of a simple, unambiguous and consensual definition, what we now have is what Peter Northouse called a "stew" of definitions.[6]

How then can we best answer the question "what is leadership"? Several strategies can guide us to an answer. Starting with an evidenced-based management approach will be more than useful: If we limit our focus only to those leadership theories that have attracted some scientific scrutiny and support, the immense literature is narrowed considerably—and informed ideas become possible.

Leadership then needs to be differentiated from management, and there are several approaches that do so. The first approach focuses on the nature of the person in differentiating leadership from management. "Managers are people who do things right, and leaders are people who do the right thing" (Bennis & Nanus, 1985, p. 21)[7] is a familiar refrain, and might suggest that managers and leaders are very different types of people, with different goals, personalities, values, and beliefs. Adding to this, John Kotter observes that "some people have the capacity to become excellent managers but not strong leaders. Others have great leadership potential but…have great difficulty becoming strong managers" (p. 52).[8] The second approach to differentiating management from leadership suggests that they involve different behaviors, that both management and leadership are critical for organizational success, but that they can be performed by the same individual. As Kotter concluded, "Once companies understand the fundamental difference between leadership and management, they can begin to groom their people to provide both" (p. 52).

A third approach to distinguishing between management and leadership *behaviors* is to emphasize how each is dependent on a different form of power. The ability to manage derives from the formal power given by the organization and is inherent in the position held. In contrast, while organizations might give someone the role or title of "leader," the ability to lead derives from the informal power that people acquire based on the quality of the relationships they develop. The discussion in this book focuses primarily on leadership behaviors.[i]

Fourth, understanding "leadership" will be helped by recognizing that there are three distinct features about leadership that have been considered and studied separately. The first feature highlights who becomes a leader in the first instance and is most frequently referred to as leadership role "emergence" or "occupancy." Research on this topic identifies the multitude of factors (e.g., early family socialization, gender, genetics) that interact so that some people are more (or less) likely to attain leadership positions than others, whether through formal organizational channels (e.g., selection, promotion), or informal channels. (Much of this will be discussed in Chapter 5.)

---

i. As will become clear later in this chapter, management and leadership behaviors are not independent; and one theory, namely that of transformational leadership, explicitly recognizes the role of both management and leadership behaviors. This will be discussed in detail.

While intriguing and important, an understanding of leader role occupancy tells us only who was imposed upon the group by the organization; it tells us nothing about how leaders behave once attaining their position. Thus, the second topic focuses on different leadership styles and behaviors. Variations of high- and poor-quality leadership behaviors have been investigated in thousands of scientific studies. Given major organizational scandals, there is also a burgeoning interest in what constitutes and leads to ethical and unethical leadership. Many of these behaviors will be considered throughout this book.

The third feature, which is often of most interest to organizational practitioners and applied researchers, centers on leadership effectiveness or success. The effects of leadership can be widespread and manifested in the behavior of employees (e.g., organizational loyalty, health, job quality), teams (e.g., cohesion), and organizational effectiveness (e.g., financial performance). Isolating these effects is sometimes complicated by the fact that they are often indirect and delayed. All of these effects will be discussed fully in the next two chapters.

The discussion so far has appropriately dealt with different aspects of leadership. But the focus of this chapter, and of this book, is on "organizational" leadership. The focus on organizational leadership does not mean that the type or style of leadership practiced successfully in work organizations would necessarily be inappropriate in other contexts. Instead, in the extent to which there are similarities across contexts, we should expect that the same leadership principles would apply. In Chapter 7, we will consider leadership in different contexts (i.e., labor unions, military, political context, schools, sports teams and organizations), and see how knowledge about leadership transfers across contexts and why it sometimes might not. In any event, any focus on organizational leadership is justified given the role of organizations in the economic well-being of our societies and the personal well being of their members, and the part that leadership plays in this.

The major part of this first chapter focuses on modern leadership theories. Because leadership theories are ultimately nothing more than different explanations and predictions about a set of behaviors, we end the chapter with some thoughts about moving from theory back to everyday behavior, with specific reference to transformational leadership.

ORGANIZATIONAL LEADERSHIP THEORIES

Paraphrasing the opening words from Andy Williams' song that was immortalized in the 1970 Academy Award–nominated movie "Love Story,"[9] where do we begin to tell the story of modern organizational leadership? We could begin with World War II, when theories of leadership emphasized the importance of traits such as height, physical appearance, and socioeconomic status. Or we could move forward to the 1950s, when research from Ohio State

University identified two separate leadership behaviors, which were referred to as "initiating and consideration structure."[ii] Or we could turn to the 1960s, when situational and "contingency" theories tried to specify the conditions under which different leadership behaviors might be more or less effective.[10]

Ever mindful that the purpose of this book is to tell the story of what we know about organizational leadership, based on available and credible research findings, and that this is not a history book, our point of departure will be with the "new-genre" leadership theories that began to make their appearance circa 1980.[11] Acknowledging the arbitrary nature of this decision, several important factors underscore the choice of 1980 as a cutoff point. First, theories about leadership prior to 1980 were largely transactional and emphasized the importance of goals, performance feedback, and employees' behaviors (both positive and negative) being followed by appropriate consequences.[12] Transactions between managers and employees were based on the formal power granted to managers by the organization. In contrast, new-genre leadership theories emphasize the relational, inspirational, and ethical nature of leadership,[13] in contrast to the hierarchical, transactional, and outcome-oriented nature of management. Second, while early theories initially attracted considerable research attention, they no longer do so; new-genre theories are now the overwhelming focus of research attention, as will be seen shortly.

Given the abundance of new-genre organizational leadership theories, where should we begin this specific discussion? Fortunately, there are data that tell us about the frequency with which the different theories receive scientific study. Timothy Judge and Joyce Bono's earlier analysis showed that together, transformational and charismatic leadership theories were studied more frequently between 1990 and 2000 than all other leadership theories combined.[14] I updated and extended this analysis to all leadership theories between 1970 and 2012[iii] to gain a more recent and in-depth appreciation of the relative frequency with which transformational leadership has been investigated and, where possible, separated transformational and charismatic leadership. The results of this analysis appear in Figure 1.1, from which it is clear that transformational leadership is now the most frequently researched leadership theory. Moreover, while research on several other theories is declining (e.g., initiation-consideration), the amount of research on transformational leadership is increasing, with well over 100 published studies in 2012 alone. Thus, the story of new-genre leadership theories appropriately begins with transformational leadership theory.

ii. Initiating structure behaviors are task-oriented, and consideration structure behaviors involve concern for employees' well-being.

iii. Only articles written in English that were peer-reviewed and published (thereby excluding theses and dissertations) are included.

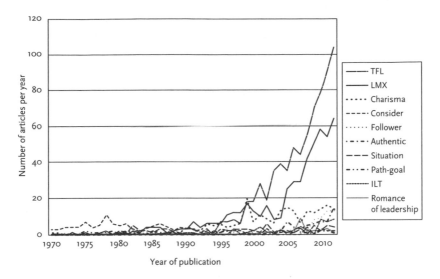

Figure 1.1
Leadership theories in research, 1970–2012. TFL, transformational leadership; LMX, leader–member exchange; ILT, implicit leadership theory.

Transformational Leadership

It is often difficult to pinpoint the precise intellectual origins of an idea or theory, but in the case of transformational leadership, the profound influence of two individuals who have had a major impact on our understanding of leadership, namely James McGregor Burns and Bernie Bass, makes this task a lot easier. Both Burns and Bass had been involved in leadership research for decades before exerting their seminal influence on the development and emergence of transformational leadership theory. They come from different intellectual traditions. McGregor Burns is a political scientist and historian, who attended the London School of Economics and received his doctoral degree from Harvard University. His 1970 study of America's 32nd president, entitled *Roosevelt: Soldier of Freedom, 1940–1945*,[15] was awarded both the Pulitzer Prize (for History) and the National Book Award in History and Biography. Burns published other books analyzing the leadership behaviors of various U.S. presidents, including the three Roosevelts,[16] all the presidents from John F. Kennedy through to George W. Bush,[17] and, most recently, Bill Clinton.[18] Burns formally differentiated between transformational and transactional leadership in his 1978 publication *Leadership*.[19]

Bernie Bass's overall contributions to our understanding of leadership are equally extensive. Bass embarked on his study of leadership in the 1940s and was credited early on with the development of the "leaderless group test." He was the author of an unbelievable 400 scientific articles.[20]

His seminal contributions to transformational leadership were crystallized in his 1985 book, *Leadership and Performance Beyond Expectations*,[21] and continued in subsequent books (e.g., *Transformational Leadership: Industrial, Military and Educational Impact*[22]) and the weighty 1,516-page *Bass Handbook of Leadership: Theory, Research and Managerial Applications*[iv] which was published after he died in 2007.[23] His books have been translated into French, German, Spanish, Portuguese, Italian, and Japanese. Together with Bruce Avolio, Bass also developed the Multifactor Leadership Questionnaire—the most widely used scale to measure transformational and transactional leadership.[24] Unquestionably, one of Bernie Bass' major contributions was to inspire generations of scholars to study and apply leadership in general, and transformational leadership in particular, within organizations and other workplace contexts (e.g., schools, the military).

The Four I's of Transformational Leadership

So what is transformational leadership? There is widespread agreement that transformational leadership comprises four separate and different behaviors: idealized influence, inspirational motivation, intellectual stimulation, and individualized consideration, each of which are described extensively in the research-based literature.[25]

Idealized influence reflects the ethical component of transformational leadership. Leaders who act in a manner consistent with idealized influence behave in ways that are good for organizations and their members and avoid acting solely on self-interest. These leaders may also go beyond what is good for the specific organization, prioritizing what is good for the physical environment[26] —in other words, these leaders are motivated by a moral commitment to the collective good, rather than what is good for themselves. Leaders who behave in this way opt to do what is right, rather than what is easy or expedient, and resist temptations to maximize their own or their organizations' short-term interests. These leaders would often be described by their followers as role models who act with integrity and humility and show a deep respect for others. The ethical nature of idealized influence can be appreciated further from Burns,[27] who differentiated between idealized influence and Maslow's[28] well-known notion of self-actualization: While Maslow regarded self-actualization as the pinnacle of psychological health and human motivation, Burns found its self-focused nature simply too inconsistent with the other-focused nature of idealized influence.

---

iv. Can too much knowledge ever be harmful? Presumably not, but carrying this handbook, weighing 5.35 lbs (or 2.43 kg), might be!

Paraphrasing the title of Bass' 1985 book, *inspirational motivation* involves leadership behaviors that help employees perform "beyond expectations"[29] — both beyond the expectations that employees hold for themselves and those that others hold for them. These leaders' vision of what needs to be accomplished forms the cornerstone of their behaviors, which they convey to their followers by telling stories and using symbols and metaphors in their conversations with their followers. They inspire by setting high but realistic goals for their followers. By doing so, they show that they believe in their followers' abilities and trust in their integrity, essentially setting up the conditions for a self-fulfilling prophesy.[30] Through all this, inspirationally motivating leaders nurture a deep sense of self-efficacy and resilience in their followers, helping them to believe in themselves so that they will first confront the internal psychological hurdles and external barriers that inhibit high levels of performance, and then persist in their efforts.

Trait theories initially assumed that leaders' intelligence was critical to their success, and intelligence has indeed been shown to be associated with leadership emergence[31] and transformational leadership behaviors.[32] Intelligence is also associated with leadership effectiveness: Dean Keith Simonton's analyses showed that intelligence scores were associated with external reputation of 342 European monarchs,[33] as well as with the presidential performance of all 42 U.S. presidents, from George Washington through George Bush.[34] Despite these findings, transformational leadership takes a different perspective: The goal of *intellectual stimulation* is not to make *leaders* more intelligent—instead, intellectually stimulating leaders elevate their followers by allowing and encouraging them to think for themselves, all the time challenging their followers to question long-held assumptions, whether about their own self-limiting expectations or the way in which work is conducted. Doing so conveys trust, and is consistent with a perspective that encourages and values employees' development and participation. Crucially, there is a long-term component to intellectual stimulation, which is epitomized in a popular 1976 quote attributed to Ralph Nader, who said, "I always thought that the function of leadership was to produce more leaders, not more followers." Because intellectual stimulation ensures that employees learn to think about their work, leaders who engage in intellectual stimulation implicitly prepare the next generation of organizational leaders.

The final component of transformational leadership is *individualized consideration*, through which leaders provide emotional and instrumental support to their employees, thereby fostering personal and work-related development. However brief and in whatever form (e.g., face-to-face, e-mail, videoconferencing), these interactions are characterized by active listening, caring, and focus on the other person. While the behaviors included within individualized consideration are by no means unique to transformational leadership, they define the quality of the leader–follower relationship and influence how followers will respond to the leaders' idealized influence, inspirational moti-vation, and intellectual stimulation. Individualized consideration makes the personal and organizational development of employees a leadership prior-ity. As a result, leaders who display individualized consideration would most likely be perceived by their followers as development-oriented, empathic, and compassionate.

A hallmark of all transformational leadership behaviors is their future-orientation (unlike the present or short-term orientation that chara-acterizes management). Whether it is through the long-term development of employees that might be accomplished through intellectual stimula-tion or individualized consideration, the explicit move away from immedi-ate self-gratification that characterizes idealized influence, or inclusion of employees in a long-term vision, transformational leadership emphasizes what is best in the long term, as will be seen later in this chapter in the behav-iors of President Franklin D. Roosevelt and New York Mayor Rudy Giuliani.

Transactional Leadership

One of Burns' and Bass' significant contributions was to recognize that lead-ers do more than just enact any or all of the four transformational behav-iors. Instead, leaders also engage in crucial transactions with their followers. Accordingly, transformational leadership was separated from "transactional leadership," which includes three different behaviors. *Contingent reward* involves behaviors considered essential within the management literature—for example, setting appropriate goals for employees and teams, providing performance-based feedback, and ensuring that behaviors in the organiza-tions have consequences. As the name implies, rewards (and punishments, if necessary) would be *contingent* on the appropriate levels of performance.

In contrast, a second form of transactional leadership, *management-by-excep-tion*, is negative, with leaders concentrating mostly on employees' mistakes, failures to meet minimal standards, and omissions. Management-by-exception can be either active or passive. Within active management-by-exception, leaders carefully monitor for performance lapses, and their responses to these lapses are immediate and often experienced as public and loud, embarrassing and intimidating by their followers. Active management-by-exception can often be experienced by employees as abusive.[35] Passive management-by-exception also describes behaviors that focus on employees' mistakes, errors, and omissions, but passive leaders wait for these lapses to occur and only intervene when the problems become too serious to ignore.

The final component of transactional leadership is *laissez-faire behavior*, a set of behaviors that would be evident when the leader equivocates and fails to provide needed direction, abdicates and denies responsibility, and avoids intervening even in serious situations. Leaders who could be characterized as laissez-faire would be seen by their employees as disengaged and psychologically absent. Later conceptualizations of transformational leadership explicitly include both the transactional and transformational components in a "full-range" leadership model and situate them on a continuum from the least to the most active leadership behaviors.[36]

Differentiating between transformational and transactional leadership is both theoretically and practically important. Transformational leaders' ability to influence employees and the trust that employees place in these leaders are rooted in their informal power in the organization, which is dependent on the quality of the relationships that they develop with their followers. In sharp contrast, while some of the behaviors included within transactional leadership are associated with more positive employee attitudes and higher levels of employee performance, transactional leadership differs from transformational leadership in the most fundamental way. Despite its name, the behaviors included within transactional "leadership" do not truly reflect leadership, because they are dependent on leaders' formal hierarchical positions and the power derived from their formal positions. As such, "transactional leadership" might best be viewed as an oxymoron: While many of these behaviors are necessary (e.g., contingent reward), they derive from one's formal position and reflect good management, not leadership.

One last question is how transformational and transactional leadership go together. To answer this, Bass originally proposed what he called the "augmentation hypothesis" to explain their relative roles and importance,[37] according to which transformational leadership "augments" or adds to any effects generated by transactional leadership. Stated somewhat differently, the effects of transformational leadership would go beyond those of transactional leadership. Consistent support has been yielded for this idea: As but one example,[38] Scott MacKenzie, Phillip Podsakoff, and Gregory Rich showed that the effect of transformational leadership was more than three times that of transactional leadership on (a) critical employee attitudes (e.g., trust in the manager, willing to engage in voluntary activities to benefit the organization) and, perhaps more important, (b) an index of objective sales performance. Clearly, unlike other leadership theories, management behaviors (or transactional leadership) are given a specific role within transformational leadership.

Charismatic Leadership

Perhaps the theory or approach closest to transformational leadership is charismatic leadership; indeed, so close are these two theories that differentiating between them can be difficult. The modern incarnations of both transformational and charismatic leadership emerged in the 1970s, and the titles of both theories ("transformational," "charismatic") are vastly overused. On occasion the two terms are even used interchangeably; there is even reference in the literature to charismatic/transformational leadership,[39] which dilutes their meaning. Nonetheless, there are small but meaningful differences between transformational and charismatic leadership.

Current approaches to charismatic leadership have their roots in the work of the famous German sociologist Max Weber. Writing initially in German in the 1920s, Weber's ideas on charismatic leadership were translated into English in 1947 by fellow sociologist Talcott Parsons.[40] Weber was initially interested in authority within organizations and suggested that charismatic authority was one of three forms of organizational authority (the other two being traditional and rational-legal authority). Given widespread belief that charismatic leaders possess extraordinary abilities or characteristics, charismatic leadership attracted widespread public and media interest, and it is still used extensively to explain the behaviors of political, religious, and cult leaders.

There are two major interpretations of charismatic leadership. Robert House's approach locates charismatic leadership in the behavior and personality of the individual leader.[41] House and colleague Jane Howell go further, identifying a series of behaviors that characterize charismatic behaviors:[42] Charismatic leaders articulate and communicate a collective, moral, optimistic, and ideological vision for the future. They merge their values and their behaviors, emphasize distal rather than proximal goals, continually reinforce their confidence in their employees' ability to meet and exceed performance expectations, and behave in ways necessary to stimulate and fulfill employees' needs and motivations. All of these traits have been shown to positively influence employees' attitudes and performance.

House and Howell also confront an issue that has bedevilled charismatic leadership researchers. Despite the positive tone and nature of their description, charismatic leadership can be used for good or evil. Instead of joining the debate as to whether charismatic leadership is inherently good *or* evil, they differentiate between two forms of charismatic leadership, namely socialized and personalized charismatic leadership. Socialized charismatic leaders are (a) democratic, (b) serve collective rather than self-interests, and (c) develop and empower others. In contrast, personalized charismatic leaders are (a) autocratic, (b) seek to maximize their own self-interest, and (c) exploit and control others.[43] Findings from research support the differentiation between socialized and personalized charismatic leadership. In a persuasive study, Jennifer O'Connor and her coauthors first put together lists of famous business, political, religious, and military leaders, differentiated them as socialized or personalized charismatic leaders, and had external raters confirm this differentiation.[44] The researchers then showed that socialized charismatic leaders were rated as significantly more likely to benefit other individuals and the broader social system, and to behave morally. Conversely, personalized charismatic leaders were more likely to cause harm to individuals and the social system, and to act aggressively.

A second modern interpretation of charismatic leadership relies less on the behaviors or personality of the leader and more on attributions that followers make about leaders and their behaviors,[45] an approach that is most closely aligned with the idea that leadership is all "in the eye of the holder." Leader behaviors are not unimportant within this perspective. Instead, what is most important is that leaders' behaviors come to be viewed or perceived as charismatic by their followers. The next step in this process is that the charisma is believed to be a part of the leader's inner dispositions.

Jay Conger and Rabindra Kanungo[46] suggested that there are three behavioral stages in this attributional model of charisma. In their view, the leader first actively scrutinizes the organization for potential or actual weaknesses, which provides ideas that can serve as the basis for the process of radical change. This sets up the second stage, in which the leader offers a vision that is dramatically different from current organizational reality, leaving themselves worthy of followers' respect, appropriate targets for identification, and role models for others. Last, through their unusual skills, risk-taking, total dedication, and willingness to lead by example, leaders develop followers' commitment to the distal goals and show how these goals can be achieved. Despite the specificity given to this attributional process, perhaps all leadership theories recognize that followers make attributions about leaders from their behaviors.

A critical point of departure differentiating both perspectives of charismatic leadership from transformational leadership is their exclusion of the transformational components of intellectual stimulation and individualized consideration from charismatic leadership. This is important, as some research has shown unique effects for intellectual stimulation (but not charismatic leadership) on enhanced return on equity and sales growth under conditions of high uncertainty.[47]

This difference notwithstanding, there is increasing agreement that the similarities between charismatic and transformational leadership may outweigh any differences, with calls for more research to understand the nature of any similarities and differences, and whether transformational and charismatic leadership have different organizational outcomes.[48] Moreover, despite the theoretical differences between the two models of charismatic leadership, the question of whether charismatic leadership is behaviorally or attributionally based is now seen as less important.[49] At the same time, interest in the distinction between socialized and personalized charismatic leadership, which reinforces the notion that charismatic leadership by itself is neither inherently good nor evil and explains the "bright" and "dark" sides of charisma, continues to attract interest.[50]

The most recently developed of the new-genre leadership theories, authentic leadership, grew out of a sense of frustration with what were seen as deficit-oriented leadership models, in which the goal was to get rid of leaders' deficits. Authentic leadership has its roots in transformational leadership (which needs no further discussion) and in the broad but related fields of positive psychology, positive organizational behavior, and positive psychological capital.[51] The positive-psychology approach itself developed out of a frustration over the dominant negative emphasis on mental illness that characterized much of psychology throughout the 20th century, and aimed to move toward a "psychology of positive human functioning...which achieves a scientific understanding and effective interventions to build thriving individuals, families, and communities."[52]

The first component in authentic leadership is leaders' *self-awareness*. Self-awareness on its own is widely believed to be important to positive leadership, but authentic leadership theory takes this further, with leaders' self-awareness being only one part of a more complex theory. Authentic leaders would be aware of strengths and weaknesses in their personalities and behaviors, as well as of the conflicts and contradictions between their strengths and weaknesses. What takes this understanding of self-awareness further, however, is that it is not sufficient for the leader to "know thyself." Instead, as Douglas May and his colleagues note, authentic leaders would go the next step and be "true to themselves,"[53] for example, by doing what they can to resolve inner conflicts and contradictions.

At one level, *unbiased processing* of external information, the second component of authentic leadership, is a core managerial challenge. However, authentic leadership goes well beyond merely processing external information and focuses on the balanced and unbiased processing of all information that is relevant to people's own selves. Even when the available information is internally disquieting or disturbing, authentic leaders would confront the information in an unbiased manner before any decisions are made. As such, unbiased or balanced processing of information—including information about oneself—is held to be at the core of personal integrity.

All new-genre theories make assumptions about the nature and/or quality of the relationship between leaders and followers. Authentic leadership is no exception, and the third component within authentic leadership theory is *relational transparency*. Authentic leaders openly share self-relevant information about their virtues and their vulnerabilities—their proudest accomplishments and their deepest doubts, and their insecurities and fears. They are motivated to ensure that others know their own authentic selves. Only through relational transparency can trust be developed between leader and follower, ultimately forming the basis for fulfilling, trusting, meaningful, and productive relationships with others in which leaders can exert an influence.

The fourth component of authentic leadership is a highly developed, *internalized moral perspective*, reinforcing the place of authentic leadership as a new-genre leadership theory. Authentic leaders resolve moral issues and dilemmas by referencing their own internal moral standards rather than by being bound by external standards, regulations, or rules. In this respect, authentic leaders have reached what some moral and developmental theorists would see as the highest stages of moral reasoning.[54] This developmental progression is central within authentic leadership theory.

Several aspects about "authentic" leadership warrant attention.[55] First, what is the evidence for the four components? In samples of high-tech manufacturing workers in the United States, university employees in the United States, part-time students who were concurrently employed on a full-time basis in the United States, and employees within a large, state-owned organization in China, Fred Walumbwa and his co-researchers found consistent support for the existence of the four components, and for the notion that they can be aggregated into a single measure of authentic leadership.[56] Second, there is no suggestion that the four components of authentic leadership (leaders' self-awareness, balanced or unbiased processing, relational transparency, an internalized moral perspective) are independent of each other,[57] nor does the initial research suggest that they are. Third, the "authentic self" is defined not in terms of interactions with others but in how people see and define themselves and the extent to which their behavior is consistent with their self-perceptions. Last, leaders are not simply "authentic" or "inauthentic"; instead, they vary in the extent to which they are authentic or not.

Acknowledging that authentic leadership remains one of the more recent leadership theories, as is evident from Figure 1.1, several conclusions are in order. First, as Timothy Judge and his colleagues suggest,[58] the challenge for researchers is now to show how authentic leadership *differs* from other similar theories, perhaps especially transformational leadership. The need to do so is evident from titles of scholarly articles in which there is complete overlap between these theories, such as "authentic transformational leadership";[59] even prominent theorists in authentic and transformational leadership are prone to using such terms.[60] Second, greater appreciation of the value of authentic leadership would derive from research that directly contrasts the effects of authentic leadership with other similar approaches and theories. Third, confidence in the effectiveness of authentic leadership would be enhanced significantly if findings were derived from teams of independent researchers working independently of each other.

Leader–Member Exchange (LMX) Theory

LMX theory represents a significant departure from other new-genre leadership theories. While transformational (and authentic) leadership focus primarily on the behavior of the leader, LMX emphasizes the quality of the leader–member relationship. Moreover, unlike other new-genre theories that at least implicitly assume that there is a consistency in how leaders interact with each of their followers, LMX theory holds that relationships within each leader–member dyad are unique, and that any approach that aggregates how a group feels about their leader ignores this uniqueness. Some early support emerged for this notion: George Graen and his colleagues showed that individual LMX relationships were a better predictor of subsequent turnover from the organization than averaged ratings of the leader that were derived from all members of the group.[61] Last, by assuming mutual influence within leader–member dyads, LMX theory again differs from other leadership theories that presume a unidirectional and downward influence from leader to follower.

What constitutes a high-quality relationship within LMX theory? Consistent with the many changes LMX theory has undergone since Graen's early writing in the 1970s, the list of attributes that characterize a high-quality relationship has changed fairly considerably. Initially, high-quality LMX relationships were based on task-related competence, interpersonal skills, and trust,[62] with aspects such as attention, support, and rewards included a little later. While different dimensions and subdimensions were added over the next decade and a half,[63] high-quality LMX relationships are now characterized by aspects such as trust, understanding, support, provision of information, opportunities for involvement in decision-making, role latitude, and autonomy. There is also some clarification as to the nature of poor-quality LMX relationships, which are not just the absence of high-quality relationships. Instead, one-way communication and downward influence, social distance, role distinctions, contractual obligations, and formal transactions that are based on distrust characterize poor-quality LMX relationships.[64]

Several concerns remain with LMX theory. Some are methodological and include inconsistent measurement of LMX across different studies, which has led to a lack of clarity of what is really meant by LMX. Other concerns are more substantive. For example, while the core of the theory is the leader–member dyad, much of the research on LMX theory asks only one of the partners of the dyad (usually the follower) to provide information on the quality of the dyadic relationship, leaving open the question of whether research has fully explored the leader–member *relationship*. In addition, LMX theory has been criticized for placing all its emphasis on the quality of the dyad, and excluding the influence of the context in which the dyad is located.[65]

Perhaps the most troublesome question is whether the quality of the leader–member dyad (as reflected by mutual support, trust, and liking within the dyad, for example) *is* leadership per se, as LMX theory implies, or whether it is a *consequence* of high-quality leadership. As will be seen in Chapter 2, enhanced trust in and liking of the leader, and mutual support between leader and follower are among the most consistent outcomes of leadership—irrespective of the particular leadership theory. Thus, it remains possible that the high-quality relationships identified by LMX theory reflect the most important consequence of leadership behaviors, rather than leadership itself. Despite these lingering questions, LMX theory remains one of the most widely researched of all leadership theories over the past three decades; and as the data in Figure 1.1 suggest, it will likely remain so for years to come.

Servant Leadership

Including servant leadership in any discussion of new-genre theories may initially seem misplaced: From a chronological perspective, Robert Greenleaf first described the nature of servant leadership in two books published in the 1970s, entitled *The Servant as Leader*[66] and *Servant Leadership: A Journey into the Nature of Legitimate Power and Greatness.*[67] (A 25th anniversary edition of the latter book was published as a set of readings in 2002, with a foreword provided by Steven Covey.[68]) Nonetheless, because servant leadership emphasizes ethical behaviors and the leader–follower relationship, it fits comfortably under the rubric of a new-genre leadership theory. Moreover, some of the core ideas inherent in servant leadership have been subjected to scientific scrutiny within the past decade.[69]

More than half a million copies of Greenleaf's books and articles had been sold worldwide by the mid-2000s.[70] Despite the popularity of "servant leadership," or more probably *because* of its popularity, pinpointing the precise nature of servant leadership is not easy because of what scholars refer to as "conceptual drift": As increasing numbers of people used the term "servant leadership" in their discussions and writings, variations from the original term became inevitable. Isolating the precise nature of servant leadership was also not helped by the fact that Greenleaf's own ideas changed and developed, even subtly, throughout his prolific career. As a result, Larry Spears, who later became president and chief executive officer (CEO) of the Robert K. Greenleaf Center for Servant Leadership,[71] identified 10 characteristics of servant leadership:[72] listening, empathy, healing, awareness, persuasion, conceptualization, foresight, stewardship, commitment to the growth of people separate from their value as employees, and, consistent with its core value of serving others, building community.

Because of the confusion as to the exact nature of servant leadership, Robert Liden and his colleagues started their research on servant leadership by developing a scale that could reliably assess the dimensions of servant leadership.[73] Their analyses showed that servant leadership is best viewed as comprising seven separate but related components or behaviors that closely reflect Greenleaf's writings: emotional healing, creating value for the community, conceptual skills, empowering, helping subordinates grow and succeed, putting subordinates first, and behaving ethically.

Like other leadership theories, many of these components would seem to overlap strongly with the diverse behaviors included in other new-genre leadership theories (e.g., transformational, authentic, and LMX leadership). However, adherents of servant leadership point to several critical differences. First, servant leadership emphasizes the development of employees, not just in the service of the organization, but for their own personal growth and advancement. Second, servant leaders go beyond advancing the needs of employees, teams, and the organizations in which they are employed and emphasize the health of communities. Third, transformational and servant leadership may be most appropriately applied to different contexts: Servant leadership may be most suitable to contexts reflecting stability and an abundance of resources, whereas transformational leadership is likely more appropriate when groups or organizations face uncertainty, ambiguity, and change.[74]

Several research studies have been conducted on servant leadership. One study focused on isolating the antecedents or precursors of servant leadership in organizations. In this study, Suzanne Peterson, Benjamin Galvin, and Donald Lange studied CEOs' servant leadership in 126 small and medium-sized enterprises (annual sales within each company was less than $5 million) in the western United States.[75] This study avoided reliance on CEO reports of their own leadership, which might be overinflated. Instead, company chief financial officers (CFOs) rated their respective CEO's servant leadership, while CEOs completed surveys assessing their own narcissism, identification with the organization, and whether they were the founder of the organization or not. Using these data, the researchers showed that CEO servant leadership was associated with firm performance as measured by return on assets. Also, given that servant leadership emphasizes personal integrity, followers' rather than leaders' needs, and a firm ethical foundation, it should not be surprising that the higher the CEO's narcissism, the lower he or she was rated on servant leadership by the CFO.

A compelling test of the tenets of servant leadership emerges from other studies that have simultaneously contrasted servant leadership with transformational leadership, or any other leadership theory. Mitchell Neubert and his research team contrasted the effects of servant leadership and the initiating structure leadership style (which focuses broadly on task performance).[76] Initiating structure was shown to be a more significant predictor of constructive and deviant work performance than servant leadership. However, servant leadership was a more significant predictor of helping behaviors and creativity than was initiating structure. In addition, while transformational leadership,

LMX, and servant leadership all predict commitment to the organization,[77] only servant leadership predicted employees' voluntary involvement within the community at large, which is consistent with the fact that servant leadership sees the health of the community as one of its primary goals.

One last finding relating to servant leadership is worth mentioning. Initially, servant leadership theorists focused on the dyadic relationship between leader and follower. Consistent with the current interest not just in leadership of individual employees but also of teams, one recent study showed that servant leadership operates equally well in the context of relationships between leaders and teams.[78]

Ethical Leadership

There have been all too many publicly visible ethical lapses by business leaders in different parts of the world over the last two decades, with sometimes devastating personal, organizational, and social consequences. Over and above the massive financial consequences for all the stakeholders involved (the organization itself, its shareholders, and employees), these ethical lapses tend to shake the public's confidence not just in the unethical leaders but in all leaders. For all these reasons, there has been a surge of interest in why leaders would choose or agree to behave ethically. In an area as fraught as ethical leadership, we should not be surprised to find that there is an array of different explanations about this complex and critical organizational issue.

Before sorting through this immense literature, however, an important reminder: This discussion centers on *ethical* behaviors performed by organizational leaders. We will deal with two different approaches to unethical leadership in Chapter 9.

Moral Reasoning

Ever since Jean Piaget's ground-breaking research with children,[79] psychologists have been interested in the question of how people grapple with moral dilemmas. Starting in the late 1960s, Lawrence Kolhberg developed a model of how people reason about the moral dilemmas they face in their everyday lives. In Kohlberg's model,[80] people's life experiences and social environments shape their cognitive reasoning abilities. As they gain more life experiences, a larger repertoire of options and perspectives becomes available to them in resolving moral dilemmas. Kolhberg proposed that people progress through three major moral development stages. In the first stage of moral reasoning, the "preconventional phase," people are egocentric and emphasize obedience, avoidance of punishment, and self-interest in how they reason about moral dilemmas. As individuals gain more experience and develop cognitively, they tend more toward equality and fairness as the principles that guide their dispute resolution. Individuals within this "conventional" phase emphasize external rules and laws in their moral conduct, and would see any relationships with others as primarily instrumental in nature. "Postconventional" moral reasoning reflects the highest stage of moral development, in which individuals use more universal principles in making moral choices and focus on the collective good.

Kohlberg's theory is relevant in the organizational context because we might expect a relationship between the postconventional stage and ethical leadership, and several studies provide support for this notion. Leanne Atwater and her colleagues studied 236 military cadets who increasingly took on leadership responsibilities during their military training.[81] They found that cadets whose moral reasoning was relatively lower upon entering military college experienced significant development in the level of moral reasoning, suggesting that experiences are important in shaping moral reasoning. They also found that cadets' levels of moral reasoning did not predict either leadership emergence or leader effectiveness, a finding which the authors themselves called "perplexing." In retrospect, however, this finding might make sense: Opportunities for translating postconventional moral values into leadership behavior in organizational contexts that emphasize and value conformity, such as an elite military academy, may be somewhat limited. Importantly, therefore, a later study did provide evidence for a link between moral reasoning and ethical leadership. Taking transformational leadership as a form of ethical leadership because of its focus away from self-interest toward the collective good, Nick Turner and his team showed in separate samples in Canada and the United Kingdom that transformational leadership was higher among postconventionalists than preconventionalists or conventionalists.[82] As these authors expected, there was no association between level of moral reasoning or any of the different aspects of transactional leadership.

An Ethic of Care

Responding initially to Kohlberg's model, which (a) emphasized the importance of cognitive reasoning within a justice orientation for resolving conflicts between individual and collective rights, and (b) recognized that his research was based on a sample of men only, Carol Gilligan offered an alternative perspective on how individuals respond to moral dilemmas.[83] Based on her own research, Gilligan showed that individuals can approach moral dilemmas from a very different perspective, one in which the maintenance and enhancement of authentic relationships is central. Gilligan's findings showed that individuals are primarily motivated to understand the personal experiences and needs of others, and to respond to these specific needs. As such, the hallmark of a care orientation in resolving moral disputes would be to find creative ways of simultaneously satisfying the competing rights and responsibilities of both parties, rather than deciding between the conflicting rights of the different parties. In this sense, Gilligan's model moves responsibility for resolving moral dilemmas from reasoning to relationships.

Subsequent research has confirmed that an ethic of care plays a significant role in ethical leadership. Taking transformational leadership as a reflection of ethical leadership because of its focus on the collective good and developing employees, Sheldene Simola, Nick Turner, and I conducted two studies which showed that leaders who reported higher levels of an ethic of care were also rated by their subordinates as higher on transformational leadership.[84] Interestingly, as was the case with Turner and colleagues' research on moral reasoning and transformational leadership, the ethic of care was not associated with transactional leadership in either of our two studies, and we suggested that the probable reason for this is that the moral foundation of transactional leadership is based on reasoning about fairness, rather than on relational needs.

Assessing Ethical Leadership

Notwithstanding the fact that there are many different approaches to understanding ethical leadership (and even more if we include unethical leadership; see Chapter 9), Michael Brown, Linda Treviño, and Michael Harrison have offered an overall definition of ethical leadership.[85] In their view, ethical leadership has multiple components. They do not specifically define the precise behaviors that constitute ethical leadership, as they acknowledge explicitly that these behaviors would be shaped and defined to some extent by the context in which they occur. They do, however, acknowledge the universality of behaviors such as "honesty, trustworthiness, fairness and care" (p. 120), some of which are included in the ethical leadership theory just discussed. Brown and his colleagues' definition requires that these leaders explicitly take the ethical consequences of their decisions into account, and that ethical behaviors are enacted personally by ethical leaders in their relationships and communications with their followers. Last, these leaders set high ethical standards, and reward their followers for meeting or exceeding the standards and punish ethical violations. Subsequent research, for example, showing how ethical leadership influences the way people experience their work and, in turn, their job performance,[86] has validated Brown and colleagues' ethical leadership framework.

The long-term influence of Brown and colleagues' research could well be far-reaching. The major outcome of their study was the development a brief,

Table 1.1. BROWN ET AL.'S ETHICAL LEADERSHIP QUESTIONNAIRE

My boss....

1. Listens to what employees have to say.
2. Disciplines employees who violate ethical standards.
3. Conducts his or her personal life in an ethical manner.
4. Has the best interests of employees in mind.
5. Makes fair and balanced decisions.
6. Can be trusted.
7. Discusses business ethics or values with employees.
8. Sets an example of how to do things the right way in terms of ethics.
9. Defines success not just in terms of results but also the way that they are obtained.
10. When making decisions, asks, "What is the right thing to do?"

Each item is responded to on a five point scale, where 1 = Strongly disagree; 2 = Disagree; 3 = Neither agree nor disagree; 4 = Agree; and 5 = Strongly agree.
From Brown, M. E., Treviño, L. K., & Harrison, D. A. (2005). Ethical leadership: A social learning perspective for construct development and testing. *Organizational Behavior and Human Decision Processes, 97*, 117–134.

reliable, and valid questionnaire that measures ethical leadership, which they accomplished in a series of rigorous studies. As their questionnaire (see Table 1.1 for the items) is freely available to researchers and practitioners, it is likely to feature prominently in future research on ethical leadership.

FROM THEORY TO DAILY BEHAVIOR: THE CASE OF TRANSFORMATIONAL LEADERSHIP

Understanding new-genre leadership theories is one thing; the challenge that looms larger for practicing leaders, however, is how such a collection of complex ideas, lofty values, and imposing behaviors can be translated into daily, workplace reality. To show how readily this can be accomplished, we will focus on the four components of transformational leadership, as it is the most widely researched leadership theory. As a starting point, it will be reassuring to know that it is neither possible nor necessary for leaders to engage in *all* four transformational leadership behaviors *all* the time. After all, leaders and their followers may not even see each other every day, and many employees are not even in the same geographical location as the leaders.[87] Thus, outstanding leaders do not engage in the right behaviors *all* the time, but they rarely miss the opportunity to do so at the *right* time.

One opportunity for leaders to demonstrate the values inherent in *idealized influence* would occur after a leader transgression or mistake, especially during difficult times when employees likely monitor their leaders' behaviors more closely. While many leaders fear that apologizing for transgressions would make them look weak, research findings show the opposite is true: offering a full apology is associated with being seen as more of a transformational leader, not less.[88] Why might apologies be so meaningful? Apologizing for the transgression requires more than just saying sorry; it involves acknowledgments of remorse, taking responsibility for the transgression, expressions of empathy, and offers of symbolic or material compensation.[89] Doing all this conveys humility, proof that leaders value employees' or followers' well-being, and an attempt to restore the dignity of the other.[90] An extraordinary demonstration of this involved Archbishop Desmond Tutu, winner of the 1984 Nobel Peace Prize. Appealing to Winnie Mandela at the Truth and Reconciliation Commission, of which he was the co-chair, to account for ethical mistakes she had made in her fight against the apartheid government, Tutu begged her to apologize: " 'Something went wrong,' said Tutu, pleading with Winnie Mandela to say publicly: I'm sorry, I'm sorry for my part in what went wrong.... 'I beg you, I beg you...I beg you, please... You are a great person. *And you don't know how your greatness would be enhanced if you were to say, "I'm sorry"' "* (italics added).[91] The lesson is clear: Leaders do not undermine their stature with an apology. To the contrary, Desmond Tutu reminded us all that just saying "I'm sorry" would be enough for Winnie Mandela to reaffirm her greatness.

A second example of how complex leadership concepts are translated into everyday behaviors is through the use of self-deprecating humor. Self-deprecating humor offers an ideal opportunity for revealing the humility that is consistent with idealized influence. Consider this distinction: in the days before the Republican National Convention in August, 2012, Mitt Romney joked in a speech in Michigan about whether President Obama could prove he was born in the United States, but the joke backfired badly. Might his leadership have been better served if the joke had been targeted at himself in some way rather than at his opponent? In contrast, Al Gore recovered from the controversy over whether he had claimed to have invented the Internet with self-deprecating humor when he went on the *Late Show with David Letterman*, and while reading Letterman's famous "Top Ten List," proclaimed "Remember, America, I gave you the Internet, and I can take it away!"[92]

Inspirational motivation can be conveyed symbolically through leaders' optimism in interactions with their followers, which symbolically shows that they believe in their abilities and trust in their intentions. Several examples of this can be offered. Irrespective of the controversies that swirled about Mayor Giuliani following the attacks of 9/11,[93] his now-famous comment in a press conference that same afternoon, that "Tomorrow New York is going to be here, and we're going to rebuild, *and we're going to be stronger than we were before...I want the people of New York to be an example to the rest of the country, and the rest of the world, that terrorism can't stop us"*[94] (italics added) shows that at the worst possible times—when followers might despair and seek revenge, they need optimism and hope from their leaders to elevate them, and to remind them just how good they are. Giuliani was by no means the first leader to demonstrate this: After numerous setbacks in World War II (such as the attack on Pearl Harbor), President Roosevelt famously looked forward to how he might confront the future, and stubbornly refused to look back in a search for someone to blame.[95]

Further support for the notion that subtle leader behaviors are sufficient to inspire others derives from the well-known Pygmalion studies conducted by Robert Rosenthal and his colleagues in the 1960s, studies which took their name from the famous George Bernard Shaw play, *Pygmalion,* on which the musical *My Fair Lady* is based.[v] In a series of studies, Rosenthal and his colleagues led elementary-school teachers to believe that some of the students who were to be in their class were early bloomers (or what they called "spurters").[96] Of course, none of these children were early bloomers; they had just been randomly assigned to this group. Despite this, achievement tests showed that children who had been described as early bloomers soon outperformed the others. How could this happen? When teachers think their students are ready to flourish, they interact differently with them. For example, they likely set more difficult problems for them to solve and monitor them less. In this way, teachers symbolically tell these children that they are talented and trusted, and the children respond accordingly.

Dov Eden and his colleagues have shown in an extensive series of studies that this powerful effect is just as pervasive in work situations.[97] They have also shown that we need to be aware of the "Golem" effect:[98] Identified initially by Elisha Babad, Jacinto Inbar, and Robert Rosenthal in their research on teachers,[99] the Golem effect reflects how subtle negative messages from leaders could also lead to declines in employee performance. Two important lessons can be learned from studies on the Pygmalion and Golem effects. First, people are remarkably sensitive to their leaders' subtle behaviors and verbal communications—especially during times of crisis—and respond accordingly. Second, the best of leadership is often reflected through the smallest behaviors (and this is true of the worst of leadership as well, as will be seen in Chapter 9).

The classic movie, *12 Angry Men,*[100] starring Henry Fonda, is often used in leadership courses. In the movie, a young Spanish-American teenager stands accused of murdering his father, and almost the entire movie takes place in the jury room, with some jurors displaying transformational or laissez-faire leadership, or management-by-exception. *12 Angry Men* is replete with examples of the successful use of *intellectual stimulation*, showing again that transformational leadership can be enacted through small but meaningful behaviors.

v. The central story behind *My Fair Lady* is how phonetics professor Henry Higgins helps Eliza Doolitle, a disheveled flower girl, to defy all social expectations and rise beyond the expectations of others.

This is exemplified in the movie by the use of the word "suppose." In an especially telling scene, Juror #7 (played by Jack Warden) is impatient for the completion of their deliberations because he has tickets for a baseball game. He is frustrated with Juror #8 (brilliantly portrayed by Henry Fonda), who initially voted not guilty to compel the jury to consider the evidence and give the accused a fair trial. Irritated by what he sees as Juror #8's obstinance, which may cost him his baseball game, he confronts him: "Suppose you are wrong and the kid's really guilty, then what?" Fonda's character is visibly shaken by the question, which forces him to reconsider all his assumptions—the very goal of intellectual stimulation. In a separate scene in the movie, Juror #3 (Lee J. Cobb) uses the word "suppose" to convey how intellectual stimulation is *not* used by his leader at work: Humbly describing his job, he says "Oh I don't do any of the supposin' at work, my boss does all the supposin.'"

12 Angry Men culminates with another vivid example of intellectual stimulation. Juror #4 (played by E.G. Marshall) is the last remaining juror who believes the boy is guilty, and needs to be persuaded otherwise. Juror #9 (Jack Sweeney), a wise old man who provides Fonda's character with support throughout the movie, has the evidence to put the boy's innocence beyond doubt, but he does not just *tell* Juror #4 what the evidence is. Instead, the turning point in *12 Angry Men* comes when Juror #9 (Sweeney) forces Juror #4 (Marshall) to confront the critical evidence by pointedly asking him: "Could those marks be made by anything other than eyeglasses?" Of course Sweeney's character knows the answer, but like any wonderful leader, he also knows that the person with the most persuasive influence over Juror #4 (Marshall) is Juror #4 himself.

With their overwhelming workload, many leaders worry how they could possibly find the time to engage in the caring, listening, and compassion that are characteristic of *individualized consideration* behaviors. But it is possible, and we would do well to remember the research of Cassie Mogilner, Zoë Chance, and Michael Norton, which showed that spending time on others left people with what they called a greater sense of "time affluence," the feeling that accomplishing something with one's time leaves us with more time.[101] Observing superlative leaders confirmed for me that high-quality leadership does not necessarily take time. As one example, one of the most meaningful things I have learned while engaged in leadership development initiatives is how leaders themselves glowingly recall receiving a "thank you" card or e-mail from their own leader, and then admit that they have kept the card for several years. But the story does not end there. Many of these leaders also acknowledge that, years later, during an especially difficult time, they go back and look at these "thank you" cards—and it picks them up again! Again, the smallest possible things that leaders do, in this case giving a thank you card that reminds people that they belong, and reaffirms that they are valued, will often have the most long-lasting effects.[102]

Individualized consideration is also epitomized in so many of the behaviors of Nelson Mandela. Coming away from even a brief meeting with Nelson Mandela, many people recount that during that brief moment, they knew they were the most important person in the world to Mandela. In one telling example, a Canadian mother and her daughter attended a mass political rally in Natal during the politically fraught and violence-riddled period leading up to the transition from apartheid to the black-majority government of the ANC in South Africa. The rally was attended by many leaders of the apartheid opposition, including Mandela. During the meeting, the mother's worst nightmare came true: Her daughter disappeared among the thousands of emotionally aroused people. After a little while, she spotted her young daughter, happily sitting on the stage—on Mandela's lap! Asked approximately two decades later what that felt like, the daughter, now an adult, declared that "Mr. Mandela was so excited to meet me!"

Last, a vivid demonstration of both idealized influence and intellectual stimulation comes from President John F. Kennedy's inaugural speech on January 20, 1961. Challenging people to go beyond their own self-interest and inviting them to think of the collective good, President Kennedy concluded his speech, saying, "And so, my fellow Americans, ask not what your country can do for you; ask what you can do for your country."[103] The lesson to be learned from all these stories is simple: While theories or explanations of leadership may be complex, the best of leadership is often seen in the smallest behaviors enacted at the right time and for the right reasons.

Before ending this discussion, it is critical to note that while most of the examples presented here depict famous leaders, this is no way implies that only people of such stature can perform behaviors of this nature. On the contrary, the everyday behaviors used as examples (e.g., apologies, self-deprecating humor, saying "thank you") are well within the daily reach of organizational leaders.

CONCLUDING THOUGHTS

Scholars and researchers have devoted themselves for decades to understanding the nature of organizational leadership. This work has resulted in many different leadership theories and in an enormous body of empirical research. From this extensive theorizing and large body of research, it is apparent that the very best of organizational leadership is relational and inspirational, ethical, future-oriented, focused on employee development, and laden with the humility that characterizes great leaders. Equally important is the knowledge that despite the loftiness of the theories, the best of leadership can be expressed through small but meaningful behaviors enacted at the right time.

That being said, two questions come to mind: Does leadership work, and if so, how? The next two chapters will deal with each of these questions.

SUGGESTED READING

Bass, B. M., & Riggio, R. E. (2006). *Transformational leadership* (2nd ed.). Mahwah, NJ: Lawrence Erlbaum.

Burns, J. M. (1978). *Leadership*. New York: Harper & Row.

Gardner, W. L., Avolio, B. J., & Walumbwa, F.O. (2005). (Eds.). *Authentic leadership theory and practice: Origins, effects and development*. Bingley, UK: Emerald Publishing.

Greenleaf, R. K., & Spears, L. C. (2002) (Eds.). *Servant leadership: A journey into the nature of legitimate power and greatness 25th anniversary edition*. Mahwah, NJ: Paulist Press.

Lazare, A. (2004). *On apology*. New York: Oxford University Press.

NOTES

1. Bass, B. M., & Bass, R. (2008). *The Bass handbook of leadership: Theory, research and managerial applications*. New York: Free Press.
2. http://www.amazon.com/ Accessed April 15, 2013.
3. Stodgill, R. A. (1974). *Handbook of leadership: A survey of theory and research*. New York: Free Press.
4. Rost, J. C. (1991). *Leadership for the twenty-first century*. New York: Praeger.
5. Burns, J. M. (1978). *Leadership*. New York: Harper & Row.
6. Northouse, P. G. (2013). *Leadership: Theory and practice* (6th ed.). Thousand Oaks, CA: SAGE Publications.
7. Bennis, W., & Nanus (1985). *Leaders: The strategies for taking charge*. New York: Harper & Row.
8. Kotter, J. P. (1999). *What leaders really do*. Cambridge, MA: Harvard Business School Press.
9. "Love Story" lyrics. Retrieved from http://www.lyricsmode.com/lyrics/a/andy_williams/love_story.html
10. Barling, J., Christie, A., & Hoption, A. (2010). Leadership. In S. Zedeck (Ed.), *Handbook of industrial and organizational psychology* (pp. 183–240). Washington, DC: American Psychological Association.
11. Avolio, B. J., Walumbwa, F. O., & Weber, T. J. (2009). Leadership: Current theories, research and future directions. *Annual Review of Psychology, 60*, 421–449.
12. Bass, B. M. (1985). *Leadership and performance beyond expectations*. New York: Free Press.
13. Bryman, A. (1992). *Charisma and leadership in organizations*. Thousand Oaks, CA: SAGE Publications.
14. Judge, T. A., & Bono, J. E. (2000). Five factor model of personality and transformational leadership. *Journal of Applied Psychology, 85*, 751–756.
15. Burns, J. M. (1970). *Roosevelt: Soldier of freedom, 1940–1945*. New York: Harcourt Brace Jovanovich.

16. Burns, J. M., & Dunn, S. (2001). *The Three Roosevelts: Patrician leaders who trans-formed America*. New York: Grove Press.
17. Burns, J. M. (2006) *Running alone: Presidential leadership—JFK to Bush II: Why it has failed and how we can fix it*. New York: Basic Books.
18. Burns, J. M., & Sorensen, G. J. (1999). *Dead center: Clinton-Gore leadership and the perils of moderation*. New York: Simon & Schuster.
19. Burns, J. M. (1978). *Leadership*. New York: Harper Collins.
20. Avolio, B. J. (2008). Bernard (Bernie) M. Bass (1925–2007). *American Psychologist, 63*, 620.
21. Bass, B. M. (1985). *Leadership and performance beyond expectations*. New York: Free Press.
22. Bass, B. M. (1998). *Transformational leadership: Industrial, military and educational impact*. Mahwah, NJ: Lawrence Erlbaum.
23. Bass, B. M., & Bass, R. (2008). *The Bass handbook of leadership: Theory, research and managerial applications*. New York: The Free Press.
24. Bass, B. M., & Avolio, B. J. (1990). *Manual for the multifactor leadership question-naire*. Palo Alto, CA: Consulting Psychologists Press.
25. Bass, B. M., & Riggio, R. E. (2006). *Transformational leadership* (2nd ed.). Mahwah, NJ: Lawrence Erlbaum.
26. Robertson, J., & Barling, J. (2013). Greening organizations through leaders' influence on employees' pro-environmental behaviors. *Journal of Organizational Behavior, 34*, 4–19.
27. Burns, J. M. (1978). *Leadership*. New York: Harper & Row.
28. Maslow, A. H. (1965). *Eupsychian management: A journal*. Homewood, IL: Dorsey.
29. Bass, B. M. (1985). *Leadership and performance beyond expectations*. New York: Free Press.
30. Eden, D. (2003). *Self-fulfilling prophecies in organizations*. In J. Greenberg (Ed.), *Organizational behavior: The state of the science* (2nd ed.) (pp. 91–122). Mahwah, NJ: Lawrence Erlbaum.
31. Ilies, R., Gerhardt, M. W., & Le, H. (2004). Individual differences in leadership emergence: Integrating meta-analytic findings and behavioral genetic estimates. *International Journal of Selection and Assessment, 12*, 207–219.
32. Cavazotte, F., Moreno, V., & Hickman, M. (2012). Effects of leader intelligence, personality and emotional intelligence on transformational leadership and managerial performance. *Leadership Quarterly, 23*, 443–455.
33. Simonton, D. K. (1984). Leaders as eponyms: Individual and situational determi-nants of monarchal eminence. *Journal of Personality, 52*, 1–21.
34. Simonton, D. K. (2006). Presidential IQ, openness, intellectual brilliance, and leadership: Estimates and correlations for 42 U.S. Chief Executives. *Political Psychology, 27*, 511–526.
35. Kelloway, E. K., Sivanathan, N., Francis, L., & Barling, J. (2005). Poor leader-ship. In J. Barling, E. K. Kelloway, & M. Frone (Eds.), *Handbook of work stress* (pp. 89–112). Thousand Oaks, CA: SAGE Publications.
36. Avolio, B. J. (1999). *Full leadership development: Building the vital forces in the organization*. Thousand Oaks, CA: SAGE Publications.
37. Bass, B. M. (1985). *Leadership and performance beyond expectations*. New York: Free Press.
38. MacKenzie, S. B., Podsakoff, P. M., & Rich, G. A. (2001). Transformational and transactional leadership and sales performance. *Journal of the Academy of Marketing Science, 29*(12), 115–134.

39. Avolio, B. J., & Gibbons, T. (1988). Developing transformational leaders: A lifespan approach. In J. A. Conger & R. N. Kanungo (Eds.), *Charismatic leadership: The elusive factor in organizational effectiveness*. San Francisco, CA: Jossey Bass.

40. Weber, M. (1947). *The theory of social and economic organizations* (T. Parsons, Transl.). New York: Free Press.

41. House, R. J. (1977). A 1976 theory of charismatic leadership. In J. G. Hunt & L. L. Larsen (Eds.), *Leadership: The cutting edge* (pp. 189–207). Carbondale, IL: Southern Illinois University Press.

42. House, R., & Howell, J. M. (1992). Personality and charismatic leadership. *Leadership Quarterly, 3*, 81–108.

43. Howell, J. M. (1988). Two faces of charisma: Socialized and personalized leadership in organizations. In J. A. Conger & R. N. Kanungo (Eds.), *Charismatic leadership* (pp. 213–236). San Francisco, CA: Jossey Bass.

44. O'Connor, J., Mumford, M. D., Clifton, T. C., Gessner, T. L., & Connelly, M. S. (1995). Charismatic leadership and destructiveness: An histiometric study. *Leadership Quarterly, 6*, 529–555.

45. Conger, J. A. (1999). Charismatic and transformational leadership in organizations: An insider's perspective oln these developing streams of research. *Leadership Quarterly, 10*, 145–179.

46. Conger, J. A., & Kanungo, R. N. (Eds.) (1998). *Charismatic leadership*. San Francisco, CA: Jossey Bass; House, R. J., & Podsakoff, P. M. (1994). Leadership effectiveness: Past perspectives and future directions. In J. Greenberg (Ed.), *Organizational behavior: The state of the science* (pp. 45–82). Mahwah, NJ: Lawrence Erlbaum.

47. Waldman, D. A., Javidan, M., & Varella, P. (2004). Charismatic leadership at the strategic level: A new application of upper echelons theory. *Leadership Quarterly, 15*, 355–380.

48. Judge, T. A., Woolf, E. F., Hurst, C., & Livingston, B. (2008). Leadership. In J. Barling & C. L. Cooper (Eds.), *The SAGE handbook of organizational behavior. Vol. 1: Micro approaches* (pp. 334 352). London: SAGE Publications.

49. Conger, J. A. (1999). Charismatic and transformational leadership in organizations: An insider's perspective oln these developing streams of research. *Leadership Quarterly, 10*, 145–179.

50. Judge, T. A., Woolf, E. F., Hurst, C., & Livingston, B. (2008). Leadership. In J. Barling & C. L. Cooper (Eds.), *The SAGE handbook of organizational behavior. Vol. 1: Micro approaches* (pp. 334–352). London: SAGE Publications.

51. Avolio, B. J., Walumbwa, F. O., & Weber, T. J. (2009). Leadership: Current theories, research, and future directions. *Annual Review of Psychology, 60*, 421–449.

52. Seligman, M. E. P., & Csikszentmihalyi, M. (2000). Positive psychology: An introduction. *American Psychologist, 55*, 5–14.

53. May, D. R., Chan, A., Hodges, T., Avolio, B. J. (2003). Developing the moral component of authentic leadership. *Organizational Dynamics, 32*, 247–260.

54. Kohlberg, L. (1969). *Stages in the development of moral thought and action*. New York: Holt, Rinehart & Winston.

55. Avolio, B. J., & Gardner, W. L. (2005). Authentic leadership development: Getting to the root of positive forms of leadership. *Leadership Quarterly, 16*, 315–338.

56. Walumbwa, F., Avolio, B. J., Gardner, W. L., Wrnsing, T. S., & Peterson, S. J. (2008). Authentic leadership: Development and validation of a theory-based measure. *Journal of Management, 34*, 89–126.

57. Ilies, R., Morgeson, F. P., & Nahrgang, J. D. (2005). Authentic leadership and eudaemonic well-being: Understanding leader-follower outcomes. *Leadership Quarterly, 16*, 373–394; Walumbwa, F. O., Avolio, B. J., Gardner, W. L., Wernsing, T. S., & Peterson, S. J. (2008). Authentic leadership: Development and validation of a theory-based measure. *Journal of Management, 34*, 89–106.

58. Judge, T. A., Woolf, E. F., Hurst, C., & Livingston, B. (2008). Leadership. In J. Barling & C. L. Cooper (Eds.), *The SAGE handbook of organizational behavior. Vol. 1: Micro approaches* (pp. 334–352). London: SAGE Publications.

59. Price, T. L. (2003). The ethics of authentic transformational leadership. *Leadership Quarterly, 14*, 67–81.

60. Zhu, W., Avolio, B. J., Riggio, R. E., & Sosik, J. J. (2011). The effects of authentic transformational leadership on follower and group ethics. *Leadership Quarterly, 22*, 801–817.

61. Graen, G. B., Liden, R. C., & Hoel, W. (1982). Role of leadership in the employee withdrawal process. *Journal of Applied Psychology, 67*, 868–872.

62. Graen, G. B. (1976). Role-making processes within complex organizations. In M. D. Dunnette (Ed.), *Handbook of industrial and organizational psychology* (pp. 1201–1245). Chicago: Rand-McNally.

63. Schriesheim, C. A., Castro, S. L., & Cogliser, C. C. (1999). Leader-member exchange (LMX) research: A comprehensive review of theory, measurement, and data-analytic practices. *Leadership Quarterly, 10*, 63–113.

64. Barling, J., Christie, A., & Hoption, A. (2010). Leadership. In S. Zedeck (Ed.), *Handbook of industrial and organizational psychology* (pp. 183–240). Washington, DC: American Psychological Association.

65. Avolio, B. J., Walumbwa, F. O., & Weber, T. J. (2009). Leadership: Current theories, research, and future directions. *Annual Review of Psychology, 60*, 421–449.

66. Greenleaf, R. K. (1970). *The servant as leader*. Newton Centre, MA: The Robert K. Greenleaf Center.

67. Greenleaf, R. K. (1977). *Servant leadership: A journey into the nature of legitimate power and greatness*. Mahwah, NJ: Paulist Press.

68. Greenleaf, R. K., & Spears, L. C. (2002) (Eds.). *Servant leadership: A journey into the nature of legitimate power and greatness 25th anniversary edition*. Mahwah, NJ: Paulist Press.

69. Van Dierendonck, D. (2011). Servant leadership: A review and synthesis. *Journal of Management, 37*, 1228–1261.

70. Spears, L. C. (2004). Practicing servant leadership. *Leader to leader, 34* (Fall), 7–11.

71. Robert K. Greenleaf Center for Servant Leadership. http://www.greenleaf.org/

72. Spears, L. C. (2004). Practicing servant leadership. *Leader to leader, 34* (Fall), 7–11.

73. Liden, R. C., Wayne, S. J., Zhao, H., & Henderson, D. (2008). Servant leadership: Development of a multidimensional measure and multi-level assessment. *Leadership Quarterly, 19*, 161–177.

74. Schaubroeck, J., Lam, S. S. K., Peng, A. C. (2011). Cognition-based and affect-based trust as mediators of leader behavior influences on team performance. *Journal of Applied Psychology, 96*, 863–871.

75. Peterson, S. J., Galvin, B. M., & Lange, D. (2012). CEO servant leadership: Exploring executive characteristics and firm performance. *Personnel Psychology, 65*, 565–596.

76. Neubert, M. J., Kacmar, K. M., Carlson, D. S., Chonko, L. B., & Roberts, J. A. (2008). Regulatory focus as a mediator of the influence of initiating structure and servant leadership on employee behavior. *Journal of Applied Psychology, 93*, 1220–1233.

77. Liden, R. C., Wayne, S. J., Zhao, H., & Henderson, D. (2008). Servant leadership: Development of a multidimensional measure and multi-level assessment. *Leadership Quarterly, 19*, 161–177.

78. Hu, J., & Liden, R. D. (2011). Antecedents of team potency and team effectiveness: An examination of goal and process clarity and servant leadership. *Journal of Applied Psychology, 96*, 851–862.

79. Piaget, J. (1965). *The moral judgment of the child*. New York: Free Press.

80. Kolhberg, L. (1969). *Stages in the development of moral thought and moral action*. New York: Holt, Rihehart & Winston; Kohlberg, L. (1976). Moral stages and moralization: The cognitive developmental approach. In T. Lickona (Ed.), *Moral development and behavior* (pp. 31–53). New York: Holt, Rinehart & Winston.

81. Atwater, L. E., Dionne, S. D., Camobreco, J. F., Avolio, B. J., & Lau, A. (1999). A longitudinal study of the leadership development process: Individual differences predicting leader effectiveness. *Human Relations, 52*, 1543–1562.

82. Turner, N., Barling, J., Epitropaki, O., Butcher, V., & Milner, C. (2002). Transformational leadership and moral reasoning. *Journal of Applied Psychology, 87*, 304–311.

83. Gilligan, C. (1982). *In a different voice*. Cambridge, MA: Harvard University Press.

84. Simola, S. K., Barling, J., & Turner, N. (2010). Transformational leadership and leader moral orientation: Contrasting an ethic of justice and an ethic of care. *Leadership Quarterly, 21*, 179–188; Simola, S. K., Barling, J., & Turner, N. (2012). Transformational leadership and leaders' mode of care reasoning. *Journal of Business Ethics, 108*, 229–237.

85. Brown, M. E., Treviño, L. K., & Harrison, D. A. (2005). Ethical leadership: A social learning perspective for construct development and testing. *Organizational Behavior and Human Decision Processes, 97*, 117–134.

86. Piccolo, R. F., Greenbaum, R., den Hartog, D. N., & Folger, R. (2010). The relationship between ethical leadership and core job characteristics. *Journal of Organizational Behavior, 31*, 259–278.

87. Howell, J. M., & Hall-Merenda, K. E. (1999). The ties that bind: The impact of leader-member exchange, transformational and transactional leadership, and distance on predicting follower performance. *Journal of Applied Psychology, 84*, 680–694.

88. Tucker, S., Turner, N., Barling, J., Reid, E. M., & Elving, C. (2006). Apologies and transformational leadership. *Journal of Business Ethics, 63*, 195–207.

89. Fehr, R., & Gelfand, M. J. (2010). When apologies work: How matching apology components to victims' self-construals facilitates forgiveness. *Organizational Behavior and Human Decision Processes, 113*, 37–50; Tucker, S., Turner, N., Barling, J., Reid, E. M., & Elving, C. (2006). Apologies and transformational leadership. *Journal of Business Ethics, 63*, 195–207.

90. Blanchard, J., & McBride, M. (2003). *The one minute apology*. New York: Harper Collins.

91. Krog, A. (1998). *Country of my skull: Guilt, sorrow, and the limits of forgiveness in the New South Africa* (p. 338). London: Jonathan Cape.

92. Gore does Dave. (2009, February 11). *CBS News*. Retrieved from http://www.cbsnews.com/stories/2000/09/14/politics/main233560.shtml

93. Buettner, R. (2007, August 17). For Giuliani, Ground Zero as linchpin and thorn. *New York Times*. Retrieved from http://www.nytimes.com/2007/08/17/us/politics/17giuliani.html; Wilson, M. (2007, June 17). Among firefighters in New York, mixed views on Giuliani. *New York Times*. Retrieved from http://www.nytimes.com/2007/06/17/us/politics/17firefighters.html?_r=1

94. New York's governor and mayor of New York City address concerns of the damage. (2001, September 11). *CNN.com/TRANSCRIPTS*. Retrieved from http://transcripts.cnn.com/TRANSCRIPTS/0109/11/bn.42.html

95. Goodwin, D. K. (1994). *No ordinary time*. New York: Simon & Shuster.

96. Rosenthal, R., & Jacobson, L. (1968). *Pygmalion in the classroom: Teacher expectation and pupils' intellectual development*. New York: Rinehart and Winston.

97. Eden, D. (2003). Self-fulfilling prophecies in organizations. In J. Greenberg (Ed.), *Organizational behavior: The state of the science* (2nd ed) (pp. 91–122). Mahwah, NJ: Lawrence Erlbaum.

98. Oz, S., & Eden, D. (1994). Restraining the Golem: Boosting performance by changing the interpretation of low scores. *Journal of Applied Psychology, 79*, 744–754.

99. Babad, E. Y., Inbar, J., & Rosenthal, R. (1982). Pygmalion, Galatea, and the Golem: Investigations of biased and unbiased teachers. *Journal of Education Psychology, 74*, 459–474.

100. Lumet, S. (Director). (1957). *12 Angry Men* (Motion picture). United States: MGM/UA Studios.

101. Mogilner, C., Chance, Z., & Norton, M. I. (2012). Giving time gives you time. *Psychological Science, 23*, 1233–1238.

102. Grant, A. M., & Gino, F. (2010). A little thanks goes a long way: Explaining why gratitude expressions motivate prosocial behavior. *Journal of Personality and Social Psychology, 98*, 946–955.

103. Kennedy, J. F. (1961, January 20). Ask not what your country can do for you [inaugural address]. Retrieved from http://www.guardian.co.uk/theguardian/2007/apr/22/greatspeeches

CHAPTER 2

Do Leaders Matter?

Do organizational leaders matter? If so, in terms of what outcomes? And do CEOs matter most? The answer to these questions might seem self-evident, but in reality these are very complex questions, made all the more difficult because our answers may be driven more by emotion than by reason. In seeking to answer these questions, much can be learned from decades of research on the extent to which leaders throughout different levels in organizations influence critical employee attitudes (e.g., commitment to the organization) and behaviors (e.g., sales performance). A separate (and surprisingly much smaller) body of research offers the opportunity to provide answers about the effects of CEOs on organizational and corporate performance; in this chapter, CEOs' leadership will be examined separately. Doing so, however, in no way implies that CEOs are the most influential or important leaders in organizations. Instead, CEOs have attracted unique research attention because of their visibility, status, and power, and we use the opportunity to examine a specific instance of the general question of whether leaders matter. We start, however, by examining the effects of those many leaders who are dispersed throughout organizations.

LEADERS DISPERSED THROUGHOUT THE ORGANIZATION

Focusing first on leaders throughout the organization might seem misguided given the exceptional prominence accorded to CEOs. Doing so is justified, however, because there are many more "regular" organizational leaders who have more frequent contact with a much larger group of employees than CEOs could ever hope to. In addition, there is a much larger body of research on leaders dispersed throughout the organization from which we can learn important lessons. This research has focused very broadly on a range of different outcomes; here we will focus on the effects of leaders on employee attitudes, different aspects of employee well-being, and employee behaviors.

Employee Attitudes: The Case of Organizational Commitment

While often belittled as "the soft stuff," employees' attitudes toward their work and their organizations simply cannot be dismissed. Decades of research findings show that employee attitudes such as loyalty or commitment to the organization, perceived fairness, job satisfaction, and trust in management are primary motivators of the behaviors that organizations cherish: attendance, retention of their most valued employees, and the voluntary behaviors that employees enact that are not required by their job descriptions but are central to organizational success.[1] Whether leaders influence these attitudes and the degree to which they do so are critical questions for scholars and practitioners alike. The sheer amount of research conducted makes it impossible to examine the full range of employee attitudes studied. As a result, we limit our focus here to one critical attitude, namely employees' commitment (or loyalty) to the organization. Commitment to the organization would be manifest through employees being proud to be members of their organization, being willing to tell others that they are members, and wanting to help their organization to be successful. Such commitment has consistent, positive effects on employees' performance.[2]

There is a large body of research linking transformational and charismatic leadership with higher levels of organizational commitment.[3] What makes employees' commitment to the organization especially interesting are profound trends over the past several decades that have seen organizations placing increasing reliance on part-time, temporary, contract, or contingent employees.[4] Doing so offers organizations greater flexibility and reduced costs, for example through decreasing employee benefit plans. In return, employees have experienced reduced job security in the short term and greater income insecurity in the long term. Because commitment to the organization is based on the notion of reciprocity, such that individuals offer their commitment if and when they believe that the organization will support them, there are questions as to whether it is possible to attract and maintain employee loyalty to the organization in the new organizational environment of tenuous employment contracts.

Possibly because of the extensive effects of organizational commitment,[5] researchers have long investigated the factors that predispose employees to high levels of such commitment. Findings from research studies leave little room for doubt: High-quality leadership is one of the key factors in employee commitment to the organization.[6] Whether we focus on transformational leadership[7] or leader–member exchange (LMX) theory,[8] consideration structure[9] or authentic leadership,[10] high-quality leadership is consistently associated with higher levels of employee commitment to the organization. More convincing are findings showing that following leadership training, positive changes in leaders' transformational behaviors over time resulted in increases in subordinates' commitment to the organization.[11]

But does this extend to employees in precarious or tenuous work situations? To understand this, Idriss Djibo, Katie Desiderio, and Norience Price surveyed a group of 126 employees who had been working in the same organization on a temporary basis for at least one month.[12] These authors were interested in the extent to which instrumental, supportive, and participative leadership might be associated with temporary employees' commitment to the organization. After controlling for any possible effects of age, gender, length of tenure with the organization, and employees' job category that could bias any findings, the researchers showed that supportive leadership behaviors were associated with higher levels of employees' affective commitment to the organization (i.e., a sense of pride in being associated with the organization) and their wish to maintain their membership of the organization. The results of this study are both clear and important: It is possible to attract the organizational commitment of temporary employees in precarious employment situations, and the role of high-quality leadership is pivotal in doing so. Thus, high-quality leadership is associated with employees' commitment to their organizations in some of the most challenging organizational situations—which mirrors the consistent effect of leadership on employees' workplace attitudes more generally.

Employee Well-Being

Employees' well-being, often in the guise of what is referred to as "occupational health and safety," has long been of concern to organizations, labor organizations, and, most especially, employees themselves. What has largely escaped public and management attention, however, is the role of leadership behaviors in this context. Researchers have recently turned their attention to employee well-being, with interesting findings.

Healthy Employees

Aside from the obvious social value of encouraging people's health and well-being, organizations themselves benefit from doing so. Almost a century ago, the notion that satisfied workers were productive workers had already piqued the interest of researchers. By 1932, Hersey reported on an intensive study which displayed an attention to detail that remains instructive today.[13] For a period of a year, he followed 12 workers on a daily basis, observing their overt behaviors (e.g., tardiness, cooperation, verbal outbursts), emotional behaviors, and physical symptoms (e.g., blood pressure, weight, sleep, and fatigue). While the conviction of some of his conclusions goes beyond what the sophistication of his statistical analyses would allow, Hersey observed that "it would seem impossible to escape the fact that in the long run, at least, men are more productive when they are in a positive emotional state than in a negative one" (pp. 356, 357). Interest in this general question among scholars persisted and became referred to as the "happy-productive worker hypothesis." Decades of research generally confirmed Hersey's early findings: Happy and healthy employees tend to be more productive.[14]

Which organizations end up with healthy employees is not just a matter of luck—organizational practices influence employees' well-being. Elsewhere in this book (Chapter 9), we will see how bad leadership hurts different aspects of psychological and physical health. This does not necessarily mean that good leaders exert positive effects on their subordinates' health and well-being; it is possible that while bad leaders exert negative effects, good leaders exert no effects on their subordinates' health. Although most articles on this topic continue to focus on the absence of poor health or sickness,[15] enough studies have been conducted on positive leadership and employee well-being to provide a data-based answer to the question.

Of the research that does exist, there are some encouraging findings. Joyce Bono and her colleagues conducted an intriguing study among 57 employees in an ambulatory health care organization.[16] Over a period of two weeks, all employees were contacted via a personal digital assistant (PDA) four times each day. Each time they were contacted, they were asked about their emotions and attitudes just before they had been contacted. What Bono and her researchers found was that over the two weeks, supervisors who engage in transformational leadership had an enduring influence on their employees' positive moods (e.g., happiness, optimism, enthusiasm).

Equally encouraging are studies showing that positive leadership is associated with more healthful choices and behaviors of employees. First, supportive leadership is associated with more successful attempts by employees at smoking cessation and weight loss, both of which constitute major health issues and are traditionally intractable behaviors.[17] Second, in a series of studies discussed later in this book (see Chapter 7), Mark Beauchamp and his colleagues showed that when teachers were trained in the behaviors that comprise transformational leadership, their students were more motivated to engage in physical exercise.[18] Finally, informal leaders in a public health care environment (what the authors called "champions") who received a one-day information session on the value of vaccinations subsequently had a 10% increase in vaccinations in their groups, while there was no increase in a comparison group whose informal leaders received no training.[19] Based on findings such as these, my colleague Kevin Kelloway and I have proposed elsewhere that leadership training and development constitutes an intervention with the potential to influence employee well-being.[20]

Recent research has gone further than documenting relationships between high-quality leadership and employee well-being by demonstrating *how* this effect occurs, with several studies finding strong support for the same explanation. Together with Kara Arnold and colleagues, we examined data from one sample of 319 Canadian employees working within a long-term care facility and, separately, a different sample of 146 Canadian funeral directors and dental hygienists.[21] Like other studies (see Chapter 3), our results showed that transformational leadership affected employees' psychological well-being indirectly. Initially, transformational leadership was positively associated with employees' beliefs that their work was meaningful, for example, that their work affected the community in which they lived. In turn, it was employees' belief that their work was meaningful that exerted a significant and direct effect on their psychological well-being. Extending support for the indirect effects of leadership on employees' well-being, Karina Nielsen and her colleagues[22] showed that transformational leadership affected employees' psychological well-being through positive work characteristics in a sample of 188 employees in a health care facility in Denmark. In this case, transformational leadership resulted in employees experiencing greater role clarity, more meaningful work, and more opportunities for development—each of which directly influenced employees' well-being. A subsequent study of 745 employees in China extends these findings,[23] showing that transformational leadership resulted in more trust in the leader and higher levels of employees' self-efficacy, both of which directly affected employees' well-being, further clarifying our understanding of the proximal and distal effects of transformational leadership.

Employee Safety

Notwithstanding technological advances that have benefitted so many organizations, the number of occupational injuries and fatalities remains unacceptably high in all countries: By one estimate of 175 countries representing all global regions, each year approximately 700,000 employees are injured at work sufficiently severely to require an absence of at least three days.[24] Thus, it is not surprising that occupational safety remains a very real concern for many employed people.

Traditionally, safety issues in organizations have been dealt with by demanding compliance with external safety regulations, meeting the terms of collective agreements, running management programs that reward all employees if no single individual suffers an injury, and providing improvements in ergonomic design. In contrast, the notion that leadership might influence occupational safety has received limited attention, despite the fact a study among enlisted U.S. naval personnel[25] reported as early as 1979 that management behaviors (e.g., emphasizing involvement in group goals and the behaviors required to achieve the goals) were associated with greater safety levels among deckhands (but not engineering personnel). (Similar effects were not found for leaders' supportive behaviors.) Despite this early interest in a link between leadership and safety, the possibility that leadership might influence safety was basically ignored by leadership researchers for the next two decades.

Given the widespread effects of leadership, and the continuing personal and organizational costs of workplace injuries and fatalities, we asked in our own research whether high-quality leadership might influence occupational safety. Together with my colleagues Catherine Loughlin and Kevin Kelloway, we introduced in 2002 the notion of context-specific leadership, in which transformational leadership behaviors have a specific focus or target.[26] Safety-specific transformational leaders would emphasize their values about safety, inspire followers to achieve safety levels previously considered unattainable, and challenge employees to think differently about safety challenges and solutions in the workplace. In making safety a priority, these leaders show their concern for their followers' well-being. One major advantage of safety-specific transformational leadership is that it provides greater clarity about leaders' values, as well as the roles and goals for leaders and their followers. In two separate samples of 174 restaurant workers and 164 young workers, for whom safety remains a very significant concern, safety-specific transformational leadership created a more positive safety climate, raised employees' awareness of safety, and reduced the number of safety-related incidents (e.g., spilling oil on the floor in a restaurant kitchen).

After this study was published, other researchers extended these findings. In one study in the United Kingdom, Stacey Conchie and Ian Donald showed that safety-specific transformational leadership exerted positive effects on what might be referred to as safety-specific citizenship behaviors—that is, voluntary employee behaviors that go beyond a concern for their own safety and include a real concern for others' safety (for example, volunteering for safety committees).[27] Kevin Kelloway and his colleagues Jane Mullen and Lori Francis verified that safety-specific transformational leadership exerted indirect effects on safety-related outcomes.[28] They went further, however, and also showed that contrary to the belief that passive leadership exerts neither positive nor negative effects, passive safety-specific leadership had negative effects on safety-related outcomes.

In a separate study, Michelle Inness and her colleagues showed that general transformational leadership influenced employees' participation in safety activities such as engaging in tasks that improve overall safety performance.[29] An even more interesting finding emerged from their study. Despite the fact that compliance with safety regulations is mandated in virtually all organizations, transformational leadership had no effect on the extent to which employees chose to comply with safety requirements. Perhaps this should not be surprising: Achieving compliance would be antithetical to the goals of the intellectual stimulation component of transformational leadership, which actively encourages employees to think for themselves. Instead, the lesson from these findings is that one cannot lead people into compliance, and that leadership affects safety not by mandating and ensuring compliance, but by allowing and encouraging people to think about others' and their own safety.

Not all research in this area has focused on transformational leadership. As one example, David Hofmann, Fred Morgeson, and Stephen Gerras[30] showed in a sample of transportation teams in the U.S. military that an LMX approach to leadership, which emphasizes the quality of the reciprocal exchanges between leader and follower, was associated with context-specific safety citizenship. Further exploration by these researchers, however, revealed that any effects of LMX leadership was dependent on the company's safety climate: Leadership only predicted safety citizenship when the safety climate was positive.

None of these findings would have any practical value if organizations were powerless to influence leadership. Jane Mullen and Kevin Kelloway implemented a half-day training initiative that concentrated on safety-specific transformational leadership with a group of 27 managers in long-term health care organizations in Nova Scotia, Canada.[31] Despite the brevity of the training, the results were very encouraging and yielded several interesting findings. Managers who received the safety-specific leadership training were subsequently more motivated to focus on safety issues and were more confident that they could do so. In addition, after the training was completed, employees whose managers had received the training saw significant changes in their managers' safety-specific transformational leadership compared to that of managers who had not received training—despite the fact that neither group knew whether their managers had received the leadership training or not. Finally, employees whose managers had received the leadership intervention also thought more highly of the company's safety climate (e.g., they believed that their company engaged in safety initiatives because they wanted to, not because they had to). This is important, as a positive safety climate has consistently been shown to result in positive safety performance.[32]

Employee Behaviors

Not surprisingly, there are countless studies linking leadership behaviors with a wide range of both positive (e.g., service quality, proactivity, citizenship behaviors) and negative behaviors (e.g., theft, absenteeism, and turnover). Indeed, so vast is this literature that providing a comprehensive discussion of all this research is beyond the bounds of this chapter. Instead, we focus on two behaviors: sales performance, because of its role in organizational success, and environmental sustainability, because of its current organizational and social relevance. (The effect of leadership on negative behaviors is considered in Chapter 9.)

Sales Performance

Successful sales performance is critical if organizations are to thrive, let alone survive. As a result, organizations devote valuable and scarce resources (e.g., financial, time) to increasing sales performance, with ample attention also given to traditional functions such as selection, supervision, ongoing-training, and appropriate compensation of sales personnel.[33] But might leadership also influence sales performance? Some research has investigated this question, and we turn first to what has been learned from these studies.

In one study, Alan Dubinsky and his colleagues investigated the simultaneous effects of transformational, transactional, and laissez-faire leadership on sales performance in a multinational medical products organization.[34] Their findings from this early study were encouraging. As the authors expected, laissez-faire leadership was not related to sales performance in any way, but both transformational and transactional leadership were. This should not be surprising, as the goal setting and performance feedback inherent in transactional leadership would enhance clarity of roles, boundaries, and expectations, which are critical for successful sales performance. There was also some support for the notion that transformational leadership added to (i.e., "augmented") the effects of transactional leadership on sales performance, which was consistent with the findings of a separate study within a forest products company.[35]

Nonetheless, Dubinsky and colleagues raised the question of whether the traditional sales role might limit the typical benefits that derive from transformational leadership, for several reasons.[36] First, sales performance is often a solitary activity that occurs physically, emotionally, and geographically separated from one's managers and colleagues—hardly conducive to the relational nature of transformational leadership. One study justifies their concern. Jane Howell and Kathryn Hall-Merenda showed that transformational (but not LMX) leadership was slightly less effective when enacted from afar than in traditional, close contexts.[37] Second, the basis for the relationship between sales manager and sales personnel is primarily economic, as a result of which Frederick Russ, Kevin McNeilly and James Comer questioned whether this might limit the effectiveness of transformational leadership,[38] with its emphasis on the leader–employee relationship.

A subsequent study of 447 sales agents' performance in a large national insurance company in the United States provides a more nuanced understanding of transformational leadership.[39] First, with respect to transactional leadership (or management issues), contingent punishment enhanced clarity of what the job entailed, which directly affected sales performance, and contingent reward was associated indirectly with citizenship behaviors through its effects on trust in the manager. Second, the measure of transformational leadership used in this study included articulating a vision, role modeling, and gaining approval of the group's goals, leaders' individualized support, and intellectual stimulation, and the authors found that different outcomes were associated with these different leadership behaviors. Like many other studies, transformational leadership enhanced trust in the leader and role clarity, both of which positively influenced sales performance. In addition, support for the augmentation effect again emerged: Transformational leadership enhanced sales performance over and above the effects of transactional leadership.

Unexpectedly, the effect of intellectual stimulation on sales performance was negative, such that the more intellectually stimulating the leader, the poorer the sales performance. The authors suggest that this is a matter of timing: Ambiguity and confusion would result when employees initially provide solutions for themselves, and the process would initially be time consuming. Any benefits of intellectual stimulation are more likely to become apparent as sales personnel become accustomed to resolving problems themselves over time. The possibility that negative effects may emerge initially would need to be taken seriously when conducting and evaluating leadership interventions.

A more recent study shows how the effects of transformational leadership on sales performance can be augmented relatively easily.[40] In a series of studies, Adam Grant showed that motivation increased when employees had some contact with the beneficiaries of their work, which would provide them with direct feedback about the social importance of their efforts and performance. In one company involved in sales of educational and marketing software within the nonprofit and university context, new hires were divided into four different groups for their initial training. In addition to their regular training, the 15 employees in the first group also met with a senior company director for 15 minutes, who explained the company's vision, and was optimistic and enthusiastic that employees could help achieve this vision—thereby displaying transformational leadership. The second group of 12 employees also received their regular training, and met someone from a different department for 10 minutes, who described how their successful sales performance would create new jobs in the company and secure current jobs like his own. The third group of 18 employees received the same initial training, and then met with both the senior director and someone from a different department who was a beneficiary of their work. Last, the fourth group of 26 new employees received the regular company training only, effectively serving as a control group.

The effects of transformational leadership together with contact with a beneficiary were substantial, and evident within seven weeks of receiving the training. Specifically, both sales per shift and revenue per shift were higher

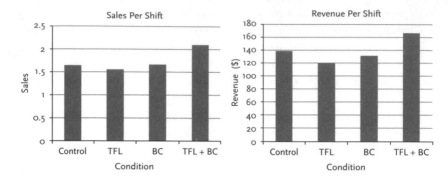

Figure 2.1
Sales and revenue per shift as a function of transformational leadership (TFL) and beneficiary contact (BC).

Data from Grant, A. M. (2012). Leading with meaning: Beneficiary contact, prosocial impact, and the performance effects of transformational leadership. *Academy of Management Journal, 55*, 458–476.

when employees received the transformational message *and* met with an internal beneficiary than for any of the three other groups (see Figure 2.1). What this shows is that minimal contact with a beneficiary was sufficient to enhance the effects of a brief transformational leadership intervention on sales and revenue even further, and the brevity of both interventions points strongly to the everyday value of this procedure for sales organizations. In addition, the brevity and negligible cost of the intervention remind us that sometimes significant effects can be achieved with small interventions.

Showing that transformational leadership and sales performance are linked is one thing; being able to show that transformational leadership can be taught, with subsequent changes in sales performance, is another. In a study I conducted with my colleagues Tom Weber and Kevin Kelloway,[41] bank managers received training for one day in transformational leadership. We followed up with all the trained managers each month for several months, and showed that changes in their transformational leadership influenced their subordinates' sales performance—despite the fact that their subordinates did not know that their branch managers had received any leadership training.

Of course, transformational leadership is not the only form of leadership associated with sales performance. John Mathieu, Michael Aherne, and Scott Taylor showed that "empowering leadership" (e.g., providing autonomy, showing confidence in the employee) raised salespeople's (a) self-confidence in using new technology relevant to sales performance and (b) their actual use of this new technology, both of which then improved actual sales performance.[42] Clearly, high-quality leadership, and transformational leadership, are associated with higher levels of sales performance. In addition, interventions exist through which appropriate leadership behaviors can be developed to improve sales performance, and these interventions can likely be enhanced through beneficiary contact.

Environmental Sustainability

Climate change is one of the great challenges of the era, and how society meets this challenge will have consequences for decades to come. Organizations contribute significantly to global climate change. Going forward, how they respond will be increasingly important both from a socially responsible perspective and in terms of whether they survive or thrive. While research on organizational responses to climate change is in its infancy, there are data suggesting that organizational leadership has a role to play.

Given widespread indications that transformational leadership is associated with both mainstream organizational outcomes (e.g., sales performance) and unconventional outcomes, such as occupational safety, Jennifer Robertson and I explored whether leadership might also influence employees' pro-environmental behaviors.[43] Consistent with our research on occupational safety, we focused on context-specific leadership, and any effects of environmentally specific transformational leadership were indirect: Environmentally specific transformational leadership was associated with employees being more passionate about environmental issues. We extended the focus beyond environmentally specific transformational leadership, however, and showed that the extent to which employees saw their leaders engaging in pro-environmental behaviors also influenced their own environmental passion. In turn, it was employees' passion for the environment that led them to engage in more pro-environmental behaviors. While we clearly need more research on the effects of organizational leadership on pro-environmental behaviors, this initial study suggests a potentially beneficial focus for leaders and scholars alike.

Does leadership matter? Studies reviewed so far support the notion that leaders throughout the organization do influence a range of outcomes of considerable importance for society, organizations, and their members. When people ask whether organizational leaders matter, however, they are often more interested in CEOs and senior executives, and it is to this question that we now turn.

DO CEOS MATTER?

Most people are fascinated by CEOs, a fascination that mirrors all the complexities of a love–hate relationship. On the positive side, many people stand in awe of CEOs, the seeming enormity of the challenges they face, and what they achieve in the face of those challenges. Many others aspire to become members of the top ranks of an organization, if not the CEO themselves. On the negative side, many people hold CEOs in contempt for what they see as unnecessary greed and the catastrophically unethical or illegal behavior of a few CEOs. Not surprisingly, therefore, CEOs routinely attract intense scrutiny from the media, investors, employees, and the lay public. Given this, understanding precisely how they affect organizations, and society more generally, is of more than passing interest. But appreciating the nature and magnitude of any such effects is complicated by several factors.

First, despite the public interest in and scrutiny of CEOs, they have received considerably less scientific attention than leaders at all other levels of the organization. One reason for this is that CEOs have less time to spend completing surveys and a phalanx of support staff dedicated to protecting their time and privacy, making it difficult to invite them to participate in research and less likely that they will accept such invitations.[44] One result of this is that the studies that do exist typically use smaller samples than studies on leaders elsewhere in the organization. Second, we cannot answer the question of whether CEOs matter by simply contrasting those organizations with and those without CEOs—indeed, any organization without a CEO for anything other than a very brief period of time would soon provide an answer to the question of whether CEOs matter! Indeed, there is research showing that return on assets declines, and investors respond negatively during short-term crisis periods when organizations are led by an "interim CEO."[45]

Thus, what we seek here is not an answer to the question of whether CEOs matter. Of course they do—just ask any CEO! Instead, we will first focus on several characteristics or attributes of CEOs that have attracted research attention. Anticipating positive outcomes, some researchers have investigated the effects of CEO transformational leadership and charisma. At the same time, other researchers have explored CEO narcissism and hubris. We will examine the effects of these four CEO behaviors or attributes on organizational and financial performance. Thereafter, we will look to the research investigating the effects of CEOs' unexpected deaths as a unique way of addressing the question of whether leaders, and specifically CEOs, matter.

CEO Transformational Leadership

Recall that transformational leadership comprises four core behaviors, and it is the nature of these four behaviors that makes transformational leadership potentially salient for CEOs. Idealized influence highlights the importance of CEOs holding values and beliefs that reflect what is best for the collective interest, rather than what is optimal for self-interest. Inspirationally motivational CEOs use symbols and stories that reveal their core values and beliefs in a way that elevates others to superior performance. In using intellectual stimulation, CEOs encourage and enable members of their senior management teams to think for themselves about why work needs to get accomplished, and the best way to do so. Last, by exhibiting individualized consideration, CEOs' behaviors are focused on the needs of their followers. Importantly, the central theme across the four transformational leadership behaviors is an other-centered, rather than self-centered, orientation.

Most of the research conducted on CEO transformational leadership focuses on its possible effects on different aspects of corporate performance. One study focused on corporate entrepreneurship in small and medium-sized enterprises in 152 firms in the United States as a context in which CEOs' transformational leadership might be especially salient.[46] Like the findings from studies on the effects of transformational leadership in general, most of the positive effects of CEO transformational leadership on corporate entrepreneurship were indirect: CEOs' transformational leadership had three important outcomes: (a) decentralization of responsibility to top management teams, (b) the extent to which risk propensity was shared amongst the 416 top management team members, and (c) behavioral integration in the top management team. In turn, each of these three outcomes affected corporate entrepreneurship.

Don Jung, Anne Wu, and Chee Chow studied the effects of CEOs' transformational leadership on firm innovation—a component of entrepreneurship—in Taiwan.[47] CEO transformational leadership was associated with company-level innovation, but this effect was even more pronounced when the climate for innovation within the organization, competition, and organizational uncertainty were high, and decentralization, formalization, and empowerment in the top team were low.

Paralleling these findings, the research on CEOs' transformational leadership on corporate performance replicates what we have learned about leaders who are dispersed throughout the organization, namely that any effects on the outcomes of interest are indirect. For example, one study of 96 credit unions in the United States showed that CEO transformational leadership initially influenced agreement about goal importance in the top management team, and it was the enhanced agreement that improved the credit union's return on assets.[48] A separate study of 170 companies in Singapore showed that higher CEO transformational leadership was associated with the extent to which the organization's human resource management (HRM) practices focused on developing human capital. In turn, when HRM practices were focused on developing human capital, employee absence in the organization was lower, and perceptions of organizational outcomes relative to the performance of industry competitors were higher.[49]

As scholars caution, we ignore differences in organizational context at our peril,[50] and accounting for the role of contextual factors highlights important nuances in CEO effectiveness. In one study, Yan Ling and her researchers suggested that the size of the organization would make a difference to the potential influence of the CEO.[51] Presumably, closer relationships between leader and follower at all levels that are possible in smaller organizations may be more challenging for CEOs of larger organizations. Data from the 121 small and medium enterprises (SMEs) in the southwest United States that these researchers studied supported their argument, as CEO transformational leadership was a significantly stronger predictor of growth in sales in smaller rather than in relatively larger organizations. Further emphasizing the role of context, the likelihood that CEO transformational leadership would predict whether annual goals for net income were realized was stronger in start-up than in established companies in the United States.[52]

The effects of CEO transformational leadership are not limited to what we might regard as traditional organizations. Christian Resick and his co-researchers investigated the effects of transformational leadership among 75 CEOs of Major League Baseball teams in the United States between 1903 and 2002,[53] and some interesting lessons emerged from their research. First, transformational CEOs were more likely to be named as one of the most influential executives in baseball history in the biographical encyclopedia of baseball[54] than those regarded as less transformational. Second, CEO transformational leadership was associated with the team's winning percentage and fan attendance, both of which influenced corporate financial performance. Last, negating a common concern that transformational leadership is a fad, these researchers found that the effects of transformational leadership were stable across the 100-year span of their research.

Given the widespread concern about unethical decisions and behaviors of some leaders, and the central place of values within the idealized influence component of transformational leadership, Jacqueline Hood's study of CEOs in 382 small to medium-sized high-tech firms in the United States has important lessons.[55] After holding the size of the organization constant, companies with transformational CEOs were significantly more likely to have a statement of ethical practices and behavior. CEOs' transactional leadership was also measured in this study and was significantly associated with the presence of diversity training for its employees, presumably because of the emphasis on equitable interpersonal treatment inherent in transactional leadership.

Relatedly, corporate social responsibility (CSR) is rooted in a positive ethical foundation. One study focused on the relationship between CEO transformational leadership and strategic CSR, that is, activities that are more closely associated with the company's competitive strategy, as indicated by environmental, product quality, and employee relations issues in the organization.[56] This study is particularly informative, as the authors investigated the charisma and intellectual stimulation components of transformational leadership separately. Based on data from 56 firms in Canada and the United

States, CEO intellectual stimulation was strongly associated with strategic CSR in the firm, but CEO charisma was not. As a result, the authors question the wisdom of ignoring the separate components of transformational leadership, and like others,[57] note that intellectual stimulation continues to be the least researched aspect of transformational leadership—despite its potential importance! A second interesting finding from this study was that again contrary to expectations, neither CEO charisma nor intellectual stimulation was associated with social CSR, that is, activities that emphasize interpersonal and social issues, such as community relations and diversity issues. Nonetheless, the researchers did not measure the individualized consideration component of transformational leadership, and it is possible that individualized consideration, with its emphasis on employee well-being, might still be significantly associated with social CSR, reinforcing the possibility that the separate components of transformational leadership might influence different behaviors.

One final study warrants mention. Given its similarity to or partial overlap with transformational leadership, Suzanne Peterson, Benjamin Galvin, and Donald Lange showed that CEOs' servant leadership predicted company return on assets.[58] Confidence in these results is increased because Peterson and her colleagues averaged return on assets over several different quarters to reduce spurious effects that can emerge from unusual performance during a single quarter.

CEO Charisma

Perhaps the most conspicuous example of CEO charisma is the President of the United States of America, an ideal context in which to examine the effects of CEO charisma given its visibility, and the immense consequences associated with the president's success and failure. Not surprisingly, there is a long-standing and immense literature on this topic, with intriguing and important findings.[59] For example, charisma is associated in the first instance with leader emergence: Research from the 1996[60] and 2008[61] U.S. elections showed that charisma was an important factor in being elected president. Presidential charisma is then positively associated with multiple and diverse ratings of the president's domestic performance.[62]

Fewer studies have focused on the organizational consequences of CEO charisma, but the positive effects of CEO charisma again become evident. In a study of U.S. and Canadian CEOs conducted by David Waldman, Mansour Javidan, and Paul Varella, charisma was associated with higher levels of corporate performance outcomes such as return on assets and the profitability of sales.[63]

Bass' idea that when confronted with crises employees become "charisma hungry" may shed more light on the nature of this relationship. Researchers have investigated whether the effects of CEO charisma are affected by the presence or absence of crisis-like situations. One study of 48 Fortune 500 companies showed that CEO charisma was associated with high levels of corporate performance (i.e., net profit margin over a five-year period) under conditions of considerable environmental uncertainty (i.e., rapid, risky, and stressful external changes).[64] This effect is not limited to the United States, as a separate study of 54 small and medium-sized organizations in the Netherlands found similar results.[65] Waldman, Javidan, and Varealla's findings also raise the possibility that it is not only CEO charisma that is associated with corporate performance under conditions of uncertainty but also CEO intellectual stimulation,[66] pointing to the importance of leaders facilitating and supporting employee problem-solving during uncertainty.

A core characteristic of charisma is persuasiveness, and researchers have investigated whether and how charismatic CEOs influence the people with whom they interact. Angelo Fanelli, Vilmos Misangyi, and Henry Tosi set up an intriguing context in which to study CEO charisma.[67] Much of the research evaluating the effects of CEO leadership uses aspects of stock value of the company as the outcome. However, the role of securities analysts' advice and recommendations in influencing the value of organizations cannot be ignored, and Fanelli et al. investigated the extent to which CEO charisma influenced analysts' recommendations (which in turn could influence organizations' stock value). To do so, they accessed the first written communication that new CEOs of 367 publicly traded corporations in the United States had with shareholders, and made an assessment of the CEOs' charisma from this communication. Importantly, because it was the first such communication, the likelihood that an analyst's assessments were based on prior knowledge of the CEO's effectiveness is minimized. Fanelli and colleagues' showed that CEOs' charisma influenced the favorability of analysts' recommendations, pointing to the importance of CEO charisma in an area not typically considered in research.

Charismatic CEOs' ability to persuade and influence others may not be limited to analysts and stockholders. In a study of 59 CEOs from large publicly traded organizations across 29 industries in the United States, Henry Tosi and his colleagues investigated whether there was a relationship between perceptions of CEO charisma and CEO compensation.[68] Their findings showed that perceived CEO charisma was associated with higher levels of CEO compensation. They suggested that one reason for this finding could be that compensation committees value the visioning skills associated with charismatic leadership. However, we should not exclude the possibility that charismatic leaders' exceptional communication and motivational skills also leave them at a distinct advantage when they negotiate their own compensation package with boards' compensation committees, resulting in higher levels of compensation for themselves.

Thus, CEOs' charisma matters in several different ways. First, CEO charisma affects diverse aspects of organizational and corporate performance. Second, under some conditions, such as environmental uncertainty, the importance of CEO charisma is increased—and this would be consistent with Bass' initial notion that, faced with a crisis, people become "charisma hungry." Finally, CEO charisma is associated with higher CEO compensation levels. Future research should investigate whether this "CEO charisma premium" is consistent with the company's performance and financial outcomes.

Both transformational and charismatic CEOs share a common characteristic: Confident in their own skills and talents, their primary emphasis is on how they can elevate the "other." In contrast to that emphasis, we now turn our attention to CEOs who harbor an unrealistic and unwarranted admiration of their own role and talents.

CEO Narcissism

Derived from a Greek myth about Narcissus, a man who fell in love with his own reflection, destructive narcissists are often charming and restless; their self-confidence reaches levels of grandiosity, and they have an exaggerated sense of entitlement. Narcissists devalue others, are willing to manipulate other people for their own purpose, and are skilled at doing so, and they prefer and develop superficial relationships. Given these characteristics, stereotypically narcissistic CEOs would raise concerns about possible negative effects on their organizations,[69] and researchers have addressed this issue.

Some workplace studies provide important insights into the nature of CEO narcissism. While not focused on CEOs, Timothy Judge and his colleagues' work showed that narcissistic leaders who were dispersed throughout the organization exaggerated their own leadership skills.[70] While this finding is to be expected, narcissism was also associated with less favorable leadership evaluations by these same leaders' subordinates—one of the findings justifying the unusually descriptive title of their article, "Loving yourself abundantly." Hwee Khoo and Giles Burch did focus on CEOs' narcissism in their study of 117 CEOs and senior managers in New Zealand. Their findings supported those of Judge and colleagues, showing that the more narcissistic the CEOs and senior managers, the less they engaged in transformational leadership.[71] Findings such as these suggest that while there are separate literatures for CEOs and other leaders spread throughout the organization, the processes and outcomes for these different leaders might be similar.

Other studies have shown that CEOs scoring higher on narcissism were rated as lower in servant leadership by their CFOs.[72] The study of CEOs of Major League Baseball teams between 1903 and 2002 mentioned previously was more specific, and showed that the higher the CEO narcissism, the lower the individualized consideration component of transformational leadership. The probable reason for this is that the self-focused nature of narcissism is antithetical to caring for others, or being focused on their development. Narcissistic CEOs in this baseball study were also less likely to enact the behaviors involved in the contingent reward component of the transformational model. Christian Resick and his coauthors suggest that the reason for this is that the narcissistic personality is incompatible with the fairness inherent in the exchange relationship that lies at the core of contingent reward.[73]

But what are the organizational consequences of narcissistic CEOs? In a major study, Arijit Chatterjee and Donald Hambrick studied the link between narcissistic CEOs and company strategy and performance in computer software and hardware organizations between 1992 and 2004.[74] In general, narcissistic CEOs tended to produce outcomes more likely to attract attention to themselves, validating the title Chatterjee and Hambrick gave to the article— "It's all about me." For example, narcissistic CEOs were more likely to prefer bold actions and strategies and to engage in a higher number of more expensive acquisitions. The findings of this study also showed that higher levels of CEO narcissism were associated with more extreme financial outcomes—both positive and negative—and more changes in financial performance.

Because narcissistic CEOs tend to make difficult decisions more hastily,[75] Nihat Aktas and colleagues followed the Chatterjee and Hambrick research by studying the effects of CEO narcissism during merger negotiations. Their focus included 656 deals negotiated between 2002 and 2006 in which both the acquirer and target companies were U.S. listed firms,[76] where the value of the transaction was greater than $1 million and reflected more than 1% of the acquiring firm's market value. As the researchers had expected, CEO narcissism was associated with a speedier completion of the private portion of merger negotiations—which could be very risky when due diligence is critical. CEO narcissism was also associated with a greater likelihood of completing the deal. Again highlighting the effects of narcissism on CEOs' leadership behavior, Wolf-Christian Gerstner and his team studied 72 CEOs within the biotech industry.[77] They showed that "audience engagement," which reflected broad interest in their industry as indicated by stories in the *New York Times* and the *Wall Street Journal*, was sufficient to influence narcissistic CEOs' decision-making and behaviors. Taken together, therefore, the research that has been conducted would suggest that influenced by their narcissism, these leaders behave in ways (e.g., more hasty decision-making, more extreme risk-taking) that are more likely to disadvantage their organizations.

How CEO narcissism is measured sheds some light on its nature. Standard personality methods have been used, in which CEOs respond to items on questionnaires such as the Hogan Development Survey,[78] the Gough Adjective Check List,[79] or the Narcissistic Personality Inventory.[80] This technique is potentially compromised, as self-report measures might be readily manipulated at the hands of skilled narcissists. More revealing, therefore, is a body of research that assesses CEO narcissism in a more unobtrusive manner. In the study on CEOs of Major League Baseball teams, senior undergraduate students served as assessors.[81] After receiving between 30 and 35 hours of training, they read all the biographical statements about the CEO published in *Baseball: The Biographical Encyclopedia*, and rated each CEO's narcissism on previously developed scales. Even more revealing is Chatterjee and Hambrick's assessment of CEO narcissism:[82] Their index of CEO narcissism was based on the prominence of CEOs' (a) photographs in the annual report (higher scores are given for narcissism when the CEO is more prominent, for example, alone in a large picture),[i] (b) names in press releases (more frequent mentions controlling for the total number of words), and (c) self-references (measured as the number of first-person singular pronouns used in interviews with the CEO). Finally, because CEOs exert substantial influence over their own pay and that of their senior team, the difference between their total compensation and that of the next-highest paid member of their senior team can provide an additional indicator of their narcissism. Wolf-Christian Gerstner and his colleagues used essentially the same criteria for their research on CEO narcissism and added one more unobtrusive item—the standing of the CEO in press releases, expressed as the number of times the CEO's name was used divided by the number of times the next-highest paid executive was named.[83]

Unobtrusive measures like these might be extremely useful not just when studying CEOs' narcissism but also when studying CEO leadership more generally. For example, U.S. presidents' inaugural speeches have been analyzed successfully for evidence of their charisma.[84] Despite the intensive efforts required to obtain unobtrusive data, they provide a picture that may not be accessible through other more traditional methods (e.g., self-rated surveys). Unobtrusive measures may also be especially useful in situations where CEOs are less willing to participate in surveys or are motivated to distort some of their responses, such as when the focus of the research is on negative aspects of leadership.

CEO Hubris

Closely related to the psychological trait of narcissism is hubris. One definition of *hubris* is an exaggerated sense of self-confidence—Nathan Hiller and Donald Hambrick speak of executives who suffer from hubris as being

i. Like virtually all other corporate annual reports, Enron's 1997 report for shareholders had a picture of its infamous CEO, Ken Lay, whose greed eventually led to the downfall of the organization. Unlike the picture of CEOs in virtually all other annual reports, however, Lay's picture was spread over an entire page. While a single case never "proves" a point, it can be more than illustrative!

"full… of themselves" (p. 306).[85] Much of what is known about CEO and executive hubris derives from Dr. David Owen, the former British Foreign Secretary and a qualified psychiatrist, who has written extensively about the existence of a "hubris syndrome" in political leaders. With the psychiatric fondness for diagnoses and labels, Dr. Owen has suggested that hubris is present if at least three or four of the following symptoms are present:[86]

- Viewing the world as a place to achieve personal power and glory
- Propensity to take actions that will make one be viewed positively
- Fixation with one's image
- Messianic manner of speaking, and use of the third-person or royal "we"
- Identification of oneself with the nation and national interest
- Excessive self-confidence bordering on invincibility, and contempt for others' advice and feedback
- A belief that one answers to history or God, rather than those one represents;
- Impulsivity and progressive isolation
- A moral rectitude that blinds one to the everyday realities of negative outcomes, which results in what Owen calls "hubristic incompetence"

Owen also points to situational characteristics of the hubris syndrome that would be unique to political leaders. For example, hubris becomes more likely as the length of time the leader has enjoyed political power increases, and unlike other forms of mental illness that are stable across contexts, hubristic symptoms usually subside when the individual is no longer in power. Many of the symptoms associated with hubris might be more likely to be present among those who seek political office (e.g., those who identify themselves with the national self-interest) or those who are more likely to be successful in elections (e.g., those most adept at messianic speech). As Malcolm Potts notes, our political system itself might favor the exaggeratedly self-confident.[87] Potts also questions whether environments in which conflict is the norm, such as the military, might favor and reward overconfidence. To date, most of the evidence in support of the hubris syndrome has derived from post hoc analyses, typically by psychiatrists or historians, of former or deceased political leaders' mental illness.[88]

But is hubris limited to political leaders and those in public sector organizations? And might CEO hubris be counterproductive? While there is a pervasive belief that with respect to leadership effectiveness, "the more self-confidence, the merrier,"[89] is it not possible that there are limits to the performance benefits of leaders' self-confidence, and that an overabundance of self-confidence might have negative effects? This is certainly the case with other presumably positive characteristics. For example, Daniel Ames and Francis Flynn showed that ever-higher levels of assertiveness can hurt leadership,[90] and Jim

McNulty and Frank Fincham point out more generally how optimism can lead gamblers astray—even in the face of significant losses.[91]

As was the case with CEO narcissism, research has focused on the effects of executive hubris on mergers and acquisitions, as hubris might influence CEOs facing decisions that have the power to transform the size, reputation, and value of their current organization. Starting almost 30 years ago with Richard Roll's research, the available evidence clearly indicates that an exaggerated sense of self affects rational decision-making by CEOs regarding large acquisitions.[92] More recent research has confirmed that CEOs' hubris[93] and overconfidence[94] are implicated in risky acquisition and investment decision-making. Refining these findings, Mathew Hayward and Hambrick showed that CEOs high in hubris were willing to overpay for large acquisitions (i.e., more than the value of the targeted organization), and that this was more likely to occur in the presence of weak governance boards (i.e., greater number of insiders, and greater likelihood that the board chair and CEO positions were held by the same person).

Importantly, this hubristic phenomenon is not limited to the United States. Overly hubristic CEOs in China were prone to the same risky decision-making, and Jiatao Li and Yi Tang showed that hubristic CEOs who were afforded higher levels of discretion in their roles were again especially vulnerable to this hubris effect.[95] What these studies collectively tell us is that there are limits to the benefits of CEO self-confidence, and that when CEO self-confidence spills over into hubris, organizations might well suffer the consequences.

We end this section with the question of whether hubristic CEOs and executives can be treated. Aside from the fact that no evidence exists suggesting that they can be, Owen and Jonathan Davidson argue cogently that it is highly unlikely that hubristic leaders would seek help in the first instance.[96] After all, they are more likely to see the very symptoms of the hubris symptom as a cause for pride, the source of their current success, and a precondition for their continued success—not as a problem worthy of treatment! Nonetheless, Owen suggests that hubris is less likely to develop in those who are more modest, willing to accept criticism, exhibit a healthy degree of skepticism, and a grounded sense of humor.[97] While treatment of hubris is unlikely at this stage, one possibility is that these characteristics might help guide selection decisions accordingly.

CEO Death and Company Performance

News of the passing of Steve Jobs, founder and former CEO of Apple, on October 5, 2011 sent journalists racing to file stories questioning whether this foreshadowed dark days for Apple's shareholders. Overall, investors' response the day after Jobs' death was mixed. The immediate response on the Frankfurt stock market was negative, with Apple shares falling as much as 5% before recovering, but trading in Apple shares swung up and down, by the end of the day showing a short-term resilience and stability that comforted investors. A year later, Apple had soared almost 75% in value. Understanding these fluctuations is complicated by the fact that the value of rival Samsung had increased by 63%.[98] What must be remembered, however, is that Jobs' death had been widely expected by investors, and the succession plan had ensured that Tim Cook assumed responsibility before Jobs' passing. Perhaps part of the answer to whether and how much CEOs matter to their organizations can be gleaned from complex situations like this.

While this has been a question of some interest to investors and organizations for a long time,[99] there are relatively few studies to guide organizations facing such situations, and the available findings show no consistent evidence of either a positive or negative effect of CEO death on financial performance. Does this mean that CEOs have no effects on the performance or shareholder value of their organizations? Not at all! One possibility is that there are no consistent, immediate effects but that there are delayed effects. Indeed, in the days following the announcement of a CEO's death, stock prices for affected companies tend to show greater dispersion.[100] This dispersion, and decisions made in particular cases such as the death of Steve Jobs, suggests that nuances within companies likely influence how a CEO's death might influence corporate and organizational performance. In particular, the situation prior to the CEO's death, the nature of the death, and characteristics about the CEO and the organization influence how a CEO's death might affect the organization and sheds additional light on the larger question of whether and how leaders matter to their organizations.

First, events occurring prior to a CEO's death shape how important stakeholders think about the organization and its future. For example, shareholders react positively to the news when the financial performance of the organization prior to the CEO's death was negative, presumably because this provides an opportunity to move forward more positively. The stock market also reacts positively if the organization had been targeted for takeover prior to the CEO's death.[101] This effect is magnified in cases where governance boards are strongly independent,[102] perhaps because they are more likely to take corrective action in the first instance. Similarly, stakeholders (e.g., shareholders, board members) are more likely to respond positively when they believe that the CEO had been clinging to power for too long. Thus, shareholder responses are more likely to be positive when the CEO who died was older,[103] had held the position of CEO[104] for a longer period of time, and held a large ownership stake in the organization.[105]

Second, whether the CEO or executive's death is sudden and unexpected or the end stage of a long illness that employees and shareholders had full knowledge of (as was the case with Steve Jobs) is of some importance. Responses to unexpected deaths are more likely to be negative, probably because share-holders will be concerned about the potential for internal disruption in the organization and have concerns about the future leadership and direction of the organization. Alternatively, when the CEO dies following a protracted illness, the market might already have reacted negatively before the death, anticipating any future negative effects.[106] In the case of Steve Jobs, his illness was common knowledge, and Apple had implemented a succession plan before he died, signaling to investors and employees alike that Apple was a well-run organization with a long-term future.

Third, the way in which the governance board responds to the challenge of selecting the new CEO also influences effects of the former CEO's death. Broadly speaking, the board can go internally or externally in selecting the new CEO, and shareholders tend to respond more positively when the successor is hired from within the organization.[107] The probable reasons for this are that internal succession signals that some succession planning had occurred within the organization, and that the board is confident with the internal talent in the organization, again suggesting to shareholders that it is a well-managed organization. In addition, transaction costs would be lower in cases of internal succession, as the process involved in an internal search for the successor would likely be less time-consuming, costly, and disruptive.

Finally, characteristics of the deceased CEO, the organization, and the board influence how the CEO's demise affects the organizations. When the deceased CEO was the founder of the organization (or a relative of the founder), the effects of the CEO's death on investor wealth are more likely to be negative,[108] probably because founder CEOs are perceived to exert a stronger influence on the organization, in some cases even reflecting the personality of the organization they led. As a result, any subsequent disruption and uncertainty would be greater. Second, scholars have speculated that the size of the organization makes a difference.[109] It would be easier for CEOs in smaller organizations to exert a greater influence on the organization; hence the sudden passing of CEOs in smaller organizations would be more disruptive. In addition, with fewer resources, smaller organizations may be more vulnerable to sudden and unexpected events such as a CEO's death. Third, research has also focused on the role of the governance board in cases of CEO deaths. Findings show that the stock market is more likely to react positively to the announcement of a CEO's death if the company has a strong, independent board (i.e., those with a greater proportion of outside members).[110] Positive effects are likely more pronounced in companies experiencing poorer financial performance, because in those situations, strong boards might be able to exert their greatest remedial effects.

To conclude this section on a less morbid note, similar lessons can be drawn from a study by Gary Ballinger, David Lehman, and David Schoorman of employees of 45 different veterinary hospitals.[111] They showed that employees who shared a high-quality relationship with their leader (the medical director) had stronger ties to the organization and were more likely to remain with the organization. None of this is surprising. However, nine of the veterinary hospitals studied by Ballinger and his team experienced a change in their organizational leadership, and employees who had enjoyed a positive LMX relationship with their medical director were *more* likely to exit the organization voluntarily after the succession. Clearly, the benefits of a high-quality relationship with one leader do not necessarily carry over to a new leader or a different leader, as Inness and her colleagues showed in their study on transformational leadership and safety.[112] What Ballinger and colleagues' study reminds us is that having a high-quality relationship with one's leader matters to employees, and precisely because it matters, employees respond accordingly.

CONCLUSION

The question posed in this chapter, "Does leadership matter?" almost invites a simple and emotionally driven "yes" or "no" response. But as the issues raised in this chapter reveal, this question is just too complex for such an answer. Instead, what findings from the many studies we have discussed demonstrate is that organizational leaders, and CEOs, do matter. An even greater appreciation of this will emerge when we examine the effects of destructive or poor leadership in Chapter 9. For now, we should remember two important points. First, despite the fact that most research has focused on transformational leadership at all levels of the organization, the research that has been conducted has not directly contrasted the effectiveness of different leadership theories. Thus, it would be premature to declare any theoretical "winners." What we can conclude, however, is that evidence supports the effectiveness of new-genre leadership theories, with their relational and inspirational, developmental and ethical emphasis. Second, organizational and corporate performance remains a function of a multitude of factors, with leadership playing a meaningful part. Whether leaders matter is shaped by a host of other factors, as will become apparent in the next chapter. For now, we can conclude that yes, indeed, leaders matter—perhaps less than some CEOs would have us believe, but more than many others might want to acknowledge. We turn our attention in Chapter 3 to understanding *how* organizational leadership "works."

SUGGESTED READING

Collingwood, H. (2009, June). Do leaders matter? *The Atlantic*. Retrieved from http://www.theatlantic.com/magazine/archive/2009/06/do-ceos-matter/307437/
Owen, D. (2008). *In sickness and in power: Illnesses in heads of government in the last 100 years*. London: Methuen.

NOTES

1. Judge, T. A., & Jammeyer-Mueller, J. D. (2012). Job attitudes. *Annual Review of Psychology, 63*, 341–367.
2. Meyer, J. P., & Allen, N. J. (1997). *Commitment in the workplace: Theory, research, and application.* Thousand Oaks, CA: SAGE Publications.
3. Jackson, T. A., Meyer, J. P., & Wang, X-H. (2013). Leadership, commitment, and culture: A meta-analysis. *Journal of Leadership and Organizational Studies, 20*, 84–106.
4. Kalleberg, A. L., Reskin, B. F., & Hudson, K. (2000). Bad jobs in America: Standard and nonstandard employment relations and job quality in the United States. *American Sociological Review, 65*, 256–278.
5. Meyer, J. P., Stanley, D. J., Herscovitch, L., & Topolnytsky, L. (2002). Affective, continuance, and normative commitment to the organization: A meta-analysis of antecedents, correlated and consequences. *Journal of Vocational Behavior, 61*, 20–52.
6. Jackson, T. A., Meyer, J. P., & Wang, X-H. (2013). Leadership, commitment, and culture: A meta-analysis. *Journal of Leadership and Organizational Studies, 20*, 84–106.
7. Avolio, B. J., Zhu, W., Koh, W., & Bhatia, P. (2004). Transformational leadership and organizational commitment: Mediating role of psychological empowerment and moderating role of structural distance. *Journal of Organizational Behavior, 25*, 951–968.
8. Eisenberger, R., Karagonlar, G., Stinglhamber, F., Neves, P., Becker, T. E., Gonzalez-Morales, M. G., & Steiger-Mueller, M. (2010). Leader-member exchange and affective organizational commitment: The contribution of supervisor's organizational embodiment. *Journal of Applied Psychology, 95*, 1085–1103.
9. Lambert, L. S., Tepper, B. J., Carr, J. C., Holt, D. T., & Barelka, A. J. (2012). Forgotten but not gone: An examination of fit between leader consideration and initiating structure needed and received. *Journal of Applied Psychology, 97*, 913–930.
10. Avolio, B. J., Gardner, W. L., Walumbwa, F. O., Luthans, F., & May, D. R. (2004). Unlocking the mask: A look at the process by which authentic leaders impact follower attitudes and behaviors. *Leadership Quarterly, 15*, 801–823.
11. Barling, J., Weber, T., & Kelloway, E. K. (1996). Effects of transformational leadership training on attitudinal and financial outcomes: A field experiment. *Journal of Applied Psychology, 81*, 827–832.
12. Djibo, I. J. A., Desiderio, K. P., & Price, N. M. (2010). Examining the role of perceived leader behaviour on temporary employees' organizational commitment and citizenship behaviour. *Human Resource Development Quarterly, 21*, 321–342.
13. Hersey, R. (1932). Rate of production and emotional state. *Personnel Journal, 11*, 355–364.
14. Judge, T. A., Thoresen, C. J., Bono, J. E., & Patton, G. K. (2001). The job satisfaction–job performance relationship: A qualitative and quantitative review. *Psychological Bulletin, 127*, 376–407.
15. Kuoppala, J., Lamminpää, A., Liira, J., & Vaino, H. (2008). Leadership, job well-being, and health effects—A systematic review and a meta-analysis. *Journal of Occupational and Environmental Medicine, 60*, 904–915; Sparks, K., Faragher, B., & Cooper, C. L. (2001). Well-being and occupational health in the 21st century. *Journal of Occupational and Organizational Psychology, 74*, 489–509.

16. Bono, J. E., Foldes, H., Vinson, G., & Muros, J. P. (2007). Workplace emotions: The role of supervision and leadership. *Journal of Applied Psychology, 92,* 1357–1367.

17. Eriksen, W. (2005). Work factors as predictors of smoking relapse in nurses' aides. *International Archives of Occupational and Environmental Health, 79,* 244–250; Whiteman, J., Snyder, D., & Ragland, J. (2001). The value of leadership in implementing and maintaining a successful health promotion program in the Naval Surface Force, US Pacific Fleet. *American Journal of Health Promotion, 15,* 96–102.

18. Beauchamp, M. R., Barling, J., & Morton, K. (2011) Transformational teaching and adolescent self-determined motivation, self-efficacy, and intentions to engage in leisure time physical activity: A randomized controlled pilot trial. *Applied Psychology: Health and Well-Being, 3,* 127–150.

19. Slaunwhite, J. M., Smith, S. M., Fleming, M., Strang, R., & Lockhart, C. (2009). Increasing vaccination rates among health care workers: Using "champions" as a motivator. *Canadian Journal of Infection Control, 24,* 159–164.

20. Kelloway, E. K., & Barling, J. (2010). Leadership development as an intervention in occupational health psychology. *Work and Stress, 24,* 260–279.

21. Arnold, K. A., Turner, N., Barling, J., Kelloway, E. K., & McKee, M. C. (2007). Transformational leadership and psychological well-being: The mediating role of meaningful work. *Journal of Occupational Health Psychology, 12,* 193–203.

22. Nielsen, K., Randall, R., Yarker, J., & Brenner, S-O. (2008). The effects of transformational leadership on followers' perceived work characteristics and psychological well-being: A longitudinal study. *Work and Stress, 22,* 16–32.

23. Liu, J., Siu, O. L., & Shi, K. (2010). Transformational leadership and employee well-being: The mediating role of trust in the leader and self-efficacy. *Applied Psychology: An International Review, 59,* 454–479.

24. Carroll, A. E., & Turner, N. (2008). Psychology of workplace safety: A thematic review of some possibilities. In J. Barling & C. L. Cooper (Eds.), *The SAGE Handbook of Organizational Behavior* (Vol. 1) (pp. 541–557). Thousand Oaks, CA: SAGE Publications.

25. Butler, M. C., & Jones, A.P. (1979). Perceived leader behavior, individual characteristics, and injury occurrence in hazardous work environments. *Journal of Applied Psychology, 64,* 299–304.

26. Barling, J., Loughlin, C., & Kelloway, E. K. (2002). Development and test of a model linking safety-specific transformational leadership and occupational safety. *Journal of Applied Psychology, 87,* 488–496.

27. Conchie, S. M., & Donald, I. J. (2009). The moderating role of safety-specific trust on the relation between safety-specific leadership and safety citizenship behaviors. *Journal of Occupational Health Psychology, 14,* 137–147.

28. Kelloway, E. K., Mullen, J., & Francis, L. (2006). Divergent effects of transformational and passive leadership in employee safety. *Journal of Occupational Health Psychology, 11,* 76–86.

29. Inness, M., Turner, N., Barling, J., & Stride, C. (2010). Transformational leadership and employee safety performance: A within-person, between-jobs design. *Journal of Occupational Health Psychology, 15,* 279–290.

30. Hofmann, D. A., Morgeson, F. P., & Gerras, S. J. (2003). Climate as a moderator of the relationship between leader-member exchange and content specific

citizenship: Safety climate as an exemplar. *Journal of Applied Psychology, 88*, 170–178.

31. Mullen, J. E., & Kelloway, E. K. (2009). Safety leadership: A longitudinal study of the effects of transformational leadership on safety outcomes. *Journal of Occupational and Organizational Psychology, 82*, 253–272.

32. Zohar, D. (1980). Safety climate in industrial organizations: Theoretical and applied implications. *Journal of Applied Psychology, 65*, 96–102; Zohar, D. (2002). Modifying supervisory practices to improve subunit safety: A leadership-based intervention model. *Journal of Applied Psychology, 87*, 156–163.

33. Comer, J. M., & Dubinsky, A. J. (1985). *Managing the successful sales force.* Lexington, MA: Lexington Books.

34. Dubinsky, A. J., Yammarino, F. J., Jolson, M. A., & Spangler, W. D. (1995). Transformational leadership: An initial investigation in sales management. *Journal of Personal Selling and Sales Management, 15*, 17–31.

35. Russ, F. A., McNeilly, K. M., & Comer, J. M. (1996). Leadership, decision making and performance of sales managers: A multi-level approach. *Journal of Personal Selling and Sales Management, 16*(Summer), 1–15.

36. Dubinsky, A. J., Yammarino, F. J., Jolson, M. A., & Spangler, W. D. (1995). Transformational leadership: An initial investigation in sales management. *Journal of Personal Selling and Sales Management, 15*, 17–31.

37. Howell, J. M., & Hall-Merenda, K. E. (1999). The ties that bind: The impact of leader-member exchange, transformational and transactional leadership, and distance on predicting follower performance. *Journal of Applied Psychology, 84*, 680–694.

38. Russ, F. A., McNeilly, K. M., & Comer, J. M. (1996). Leadership, decision making and performance of sales managers: A multi-level approach. *Journal of Personal Selling and Sales Management, 16* (Summer), 1–15.

39. MacKenzie, S. B., Podsakoff, P. M., & Rich, G. A. (2001). Transformational and transactional leadership and sales performance. *Journal of the Academy of Marketing Science, 29*, 115–134.

40. Grant, A. M. (2012). Leading with meaning: Beneficiary contact, prosocial impact, and the performance effects of transformational leadership. *Academy of Management Journal, 55*, 458–476.

41. Barling, J., Weber, T., & Kelloway, E. K. (1996). Effects of transformational leadership training on attitudinal and financial outcomes: A field experiment. *Journal of Applied Psychology, 81*, 827–832.

42. Mathieu, J., Ahearne, M., & Taylor, S. R. (2007). A longitudinal cross-level model of leader and salesperson influences on sales force technology use and performance. *Journal of Applied Psychology, 92*, 528–537.

43. Robertson, J., & Barling, J. (2013). Greening organizations through leaders' influence on employees' pro-environmental behaviors. *Journal of Organizational Behavior, 34*, 176–194.

44. Cycyota, C. S., & Harrison, D. A. (2006). What (not) to expect when surveying executives: A meta-analysis of top manager response rates and techniques over time. *Organizational Research Methods, 9*, 133–160.

45. Ballinger, G. A., & Marcel, J. J. (2010). The use of an interim CEO during succession episodes and firm performance. *Strategic Management Journal, 31*, 262–283.

46. Ling, Y., Simsek, Z., Lubatkin, M. H., & Veiga, J. F. (2008). Transformational leadership's role in promoting corporate entrepreneurship: Examining the CEO-TMT interface. *Academy of Management Journal, 51*, 557–576.

47. Jung, D., Wu, A., & Chow, C. W. (2008). Towards understanding the direct and indirect effects of CEOs' transformational leadership on firm innovation. *Leadership Quarterly, 19*, 582–594.

48. Colbert, A. E., Kristof-Brown, A. I., Bradley, B. H., & Barrick, M. R. (2008). CEO transformational leadership: The role of goal importance in top management teams. *Academy of Management Journal, 51*, 81–96.

49. Zhu, W., Chew, I. K. H., & Spangler, W. D. (2005). CEO transformational leadership and organizational outcomes: The mediating role of human-capital-enhancing human resource management. *Leadership Quarterly, 16*, 39–52.

50. Johns, G. (2006). The essential impact of context on organizational behavior. *Academy of Management Review, 31*, 386–408.

51. Ling, Y., Simsek, Z., Lubatkin, M. H., & Veiga, J. F. (2008). The impact of transformational CEOs on the performance of small- to medium-sized firms: Does organizational context matter? *Journal of Applied Psychology, 93*, 923–934.

52. Peterson, S. J., Walumbwa, F. O., Byron, K., & Myrowitz, J. (2009). CEO positive psychological traits, transformational leadership, and firm performance in high-technology start-up and established firms. *Journal of Management, 35*, 348–368.

53. Resick, C. J., Whitman, D. S., Weingarden, S. M., & Hiller, N. J. (2009). The bright-side and the dark-side of CEO personality: Examining core-self evaluations, narcissism, transformational leadership and strategic influence. *Journal of Applied Psychology, 94*, 1365–1381.

54. Pietrusza, D., Silverman, M., & Gershman, M. (2000). *Baseball: The biographical encyclopedia*. Kingston, NY: Total/Sports Illustrated.

55. Hood, J. (2003). The relationship of leadership style and CEO values to ethical practices in organizations. *Journal of Business Ethics, 43*, 263–273.

56. Waldman, D. A., Siegel, D. S., & Javidan, M. (2006). Components of CEO transformational leadership and corporate social responsibility. *Journal of Management Studies, 43*, 1703–1725.

57. Locke, E. A. (2003). Foundations for a theory of leadership. In S. E. Murphy & R. E. Riggio (Eds.), *The future of leadership development* (pp. 121–137). Mahwah, NJ: Lawrence Erlbaum Associates.

58. Peterson, S. J., Galvin, B. M., & Lange, D. (2012). CEO servant leadership: Exploring executive characteristics and firm performance. *Personnel Psychology, 65*, 565–596.

59. Simonton, D. K. (1987). *Why presidents succeed: A political psychology of leadership*. New Haven, CT: Yale University Press.

60. Pillai, R., & Williams, E. A. (1998). Does leadership matter in the political arena? Voters' perceptions of candidates' transformational and charismatic leadership and the 1996 U.S. presidential vote. *Leadership Quarterly, 9*, 397–406.

61. Bligh, M. C., & Kohles, J. C. (2009). The enduring allure of charisma: How Barack Obama won the historic 2008 presidential election. *Leadership Quarterly, 20*, 483–492.

62. House, R. J., Spangler, W. D., & Woycke, J. (1991). Personality and charisma in the U.S. Presidency: A psychological theory of leader effectiveness. *Administrative Science Quarterly, 36*, 364–396.

63. Waldman, D. A., Javidan, M., & Varella, P. (2004). Charismatic leadership at the strategic level: A new application of upper echelons theory. *Leadership Quarterly, 15*, 355–380.

64. Waldman, D. A., Ramirez, G. G., House, R. J., & Puranam, P. (2001). Does leadership matter? CEO leadership attributes and profitability under conditions of perceived environmental uncertainty. *Academy of Management Journal, 44,* 134–143.
65. De Hoogh, A. H. N., den hartog, D. N., Koopman, P. L., Thierry, H., van den Berg, P. T., van der Weide, J. G., & Wilderdom, C. P. M. (2004). Charismatic leadership, environmental dynamism, and performance. *European Journal of Work and Organizational Psychology, 13,* 447–471.
66. Waldman, D. A., Javidan, M., & Varella, P. (2004). Effects of transformational leadership training on attitudinal and financial outcomes: A field experiment. *Journal of Applied Psychology, 81,* 827–832.
67. Fanelli, A., Misangyi, V. F., & Tosi, H. L. (2009). In charisma we trust: The effects of CEO charismatic visions on security analysts. *Organization Science, 20,* 1011–1033.
68. Tosi, H. L., Misangyi, V. F., Fanelli, A., Waldman, D. A., & Yammarino, F. J. (2004). CEO charisma, compensation, and firm performance. *Leadership Quarterly, 15,* 405–420.
69. Lubit, R. (2002). The long-term organizational impact of destructively narcissistic managers. *Academy of Management Executive, 16(1),* 127–138.
70. Judge, T. A., LePine, J. A., & Rich, B. L. (2006). Loving yourself abundantly: Relationship of the narcissistic personality to self- and other perceptions of workplace deviance, leadership, and task and contextual performance. *Journal of Applied Psychology, 91,* 762–776.
71. Khoo, H. S., & Burch, G. St. J. (2008). The "dark side" of leadership personality and transformational leadership: An exploratory study. *Personality and Individual Differences, 44,* 86–97.
72. Peterson, S. J., Galvin, B. M., & Lange, D. (2012). CEO servant leadership: Exploring executive characteristics and firm performance. *Personnel Psychology, 65,* 565–596.
73. Resick, C. J., Whitman, D. S., Weingarden, S. M., & Hiller, N. J. (2009). The bright-side and the dark-side of CEO personality: Examining core-self evaluations, narcissism, transformational leadership and strategic influence. *Journal of Applied Psychology, 94,* 1365–1381.
74. Chatterjee, A., & Hambrick, D. C. (2007). It's all about me: Narcissistic chief executive officers and their effects on company strategy and performance. *Administrative Science Quarterly, 52,* 351–386.
75. Lubit, R. (2002). The long-term organizational impact of destructively narcissistic managers. *Academy of Management Executive, 16(1),* 127–138.
76. Aktas, N., de Bodt, E., Bollaert, H., & Roll, R. (2010). *CEO narcissism and the takeover process: From private initiation to deal completion.* Retrieved from https://fisher.osu.edu/blogs/efa2011/files/BEH_2_3.pdf
77. Gerstner, W-C., König, A., Enders, A., & Hambrick, D. E. (2013). CEO narcissism, audience engagement, and organizational adoption of technological discontinuities. *Administrative Science Quarterly, 58,* 257–291.
78. *Hogan Development.* Tulsa, OK: Hogan Assessment Systems.
79. Gough, H. G., & Heilbrun, A. B. (1965). *The Adjective Check List Manual.* Palo Alto, CA: Consulting Psychologists Press.
80. Raskin, R., & Terry, H. (1988). A principal-components analysis of the Narcissistic Personality Inventory and further evidence of its construct validity. *Journal of Personality and Social Psychology, 54,* 890–902.

81. Resick, C. J., Whitman, D. S., Weingarden, S. M., & Hiller, N. J. (2009). The bright-side and the dark-side of CEO personality: Examining core-self evaluations, narcissism, transformational leadership and strategic influence. *Journal of Applied Psychology, 94*, 1365–1381.

82. Chatterjee, A., & Hambrick, D. C. (2007). It's all about me: Narcissistic chief executive officers and their effects on company strategy and performance. *Administrative Science Quarterly, 52*, 351–386.

83. Gerstner, W-C., König, A., Enders, A., & Hambrick, D. E. (2013). CEO narcissism, audience engagement, and organizational adoption of technological discontinuities. *Administrative Science Quarterly, 58*, 257–291.

84. Emrich, C. G., Brower, H. H., Feldman, J. M., & Garland, H. (2001). Images in words: Presidential rhetoric, charisma, and greatness. *Administrative Science Quarterly, 46*, 527–557.

85. Hiller, N. J., & Hambrick, D. C. (2005). Conceptualizing executive hubris: The role of (hyper-) core self-evaluations in strategic decision-making. *Strategic Decision Making, 26*, 2005–2319.

86. Owen, D. (2008). Hubris syndrome. *Clinical Medicine, 8*, 428–432; Owen, D. (2011). Psychiatry and politicians—afterword. *The Psychiatrist, 35*, 145–148.

87. Potts, M. (2007). Overconfident in warfare. *Journal of the Royal Society of Medicine, 100*, 63.

88. Owen, D. (2008). *In sickness and in power: Illnesses in heads of government in the last 100 years*. London: Methuen.

89. Judge, T. A., & Bono, J. E. (2001). Relationship of core self-evaluation traits—self-esteem, generalized self-efficacy, locus of control, and emotional stability—with job satisfaction and job performance: A meta-analysis. *Journal of Applied Psychology, 86*, 80–92.

90. Ames, D. R., & Flynn, F. J. (2007). What breaks a leader: The curvilinear relation between assertiveness and leadership. *Journal of Personality and Social Psychology, 92*, 307–324.

91. McNulty, J. K., & Fincham, F. D. (2012). Beyond positive psychology? Toward a contextual view of psychological approaches and well-being. *American Psychologist, 67*, 101–110.

92. Roll, R. (1986). The hubris hypothesis of corporate takeovers. *Journal of Business, 59*, 197–216.

93. Hayward, M. L., & Hambrick, D. C. (1997). Explaining the premiums paid for large acquisitions: Evidence of CEO hubris. *Administrative Science Quarterly, 42*, 103–127.

94. Malmandier, U., & Tate, G. (2005). CEO overconfidence and corporate investment. *Journal of Finance, 60*, 2661–2770.

95. Li, J., & Tang, Y. (2010). CEO hubris and firm risk taking in China: The moderating role of managerial discretion. *Academy of Management Journal, 53*, 45–68.

96. Owen, D., & Davidson, J. (2011). Hubris syndrome: An acquired personality disorder? A study of US presidents and UK prime ministers over the last 100 years. *Brain, 132*, 1396–1406.

97. Owen, D. (2008). *In sickness and in power: Illnesses in heads of government in the last 100 years*. London: Methuen Publishing.

98. Rushton, K. (2012, October 4). How Apple has performed in the year since Steve Jobs' death. *The Telegraph*. Retrieved from http://www.telegraph.co.uk/technology/apple/9589295/Graphic-How-Apple-has-performed-in-the-year-since-Steve-Jobs-death.html

99. Worrell, D. L., Davidson, W. N., Chandy, P. R., & Garrison, S. L. (1986). Management turnover through deaths of key executives: Effects on investor wealth. *Academy of Management Journal, 29*, 674–694.

100. Johnson, W. B., Magee, R. P., Nagarajan, N. J., & Newman, H. A. (1985). An analysis of the stock price reaction to sudden executive deaths. *Journal of Accounting and Economics, 7*, 151–174.

101. Salas, J. M. (2010). Entrenchment, governance, and the stock price reaction to sudden executive deaths. *Journal of Banking and Finance, 34*, 656–666.

102. Borokhovich, K. A., Brunarski, K. R., Donahue, M. S., & Harman, Y. S. (2006). The importance of board quality in the event of a CEO death. *Financial Review, 41*, 307–337.

103. Combs, J. G., Kethcen, D. J., Perryman, A. A., & Donahue, M. S. (2007). The moderating effect of CEO power on the board composition-firm performance relationship. *Journal of Management Studies, 44*, 1299–1323.

104. Salas, J. M. (2010). Entrenchment, governance, and the stock price reaction to sudden executive deaths. *Journal of Banking and Finance, 34*, 656–666.

105. Combs, J. G., Kethcen, D. J., Perryman, A. A., & Donahue, M. S. (2007). The moderating effect of CEO power on the board composition-firm performance relationship. *Journal of Management Studies, 44*, 1299–1323.

106. Worrell, D. L., Davidson, W. N., Chandy, P. R., & Garrison, S. L. (1986). Management turnover through deaths of key executives: Effects on investor wealth. *Academy of Management Journal, 29*, 674–694.

107. Worrell, D. L., & Davidson, W. N. (1987). The effects of CEO succession on stockholder wealth in large firms following the death of the predecessor. *Academy of Management Journal, 13*, 509–515.

108. Worrell, D. L., Davidson, W. N., Chandy, P. R., & Garrison, S. L. (1986). Management turnover through deaths of key executives: Effects on investor wealth. *Academy of Management Journal, 29*, 674–694.

109. Worrell, D. L., Davidson, W. N., Chandy, P. R., & Garrison, S. L. (1986). Management turnover through deaths of key executives: Effects on investor wealth. *Academy of Management Journal, 29*, 674–694.

110. Borokhovich, K. A., Brunarski, K. R., Donahue, M. S., & Harman, Y. S. (2006). The importance of board quality in the event of a CEO death. *Financial Review, 41*, 307–337.

111. Ballinger, G. A., Lehman, D. W., & Schoorman, F. D. (2010). Leader-member exchange and turnover before and after succession events. *Organizational Behavior and Human Decision Processes, 113*, 25–36.

112. Inness, M., Turner, N., Barling, J., & Stride, C. (2010). Transformational leadership and employee safety performance: A within-person, between-jobs design. *Journal of Occupational Health Psychology, 15*, 279–290.

CHAPTER 3
How Does Leadership Work?

We now know that leadership "works." An intriguing set of questions, however, asks not whether leadership works, but *how* it works. Quite simply, just having a high-quality leader does not mean that someone would automatically or immediately perform at a superior level—the process is much more complex. Considerable strides have been made in understanding the process through which leadership influences individuals, teams, and organizations, and under what conditions any effects of leadership are heightened or minimized. We explore the lessons learned from this large body of research in this chapter. Any understanding of *how* leadership works will be enhanced by knowing *when* its effects become apparent, and we turn to this question at the end this chapter.

MEDIATING THE EFFECTS OF LEADERSHIP ON OUTCOMES

Leadership behaviors (irrespective of the particular theory) primarily exert indirect effects on outcomes. As an example of this process that will be discussed more fully in this chapter, high-quality leadership enables employees to place more trust in their leaders, and it is predominantly this trust that directly affects employee performance. In this respect, trust serves to mediate[i] the effects of leadership on outcomes; some have referred to this as a "downstream" effect of leadership. What we have learned to date is that, broadly speaking, leadership affects the way in which followers view (a) themselves and (b) their work, and (c) their relationships with their leaders—each of which then directly influences employees' workplace attitudes and behaviors (the entire process is shown in Figure 3.1). Thus, mediating variables tells us

i. In this sense, a mediator is an intervening variable through which the effects of leadership must pass to influence the ultimate outcome.

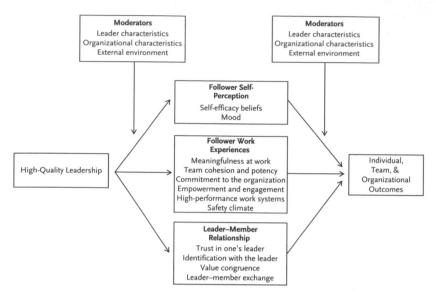

Figure 3.1
The leadership process.

about the process of leadership. We now consider each of these broad mediators in more detail.

Followers' Self-Perceptions

Employees' Self-Efficacy Beliefs

Albert Bandura, arguably the most influential psychologist over the past century, introduced the idea of self-efficacy beliefs in the 1970s. Simply stated, self-efficacy reflects individuals' beliefs that, given sufficient effort, they can succeed in specific behaviors.[1] Ever since Bandura's early theorizing in the 1970s, self-efficacy theory has become one of the most widely studied topics in the social sciences, and research consistently confirms the depth and pervasiveness of its effects. Initial research by Bandura, Nancy Adams, and Janice Beyer demonstrated the effects of self-efficacy beliefs on clinical phenomena such as snake phobias.[2] Since then, research has shown how self-efficacy beliefs predict the initiation, maintenance, and persistence of behavior in diverse situations such as academic performance in children, health behaviors, athletic and sports performance, and work organizations. Self-efficacy is more focused or specific than self-esteem and self-confidence, and a stronger predictor of performance than individual skill levels. Self-efficacy beliefs go beyond the individual, as groups' collective efficacy beliefs also predict group-level performance.[3] Not surprisingly, therefore, Roger Bruning and his colleagues maintain that "Few perceptions about the self are more important than self-efficacy beliefs" (p. 35).[4]

The three most important factors in the development of self-efficacy are (a) personal mastery experiences, (b) vicarious experiences, and (c) verbal persuasion, all of which would be strongly influenced by high-quality leadership. For example, transformational leaders ensure that their followers enjoy sufficient autonomy to engage in new behaviors, and they increase the likelihood of their followers' success through guided mastery experiences. Employees' self-efficacy beliefs would also be enhanced as they watch their leaders serve as role models; in the study I conducted with Jennifer Robertson mentioned in Chapter 2, watching one's leader engage in pro-environmental behaviors indirectly affected one's own pro-environmental behaviors.[5] While still important, any effects of leaders' verbal persuasion (e.g., through feedback and encouragement) would be less influential, as it lacks a personal experiential basis.

Several studies have now documented that leadership—whether transformational,[6] leader–member exchange (LMX)[7] empowering,[8] ethical,[9] or visionary[10]—positively affects diverse organizational outcomes by raising employees' self-efficacy beliefs. These outcomes include employees' willingness to go beyond minimal job requirements,[11] employee well-being,[12] customer satisfaction and employee sales performance,[13] supervisor-rated job performance,[14] and the extent to which supervisors rate their employees as high in potential for promotion.[15] Thus, the role of self-efficacy beliefs as a mediator of the effects of leadership is evident through (a) the sheer breadth of outcomes affected and (b) the fact that support for the mediating role of self-efficacy beliefs emanates not just from the United States but from numerous other countries as well (e.g., Denmark, Portugal, the People's Republic of China, and Hong Kong).

Karoline Strauss, Mark Griffin, and Alannah Rafferty have refined our understanding of how self-efficacy mediates any effects of transformational leadership.[16] They asked participants in their study (employees working for an Australian public sector agency) to rate the transformational leadership of both their own unit leaders and senior leaders in their agency, with whom they presumably had less contact. Their analyses showed that employees' role breadth (or general) self-efficacy beliefs mediated the effects of their *unit* leaders' transformational leadership on four outcomes of importance to the organization (essentially, perceptions of individual and team member potency and competence). Higher-level organizational leaders' transformational leadership was unrelated to employees' self-efficacy beliefs, presumably because they are not as interpersonally or physically close to or involved with employees as are unit leaders, and thus have fewer opportunities to influence employees' mastery experiences or to act as role models to employees. As a result, self-efficacy beliefs did not mediate the effects of senior leadership on these same outcomes. What this means is that if organizations are intent on enhancing employees' self-efficacy beliefs, reliance on the behaviors of the most proximal leader would be the most effective approach.

Findings such as these highlight the importance of individuals' personal self-efficacy beliefs. Collective efficacy is equally important and reflects a team or group's shared belief (i.e., "we can do it" vs. "I can do it") in its ability to complete the activities required for successful task performance.[17] Collective efficacy has been shown to mediate the effects of leadership on team performance in different contexts. For example, one study of management teams in medium-sized hotels in the United States[18] showed that empowering leadership behaviors (e.g., participative decision-making, coaching, demonstrating concern) were associated with significantly higher levels of collective efficacy within the management teams, which in turn predicted the hotel's financial performance (i.e., revenue generated from room rentals over a 28-day period relative to local competitors). Similarly, collective efficacy mediated the effects of transformational leadership on self-assessed effectiveness in a sample of 47 teams in Korea.[19] The fact that both individual and collective self-efficacy mediate the effects of leadership on organizational outcomes only increases its importance to organizations.

Thus, employees' and teams' self-efficacy beliefs are enhanced by high-quality leadership and in turn exert meaningful and pervasive effects on a range of organizational outcomes. But what about leaders' own self-efficacy beliefs? Might they also play an important role in the leadership process? Self-efficacy theory would suggest that leaders with higher efficacy beliefs would be more likely to engage in high-quality leadership behaviors, expend greater levels of energy to fulfill their leadership responsibilities, and persist in the face of challenges. There is some support for the role of leadership self-efficacy in predicting leadership effectiveness. Based on a sample of military recruits in Singapore,[20] higher levels of recruits' own leadership self-efficacy were associated with superiors' ratings of their recruits' leadership effectiveness, even though their superiors were unaware of the self-efficacy ratings.

Employees' Mood

Moving away from self-efficacy as an exemplar of employees' self-perceptions, high-quality leadership also affects how followers feel about themselves more generally. A study in 10 different insurance firms in Taiwan showed that employees' moods mediated the effects of transformational leadership on supervisor-rated performance. In this study, higher levels of transformational leadership were associated with followers' positive moods (e.g., the extent to which the followers felt happy, pleased, and even joyful over the prior week).[21] In turn, followers' positive moods were associated with supervisors' general ratings of their employees' overall task performance, as well as the extent to which they assisted coworkers in their tasks.

Followers' Work Experiences

Leadership affects not only the way people feel about themselves, but also how they experience their work generally. And the way in which people experience their work has important and widespread implications. Research findings show consistently that people who enjoy positive work experience are more productive and healthy; the opposite is true for those who have the misfortune to experience their work negatively. Moreover, the benefits of positive work experiences extend beyond any health or productivity benefits. Because our different social roles (e.g., work, parent) intersect and overlap,[22] the way in which people experience their work spills over into the quality of family and community functioning.[23] A large body of research shows how leadership is implicated in the nature and quality of followers' work experiences, several of which are examined next.

Meaningfulness of Work

While the extrinsic functions of work (i.e., financial remuneration) are obviously important, social scientists have emphasized for decades that we seek more from our work than financial remuneration. In fact, once people are paid above the poverty line, financial remuneration may no longer be the most salient attribute they seek from their work. Based on more than 50 years of research and personal observation, Marie Jahoda suggested in her 1982 book, *Employment and Unemployment: A Social Psychological Analysis*,[24] that over and above the manifest functions of employment (namely financial remuneration), individuals seek out latent or psychological functions from employment, which include time structure, social contacts, purposefulness, an identity, and regular activities. By the mid-1970s, Richard Hackman and Greg Oldham[25] had identified five core job characteristics that shape individuals' psychological experience of their work: the extent to which different skills are used ("task variety"), whether employees are responsible for the whole job or just components of the job ("task identity"), whether the job affects other people ("task significance"), how much "autonomy" people have on the job, and whether employees receive regular and clear "feedback" about their performance. More recently, as we saw in Chapter 2, Adam Grant's research has underscored the importance of the relational component of work and shown how work gains meaning when we affect the lives of others.

Transformational leaders have the potential to influence their employees' experience of the meaningfulness of their work. For example, by emphasizing collective values and higher goals, transformational leaders give work a higher purpose and a sense of meaningfulness. By showing confidence in employees' ability to do their job and encouraging employees to think for themselves, employees' sense of autonomy and independence are enhanced. Finally, through leaders' individualized consideration behaviors, social contacts and relational aspects of job design are enhanced.

Several recent studies involving German, Danish, and Canadian employees support the notion that transformational leadership boosts employees' experienced meaningfulness of their work. For example, studies have confirmed that high-quality transformational leadership is associated with employees' beliefs that their work is meaningful. Adam Grant's extensive research program suggests that the effects of transformational leadership on experienced meaningfulness are heightened significantly when leaders create opportunities for employees to interact with the beneficiaries of their work.[26] In turn, believing that one's work is meaningful has positive effects on critical organizational outcomes, such as intrinsic motivation, goal commitment, task performance and citizenship behaviors,[27] and affective commitment to the organization.[28] In addition, employees' work experiences also influence their well-being.[29]

These studies confirm that experienced meaningfulness of work explains the indirect effects of leadership. Further support for this process would follow from studies showing that destructive leadership has a negative effect on employees' beliefs that their work is meaningful, which in turn would negatively affect organizational outcomes, and some support for this process exists. Based on data obtained from a sample of bank employees in the Philippines, for example, Alannah Rafferty and Simon Restubog showed that abusive supervision reduced the belief that work is meaningful. In turn, the belief that one's work was not meaningful was associated with a decreased willingness among employees to keep information confidential, which was a necessary requirement of the job.[30]

Of course, isolating one way in which the experience of work transmits the effects of leadership on work outcomes does not preclude the existence of other mediating variables. Indeed, social scientists have uncovered several other diverse ways in which leadership exerts its effects, and it is to these that we now turn our attention.

Commitment to the Organization

High-quality leadership affects not only the way in which employees' experience their work, but as we saw in Chapter 2, there is compelling support for the notion that high-quality leadership affects the way in which people view their employing organizations. More specifically, high-quality leadership—whether expressed in the form of leader consideration, supervisor support, leader–member exchanges, or transformational leadership—is consistently and strongly associated with employees feeling a deep sense of pride in being a member of the organization (what is now widely referred to as "affective commitment"[ii]).[31] One explanation for this is that one's direct leader reflects the most proximal contact an employee has with the organizational hierarchy and comes to be viewed as a representative of the organization. All of this is important, because employees who feel a deep attachment to and pride in the organization and want to retain membership for the rest of their careers will be motivated to do what they can to help the organization thrive.[32]

Together with the voluminous body of knowledge that has been developed on the antecedents and outcomes of affective commitment,[33] there is a vibrant research literature linking leadership and affective commitment. Timothy Jackson, John Meyer, and Frank Wang identified 102, 29, and 27 studies linking affective, normative, and continuance commitment, respectively, with transformational leadership.[34] They even uncovered enough research to be able to study the link between commitment and the separate components of transformational and transactional leadership. As might be expected, transformational leadership and its four separate components were all positively associated with affective (but not continuance) commitment. In addition, while high levels of contingent reward were positively related to affective commitment, higher levels of passive management-by-exception and laissez-faire leadership were associated with lower levels of affective commitment.

Karoline Strauss and colleagues' study of Australian public sector workers provides the most nuanced understanding of how affective commitment mediates the effects of transformational leadership.[35] As noted in the earlier discussion on self-efficacy, these authors were interested in understanding the differential effects of supervisors' proximal transformational leadership, as opposed to the more distal transformational leadership behaviors of those higher up in the organizational hierarchy. Several interesting findings emerged. First, employees' feelings of commitment to their work unit and to their employing organization could be separated. Second, commitment to the organization transmitted the effects of transformational leadership on proactivity. Third, although distal transformational leadership (i.e., higher up the organizational hierarchy) affected commitment to the organization, only

ii. John Meyer and Natalie Allen differentiate between three forms of commitment: "affective commitment" (e.g., "I 'want' to be a member of the organization"), "continuance commitment" (e.g., "I 'have' to be a member of the organization because of the costs of leaving"), and "normative commitment" (e.g., "I 'ought' to stay a member of the organization because that is what good people do"). Affective commitment has the most consistently positive effects on employee attitudes and performance.

proximal transformational leadership by the supervisor influenced commitment to the team. The effects of team and organizational commitment were specific: Commitment to the team only affected team-based performance, and commitment to the organization only affected organizational-level outcomes.

Empowerment and Work Engagement

The object of much organizational research, "empowerment" is a form of intrinsic task motivation combining individuals' beliefs about their competence, the impact of their work on task achievement, the subjective importance they ascribe to particular tasks, and the autonomy they enjoy in work-related decision-making.[36] Transformational leadership is critical in enhancing empowerment. In turn, feeling empowered leaves individuals wanting to engage in their work and help their organizations. Studies have now shown, for example, that empowerment mediates the effects of transformational leadership on employees' commitment to the organization; this was shown in a sample of more than 500 nurses in Singapore.[37] Similar findings have been demonstrated at the group level: Empowerment mediated the effects of transformational leadership on collective efficacy in a Korean sample of 47 teams.[38] In addition, given the similarity between empowerment and intrinsic motivation, it is worth noting that intrinsic motivation has also been found to mediate the effects of transformational leadership on coaches' ratings of athletes' sports performance.[39]

Perhaps the most informative study on the role of empowerment was conducted by Gilad Chen and his co-researchers.[40] While many of the studies discussed thus far investigated *either* the individual effects of leadership *or* leadership climate separately, Chen and colleagues asked whether individual *and* team empowerment would mediate the effects of leadership climate and LMX on team and individual performance. They also investigated whether overall leadership climate affected individual empowerment, using a very large sample of 445 employees who were members of 62 different teams from 31 different stores of a Fortune 500 company specializing in home improvement products. The 31 store managers were also included in the sample. What did the investigators find? Individuals' feelings of empowerment mediated the effects of LMX on individual performance, and this same process emerged at the team level: Team empowerment mediated the effects of overall leadership climate on team performance. Highlighting the importance of the joint effects of individual and team empowerment, high team empowerment counteracted any effects of low individual empowerment. In addition, any effects of individual empowerment on individual performance were greater when team empowerment levels were higher (although predictably, this effect only emerged for teams whose work was highly interdependent).

Important practical lessons can be derived from Chen et al.'s study. A dilemma frequently encountered is whether to focus motivational efforts on teams or on individuals. As the authors note in their report, team and individual empowerment are positively related, thus concerns that empowering teams and empowering individuals are mutually exclusive can be discounted. Similarly, because individual and team performance are related, managers can enhance team performance by focusing on individuals' personal needs, without compromising team performance.

Like empowerment, the term "work engagement" is used extremely frequently. Common to most definitions is that work engagement involves an intensity that transcends feelings of (job) satisfaction. It is typically experienced as a passion for and commitment to the specific work in which the individuals are engaged. Given this, the role of high-quality leadership in increasing employees' work engagement might be expected. In turn, work engagement has diverse positive organizational outcomes; several studies have investigated whether employee work engagement mediates any effects of leadership.

In the first of these studies, Marisa Salanova and her colleagues used a sample of 17 nursing supervisors and the 364 nurses who reported to them in a large Portuguese hospital to show that nursing supervisors' transformational leadership was associated with higher levels of work engagement. In turn, higher levels of work engagement were associated with a willingness to voluntarily go beyond the requirements of the job description to help the organization.[41] A second study focused on encouraging employees' knowledge creation given the prominence accorded to knowledge creation in organizational success. Because the behaviors involved in knowledge creation are voluntary,[42] Hoon Song and colleagues' findings from lower level employees and middle managers in six different organizations in South Korea[43] are revealing: They showed that transformational leadership was associated with higher levels of employee work engagement. In turn, higher levels of work engagement predicted knowledge creation initiatives at the team level.

A note of caution about work engagement is in order here. One seemingly logical conclusion from these studies is that organizations should do whatever is feasible to encourage the highest possible levels of employee work engagement. However, this could result in unintended negative consequences, what some management scholars refer to as the "too-much-of-a-good-thing" phenomenon.[44] Somewhat similar to the effects of extreme identification with the organization,[45] very high levels of work engagement (and empowerment) may have detrimental effects on individuals (e.g., work stress, burnout, ill health) and organizations (e.g., absenteeism, diminished job performance).

There is tremendous variation in human resource practices within different organizations. On one side is a control orientation in which organizational goals include reduced costs and greater efficiency that would be achieved through external rules, regulations, and monitoring, all of which are intended to induce compliance. On the other side is a commitment orientation, in which organizational goals are accomplished through practices that encourage employee involvement, commitment, and trust[46] (often referred to as a "high-performance" work system). The variation in human resource practices reflects not just a difference in style; recent research confirms that high-performance work systems (which invariably reflect a commitment orientation) are associated with job satisfaction, organizational commitment and psychological empowerment,[47] diverse aspects of the organization's financial performance,[48] employee safety,[49] employee turnover,[50] service quality,[51] and overall firm performance.[52] As one example, Mark Huselid showed that an increase in high-performance work practices of approximately 15% resulted in an increase of $27,044 in sales and $3,814 in profits per employee, and a decrease in turnover of 7% compared to the average.[53] Despite widespread interest in the effects of high-performance work systems, very little research has focused on what factors influence the choice of different systems.

CEOs play a significant role in the type of human resource practices adopted by an organization. Weichun Zhu, Irene Chew, and William Spangler argued that CEOs who exhibit transformational leadership behaviors, which include the belief that employees can be motivated to exceed expectations and a concern for employees' personal needs, would be more likely to implement "human capital–enhancing" human resource management practices,[54] in which the development of employees who are committed to the organization, and have the skills necessary for superior task performance, are viewed as key to organizational success. To investigate this, Wu and his team obtained data from human resource managers and CEOs in 170 diverse organizations located in Singapore and collected information on employee absence and sales performance from organizational records. As expected, CEOs higher in transformational leadership were more likely to ensure that human capital–enhancing human resource practices were implemented in their organizations. In turn, these practices were associated with positive perceptions of organizational performance, lower absenteeism rates, and higher levels of sales performance. On the basis of these findings, Zhu and colleagues concluded that CEO transformational leadership constitutes a competitive advantage for the organization.

Dov Zohar was the first researcher to bring attention to the nature and importance of workplace safety climate.[55] What drove Zohar to this was the realization that companies with a positive occupational safety record shared several characteristics, such as the conviction that safety is critical to overall job performance, and the greater likelihood that employees believe that management cares about occupational safety, which in turn influences safety behaviors. What might be regarded as the first generation of research on safety climate following Zohar's initial publication confirmed two important findings. First, safety climate reflects employees' shared perceptions concerning the organizational policies, procedures, and practices regarding safety and its management. Second, perceptions of safety climate consistently predict employees' safety behaviors and injuries, as well as organization-wide safety performance.[56]

As is evident from Chapter 2, high-quality leadership in general and safety-specific transformational leadership in particular are associated with higher levels of workplace safety behaviors and lower levels of injuries. Research now goes further, examining how such effects occur, thereby isolating the mediating role of employees' perceptions of safety climate. In a series of studies, the presence of safety-specific transformational leadership (i.e., transformational leadership in which the focus is specifically on safety and its importance) resulted in individual employees enjoying more positive perceptions of the company's safety climate (i.e., these employees viewed safety as important and believed that management's commitment to safety derived from an intrinsic commitment rather than compliance with external requirements). In turn, these climate perceptions predicted fewer adverse safety events and injuries. Importantly, this effect has been demonstrated with young workers and restaurant employees who typically are more vulnerable to workplace injuries,[57] employees engaged in the construction and maintenance of heavy-duty equipment,[58] and university students employed on a part-time basis.[59]

Three particular findings enhance credibility in the mediating role of safety climate perceptions. First, the effects of transformational leadership on team-level injury rates were also explained by groups' shared perceptions of safety climate.[60] Second, when safety-specific transformational leadership increased following a leadership training intervention, employees' perceptions of safety climate increased. In turn, this resulted in enhanced participation in safety activities, and fewer injuries.[61] Finally, safety climate can also mediate the effects of negative leadership on safety outcomes. Specifically, passive leadership is associated with poorer perceptions of safety climate,[62] which in turn predict individual and group-level injury rates.[63]

Organizations are no longer interested only in the work performance of individual employees. Instead, the performance and output of groups and teams are equally important to effective organizational functioning, and the quality of team performance remains one of the most important challenges faced by leaders. While none of this is new,[64] research on leadership in general and that on transformational leadership continue to focus primarily on individual effects of leadership. Several studies now point to how effects of leadership on team performance are transmitted.

Bernie Bass and his colleagues studied how transformational leadership influenced team performance in 72 U.S. military platoons (units) that were engaged in noncritical operations.[65] They showed that transformational leadership (but neither transactional leadership nor passive leadership) resulted in high levels of team potency. In turn, team potency predicted performance in the field. More recently, John Schaubroeck, Simon Lam, and Sandra Cha focused on transformational leadership and branch-level performance in 218 financial service teams located in the United States or Hong Kong.[66] Like Bass et al.'s findings from military units, it was again team potency that linked transformational leadership with financial outcomes. To appreciate how teams transmit the effects of transformational leadership onto group performance, it is instructive to note how both groups of researchers measured team "potency." For example, Bass and colleagues used items such as "our platoon has confidence in itself" (p. 210), and Schaubroeck et al. measured team potency with items such as "The unit I work with has above average ability," and "The members of this department have excellent job skills." In both cases, therefore, transformational leadership enabled group members to experience a higher level of confidence or belief in each other's ability to get the job done—which reflects a sense of collective efficacy. It was then through this manifestation of team cohesion and potency that transformational leadership resulted in higher levels of group performance.

Influencing the Leader–Member Relationship

Just as high-quality leadership influences how people experience their work, high-quality leadership also affects the quality of the leader–member relationship. This should be no surprise, as it reflects what we know from so many different aspects of our lives: When we are well treated by someone who has influence over us—be it a parent, romantic partner, or teacher—our relationship with that person is better for it. In turn, the nature and quality of the leader—member relationship affects how employees behave at work.

Trust in one's leader is not a right automatically given by employees to leaders by virtue of their position in the organizational hierarchy. To understand why this might be the case, the nature of interpersonal trust needs to be appreciated. Some two decades ago, Roger Mayer, James David, and David Schoorman offered what remains the most cogent definition of interpersonal trust within organizations.[67] According to these authors, trust reflects (a) a willingness by subordinates to leave themselves vulnerable at the hands of their leaders (b) in the expectation that, in return, their leaders will behave in a way that they personally value, (c) despite employees' inability to constantly monitor their leader's behavior. Employees would likely be more willing to leave themselves vulnerable to, and feel much less need to constantly scrutinize, the behavior of transformational leaders who believe in their employees, allow and encourage them to think for themselves, and who emphasize other-centered values and the collective good rather than the pursuit of their own interests. Moreover, the listening, caring, and mentoring behaviors consistent with individualized consideration would help create the social bond between leader and follower that facilitates the development of trust.[68] Going forward, employees who trust their leaders, who are willing to "to suspend their questions, doubts and personal motives" (p. 1009),[69] would be able to concentrate fully on individual and team performance; this explains why trust in one's leader would mediate the effects of leadership on valued outcomes.

Numerous studies have investigated this process. As might be expected, high-quality leadership, whether expressed through servant leadership,[70] transformational leadership, or interactional justice,[71] is consistently associated with higher levels of trust in one's leader, with most of the research focusing on transformational leadership and interactional justice. In turn, trust in one's leader consistently results in positive organizational outcomes, such as employee attitudes (e.g., job satisfaction, organizational commitment and retention), organizational citizenship behaviors,[72] employee well-being,[73] greater tenure with the organization, and even NCAA basketball performance.[74]

One study demonstrating how trust mediates the effects of leadership is particularly instructive, as it did not just measure employees' self-reports of their trust in their leader. Abhishek Srivastava, Kathryn Bartol, and Ed Locke viewed the extent to which team members were willing to share task-appropriate information, knowledge, and thoughts as a behavioral expression of trust.[75] Sharing knowledge is vital, because organizations cannot compel employees to do so. Instead, employees share knowledge according to the extent to which they trust in their leaders and peers.[76] Srivastava et al. showed that sharing knowledge as a behavioral expression of trust mediated the effects of empowering leadership on financial performance of management teams (revenue based on room rentals relative to other local establishments) in hotels.

Identification with the Leader

Employees are likely to identify with their leaders under several conditions. First, as employees learn that their leaders' values can be respected and that their leaders' intentions and behaviors can be trusted, the moral bond between the parties will foster identification with the leader. Second, as employees come to appreciate that their leaders care for them as individuals, employees, and team members, and such behaviors are reciprocated, identification with the leader will be strengthened. This identification is critical for effective leadership. Conger and Kanungo have argued, for example, that it is through this identification that charismatic leaders will indirectly affect employees.[77] Not surprisingly, the possible role of employees' identification with leaders has been explored in several studies.

In one study, Frank Wang and Jane Howell focused on both individual and group-focused transformational leadership in a Canadian sample of 60 leaders and 200 team members.[78] As expected, individuals' identification with one's own leader explained the effects of transformational leadership on supervisor-rated performance. However, these researchers went further, and showed that transformational leaders heightened employees' identification not just with themselves, but also with their direct work groups, which then explained the effects of group-focused transformational leadership on groups' collective efficacy. A second study in six separate U.S. banks also showed that transformational leadership enhanced employees' identification with their work groups, which then predicted supervisor-rated performance.[79] Finally, in a more extensive study conducted in a sample of 76 branch managers and 888 employees in an Israeli bank, Ronit Kark, Boas Shamir, and Gilad Chen found that the relationship between managers' transformational leadership and their employees' empowerment was fully mediated through personal identification with the leader.[80]

Following their earlier work on personalized and socialized charisma, Kark and her colleagues shed light on the mediating role of psychological identification with the leader by differentiating between personal identification with a leader and social identification with the work group. They argued that personal identification with the leader might unintentionally lead to dependence on the leader (which could then inadvertently detract from performance). In contrast, social identification with the group is more likely to lead to feelings of empowerment. The reason offered for this is that when individuals identify with their group, any success experiences are likely to be attributed to the group, strengthening the rationale for future team efforts. Yet when employees identify strongly with a leader, success is likely to be attributed to the leader, not themselves, with potentially negative motivational consequences. After all, if success is a function of the leader, employees might well ask themselves whether it makes sense to increase their own efforts.

Results from Kark and her colleagues' study in an Israeli bank supported their hypotheses.[81] The effects of managers' transformational leadership on employees' empowerment (reflected by self- and collective efficacy and collective esteem) was fully explained by the social identification with the group that resulted from high levels of transformational leadership. Like other studies, transformational leadership also predicted personal identification with the leader, but personal identification predicted dependence on the leader (not empowerment), which would have to be of some considerable concern. By clarifying the different roles of personal and social identification with a leader, Kark et al. have helped explain when and why the outcomes of transformational leadership might sometimes be detrimental.

Finally, a comment on the complex role of the level of identification warrants mention. In research unrelated to leadership, Lorenzo Avanzi and his colleagues were concerned about potential drawbacks that might ensue when identification becomes too strong.[82] In two separate studies in Italy on 195 law clerks and 140 teachers, they showed that as organizational identification initially increased, workaholism decreased, and well-being increased. However, when levels of identification reached unusually high levels, workaholism increased in both of their samples, in turn resulting in lower levels of well-being. Thus, levels of identification that are so high that individuals tend to "lose themselves" can potentially harm well-being. Leaders need to appreciate that both the source and level of identification are critical in determining whether beneficial or harmful effects will emerge on performance outcomes.

Value Congruence

Closely related to the notion of psychological identification with the leader is the extent to which leaders and their followers enjoy shared values, which itself is important because of the organizational benefits (e.g., employee commitment and satisfaction) that flow from value congruence.[83] When leaders clearly articulate other-centered values and a compelling vision for the future, employees become inspired to work together toward common goals, and focus their energy on achieving collective rather than individual goals. Several studies document the benefits of value congruence.

Dong Jung and Bruce Avolio's early research showed that value congruence mediates the effects of transformational leadership on performance quantity and quality, as well as satisfaction with the leader.[84] Making this more compelling was their finding that transactional leadership had no influence on leader–follower value congruence, and thus had no mediating role at all. A subsequent study on 177 work groups and their leaders within a nationwide U.S. health care organization provided an interesting refinement, as the focus in that study was on the way in which high-quality leadership might result in fewer destructive behaviors.[85] As expected, this second study showed that higher levels of socialized (or positive) charismatic leadership were associated with greater leader–follower value congruence. In turn, higher levels of value congruence with the leader resulted in fewer acts of interpersonal and organizational deviance by employees within the organization. Additional support for the role of value concordance derives from a study in Taiwan which showed that the match between employees' values and what they believed were the organization's values, linked CEO charismatic leadership and employees' commitment to the organization and satisfaction with their leader.[86]

Leader–Member Exchange

In most leadership research, leader–member exchange (LMX) is treated as a leadership theory in its own right, and it has received considerable research attention as such (see Chapter 1 and Table 1.1). A few studies have taken a slightly different approach, however, assessing whether the quality of exchanges between leader and follower mediate the effects of leadership, an approach based on the assumption that high-quality leadership stimulates positive leader–member exchanges,[87] and on considerable data showing that high-quality leader–member exchanges predict positive employee and organizational outcomes.

In one study on 162 supervisor–subordinate dyads in a city in northern China,[88] higher levels of transformational leadership resulted in employee reports of higher quality exchanges with their supervisors. Higher quality leader–member exchanges were then shown to enhance external ratings of subordinates' task performance, as well as subordinates' willingness to voluntarily go beyond the formal requirements of their jobs and engage in behaviors that would benefit their organizations. The authors of this study point to an additional lesson from their findings. Specifically, where high-quality leader–member exchanges between leaders and followers are deemed to be important by organizations, thought should be given to explicitly developing transformational behaviors amongst the organization's leaders.

In a separate research study, Fred Walumbwa and colleagues were interested in explaining the effects of ethical leadership[89] and focused on the mediating role of the quality of leader–member exchanges in a pharmaceutical company in China. Their findings showed that ethical leadership was associated indirectly with their followers' supervisor-rated job performance, and that this effect could be explained by the positive effects of ethical leadership on the quality of leader–member exchanges. The researchers point to an important practical implication from their findings that is sometimes over-looked, namely, that ethical leadership has positive organizational benefits!

We leave this section with one concluding thought. The preceding dis-cussion on mediators of the effects of leadership on valued outcomes was somewhat limited by the available literature to a consideration of mediators acting in isolation. In reality, the process is more complex, and the effects of leadership are probably mediated by many factors simultaneously. As but one example, Fred Walumbwa and colleagues studied the effects of authentic leadership on performance and citizenship behaviors at the group level in a large bank in the United States.[90] Their findings showed that group trust and collective psychological capital (i.e., collective efficacy, hope, optimism, and resilience) jointly mediated the effects of authentic leadership on the desired group outcomes.

MODERATORS

Our understanding of how leadership works has gone beyond a focus on medi-ators, or the process of leadership. Countless studies have also focused on the conditions under which the effects of leadership are enhanced or even nulli-fied. One example of this which will be discussed elsewhere is the way in which crises can leave employees hungry for charismatic leadership, increasing the probability that charismatic leadership might become more effective during crises. A separate line of research has focused on factors that may nullify the effects of leadership, what Kerr and Jermier long ago referred to as "substi-tutes" for leadership.[91] Considerable strides have been made in identifying many of these characteristics, and how they enhance or decrease the effects of leadership. In this discussion, we will consider how characteristics of the leader, the organization, and the external environment moderate effects of leadership.[iii]

Leader Characteristics

How characteristics of the leader influence leadership effectiveness has been extensively studied. Two of the most prominent characteristics are gen-der and personality, and each has attracted a very large number of studies.

iii. A moderator variable shapes or influences the relationship between two other variables. Thus, as one example, organizational size moderates the effects of CEO lead-ership on outcomes, inasmuch as this effect is considerably stronger in smaller orga-nizations and weaker in larger organizations. In this sense, moderator variables create boundary conditions for the effects of CEO leadership.

Neither are discussed at this stage, however, as they are each discussed extensively elsewhere in this book. We will delve into the issue of gender and leadership in Chapter 8, and leaders' personality will be studied in greater detail in Chapter 10.

CEO Ownership Status

While the view from below might suggest that all CEOs enjoy the same elevated level of status within their organization, this is not the case. For example, CEOs differ in terms of whether they are the owners[92] and/or founders of the organization, or have been hired as CEO by a board of directors or could be a member of the board of directors. These differences could have meaningful practical and psychological implications. Being the owner or founder would enhance psychological engagement and a focus on the long-term performance of the organization. In contrast, CEOs hired to their position are accountable to an external group that has the power to monitor, influence, and reward the consequences of their leadership behaviors, and thus these CEOs would be limited in the decisions they make and the actions they take.[93] Similar effects might depend on whether someone is a CEO of a publicly traded or privately owned organization. As SAS CEO and majority-owner, Jim Goodnight, who chose to retain ownership and control of the organization he founded in 1976, said of decisions he made to increase his staff size in 2001, 2002, and 2003 that bucked industry-wide trends, "If we were public, I wouldn't have been able to do that."[94]

From a psychological perspective, studies over several decades have consistently documented the performance and health benefits of feeling that one has some control in a given situation. In this respect, the benefits of ownership are far-reaching. As one example, Lois Tetrick and her colleagues showed that despite the fact that licensed morticians who were CEO/owners of funeral homes received less social support from people at work than either funeral home managers or employees, they enjoyed higher levels of work fulfillment and less work stress and emotional exhaustion from their work than non-owners.

Other studies have investigated the organizational consequences of CEO status. One study in the Netherlands investigated 54 small and medium-sized organizations in which just over half (28) of the CEOs were owners[95] and showed that company profitability was significantly higher for charismatic CEOs who were owners than similarly charismatic CEOs who were not owners of the organization. Importantly, the level of charismatic leadership did not differ between the two groups of CEOs, further supporting the notion that CEO status moderates the effectiveness of CEO leadership. It is also worth noting that employees whose CEO was an owner exhibited more positive work attitudes than employees whose CEOs were not owners. A separate and larger study of CEOs of small and medium-sized organizations (68 of the CEOs were founders, and the remaining 53 non-founders) focused on the effects of founder status.[96] This study was conducted in the northeastern United States, and the researchers showed that founder CEOs' transformational leadership was strongly associated both with annual sales growth and how CEOs believed their organization was faring relative to their competitors. In contrast, non-founder CEOs' transformational leadership was only weakly associated with these same two outcomes.

What lessons can be learned from the studies on CEO ownership status? Simply being an owner or founder does not automatically or directly convey any performance benefits to organizations. Instead, being an owner or founder provides greater managerial discretion and decision latitude, both of which enable more effective leadership (and, it should be noted, CEO health). The lesson is not simply that founders should be retained as CEOs as long as possible. Rather, the challenge is to find ways in which non-owner/ founder CEOs can enjoy similar levels of managerial discretion and decision latitude.

One factor limiting this discretion would be the requirement for the CEO to report to a board. But must boards necessarily constrain CEOs' discretion? Jianyun Tang, Mary Crossan, and Glenn Rowe were interested in whether and how boards might moderate the performance effects of dominant CEOs. One of the five contributing factors to their dominance index was whether the CEO was the founder or a relative of the founder.[97] They studied 51 publicly traded companies in the computer industry in the United States, and demonstrated that dominant CEOs produced more extreme financial outcomes for the organization—both positive and negative. However, in the presence of powerful boards (e.g., those on which the CEO was not also the board chairperson), dominant CEOs produced less extremes in financial performance and more positive financial performance in general. In contrast, in the presence of less powerful boards, dominant CEOs were more likely to generate lower levels of, and more extremes in, financial performance.

Jiatao Li and Yi Tang's extensive study of CEO hubris among 2,790 CEOs of manufacturing companies in China[98] lends credibility to these findings. They showed that when the CEO was also the board chairperson, the statistical relationship between CEO hubris and firm risk-taking was significantly higher than in companies in which the CEO–board chair roles were separated, presumably because separating the two roles allows for greater monitoring of and less discretion for the CEO. Given the importance of maintaining managerial discretion and decision latitude, discussed elsewhere in this chapter, the authors of this study viewed their findings as a call more generally for a greater balance of power between boards and CEOs.

Organizational Context

Organizations are not homogenous entities. They differ from each other in meaningful ways, such as organizational size, whether they operate in the public or private sector, and their geographical location, to name just a few factors. Despite this, the role of context is underresearched in the organizational sciences, a critical omission because, as Gary Johns notes, contextual factors affect the frequency, meaning, and effects of behaviors in organizations.[99] Organizational context also exerts complex effects on leadership.[100] In some contexts, the effects of leadership are magnified; in others, they are reduced significantly if not nullified. In this section, we examine how organizational size, physical distance between leaders and followers, and extreme or crisis contexts influence the effectiveness of leadership behaviors.

Organizational Size

The idea that organizational or unit size might influence leadership effectiveness is based largely on the notion that as the number of employees or scope of responsibilities increases, the opportunity to maximize many of the elements central to new-genre leadership theories (e.g., charisma, interpersonal relationships) is minimized. Supporting this idea, John Hemphill showed as long ago as 1950 that the size of the organizational unit affected the demands on leaders, and leaders' task-related behavior.[101] More recent research has focused not just on unit size (as was the case with most earlier research) but also on organizational size, and the question raised is whether any beneficial effects of leadership are lost or minimized in larger organizations.

Yair Berson and his colleagues studied a group of leaders whose span of control ranged from 4 to 90 people.[102] Their findings showed that larger organizational size was associated with lower levels of leaders' optimism and confidence and with diminished beliefs in leaders' vision statements regarding what they believed they could achieve. The researchers suggest that this occurred because leaders in larger organizations feel they have diminished control and influence, which constrains the content of their organizational vision.

Other research already discussed solidifies our understanding of the role of organizational size. Ling and colleagues studied whether organizational size influenced leadership effectiveness in small and medium-sized firms involved in manufacturing, construction, scientific, and technical organizations.[103] To do so, they obtained data on 121 CEOs' transformational leadership from members of their top management teams. On average, the firms had 62 employees and $4.9 million in annual sales. Their findings strongly support theorizing about organizational size: CEO transformational leadership exerted direct effects on organizational performance (as reflected by annual sales growth) in smaller organizations; this direct effect was not significant in medium-sized organizations.

Physical Distance

Globalization has resulted in many intended and unintended consequences throughout society, and organizations have not been unaffected. As a result of globalization, many leaders are now responsible for people who are not in the same physical or geographical location as themselves. There is also the challenge of leading employees who speak different languages and/or are in different time zones,[104] or are in domestic organizations in the same city as their leaders but who work from home for much or all of the workweek. The challenge of physical distance between leaders and followers is apparent.[105] Not surprisingly, therefore, researchers are interested in understanding how physical distance between leaders and followers might influence the effectiveness of leadership. Initial speculation was that physical distance would have a negative effect on the relationship between leader and follower[106] because of diminished opportunities for performance monitoring and correction, as well as decreased frequency and quality of leader–follower communication to the point that physical distance would render effective leadership impossible.[107]

Early research supported this gloomy perspective. Phillip Podsakoff and his team of researchers first showed that with greater physical distance, contingent reward was less effective in generating high performance.[108] Subsequent research, however, did not consistently find similar negative effects. Jane Howell and Kathryn Hall-Merenda studied 109 bank managers, each of whom was responsible for the performance of between four and six geographically isolated branch managers.[109] Their results were more mixed, showing that contingent reward and active management-by-exception were strongly associated with follower performance when physical distance was greatest. In contrast, transformational leadership was more effective, and passive management-by exception less detrimental with less physical distance between leader and follower. Similar effects emerged in a later study by Howell, Derrick Neufeld, and Bruce Avolio in which the outcome was business unit performance.[110] These authors note that the diminished effects for passive management-by-exception emerged because as physical distance increases, the opportunity for punishing others decreases. Likewise, transformational leadership was less effective because its expression requires opportunities for interpersonal interactions.

Despite these findings, it would be premature to conclude that physical distance necessarily nullifies any benefits of leadership. Technological innovations offer leaders opportunities to minimize the *perceived* distance between themselves and their followers. Ann Majchrzak and her colleagues reported on interviews they conducted with team members and team leaders who had learned to successfully navigate the challenges of geographically dispersed teams.[111] Key to any success was the way in which these team members and leaders (a) relied on technology as best they could to minimize geographical distance; (b) recognized, valued, and took advantage of the diversity within dispersed teams; and (c) used frequent and high-quality communication to avoid divisions in dispersed teams.

Along similar lines, Kevin Kelloway and I conducted a laboratory study with a group of colleagues on what we termed remote transformational leadership. Undergraduate students participating in this study received the information about the tasks that needed to be completed via e-mail, using a transformational leadership (charismatic or intellectually stimulating) or a neutral (i.e., non-leadership) message.[112] Not only could the recipients of the e-mail correctly identify whether they had received a leadership vs. non-leadership message, but task motivation was significantly greater after receiving the intellectually stimulating message, and task performance was higher after receiving the leadership messages.

A study by Adam Grant and Francesca Gino takes this an important step further. Within the context of a laboratory study, student participants signed up for a study on writing skills and feedback. As part of the study, they received an e-mail from someone they believed to be a student. Including an exceptionally brief expression of gratitude ("Thank you so much! I am really grateful") in the e-mail, which is consistent with individualized consideration, was sufficient to motivate more voluntary helping behavior. Similar productivity effects emerged in a sample of university fundraisers when, in addition to their regular feedback, the director of their department told them, "I am very grateful for your hard work. We sincerely appreciate your contributions to the university" (p. 951).[113] Clearly, the potential exists to use existing technologies to confront leadership disadvantages that emerge from physical distance.

Thus, the extent to which geographically dispersed teams is becoming the norm does not have to threaten leadership effectiveness. What is now required is more concerted action to learn to harness the potential benefits of technology. Gil Luria, Dov Zohar, and Ido Erev's research on occupational safety interventions provides further guidance in this respect.[114] Not surprisingly, their findings demonstrated that being visible to one's supervisor was associated with higher levels of safety behavior. More importantly, however, they showed that the reason for this was that supervisors spent more time interacting with subordinates who were clearly and readily visible. One lesson from their findings is that leaders who find themselves visibly removed from their subordinates need to do whatever they can to ensure that the frequency and quality of their interactions are not compromised.

Maximum (vs. Typical) Contexts

While the benefits of leadership are pervasive, leadership is often assumed to be most important when organizations or their members are in crisis or experiencing unusually high levels of stress, uncertainty, confusion, and change.[115] Given this, it is somewhat surprising that there are no differences in effectiveness of transformational leadership in the public sector and military, business, and educational contexts.[116] One plausible reason for this is that there is more variation within any of these four contexts than between them. Just taking the military context as one example, leadership occurs in non-combat, headquarters-based administrative units all the way through to time-sensitive, combat missions in enemy territory that have a high risk for capture, injury, or death. Another plausible reason for the fact that no such differences have emerged between contexts is that more often than not, research on military contexts has not focused on leadership during active combat.

Instead of focusing only on the nature of the overall organization, Paul Sackett, Sheldon Zedeck, and Larry Gogli introduced what they called "maximum performance contexts," in which individuals (a) know that their performance is being evaluated and (b) accept the need to maximize their effort, and (c) the task is of sufficiently short duration so that those involved can maintain maximum effort throughout.[117] Beng Chong Lim and Robert Ployhart studied the moderating role of typical vs. maximum performance contexts on leadership effectiveness in a sample of combat teams in the Singapore Armed Forces.[118] Performance in maximum contexts involved tasks such as evacuating an injured soldier; performance in typical contexts required the same behaviors as those used during training. Transformational leadership was significantly more effective in predicting team performance in maximum than in typical contexts.

Revisiting Safety Climate

As already noted earlier in this chapter, safety climate reflects employees' shared perceptions about organizational policies, procedures, and practices regarding occupational safety. While we now know that safety climate mediates any effects of leadership on organizational outcomes, safety climate can also influence the strength of any effects of leadership on desired outcomes. As one example, David Hofmann and his colleagues studied 29 teams of a U.S. military unit whose responsibility was to transport materials for deployment.[119] They showed that in teams in which there was a more positive safety climate, high-quality LMX relationships resulted in employees viewing safety-related behaviors as a regular part of their jobs. In contrast, high-quality LMX relationships were not related to similar safety behaviors when the safety climate was low. Aside from demonstrating the important moderating role of safety climate on the leadership–safety behavior relationship, Hoffman and colleagues' findings suggest that high levels of other "micro-climates" (e.g., customer-service climate) might also moderate leadership effectiveness in other domains, a topic well worth investigating.

External Environment

Just as contextual factors within the organization moderate the effects of leaders' behaviors, so too does the wider social context in which the organization finds itself, probably because the environment in which leaders find themselves shapes the meaning of their leadership behaviors and establishes boundaries for leaders' behaviors and leader effectiveness.[120]

Environmental Uncertainty

Organizations operate today in an environment characterized by varying degrees of uncertainty and ambiguity, affecting both leaders and employees alike. Uncertainty is experienced as stressful by employees. As a result, under extreme levels of environmental uncertainty, a sense of crisis could become pervasive within which employees become "charisma hungry," looking more to transformational and charismatic leaders with their overt confidence and greater optimism. While environmental uncertainty might seem to create undue difficulties for leaders, some researchers have taken the opposite perspective, suggesting that uncertainty and ambiguity provide leaders with a window of opportunity.

David Waldman and his colleagues were among the first to examine how environmental uncertainty moderates the effectiveness of CEOs' charismatic behavior.[121] They collected data from CFOs, comptrollers, treasurers, and senior vice presidents on 131 CEOs of Fortune 500 companies. At the same time, they carefully controlled for several factors that might affect their findings (e.g., prior organizational performance, CEO tenure, organizational size). Their findings were particularly interesting: As they had initially imagined, charismatic leadership behavior was strongly associated with the organization's industry-adjusted net profit margin (calculated as net income/net sales) when environmental uncertainty was high (i.e., changes were perceived as dynamic, risky, rapid, and stressful). However, just as interesting were the findings showing that under conditions of low environmental uncertainty, high levels of CEO charisma were associated with lower levels of net profit margin, supporting the role of the external environment in moderating any effects of leadership effectiveness.

Other researchers then investigated this effect further. Henry Tosi and his colleagues studied a sample of 59 Fortune 500 companies in the United States.[122] They showed that under high (but not low) levels of perceived market uncertainty, CEOs' charismatic leadership was positively associated with shareholder value (but not with higher levels of return on assets). More recently, Peterson et al. analyzed the effects of transformational leadership on the extent to which annual goals for net income were achieved in start-up and established technology firms, because of the greater uncertainty and challenges that pervade start-ups.[123] Their findings again showed that transformational leadership was indeed more strongly associated with meeting net income targets in start-ups than in established firms.

Given that context can affect the level, meaning, and effectiveness of leadership, it is important to know whether any effects of environmental uncertainty are limited to organizations in the United States. Annabel De Hoogh and her researchers found some support for the effects of environmental uncertainty in their sample of small and medium-sized enterprises in the Netherlands.[124] Specifically, CEO charismatic leadership was again positively related to employees' positive work attitudes under high (but not low) levels of environmental uncertainty, demonstrating the cross-national effects of environmental uncertainty on leadership effectiveness.

To conclude, the findings on environmental uncertainty and ambiguity make it clear that the effects of transformational leadership are not uniform across all contexts. Instead, what should be encouraging is that leadership in general and transformational leadership in particular yield their strongest effects precisely in situations when it is most needed.

HOW LONG DOES IT TAKE FOR LEADERSHIP TO EXERT ITS EFFECTS?

A pervasive and deeply ingrained belief among scholars and practitioners alike is that it takes time for leadership to exert its effects. Widespread evidence for the indirect (or mediated) effects of leadership discussed above explains why delayed effects should be expected. To reiterate, people do not automatically elevate their behaviors in the presence of high-quality leadership. To take one example, high-quality leadership earns the trust of employees over time, and it is largely this trust that predicts specific outcomes—in due course. Thus, much needs to happen between the enactment of high-quality leadership behaviors and desired outcomes. Yet this still only tells us that some delay must be expected; it provides no information about precisely when any effects might emerge.

Complicating matters, the length of time it takes for leadership to exert its effects may be moderated by situational factors, making predictions of when desired effects might emerge even more difficult. For example, consistent with the fact that contexts shape the experience and effectiveness of leadership, one possibility is that certain types of leadership might exert effects almost immediately during the most dangerous crises, when followers fear for their safety if not their lives. In any event, understanding when leadership might exert its effects is not just of academic interest, but would also enable organizations to set their expectations more realistically and plan more efficiently, and would provide a set of intriguing questions for future researchers.

Given the importance of understanding how long it might take for leadership to exert any effects, and just as importantly, how long any effects might be maintained, it is unfortunate that there appear to be no research findings to guide this discussion. Clearly, research is needed to begin to understand these issues more thoroughly.

CONCLUSION

Research over the past two decades has resulted in an understanding of *how* leadership exerts its effects. Simply stated, leadership does not exert direct and immediate effects on followers. Instead, any such effects are invariably indirect and occur because high-quality leaders help people think differently about themselves and their work and improve the quality of the leader–follower relationship. All of this helps explain why leadership probably exerts delayed rather than immediate effects. At the same time, research has pointed to the contexts and situations in which any effects of leadership are magnified or even nullified. But what enables us to draw these conclusions? In the next chapter, we examine how leadership researchers go about their craft that underlies this knowledge.

SUGGESTED READING

Bass, B. M., & Riggio, R. E. (2006). *Transformational leadership* (2nd ed.). Mahwah, NJ: Lawrence Erlbaum.

Grant, A. (2013). *Give and take: A revolutionary approach to success*. New York: Viking.

NOTES

1. Bandura, A. (1997). Self-efficacy: Toward a unifying theory of behavior change. *Psychological Review, 84,* 191–215.
2. Bandura, A., Adams, N. E., & Beyer, J. E. (1977). Cognitive processes mediating behavioral change. *Journal of Personality and Social Psychology, 35,* 125–139.

3. Bandura, A. (1995). *Self-efficacy in changing societies*. Cambridge, UK: Cambridge University Press; Bandura, A. (1997). *Self-efficacy: The exercise of control*. New York: Freeman.

4. Bruning, R., Dempsey, M., McKim, C., Kauffman, D. F., & Zumbrunn, S. (2013). Examining dimensions of self-efficacy for writing. *Journal of Educational Psychology, 105*, 25–38.

5. Robertson, J., & Barling, J. (2013). Greening organizations through leaders' influence on employees' pro-environmental behaviors. *Journal of Organizational Behavior, 34*, 176–194.

6. Aryee, S., & Chu, C. W. L. (2012). Antecedents and outcomes of challenging job conditions: A social cognitive perspective. *Human Performance, 25*, 215–234; Liu, J., Siu, O. L., & Shi, K. (2010). Transformational leadership and employee well-being: The mediating role of trust in the leader and self-efficacy. *Applied Psychology: An International Review, 59*, 454–479; Nielsen, K., & Munir, F. (2009). How do transformational leaders influence followers' affective well-being? Exploring the mediating role of self-efficacy. *Work and Stress, 23*, 313–329; Salanova, N., Lorente, L., Chambel, M. J., & Martinez, I. M. (2011). Linking transformational leadership to nurses' extra-role performance: The mediating role of self-efficacy and work engagement. *Journal of Advanced Nursing, 67*, 2256–2266; Walumbwa, F. O., Avolio, B. J., & Zhu, W. (2008). How transformational weaves its influence on individual job performance: The role of identification and efficacy beliefs. *Personnel Psychology, 61*, 793–825.

7. Walumbwa, F. O., Cropanzano, R., & Goldman, B. M. (2011). How leader–member exchange influences effective work behaviors: Social exchange and internal–external efficacy perspectives. *Personnel Psychology, 64*, 739–770.

8. Ahearne, M., Mathieu, J., & Rapp, A. (2005). To empower or not empower your sales force? An empirical examination of the influence of leadership empowerment behavior on customer satisfaction and performance. *Journal of Applied Psychology, 90*, 945–955; Srivistava, A., Bartol, K. M., & Locke, E. A. (2006). Empowering leadership in management teams: Effects on knowledge sharing, efficacy, and performance. *Academy of Management Journal, 49*, 1239–1251.

9. Walumbwa, F. O., Mayer, D. M., Wang, P., Wang, H., Workman, K., & Christensen, A. L. (2011). Linking ethical leadership to employee performance: The roles of leader-member exchange, self-efficacy, and organizational identification. *Organizational Behavior and Human Decision Processes, 115*, 204–213.

10. Griffin, M. A., Parker, S. K., & Mason, C. M. (2010). Leader vision and the development of adaptive and proactive performance: A longitudinal study. *Journal of Applied Psychology, 95*, 174–182.

11. Salanova, M., Lorente, L., Chambel, M. J., & Martinez, I. M. (2011). Linking transformational leadership to nurses' extra-role performance: The mediating role of self-efficacy and work engagement. *Journal of Advanced Nursing, 67*, 2256–2266.

12. Liu, J., Siu, O. L., & Shi, K. (2010). Transformational leadership and employee well-being: The mediating role of trust in the leader and self-efficacy. *Applied Psychology: An International Review, 59*, 454–479; Nielsen, K., & Munir, F. (2009). How do transformational leaders influence followers' affective well-being? Exploring the mediating role of self-efficacy. *Work and Stress, 23*, 313–329.

13. Ahearne, M., Mathieu, J., & Rapp, A. (2005). To empower or not empower your sales force? An empirical examination of the influence of leadership

empowerment behavior on customer satisfaction and performance. *Journal of Applied Psychology, 90*, 945–955.

14. Aryee, S., & Chu, C. W. L. (2012). Antecedents and outcomes of challenging job conditions: A social cognitive perspective. *Human Performance, 25*, 215–234; Walumbwa, F. O., Avolio, B. J., & Zhu, W. (2008). How transformational weaves its influence on individual job performance: The role of identification and efficacy beliefs. *Personnel Psychology, 61*, 793–825.

15. Aryee, S., & Chu, C. W. L. (2012). Antecedents and outcomes of challenging job conditions: A social cognitive perspective. *Human Performance, 25*, 215–234.

16. Strauss, K., Griffin, M. A., & Rafferty, A. E. (2009). Proactivity directed toward the team and organization: The role of leadership, commitment and role-breadth self-efficacy. *British Journal of Management, 20*, 279–291.

17. Bandura, A. (1986). *Social foundations of thought and action: A social cognitive theory*. Upper Saddle River, NJ: Prentice Hall.

18. Srivastava, A., Bartol, K. M., & Locke, E. A. (2006). Empowering leadership in management teams: Effects on knowledge sharing, efficacy, and performance. *Academy of Management Journal, 49*, 1239–1251.

19. Jung, D. I., & Sosik, J. J. (2002). Transformational leadership in work groups: The role of empowerment, cohesiveness, and collective efficacy on perceived group performance. *Small Group Research, 33*, 313–336.

20. Ng, K. Y., Ang, S., & Chan, K. Y. (2008). Personality and leadership effectiveness: A moderated mediation model of leadership self-efficacy, job demands and job autonomy. *Journal of Applied Psychology, 93*, 733–743.

21. Tsai, W-C., Chen, H-W., & Cheng, J-W. (2009). Employee positive moods as a mediator linking transformational leadership and employee work outcomes. *International Journal of Human Resource Management, 20*, 206–219.

22. Katz, D., & Kahn, R. L. (1978). *The social psychology of organizations* (2nd ed.). New York: John Wiley & Sons.

23. Barling, J. (1990). *Employment, work and family functioning*. London: Wiley.

24. Jahoda, M. (1982). *Employment and unemployment: A social psychological analysis*. New York: Cambridge University Press.

25. Hackman, J. R., & Oldham, G. R. (1980). *Job redesign*. Boston: Addison-Wesley.

26. Grant, A. M. (2012). Leading with meaning: beneficiary contact, prosocial impact, and the performance effects of transformational leadership. *Academy of Management Journal, 55*, 458–476.

27. Piccolo, R. F., & Colquitt, J. A. (2006). Transformational leadership and job behaviors: The mediating role of core job characteristics. *Academy of Management Journal, 49*, 327–340.

28. Korek, S., Felfe, J., & Zaepernick-Rothe, U. (2010). Transformational leadership and commitment: A multilevel analysis of group-level influences and mediating processes. *European Journal of Work and Organizational Psychology, 19*, 364–387.

29. Arnold, K. A., Turner, N., Barling, J., Kelloway, E. K., & McKee, M. (2007). Transformational leadership and psychological well-being: The mediating role of meaningful work. *Journal of Occupational Health Psychology, 12*, 193–203.

30. Rafferty, A. E., & Restubog, S. L. D. (2011). The influence of abusive supervision on followers' organizational citizenship behaviours: The hidden costs of abusive supervision. *British Journal of Management, 22*, 270–285.

31. Jackson, T. A., Meyer, J. P., & Wang, X-H. (2013). Leadership, commitment, and culture: A meta-analysis. *Journal of Leadership and Organizational Studies, 20*, 84–106.

32. Levinson, H. (1965). Reciprocation: The relationship between man and organization. *Administrative Science Quarterly, 9*, 370–390.

33. Klein, H. J., Becker, T. E., & Meyer, J. P. (Eds.) (2009). *Commitment in organizations: Accumulated wisdom and new directions.* New York: Routledge/Taylor & Francis Group.

34. Jackson, T. A., Meyer, J. P., & Wang, X-H. (2013). Leadership, commitment, and culture: A meta-analysis. *Journal of Leadership and Organizational Studies, 20*, 84–106.

35. Strauss, K., Griffin, M. A., & Rafferty, A. E. (2009). Proactivity directed toward the team and organization: The role of leadership, commitment and role-breadth self-efficacy. *British Journal of Management, 20*, 279–291.

36. Spreitzer, G. M. (1995). Psychological empowerment in the workplace: Dimensions, measurement and validation. *Academy of Management Journal, 38*, 1442–1465.

37. Avolio, B. J., Zhu, W., Koh, W., & Bhatia, P. (2004). Transformational leadership and organizational commitment: Mediating role of psychological empowerment and moderating role of structural distance. *Journal of Organizational Behavior, 25*, 951–969.

38. Jung, D. I., & Sosik, J. J. (2002). Transformational leadership in work groups: The role of empowerment, cohesiveness, and collective-efficacy on perceived group performance. *Small Group Research, 33*, 313–336.

39. Charbonneau, D., Barling, J., & Kelloway, E. K. (2001). Transformational leadership and sports performance: The mediating role of intrinsic motivation. *Journal of Applied Social Psychology, 31*, 1521–1534.

40. Chen, G., Kirkman, B. L., Kanfer, R., Allen, D., & Rosen, B. (2007). A multilevel study of leadership, empowerment, and performance in teams. *Journal of Applied Psychology, 92*, 331–346.

41. Salanova, M., Lorente, L., Chambel, M. K., & Martinez, I. M. (2011). Linking transformational leadership to nurses' extra-role performance: The mediating role of self-efficacy and work engagement. *Journal of Advanced Nursing, 67*, 2256 2266.

42. Kelloway, E. K., & Barling, J. (2000). Knowledge work as organizational behavior. *International Journal of Management Reviews, 2*, 287–304.

43. Song, J. H., Kolb, J. A., Lee, U. H., & Kim, H. K. (2012). Role of transformational leadership in effective organizational knowledge creation practices: Mediating effects of employees' work engagement. *Human Resource Development Journal, 23*, 65–101.

44. Pierce, J. R., & Aguinas, H. (2013). The "too-much-of-a-good-thing" effect in management. *Journal of Management, 39*, 313–338.

45. Avanzi, L., van Dick, R., Fraccaroli, F., & Sarchielli, G. (2012). The downside of organizational identification relations between identification, workaholism and well-being. *Work & Stress, 26*, 289–307.

46. Walton, R. E. (1985). From control to commitment in the workplace. *Harvard Business Review, 63*(2), 77–84.

47. Messersmith, J. G., Patel, P. C., Lepak, D. P., & Gould-Williams, J. S. (2011). Unlocking the black box: Exploring the link between high-performance work systems and performance. *Journal of Applied Psychology, 96*, 1105–1118.

48. Bae, J., & Lawler, J. J. (2000). Organizational and HRM strategies in Korea: Impact on firm performance in an emerging economy. *Academy of Management Journal, 43*, 502–517; Bjorkman, I., & Xiucheng, F. (2002).

Human resource management and the performance of Western firms in China. *International Journal of Human Resource Management, 13*, 853–864; Razouk, A.A. (2011). High-performance work systems and performance of French small- and medium-sized enterprises: Examining causal order. *International Journal of Human Resource Management, 22*, 311–330.

49. Zacharatos, A., Barling, J., & Iverson, R. D. (2005). High performance work systems and occupational safety. *Journal of Applied Psychology, 90*, 77–93.
50. Huselid, M. A. (1995). The impact of human resource management practices on turnover, productivity, and corporate financial performance. *Academy of Management Journal, 38*, 635–672.
51. Aryee, S., Walumbwa, F. O., Seidu, E. Y. M., & Otaye, L. W. (2012). Impact of high-performance work systems on individual- and branch-level performance: Test of a multilevel model of intermediate linkages. *Journal of Applied Psychology, 97*, 287–300; Liao, H., Toya, K., Lepak, D. P., & Hong, Y. (2009). Do they see eye to eye? Management and employee perspectives of high-performance work systems and influence processes on service quality. *Journal of Applied Psychology, 94*, 371–391.
52. Takeuchi, R., Lepak, D. A., Wang, H., & Takeuchi, K. (2007). An empirical examination of the mediating mechanism mediating between high-performance work systems and the performance of Japanese organizations. *Journal of Applied Psychology, 92*, 1069–1083.
53. Huselid, M. A. (1995). The impact of human resource management practices on turnover, productivity and corporate financial performance. *Academy of Management Journal, 38*, 635–672.
54. Zhu, W., Chew, I. K. H., & Spangler, W. D. (2005). CEO transformational leadership and organizational outcomes: The mediating role of human-capital-enhancing human resource management. *Leadership Quarterly, 16*, 39–52.
55. Zohar, D. (1980). Safety climate in industrial organizations: Theoretical and applied implications. *Journal of Applied Psychology, 65*, 96–102.
56. Zohar, D. (2010). Thirty years of safety climate research: Reflections and future directions. *Accident Analysis and Prevention, 42*, 1517–1522.
57. Barling, J., Loughlin, C., & Kelloway, E. K. (2002). Development and test of a model linking safety-specific transformational leadership and occupational safety. *Journal of Applied Psychology, 87*, 488–496.
58. Zohar, D. (2002). The effects of leadership dimensions, safety climate, and assigned work priorities on minor injuries in work groups. *Journal of Organizational Behavior, 23*, 75–92.
59. Kelloway, E. K., Mullen, J., & Francis, L. (2006). Divergent effects of transformational and passive leadership on employee safety. *Journal of Occupational Health Psychology, 11*, 76–86.
60. Zohar, D. (2002). The effects of leadership dimensions, safety climate, and assigned work priorities on minor injuries in work groups. *Journal of Organizational Behavior, 23*, 75–92.
61. Mullen, J., & Kelloway, E. K. (2009). Safety leadership: A longitudinal study of the effects of transformational leadership on safety outcomes. *Journal of Occupational and Organizational Psychology, 82*, 253–272.
62. Kelloway, E. K., Mullen, J., & Francis, L. (2006). Divergent effects of transformational and passive leadership on employee safety. *Journal of Occupational Health Psychology, 11*, 76–86.

63. Kelloway, E. K., Mullen, J., & Francis, L. (2006). Divergent effects of transformational and passive leadership on employee safety. *Journal of Occupational Health Psychology, 11*, 76–86; Zohar, D. (2002). The effects of leadership dimensions, safety climate, and assigned work priorities on minor injuries in work groups. *Journal of Organizational Behavior, 23*, 75–92.

64. Hackman, J. R., & Walton, R. E. (1986). Leading groups in organizations. In P. S. Goodman (Ed.), *Designing effective work groups* (pp. 72–119). San Francisco: Jossey-Bass; Lim, B. C., & Ployhart, R. E. (2004). Transformational leadership: Relations to the five-factor model and team performance in typical and maximum contexts. *Journal of Applied Psychology, 89*, 610–621.

65. Bass, B. M., Avolio, B. J., Jung, D. I., & Berson, Y. (2003). Predicting unit performance by assessing transformational and transactional leadership. *Journal of Applied Psychology, 88*, 207–218.

66. Schaubroeck, J., Lam, S. S. K., & Cha, S. E. (2007). Embracing transformational leadership: Team values and the impact of leader behavior on team performance. *Journal of Applied Psychology, 92*, 1020–1030.

67. Mayer, R. C., David, J. H., & Schoorman, F. D. (1995). An integrative model of organizational trust. *Academy of Management Review, 20*, 709–734.

68. Tyler, T. R., & Degoey, P. (1996). Trust in organizational authorities: The influence of motive attributions on willingness to accept decisions. In R. M. Kramer & T. R. Tyler (Eds.) *Trust in organizations: Frontiers of theory and research* (pp. 331–350). Thousand Oaks, CA: SAGE Publications.

69. Dirks, K. T. (2000). Trust in leadership and team performance: Evidence from NVAA basketball. *Journal of Applied Psychology, 85*, 1004–1012.

70. Senjaya, S., & Pekerti, A. (2010). Servant leadership as antecedent of trust in organizations. *Leadership & Organization Development Journal, 31*, 643–663.

71. Dirks, K. G., & Ferrin, D. L. (2002). Trust in leadership: Meta-analytic findings and implications for research and practice. *Journal of Applied Psychology, 87*, 611–628.

72. Dirks, K. G., & Ferrin, D. L. (2002). Trust in leadership: Meta-analytic findings and implications for research and practice. *Journal of Applied Psychology, 87*, 611–628.

73. Kelloway, E. K., Turner, N., Barling, J., & Loughlin, C. (2012). Transformational leadership and employee psychological well-being: The mediating role of employee trust in leadership. *Work and Stress, 26*, 39–55; Liu, J., Siu, O. L., & Shi, K. (2010). Transformational leadership and employee well-being: The mediating role of trust in the leader and self-efficacy. *Applied Psychology: An International Review, 59*, 454–479.

74. Dirks, K. T. (2000). Trust in leadership and team performance: Evidence from NVAA basketball. *Journal of Applied Psychology, 85*, 1004–1012.

75. Srivastava, A., Bartol, K. M., & Locke, E. A. (2006). Empowering leadership in management teams: Effects of knowledge sharing, efficacy, and performance. *Academy of Management Journal, 49*, 1239–1251.

76. Kelloway, E. K., & Barling, J. (2000). Knowledge work as organizational behavior. *International Journal of Management Reviews, 2*, 287–304.

77. Conger, J. A., & Kanungo, R. N. (1998). *Charismatic leadership in organizations*. Thousand Oaks, CA: SAGE Publications.

78. Wang, X. H., & Howell, J. M. (2012). A multilevel study of transformational leadership, identification, and follower outcomes. *Leadership Quarterly, 23*, 775–790.

79. Walumbwa, F. O., Avolio, B. J., & Zhu, W. (2008). How transformational weaves its influence on individual job performance: The role of identification and efficacy beliefs. *Personnel Psychology, 61*, 793–825.
80. Kark, R., Shamir, B., & Chen, G. (2003). The two faces of transformational leadership: Empowerment and dependency. *Journal of Applied Psychology, 88*, 246–255.
81. Kark, R., Shamir, B., & Chen, G. (2003). The two faces of transformational leadership: Empowerment and dependency. *Journal of Applied Psychology, 88*, 246–255.
82. Avanzi, L., van Dick, R., Fraccaroli, F., & Sarchielli, G. (2012). The downside of organizational identification: Relations between identification, workaholism and well-being. *Work and Stress, 26*, 289–307.
83. Meglino, B. M., Ravlin, E. C., & Adkins, C. L. (1989). A work values approach to corporate culture: A field test of the congruence process and its relationship to individual outcomes. *Journal of Applied Psychology, 74*, 424–432.
84. Jung, D. I., & Avolio, B. J. (2000). Opening the black box: An experimental investigation of the mediating effects of trust and value congruence on transformational and transactional leadership. *Journal of Organizational Behavior, 21*, 949–964.
85. Brown, M. E., & Trevino, L. K. (2006). Socialized charismatic leadership, values congruence, and deviance in work groups. *Journal of Applied Psychology, 91*, 954–962.
86. Huang, M. P., Cheng, B. S., & Chou, L. F. (2005). Fitting in organizational values: The mediating role of person-organization fit between CEO charismatic leadership and employee outcomes. *International Journal of Manpower, 26*, 35–49.
87. Deluga, R. J. (1992). The relationship of leader-member exchanges with laissez faire, transactional, and transformational leadership. In K. E. Clark, M. B. Clark, & D. R. Campbell (Eds.), *Impact of leadership* (pp. 237–247). Greensboro, NC: Centre for Creative Leadership.
88. Wang, H., Law, K. S., Hackett, R. D., Wang, D., & Chen, Z. X. (2005). Leader-member exchange as a mediator of the relationship between transformational leadership and followers' performance and organizational citizenship behavior. *Academy of Management Journal, 48*, 420–432.
89. Walumbwa, F. O., Mayer, D. M., Wang, P., Wang, H., Workman, K., & Christensen, A. L. (2011). Linking ethical leadership to employee performance: The roles of leader-member exchange, self-efficacy, and organizational identification. *Organizational Behavior and Human Decision Processes, 115*, 204–213.
90. Walumbwa, F. O., Luthans, F., Avey, J. B., & Oke, A. (2011). Authentically leading groups: The mediating role of collective psychological capital and trust. *Journal of Organizational Behavior, 32*, 4–24.
91. Kerr, S., & Jermier, J. M. (1978). Substitutes for leadership: Their meaning and measurement. *Organizational Behavior and Human Performance, 22*, 375–403.
92. Tetrick, L. E., Slack, K. J., Da Silva, N., Sinclair, R. R. (2000). A comparison of the stress–strain process for business owners and nonowners: Differences in job demands, emotional exhaustion, satisfaction, and social support. *Journal of Occupational Health Psychology, 5*, 464–476.
93. Hambrick, D., & Finkelstein, S. (1987). Managerial discretion: A bridge between two polar views of organizations. In B. M. Staw & L. L. Cummings (Eds.), *Research in organizational behavior* (Vol. 9, pp. 369–406). Greenwich, CT: JAI Press.

94. Maney, K. (2004). SAS workers won when greed lost. *USA Today*. Retrieved from http://www.usatoday.com/money/industries/technology/2004-04-21-sas-culture_x.htm

95. De Hoogh, A. H. B., den Hartog, D. N., Koopman, P. L., Thierry, H., ven den Berg, P. T., van der Weide, J. G., & Wilderom, C. P. M. (2004). Charismatic leadership, environmental dynamism, and performance. *European Journal of Work and Organizational Psychology, 13*, 447–471.

96. Ling, Y., Simsek, Z., Lubatkin, M. H., & Veiga, J. F. (2008). The impact of transformational CEOs on the performance of small- to medium-size firms: Does organizational context matter? *Journal of Applied Psychology, 93*, 923–934.

97. Tang, J., Crossan, M., & Rowe, W. G. (2011). Dominant CEO, deviant strategy, and extreme performance: The moderating role of a powerful board. *Journal of Management Studies, 48*, 1479–1503.

98. Li, J., & Tang, Y (2011). CEO hubris and firm risk taking in China: The moderatiung role of managerial discretion. *Academy of Management Journal, 53*, 45–68.

99. Johns, G. (2006). The essential impact of context on organizational behavior. *Academy of Management Review, 31*, 386–408.

100. Porter, L. W., & Mclaughlin, G. B. (2006). Leadership and the organizational context: Like the weather? *Leadership Quarterly, 17*, 559–576.

101. Hemphill, J. K. (1950). Relations between the size of the group and the behavior of superior leaders. *Journal of Social Psychology, 32*, 11–22.

102. Berson, Y., Shamir, B., Avolio, B. J., & Popper, M. (2001). The relationship between vision strength, leadership style, and context. *Leadership Quarterly, 12*, 53–73.

103. Ling, Y., Simsek, Z., Lubatkin, M. H., & Veiga, J. F. (2008). The impact of transformational CEOs on the performance of small- to medium-size firms: Does organizational context matter? *Journal of Applied Psychology, 93*, 923–934.

104. Weisband, S. (2008). *Leadership at a distance: Research in technologically supported work*. Hillside, NJ: Lawrence Erlbaum.

105. O`Leary, M. B., & Cummings, J. N. (2007). The spatial, temporal and configural characteristics of geographic dispersion in teams. *MIS Quarterly, 321*, 433–454.

106. Napier, B. J., & Ferris, G. R. (1993). Distance in organizations. *Human Resource Management Review, 3*, 321–357.

107. Kerr, S., & Jermier, J. M. (1978). Substitutes for leadership: Their meaning and measurement. *Organizational Behavior and Human Performance, 22*, 375–403.

108. Podsakoff, P. M., Todor, W. D., Grover, R. A., & Huber, V. L. (1984). Situational moderators of leader reward and punishment behaviors: Fact or fiction? *Organizational Behavior and Human Performance, 34*, 21–63.

109. Howell, J. M., & Hall-Merenda, K. E. (1999). The ties that bind: The impact of leader member-exchange, transformational and transactional leadership, and distance on predicting follower performance. *Journal of Applied Psychology, 84*, 680–694.

110. Howell, J. M., Neufeld, D. J., & Avolio, B. J. (2005). Examining the relationship of leadership and physical distance with business unit performance. *Leadership Quarterly, 16*, 273–285.

111. Majchrzak, A., Malhotra, A., Stamps, J., & Lipnack, J. (2004, May). Can absence make a team grow stronger? *Harvard Business Review, 20*, 1–8.

112. Kelloway, E. K., Barling, J., Kelley, E., Comtois, J., & Gatien, B. (2002). Remote transformational leadership. *Leadership and Organizational Development Journal, 24(3)*, 163–171.

113. Grant, A. M., & Gino, F. (2010). A little thanks goes a long way: Explaining why gratitude expressions motivate prosocial behavior. *Journal of Personality and Social Psychology, 98,* 946–955.

114. Luria, G., Zohar, D., & Erev, I. (2008). The effect of workers' visibility on effectiveness of intervention programs: Supervisory-based safety interventions. *Journal of Safety Research, 39,* 273–280.

115. Bass, B. M. (1998). *Transformational leadership: Industry, military and educational impact.* Hillside, NJ: Lawrence Erlbaum.

116. Judge, T. A., & Piccolo, R. F. (2004). Transformational and transactional leadership: A meta-analytic tests of their relative validity. *Journal of Applied Psychology, 89,* 755–768.

117. Sackett, P. R., Zedeck, S., & Fogli, L. (1988). Relations between measures of typical and maximum job performance. *Journal of Applied Psychology, 73,* 482–486.

118. Lim, B. C., & Ployhart, R. E. (2004). Transformational leadership: Relations to the five-factor model and team performance in typical and maximum contexts. *Journal of Applied Psychology, 89,* 610–621.

119. Hofmann, D. A., Morgeson, F. P., & Gerras, S. J. (2003). Climate as a moderator of the relationship between leader-member exchange and content specific citizenship. Safety climate as an exemplar. *Journal of Applied Psychology, 88,* 170–178.

120. Katz, D., & Kahn, R. L. (1968). *The social psychology of organizations.* New York: Wiley.

121. Waldman, D. A., Ramirez, G. G., House, R. J., & Ruranam, P. (2001). Does leadership matter? CEO leadership attributes and profitability under conditions of perceived environmental uncertainty. *Academy of Management Journal, 44,* 134–143.

122. Tosi, H. L., Misangyi, V. F., Fanelli, A., Waldman, D. A., & Yammarino, F. J. (2004). CEO charisma, compensation, and firm performance. *Leadership Quarterly, 15,* 405–420.

123. Peterson, S. J., Walumbwa, F. O., Byron, K., & Myrowitz, J. (2009). CEO positive psychological traits, transformational leadership, and firm performance in high-technology start-up and established firms. *Journal of Management, 35,* 348–368.

124. De Hoogh, A. H. B., den Hartog, D. N., Koopman, P. L., Thierry, H., ven den Berg, P. T., van der Weide, J. G., & Wilderom, C. P. M. (2004). Charismatic leadership, environmental dynamism, and performance. *European Journal of Work and Organizational Psychology, 13,* 447–471.

CHAPTER 4

The Typical Leadership Study

How Do We Know What We Know?

Given the thousands of peer-reviewed, English-language articles published on organizational leadership during the past 40 or more years, one would be forgiven for throwing up one's hands and asking, "But how do we know all this?" The answer to this question is of considerable importance: Several hundreds of research studies on leadership are published each year across different contexts (e.g., business, sports, politics), by researchers in different disciplines (e.g., sociology, psychology, management, economics), across all continents. Understanding *how* leadership research is conducted, and appreciating the methodological rigor and creativity that characterizes this research despite substantial practical constraints (e.g., financial, access to leaders and organizations), will help provide the credibility that is critical if the findings from the research are to be taken seriously and the gap between leadership researchers and practitioners is to be bridged. Thus, answering the question of how we know what we know forms the basis of the current chapter.

To understand what the "typical" leadership study looks like, we turn to four different academic journals. To gain a reasonable sample of current research on the psychological and behavioral aspects of organizational leadership, I performed an electronic search of all leadership research conducted since 2000 using the extensive electronic PsychINFO database. Practical necessity dictated that this search be limited to four journals that typically publish the highest quality organizational research. Included in this analysis were peer-reviewed, English-language articles appearing in three generalist journals: *Academy of Management Journal*, the *Journal of Applied Psychology*, and the *Journal of Organizational Behavior*. This analysis was then extended to include articles published in *Leadership Quarterly*, as it is arguably the most prestigious of all the journals devoted specifically to the topic of leadership. On the basis of this analysis, I will first outline the "what, who, and where" of current leadership research, then consider how these studies are conducted, and close with thoughts on how leadership is measured in the "typical" leadership study. This last section includes an invitation to go online and try out some of the most widely used leadership questionnaires.

TOPICS COVERED IN THE STUDY OF LEADERSHIP

Several substantive issues can be identified in this set of articles that help place our understanding of leadership in context. Specifically, we can identify (a) what theories are studied, (b) who is more likely to be studied—males or females or executives, middle management, or supervisors, (c) in which countries leadership research tends to take place, and (d) in what contexts or sectors leadership is studied, i.e., the public or private sectors. Understanding these issues can help inform us of the basis of our current knowledge and perhaps guide us toward the issues that are most likely to be studied in the near future.

What Leadership Theories Are Studied?

Our analysis of which leadership theories are studied relies on the more extensive data depicted in Figure 1.1. Understanding which theories attract more (or less) research is not just an abstract, intellectual topic of concern to researchers; the answer to this question also has important practical consequences. Interest in certain leadership behaviors and disinterest in others might well be influenced by the availability (or paucity) of knowledge, and leaders themselves might gravitate to areas where knowledge about leadership and leadership advances is more readily available. Thus, the leadership theories that researchers choose to study (or to ignore) is of academic and practical interest.

A look back at leadership research over the past several decades reveals some interesting trends. First, Tim Judge and Joyce Bono[1] were interested in the popularity of transformational leadership, and their analysis showed that more articles cited transformational or charismatic leadership during the 1990s than all other theories of leadership combined. This remained the case in the analysis I conducted with Amy Christie and Colette Hoption,[2] as well as the current analysis of research between 1970 and 2012. Just as importantly, these last two analyses also show that the research focus on transformational leadership is steadily increasing. In addition, as noted in Chapter 1, transformational and charismatic leadership are sometimes considered together. If we include charismatic leadership together with transformational leadership, the increasing ascendancy of research on transformational leadership is even more remarkable. Second, as was the case with our earlier analysis, leader–member exchange (LMX) remains the second most widely studied theory, and the amount of research on LMX theory is also increasing. The current focus on the dyadic nature of this relationship might also help explain this, and the emerging interest in the nature and effects of "followership"[3] (see Figure 1.1 and Chapter 10).

Third, not only can we make predictions about which leadership theories will most likely receive increasing attention in the future, these data also highlight several theories that were of considerable historical significance in early leadership research but that now receive very little scientific attention. The classic Ohio State studies identified and investigated two leadership behaviors, namely initiating structure and consideration, and this body of research was of considerable significance in the initial development of leadership theory after World War II. As the data in Figure 1.1 show, however, at best there is now sporadic interest in this theory. Indeed, so little research now focuses on these behavioral dimensions that we spoke of the "disappearance of the Ohio State leadership dimensions from the literature" (p. 186) in our earlier publication.[4] Contingency theories of leadership (e.g., path-goal theory) dominated the literature in the 1960s and 1970s, but again, it is unlikely that much new knowledge will be provided on these theories of leadership in the future.

Thus, inasmuch as it is possible to predict the future, it is highly unlikely that we will see new knowledge being developed about the old, historically important theories anytime soon. Instead, what we are likely to witness is increasing knowledge being developed about theories of leadership that are ethical, inspirational (inasmuch as they emphasize charisma and inspiration), and relational (they underscore the quality of the relationship between leader and follower). This is consistent with the increasing focus on LMX, transformational, and charismatic leadership. At the same time, consistent with the relatively new focus on the dyadic nature of leadership, we may also see more research being conducted that focuses specifically on followership.

Whom Do We Study: Males or Females?

The question of the extent to which leadership research has included both males and females is important for several reasons. First, science has not always been gender-blind. For example, concerns that medical science was based primarily on male "subjects," with lessons learned from such studies inappropriately applied to women, have not yet been put to rest.[5] Social science research is not immune from similar concerns, as noted in earlier criticisms of Kohlberg's moral reasoning theory, which was initially based on male samples only.[6] Second, women leaders are still not free from the effects of bias in the workplace, and it is critical not to perpetuate this bias in leadership research. Reassuringly, most of the leadership studies (88% of those that reported the gender of their participants) in our analyses included both female and male leaders. Of those that did not, most of the remainder focused exclusively on male leaders (10%) rather than on female leaders (2%). Whether this is problematic and a continuation of lingering gender bias is not straightforward, for several reasons. Just because research shows differences in the inclusion of male and female research participants' behavior is not by itself an indication of bias.[7] In some circumstances, it could be appropriate to conduct within-gender studies to learn more about gender-specific nuances in leadership behaviors. However, one would then want to see an equal number of male-only and female-only leadership studies. Thus, the disproportionate focus on male leaders might indicate a lingering stereotype favoring male leaders in organizations, and may perpetuate such stereotypes in organizations (an issue that will be considered in Chapter 8).

Whom Do We Study: Top Management, Middle Management, or Supervisors?

Based on descriptions provided in research reports, participants in leadership research were classified as occupying senior-management, middle-management, or supervisory positions. Of the studies providing this information, only 15% focused on the leadership of senior management, with approximately equal numbers of the remaining studies focusing on middle management (40%) and supervisors (45%). The limited focus on leaders in senior-management positions is somewhat surprising given the media obsession with CEOs and senior management, and the presumed role that senior management plays in most organizations. Several factors might account for the relative lack of attention to top management in leadership research. From the researchers' perspective, it is often extremely difficult to get senior management to agree to complete questionnaires or, even more so, to participate in laboratory-based research. In addition, the questions that need to be asked about top-level leadership might be much more complex, requiring more complicated surveys that are more demanding of senior leaders (and the researchers, too!). It would not be surprising, then, if the investment in time needed by senior management to participate in research would be seen as simply too onerous.

Two observations concerning the emphasis on middle-management and supervisory positions are worth noting. First, this relative focus parallels research on teams and union leaders. Within the explosion of research on teams within organizations over the past 15 years or so, there has been far less research on what is often referred to as top-level teams. Similarly, as will be apparent in Chapter 7, most of the research on union leadership has focused on shop stewards rather than on union presidents. In both of these cases, it is likely that problems of access and time reduced the focus on top-level teams and union presidents. Second, while more research on CEOs and those holding senior-management positions could provide useful information, this should not happen at the expense of research on leaders dispersed throughout middle-management or supervisory positions. Middle management and supervisors remain at the forefront of leadership on a daily basis, and providing a solid body of knowledge that might assist them in their endeavors should be welcomed.

The fact that the primary focus has been on middle management and those holding supervisory positions would only be problematic if it meant (a) that we were developing a body of knowledge that was of little or limited value to leadership in organizations, (b) that an appropriate body of knowledge about senior management was not being developed, or (c) that there were substantial differences in the way in which top-level leaders, middle managers, and supervisors executed their leadership function. There is no indication that the body of knowledge developed on leadership is compromised in any of these ways.

Cross-National Issues in the Study of Leadership

Looking back over the past few decades, globalization has profoundly changed how countries and individuals interact with each other,[8] and globalization has also disrupted organizations. If the future of business is to take place at a global level, we need a comprehensive understanding of leadership across the world. The question asked here is whether leadership research is providing the kind of knowledge that organizations need to be able to cope with this new global reality.

Our analysis of research trends in several major management journals does not provide an encouraging picture. Of the articles published from 2000 on that focused on leadership, the overwhelming majority (approximately 70%) limited their focus to the United States. Approximately 10% of the remaining articles focused on the Netherlands, Israel, and the United Kingdom. Notably, very little of the research (some 6%) was conducted on leadership in any of the so-called BRICS countries (Brazil, Russia, India, China, South Africa), which are becoming increasingly significant in terms of economic power.[9]

While this initially paints a picture of a narrow research focus that might not be capable of providing the broad-based knowledge required, there are two redeeming features. First, several regional psychological journals, for example in Europe (e.g., *European Journal of Work and Organizational Psychology*) and the United Kingdom (e.g., the *Journal of Organizational and Occupational Psychology*), regularly feature interesting and high-quality research on organizational leadership. Not surprisingly, given the psychological nature of these journals, much of this research is theoretically based and has advanced our understanding of leadership. Nonetheless, even though these journals are published outside of North America, the usefulness of the knowledge gained for a global perspective is somewhat limited, as the research in these journals is often as Eurocentric as the North American research is self-focused—and likely for the same reasons—namely the expertise, costs, and time involved in cross-national research. Research on paternalistic leadership in Taiwanese organizations would exemplify this.[10] In addition, given their psychological focus, these journals are one step further removed from management, and interesting findings published in such journals might be expected to have more of a distal and delayed effect on leadership practice.

Second, in evaluating what is known about cross-national leadership, the GLOBE (Global Leadership and Organizational Effectiveness) leadership study cannot be ignored. The GLOBE project was the brainchild of the late Robert (Bob) House at the Wharton School of Management,[11] and is simply too large and extensive to be considered as a single study. Initially started at a conference hosted at the University of Calgary in 1994 and attended by 54 researchers from 38 different countries, the GLOBE study now has over 150 collaborative researchers spanning 60 countries. If there is a "typical" GLOBE study, it might be characterized by the use of self-reported surveys among a very large sample spanning at least 2 of the more than 60 countries represented in the project. In essence, the purpose of the GLOBE project is to relate culturally specific attributes within the specific country to particular leadership styles and behaviors and leadership effectiveness. As such, research findings from the GLOBE project should contribute significantly to our understanding of cross-national leadership, with one caveat. When the GLOBE project was initiated in the early 1990s, Geert Hofstede's conceptualization of culture was widely accepted, and his dimensions of culture featured prominently in the framework assumed within the GLOBE project.[12] Three decades later, there are questions concerning the validity of Hofstede's framework. Without substantial revisions to the GLOBE program, the extent to which GLOBE research is published in leading international journals or the results influence leadership researchers and practitioners may be limited.[13]

In summary, therefore, significant challenges remain for researchers to expand the research focus to be more internationally representative. From a development perspective, businesses are looking to the BRICS countries for future opportunities, and yet leadership research has been very slow to follow. One explanation for this is the practical difficulty (e.g., costs, language barriers) and complexity involved in conducting cross-national leadership research. Nonetheless, if leadership research is to be relevant to practitioners, new knowledge about leadership needs to be developed in those countries where business is located, or might soon be located, not in those countries that researchers find most convenient, despite the dramatic increases in expertise, time, and financial resources required.

Organizational Context

Contrary to what many media reports might have us believe, not all leaders are employed in the private sector. Leaders are employed wherever work occurs, and this is important because context matters. The context within which leaders find themselves shapes the way in which leadership behaviors might be expressed and accepted, presents different challenges, and offers different resources and opportunities. For example, being a leader in a large and successful multinational organization responsible for thousands of employees might be a very different experience from being a leader in a voluntary organization motivating volunteers to embark on a door-to-door fund-raising campaign.

So which contexts are studied? The results from the studies for which relevant data are available tell a clear story: Most of the research (58%) has focused on leadership within the private sector, with 38% of the leadership research being conducted in the public sector. The rest of the research (4%) is scattered throughout military, unions, sports, and volunteer organizations, where unique characteristics of the different contexts would again present very different challenges in the pursuit of effective leadership.

Is this relative emphasis in leadership studies on private-sector organizations appropriate? One criterion by which this question might be answered is whether the research focus matches employment and economic activities across different sectors,[14] and by this criterion the emphasis on the private sector within leadership research is appropriate. However, some concern should be expressed on the contexts studied *within* the private sector, in which *large* organizations continue to attract researchers' interest significantly more than small and medium-sized organizations.[15] While this matches the interests of media, political lobbyists, legislators, and labor organizers, the overemphasis on large organizations is problematic for several reasons. First, in most industrialized and developing countries, including the United States and Canada,[16] employment in small and medium-sized enterprises (SMEs) vastly outnumbers that in large organizations. Second, the resources (e.g., training) available to leaders in SMEs and large organizations differ substantially. Third, as was apparent in Chapter 3, leadership effectiveness differs in small and large organizations. As a result, more leadership research in small and medium-sized businesses should be encouraged.

Researchers use an array of different techniques and methods when investigating leadership. Understanding the nature of these techniques, their strengths, and their weaknesses is an important step in appreciating findings from the wide range of studies that have been conducted on leadership. In this section, I briefly outline these different methodologies, which include survey, experimental, archival and qualitative research, and meta-analyses. From this overview it will become evident that leadership researchers have been remarkably inventive in the ways in which they have set about uncovering new knowledge.[i]

Survey Research

In survey research, a group of respondents is asked to complete a set of questionnaires focusing on a variety of different topics. Survey research remains the most frequent methodology used in studies on leadership; of all possible methodologies that can be used, survey research accounted for 60% of the studies that I identified.

The plethora of available survey-based studies on leadership complicates the choice of any one article to represent survey research. Nonetheless, Jiayan Liu, Oi-Ling Siu, and Kan Shi's recent study[17] serves as an appropriate example of survey research, as it addresses an issue of topical importance.[18] We know from prior research that the quality of leadership behaviors influences employees' well-being, but how does this influence take place? Liu and colleagues initially surveyed two groups of employees (one from Beijing, and the second from Hong Kong) to enhance the generalizability of their findings. Their survey contained items on transformational leadership, trust in the leader, the respondents' own self-efficacy beliefs, job satisfaction, perceived work stress, and stress symptoms. As predicted, their results showed that higher levels of transformational leadership were associated with higher levels of employee self-efficacy and job satisfaction, and lower levels of employee work stress and stress symptoms. These researchers then used advanced statistical techniques to tease out *how* transformational leadership influenced employees' well-being. Consistent with the indirect effect of leadership discussed in Chapter 3, they found that transformational leadership was first associated

i. The goal of this section is to introduce those more intimately involved in the practice of leadership to the broad techniques used in leadership research. As such, a broad picture of the research techniques is presented at the expense of nuance within the techniques (e.g., within- vs. between-subjects experimental designs, or case studies vs. semi-structured interviews vs. participant observation approaches in qualitative research.)

with higher levels of employees' trust in their leaders (their relationship with the leaders) and beliefs about their own efficacy (the way in which they see themselves). In turn, all the effects of transformational leadership on employees' work stress and stress symptoms were transmitted via trust in management and employees' self-efficacy beliefs. In terms of the knowledge generated, the same pattern of findings emerged in both the Beijing and Hong Kong samples, suggesting that the effects of transformational leadership are generalizable, at least across these two cities.

While survey-based questionnaires will likely remain the most frequently used technology, the issue of response rates obtained in survey-based leadership research needs to be addressed. Most leaders already have more to do at work than worry about completing some time-consuming questionnaires to advance knowledge. But achieving a satisfactory response rate is important: Researchers need a sufficient number of surveys to allow for appropriate statistical analyses. Response rates become an even more salient issue when research targets senior executives' leadership, and it should not be surprising to learn that there was a decline in responding to surveys among senior executives between 1992 and 2003.[19] More troublesome is that traditional methods used to boost response rates (e.g., providing advance notice, follow-up, and personalizing the invitation to participate) were ineffective, although some factors (i.e., the salience of the research and endorsement from executives' peers) did prove useful in boosting the likelihood that they would complete the questionnaires.

One last comment on the use of surveys in leadership research is in order. Going forward, we will see a proliferation of the use of social media to distribute surveys. Available technologies make Web-based surveys easily accessible, less time-consuming, and far less costly to researchers. Adding to these significant benefits, researchers using electronically based surveys will also be able to reach vastly more potential respondents across the world.

Cross-Sectional vs. Longitudinal Data

One consistent issue in the context of survey research (but less so with laboratory studies) is the use of cross-sectional vs. longitudinal data. Briefly, cross-sectional data are collected at one point in time, while longitudinal data involve two or more different phases of data collection, typically answering the same questions, with the same group of respondents. Given the amount of time involved in collecting data over time, the increased financial costs of repeatedly conducting surveys, the escalating dropout rate as the time period between administration of the different surveys increases, and the natural impatience of researchers (or organizations) to see the results, it should come as no surprise that fully 85% of the articles in our analysis were based on cross-sectional rather than longitudinal data.

Interpreting the data from cross-sectional surveys suffers from one major drawback: the inability to make any causal inferences. For example, if a researcher was investigating the link between transformational leadership and employees' job performance, even a strong positive statistical correlation would not allow the researcher to conclude that transformational leadership *causes* higher levels of job performance. It is statistically as likely that high-performing employees allow or encourage their leaders to behave in a transformational manner, which is not implausible, as Bill Curtis and his coauthors argued in their early research on leadership in the sports context (see Chapter 7).[20] In addition, what is referred to as "unmeasured third variables" (which could be an aspect about the organizational context, team cohesion, or industry sector) might influence both the leadership behaviors and job performance. For this reason, more confidence can be placed on data drawn from longitudinal designs to advance our understanding of leadership.

Paul Bartone and colleagues' study provides a noteworthy example of longitudinal research. They investigated the process of leadership development and change in military cadets from the time of their arrival at West Point Military Academy to their graduation four years later.[21] A small group of participants were randomly selected from all entering cadets and were interviewed three times: first upon their arrival, during the second year, and again during their final year of studies. Although the relatively small sample size limited the sophistication of their statistical analyses, Bartone and his researchers were able to show that meaningful psychosocial development occurred among the cadets over the four-year period, and that increasing psychosocial development was positively associated with leader performance in the final year at the academy. The major advantage of extended longitudinal studies is their potential to investigate changes over time, which was central to these researchers' investigation of the role of psychosocial development. In this case, the longer the span of time over which the study was conducted, and the greater the number of assessments conducted, the more likely it was that changes could be detected.

At the same time, one of the major practical and methodological challenges inherent in extended longitudinal research is the reality of participants dropping out during the study. There was significant attrition in Bartone et al.'s study. Approximately 20% of the initial sample was not available for subsequent follow-up, paralleling the normal dropout rates for West Point cadets. The challenge posed is that if participants dropped out of the study because poor leadership or academic performance resulted in their being excluded from the academy, the validity of any lessons drawn about leadership in general could be compromised by the fact that they were drawn from a sample of unusually skilled cadets.

Deciding to collect longitudinal data, however, is just the beginning. A more fundamental (and difficult) decision is how much time should separate the different time points. From studies based on longitudinal data, two observations become clear. First, the time elapsed between the two measurements is typically relatively short, and second, the reasons for choosing the specific time intervals are more likely a function of practical opportunity (i.e., when organizations grant access) than theoretical choice. (To be fair to researchers, there is very little theory to help guide the choice of an appropriate time lag.) But just what time lag should exist in longitudinal research is critical if we are to discern changes in leadership over time. It is possible that with short time lags (e.g., three months), the research study could be over before any delayed changes in the effects of leadership could emerge. A second possibility is that the lag between the two measurements is so long that any changes that did occur have diminished or dissipated by the end of the study. In both of these cases, the choice of the time lag would inadvertently make it appear as if no leadership changes had taken place. A third possibility exists, and that is that any change occurs unevenly. For example, change might not be seen initially while new leadership skills are practiced and learned,[22] change might start slowly and then accelerate, or change may emerge quickly and decelerate—all of which could lead to erroneous conclusions. What this suggests is that the benchmark for longitudinal research should be the inclusion of more than two time lags—carefully chosen on the basis of when changes might be expected to occur—to adequately capture the complex patterns of behavioral change, which would also allow researchers to use complex statistical procedures that can detect subtle changes.

Experimental Research

Laboratory Experiments

Viewed as the gold standard by many academic researchers, tightly controlled laboratory-based leadership research is not done as frequently as one might expect. Indeed, my analysis of leadership research from 2000 on suggests that approximately 15% of all studies were conducted in laboratory settings. Practical difficulties and concerns about generalizing findings from the laboratory to the field no doubt limit the extent to which laboratory studies are conducted. Nonetheless, rigorous laboratory research does have a place in the development of new knowledge, given the causal inferences that can be made from their findings. We will return to this issue shortly.

Shelley Kirkpatrick and Ed Locke's study provides an interesting example of laboratory-based leadership research.[23] They were interested in the effects of charismatic and transformational leadership and their specific components (e.g., visioning, task cues, a charismatic communication style, emphasis on quality) on relevant outcomes, and whether any effects of charismatic and transformational leadership on outcomes are mediated through their effects on followers' self-efficacy beliefs and quality goals. Answering this question required a complex experimental design ideal for laboratory-based research, and their study provides an example of what is possible using a laboratory study.

Students volunteered to participate in this study and were selected randomly to be in either the experimental or control group. Experimental sessions took two hours, with groups of between 4 and 12 students attending each session. Professional actors who received more than 30 hours of training served as the leaders in this laboratory study. Because the gender of the leader can exert subtle effects, half of the participants in each of the experimental and control groups interacted with a female leader, the other half viewed a male leader. Each session began with the designated leader providing brief background information and explaining that the study focused on "task design" so as not to alert the participants to the true nature of the study, which might have biased their responses. After a practice trial, student participants completed two 15-minute trials; the task itself was designed deliberately to be routine, so that any motivation or inspiration that did occur could not be a function of an interesting task but only the result of inspiring leadership. After participants finished their tasks, they provided ratings of their attitudes toward the leader and toward the leader's performance. Researchers conducting laboratory research typically quiz participants at the end of the study to ensure that the participants viewed the manipulation as it was intended. All the participants in this study viewed the role of the leaders as equally credible irrespective of the group to which they were assigned. Thus we can conclude that the manipulation used in the experiment was successful.

Like most other laboratory based-leadership research, this study examined student participants on a simulated task. Questions about the generalizability of the findings often loom large after laboratory-based research, and can limit the extent to which findings from laboratory research are readily accepted by management practitioners and are incorporated into daily practice. However, generalizability was never meant to be a primary focus of laboratory research. Instead, when conducted properly (i.e., there is a control group that does not receive the intervention, participants are assigned to the control and intervention groups on a random basis, and pre- and post-intervention assessments are conducted), laboratory research allows inferences about causality—that it was the leadership intervention that "caused" any changes in the outcomes. Thus, laboratory-based research has a critical place in the development of new knowledge about leadership and needs to be encouraged, with results from these studies given the attention they deserve.

Vignette Studies

Vignette studies offer researchers the opportunity of carefully controlling variables that could not normally be dealt with in field studies and might be even more difficult to control in a traditional laboratory context. In a typical vignette study, two groups of individuals (e.g., an experimental and a control group) read a scenario in which virtually all the material is identical. However, there would be minor but meaningful changes within the vignettes viewed by the different groups, and the researchers would be interested in understanding whether the two groups responded differently to the subtle differences.

As one example of a vignette study, Tori Brescoll, Erica Dawson, and Eric Uhlmann were interested in the precarious position of male and female leaders in what the researchers referred to as gender-stereotypic-incongruent occupations,[24] examples of which were male presidents of a women's university or college, or female campus police chiefs. All participants in their study were randomly assigned to read one scenario (vignette) in which the target leader (either a university president of a women's college or a campus police chief), described as either a man or a woman, performed appropriately in the job or made a mistake—for example, dispatched an appropriate number of campus police officers or too few to a protest meeting. After reading the scenarios, participants responded to questions about their perceptions of the leader and the situation. The results of Brescoll and colleagues' study showed that when leaders' performance was satisfactory, there were no effects of gender incongruence. When performance errors were made, however, leaders in status-incongruent situations were perceived as being of lower status and less competent. These findings help explain the fragile condition of leaders in status-incongruent conditions, and as the research by Brescoll and her team confirm, vignette studies can provide interesting information about leadership.

Vignette studies are most likely to take place in a laboratory context (but could also be conducted online irrespective of where the participants may be) and are particularly useful in the early phases of researching a particular idea. Ideas supported from vignette studies can then be extended to field settings. As our analysis of prior leadership research confirms, vignette studies remain infrequent, possibly because questions about the generalizability of any findings loom large following their use. Only 4% of the studies we located used a vignette approach, and it is unlikely that we will see an increase in these studies.

Field Research

Field research takes place in the actual context in which the phenomenon under investigation occurs, which in this case means in organizational settings. As an example, if the focus of the research was on military leadership, the research would take place in situ (rather than in a laboratory or classroom setting, for example). The major advantage of field studies is that they provide confidence that we are accounting for finite nuances of the behavior and context under consideration, and field studies enhance our ability to generalize any findings back to organizations. Given the applied nature of leadership, 20% of leadership studies have used a field research approach—more than the number of laboratory-based studies.[ii]

Dov Eden's extensive research best characterizes the tradition of field research on leadership, and we take just one of the many field studies he conducted to illustrate how well-conducted field research can advance our understanding of leadership. In one study, Taly Dvir, Dov Eden, Bruce Avolio, and Boas Shamir compared the effectiveness of training military leaders in either transformational leadership or the routine leadership training. Their study was embedded in the regular training of infantry officer cadets in the Israeli military.[25] The seven trainers who delivered the transformational leadership training each received five full days of instruction in how to deliver transformational leadership training. In contrast, the five trainers who were to provide the routine leadership workshop required no special training, as they already had the appropriate expertise. Squads of preselected cadets who were already scheduled to undergo leadership training were randomly assigned to receive either the transformational or routine leadership interventions, both of which lasted three full days. Delivery of both transformational and routine leadership used standard training techniques (e.g., role-playing, group discussions, feedback, cases, and simulations). Six weeks after the completion of the three-day training session, the participants in the transformational leadership training group received a three-hour booster session to support what had been learned. (Budgetary concerns precluded the booster session being offered to those in the routine training group.[iii])

Practical constraints that frequently emerge when conducting field studies usually limit the ability to randomly assign participants to intervention or control groups. In reviewing the contribution of field studies to our understanding of the nature and outcomes of leadership, however, what is lost in experimental rigor is recovered in the ability to generalize the findings beyond

ii. An important distinction: While many field studies would use surveys, they would take place in situ and usually involve some form of planned or naturally occurring intervention.

iii. After the study was completed, the identical training that leaders in the transformational leadership group had received was offered to leaders who had been assigned randomly to routine leadership training, for ethical reasons. It would make little ethical sense to deprive some participants of the opportunity to develop their leadership simply because they were randomly assigned to the "wrong" group, sometimes after volunteering to participate in research.

the laboratory. In addition, factors that cannot be controlled as readily in field studies as they might be within laboratory research can often be controlled statistically. In this sense, field studies are neither better nor worse than laboratory-based research. Instead, the strengths of field research often compensate for the weaknesses of laboratory-based research, and vice versa, and both field and laboratory studies can provide an understanding of different aspects of the nature and effects of leadership.

Archival Research

Researchers have always made use of archival research. One of the earliest examples of archival research is the Oakland Growth Study, which was started in 1931 to understand the social, intellectual, and physical growth of 167 children who were born in 1920 or 1921 and at the time of the first interviews were in fifth or sixth grade. The study only ended in 1981, with the participants being interviewed a total of five times over many years. Glen Elder's use of these data for his now-classic study on the effects of economic privation on long-term development is a fitting example of archival research.[26] Of course, Elder was not present throughout all phases of the study, but he subsequently gained access, analyzed all the available data, and showed why some children were not harmed by the adverse economic conditions and even thrived.

One source of archival data that has featured prominently in leadership research is U.S. presidents' speeches. An example of how such data have been used to enhance knowledge on leadership is Jeffery Scott Mio and colleagues' research on the use of metaphor in presidential inaugural speeches, from George Washington to Bill Clinton.[27] Two independent and skilled raters examined each speech and generated a metaphor density score, which reflected the number of metaphors in the speech divided by the number of words in the speech. The results from their analyses enabled them to pinpoint how metaphor is used as a rhetorical tool for inspiration by charismatic U.S. presidents.

Lest the impression be created that archival data are only useful for analyzing political leaders, Michelle Ryan and Alex Haslam accessed the 2003 Cranfield Index[28] and the online Share Monitoring Service of the London Stock Exchange. As will be discussed in more detail in Chapter 8, they were able to provide some support for the "glass cliff" phenomenon from these data, which showed that women were more likely to be appointed as members of boards of directors during periods of poor performance, while men were more likely to be appointed during periods of stability.[29] In addition, to appreciate the range of archival data available, recall from Chapter 2 how Chatterjee and Hambrick accessed (a) companies' annual reports to analyze the relative size of the CEO's picture, (b) company press releases to examine how prominently

CEOs were featured in media stories, (c) digital data to quantify the number of times CEOs used the first-person singular pronoun in media interviews, and (d) salaries of the CEO and members of the top management team. They then created their measure of CEO narcissism from these diverse sources.[30] In an electronic world, the opportunity to identify archival data for leadership research is becoming increasingly apparent.

Meta-Analysis

A meta-analysis is a statistical process in which the researcher takes all possible articles on a particular topic (e.g., leadership and performance outcomes), amalgamates the data from all the studies, and quantitatively analyses all the data together. Meta-analyses have become a very popular research tool. Factors within different studies that might have affected the findings (e.g., sample size, reliability of the measures used) can be controlled statistically in a meta-analysis, thus meta-analyses are said to provide "true" relationships between variables. Issues addressed through the use of meta-analysis include gender and leadership,[31] leadership effectiveness,[32] and the validity of different leadership theories.[33]

There are numerous meta-analytic studies on leadership. Timothy Judge and Ronald Piccolo's meta-analysis on the relationship between transformational and transactional leadership, and different outcomes (e.g., followers' job satisfaction and motivation, leadership satisfaction, perceived leader effectiveness, and group or organizational performance)[34] provides an excellent example of this form of research. They amalgamated all empirical articles that were published on this topic up until 2003. As a result, some of their analyses were based on samples ranging from a few thousand to as many as 22,300 participants in one particular analysis. Their findings showed that, as predicted, transformational and transactional forms of leadership were significantly associated with the job performance outcomes. Follow-up analyses also showed that, in most instances, transformational leadership correlated more highly with the outcome criteria than transactional leadership. In addition, they showed that laissez-faire leadership was negatively associated with the leadership outcome.

An additional benefit of meta-analysis is that it allows researchers to search for more nuanced results. In this respect, Judge and Piccolo's analyses also showed important differences between transformational and transactional leadership (specifically, contingent reward). While transformational leadership was consistently effective across diverse settings (business, college, military, and the public sector), contingent reward was effective in business contexts, less so in military and public-sector contexts, and of questionable effectiveness in college settings. In addition, while transformational leadership was effective in both cross-sectional and longitudinal designs, contingent reward was only effective when researched using relatively weaker cross-sectional designs. What this means is that the demonstrated effectiveness of transformational leadership is more robust than that of contingent reward.

As research on leadership increases in frequency and scope, we are likely to see more meta-analytic investigations integrating the findings of these studies, as it is an appropriate technique for integrating large amounts of data.

Qualitative Research

A common characteristic of the methods discussed so far is their reliance on numerical data and quantitative analyses. Kevin Lowe and William Gardner estimated that about two-thirds of research in the journal *Leadership Quarterly* made use of some form of quantitative data analysis.[35] Beginning in the late 1980s, the study of organizational leadership started to make more frequent use of qualitative-research techniques.[36] Qualitative and quantitative studies generally confront the same basic questions. However, qualitative research is often used when there is greater interest in delving more deeply into the phenomenon of interest, and perhaps in gaining a more nuanced understanding of the causes and consequences of the same phenomenon under investigation. Qualitative research is also useful in initially gaining some understanding of the topic, but is less useful in establishing how a set of findings might generalize to whole populations. One consequence of this is that qualitative research generally requires far fewer participants than quantitative research. An array of different techniques (e.g., textual analysis, structure, semi- and unstructured interviews, focus groups, participant observation) can be used to provide the data that would be amenable to qualitative analysis.

Given the array in possible methods, selecting one study as an example of qualitative research is by no means easy. I chose Susan Murphy and Ellen Ensher's study because of their unusual focus on the effects of television directors' charismatic leadership on creativity in teams.[37] These researchers conducted interviews with 21 directors that lasted approximately one hour each. Interviews were tape recorded, and the interviewers took careful notes during the interview. After the interviews were transcribed (providing an average of 20 single-spaced pages of information each), the information was analyzed using software specifically designed to categorize themes within the interview responses. In addition, each interview was sorted by specially trained coders according to the themes inherent in charismatic leadership.

Using this qualitative approach, the authors obtained rich data that confirmed how creative TV directors use different aspects of charismatic leadership. For example, one director commented on how the director's vision was communicated to everyone on the set: "I have a clear vision for how I want to proceed, what I want the show to look like. I break it down into a smaller piece, so on the first day you get a rehearsal of the first scene. Within that rehearsal, I make a series of decisions that are communicated to everybody" (p. 342). Displaying consideration for actors' personal need not to be publicly humiliated, which arose from his own awareness as an actor, one director insisted, "I never, never yell across the set" (p. 343). Finally, charismatic leaders take risks and overcome their own fears, as exemplified by one director who said, "You know it's important that you get chills yourself from others coming up with ideas that you had not thought of. Don't be afraid to hire people who are more talented than you" (p. 346).

One concluding observation warrants mention. Each of the research methods discussed here have been described in isolation, and they each have different strengths and weaknesses. To maximize inferences that can be made from any single research project, researchers are invariably encouraged to conduct more than one study using different methods to answer the same question. For example, Satu Koivisto, Jukka Lipponen, and Michael Platow used both a vignette and experimental study to show that supervisors' interpersonal fairness shapes the way in which team members view whether changes are threatening or not.[38]

MEASUREMENT ISSUES IN THE STUDY OF LEADERSHIP

As already noted, the most frequent method for measuring leadership behaviors is through questionnaires. The sheer number of questionnaires used to measure different types of high-quality, destructive, and poor leadership, however, makes it impossible to discuss each of them in detail in this book. Nonetheless, some comments on the measurement of transformational leadership, which remains the most widely studied theory of positive leadership (see Figure 1.1), are in order. The most frequently used questionnaire to assess transformational leadership is the Multifactor Leadership Questionnaire (MLQ),[39] and accordingly, much of the discussion here is limited to the MLQ. Although the MLQ can be used within the framework of 360-degree feedback, in a research context it is most likely to be completed by subordinates about their leaders.

The MLQ purports to separately measure the different dimensions of both transformational and transactional leadership. From the MLQ, scores on the four components of transformational leadership (idealized influence, inspirational motivation, intellectual stimulation, individualized consideration), as well as transactional leadership (contingent reward, active and passive management-by-exception, and laissez-faire) are provided. Most of the focus in the leadership literature has been on transformational leadership, and the major questions raised concern its four dimensions.

Specifically, numerous studies over the past two decades have questioned whether the four dimensions should be measured separately, because data from leadership studies consistently show that the relationships between the four factors are extremely high. Our attempt to measure the four dimensions separately with respect to what is referred to as transformational teaching proved no more successful, suggesting that the issue is not limited to the MLQ alone.[40] Making matters more complicated is the finding that there are also consistently high correlations between transformational and transactional leadership, in all cases higher than one might expect given the underlying theory.

As a result, interpreting data obtained on the MLQ is complicated. One possible reason for the high correlation between the four components is that the questionnaire is flawed, and cannot isolate the real differences that exist between the four components of transformational leadership. A second possibility is that the MLQ provides an appropriate picture, but that the four dimensions are not as separate as the theory might have us believe, which would be consistent with our data from the Transformational Teaching Questionnaire. Because of this uncertainty, and because copyright restrictions make it difficult for researchers to freely use items from the MLQ, there is now some interest in alternative questionnaires, and several publicly available questionnaires do now exist.

Sally Carless, Alexander Wearing, and Leon Mann[41] were amongst the first to attempt to create an alternative measure and developed the Global Transformational Leadership Scale, a short, seven-item measure of transformational leadership that makes no attempt to differentiate between the four different transformational components. At about the same time, Beverly Alimo-Metcalfe and Robert Alban-Metcalfe went in the opposite direction, generating a nine-dimensional Transformational Leadership Questionnaire which separately assesses different aspects of transformational leadership.[42] While ignoring the separate nature of the four dimensions of transformational leadership is a potential pitfall in the Carless et al. scale, the sheer complexity of Alimo-Metcalfe and Alban-Metcalfe's questionnaire will likely limit its use. Across several studies, Philip Podsakoff and his colleagues[43] have developed the Transformational Leader Behavior Inventory (TLI), a well-validated scale that assesses both transformational leadership (22 items) and the contingent reward component of transactional leadership (five items), which has been used successfully in subsequent research.[44] Their items are reproduced in Table 4.1.

In addition to addressing how best to measure leadership, some consideration of *when* we might measure leadership is in order. The reason for this is that two psychological factors may bias followers' ratings of their leaders at different stages of the leader–follower relationship. The first such bias is the "honeymoon effect."[45] As its name implies, the honeymoon effect

Table 4.1. THE TRANSFORMATIONAL LEADER BEHAVIOR INVENTORY

Transformational Leadership:

I believe my leader . . .

1. Is always seeking new opportunities for the unit/department/organization.
2. Paints an interesting picture of the future for our group.
3. Has a clear understanding of where we are going.
4. Inspires others with his/her plans for the future.
5. Is able to get others committed to his/her dream of the future.
6. Fosters collaboration among work groups.
7. Encourages employees to be "team players."
8. Gets the group to work together for the same goal.
9. Develops a team attitude and spirit among his/her employees.
10. Acts without considering my personal feelings. (R)
11. Shows respect for my personal feelings.
12. Behaves in a manner that is thoughtful of my personal needs.
13. Treats me without considering my personal feelings.
14. Shows us that he/she expects a lot from us.
15. Insists on only the best performance.
16. Will not settle for second best.
17. Leads by "doing" rather than simply by "telling."
18. Provides a good model to follow.
19. Leads by example.
20. Has provided me with new ways of looking at things which used to be a puzzle to me.
21. Has ideas that have forced me to rethink some of my own ideas I have never questioned before.
22. Has stimulated me to think about old problems in new ways.

Contingent Reward Behavior:

1. Always gives me positive feedback when I perform well.
2. Gives me special recognition when my work is very good.
3. Commends me when I do a better than average job.
4. Personally complements me when I do outstanding work.
5. Frequently does not acknowledge my good performance. (R)

(R) = reverse coded.
From Rubin, R. S., Munz, D. C., & Bommer, W. H. (2005). Leading from within: The effects of emotion recognition and personality on transformational leadership behavior. *Academy of Management Behavior, 48,* 857.

characterizes the relationship of newly married couples: At the outset of a marriage, one would expect to find virtually all marital partners reporting high relationship satisfaction, with little variation between couples. Over time, however, the average of the relationship satisfaction scores would likely decrease, and the range of scores would increase as many people remain satisfied but others start to experience dissatisfaction. The honeymoon effect can also characterize employees' motivation upon joining an organization: there is a tendency for most employees to be highly motivated at first, with the average motivation decreasing (and the range of motivation increasing) eight months into the job.[46] It follows that obtaining follower ratings of leadership behavior early in the leader–follower relationship may result in artificially optimistic estimates of leadership. Questions of when to assess leadership must also be sensitive to the fact that followers need time to get to know what lies beneath the surface, as assessments of ethical leadership (or what will be referred to as "pseudo-transformational leadership" in Chapter 9) may be misleading if undertaken too soon in the relationship. Second, and related to the honeymoon effect, is the "hangover effect,"[47] which speaks to the period during which ratings of leadership are in decline and then become stable. As such, leadership researchers (and practitioners, too—for example, during 360-degree feedback exercises) should be sensitive to possible honeymoon effects when leaders and followers find themselves together for the first time, as followers' leadership ratings might well be inflated artificially. Later on, concern about hangover effects should be considered just as seriously.

An Invitation

Before concluding this chapter, I invite you to see firsthand how leadership is measured. At the end of this paragraph, you will find a URL. If you visit this Web site, you will find three questionnaires: Podsakoff and colleagues' Transformational Leader Behavior Inventory (TLI), which was introduced in this chapter; Brown and colleagues' Ethical Leadership Questionnaire, which was discussed in Chapter 1; and Tepper's Abusive Supervision Scale, which will be considered in Chapter 9, on destructive leadership. You can rate your own leader (and pass the link on to others as well), and if you do so, you will receive some feedback on your leader in terms of her or his transformational leadership, abusive supervision, and ethical leadership. http://www.oup.com/us/barling

CONCLUSION

Clearly, our current knowledge about leadership has been based on an extensive array of different methodologies. As we move forward, researchers will continue to refine the topics, techniques, and measurement tools, advancing the research-based knowledge on organizational leadership. The next time you receive an invitation to participate in the kind of leadership research described in this chapter, please consider participating. By doing so, you will have the opportunity to participate in the kind of research presented in this chapter, and contribute to the ever-expanding knowledge on the nature, causes, and consequences of organizational leadership.

SUGGESTED READING

Aronson, A., & Aronson, J. (2011). *The social animal*, 11th ed. New York: Worth. See especially Chapter 9: Social psychology as a science. pp. 405–429.

Klenke, K. (2008). *Qualitative research in the study of leadership*. Bingley, UK: Emerald Group Publishing.

NOTES

1. Judge, T. A., & Bono, J. E. (2000). Five-factor model of personality and transformational leadership. *Journal of Applied Psychology, 85*, 751–765.
2. Barling, J., Christie, A., & Hoption, C. (2010). Leadership. In S. Zedeck (Ed.), *Handbook of industrial and organizational psychology* (Vol. 1, pp. 183–240). Washington, DC: American Psychological Association.
3. Kellerman, B. (2008). *Followership*. New York: McGraw-Hill.
4. Barling, J., Christie, A., & Hoption, C. (2010). Leadership. In S. Zedeck (Eds.), *Handbook of industrial and organizational psychology* (Vol. 1, pp. 183–240). Washington, DC: American Psychological Association.
5. Holdcroft, A. (2007). Gender bias in research: How does it affect evidence-based medicine? *Journal of the Royal Society of Medicine, 100*(1), 1–2.
6. Gilligan, C. (1982). *In a different voice*. Cambridge, MA: Harvard University Press.
7. Eagly, A. H. (1995). The science and politics of comparing women and men. *American Psychologist, 50*, 145–158.
8. Friedman, T. L. (2005). *The world is flat: A brief history of the 21st century*. New York: Farrar, Straus & Giroux.
9. Desai, R. (2013, April 2). The BRICS are building a challenge to Western economic supremacy. *The Guardian*. Retrieved from http://www.guardian.co.uk/commentisfree/2013/apr/02/brics-challenge-western-supremacy
10. Cheng, B., Chou, L., & Wu, T. (2004). Paternalistic leadership and subordinate responses: Establishing a leadership model in Chinese organizations. *Asia Journal of Social Psychology, 7*, 89–117.
11. House, R., Javidan, M., Hanges, P., & Dorfman, P. (2002). Understanding cultures and implicit leadership theories across the globe: An introduction to project GLOBE. *Journal of World Business, 37*, 3–10.
12. Hofstede, G. H. (1980). *Culture's consequences: International differences in work related values*. Thousand Oaks, CA: SAGE Publications.
13. Taras, V., Kirkman, B., & Steel, P. (2010). Examining the impact of culture's consequences: A three-decade, multilevel, meta-analytic review of Hofstede's cultural value dimensions. *Journal of Applied Psychology, 95*, 405–439.
14. O'Leary, M. B., & Almond, B. A. (2009). The industry settings of leading organizational research: The role of economic and non-economic factors. *Journal of Organizational Behavior, 30*, 497–524.
15. Dionisi, A., & Barling, J. (2011). Sexual harassment: A big issue for small and medium enterprises? In E. K. Kelloway & C. L. Cooper (Eds.), *Occupational health and safety in small and medium enterprise* (pp. 129–158). London: Elgar.

16. Headd, B. (2000). The characteristics of small-business employees. *Monthly Labor Review, April*, 13–18; Wong, Q. (2009). *Small business profile: An overview of Canada's small and mid-sized enterprises*. Toronto: Canadian Federation of Independent Business.

17. Liu, J., Siu, O. L., & Shi, K. (2010). Transformational leadership and employee well-being: The mediating role of trust in the leader and self-efficacy. *Applied Psychology: An International Review, 59*, 454–479.

18. Arnold, K. A., Turner, N., Barling, J., Kelloway, E. K., & McKee, M. C. (2007). Transformational leadership and well-being: The mediating role of meaningful work. *Journal of Occupational Health Psychology, 12*, 193–203.

19. Cycyota, C. S., & Harrison, D. A. (2006). What (not) to expect when surveying executives: A meta-analysis of top manager response rates and techniques over time. *Organizational Research Methods, 9*, 133–160.

20. Curtis, B., Smith, R. E., & Smoll, F. L. (1979). Scrutinizing the skipper: A study of leadership behaviors in the dugout. *Journal of Applied Psychology, 64*, 391–400.

21. Bartone, P. T., Snook, S. A., Forsythe, G. B., Lewis, P., & Bullis, R. C. (2007). Psychosocial development and leader performance of military cadets. *Leadership Quarterly, 18*, 490–504.

22. Hirst, G., Mann, L., Bain, P., Lirola-Merlo, A., & Richver, A. (2004). Learning to lead: The development and testing of a model of leadership learning. *Leadership Quarterly, 15*, 311–327.

23. Kirkpatrick, S. A., & Locke, E. A. (1996). Direct and indirect effects of three core charismatic leadership components on performance and attitudes. *Journal of Applied Psychology, 81*, 36–51.

24. Brescoll, V. L., Dawson, E., & Uhlmann, E. L. (2010). Hard won and easily lost: The fragile status of leaders in gender stereotype-incongruent occupations. *Psychological Science, 21*, 1640–1642.

25. Dvir, T., Eden, D., Avolio, B. J., & Shamir, B. (2002). Impact of transformational leadership on follower development and performance: A field experiment. *Academy of Management Journal, 45*, 735–744.

26. Elder, G. H., Jr. (1974). *Children of the Great Depression: Social change in life experience*. Chicago: University of Chicago Press.

27. Mio, J. S., Riggio, R. E., Levin, S., & Reese, R. (2005). Presidential leadership and charisma: The effects of metaphor. *Leadership Quarterly, 16*, 287–294.

28. The FTSE female index. Retrieved from http://www.som.cranfield.ac.uk/som/ftse

29. Ryan, M. K., & Haslam, S. A. (2005b). The glass cliff: Evidence that women are over-represented in precarious leadership positions. *British Journal of Management, 16*, 81–90.

30. Chatterjee, A., & Hambrick, D. C. (2007). It's all about me: Narcissistic chief executive officers and their effects on company strategy and performance. *Administrative Science Quarterly, 52*, 351–386.

31. Eagly, A. H., Johannesen-Schmidt, M. C., & van Engen, M. L. (2003). Transformational, transactional and laissez-faire leadership studyles. A meta-analysis comparing men and women. *Psychological Bulletin, 129*, 569–591; Eagly, A. H., Karay, S. J., & Makhijani, M. G. (1995). Gender and the effectiveness of leaders: A meta-analysis. *Psychological Buleetin, 117*, 125–145; van Engen, M. L., & Willemsen, T. M. (2004). Sex and leadership styles: A meta-analysis of research published in the 1990's. *Psychological Reports, 94*, 3–18.

32. Avolio, B. J., Reichard, R. J., Hannah, S. T., Walumbwa, F. O., & Chan, A. (2009). A meta-analytic review of leadership impact research. Experimental and quasi-experimental studies. *Leadership Quarterly, 20,* 764–784; Burke, C. S., Stagl, K. C., Cameron, G. F., Salas, E., & Halpin, S. M. (2006). What type of leadership behaviors are functional in teams? A meta-analysis. *Leadership Quarterly, 17,* 288–307; Gastil, J. (1994). A meta-analytic review of the productivity and satisfaction of democratic and autocratic leadership. *Small Group Research, 25,* 384–410.

33. Sin, H. P., Nahrgang, J. D., & Morgeson, F. P. (2009). Understanding why they don't see eye to eye: An examination of leader-member exchange (LMX) agreement. *Journal of Applied Psychology, 94,* 1048–1057; Judge, T. A., & Piccolo, R. F. (2004). Transformational and transactional leadership: A meta-analytic test of their relative validity. *Journal of Applied Psychology, 89,* 755–768.

34. Judge, T. A., & Piccolo, R. F. (2004). Transformational and transactional leadership: A meta-analytic test of their relative validity. *Journal of Applied Psychology, 89,* 755–768.

35. Lowe, K. B., & Gardner, W. L. (2000). Ten years of the Leadership Quarterly: Contributions and challenges for the future. *Leadership Quarterly, 11,* 459–514.

36. Bryman, A. (2004). Qualitative research on leadership: A critical but appreciative review. *Leadership Quarterly, 15,* 729–769.

37. Murphy, S. E., & Ensher, E. A. (2008). A qualitative analysis of charismatic leadership in creative teams: The case of television directors. *Leadership Quarterly, 19,* 335–353.

38. Koivisto, S., Lipponen, J., & Platow, M. J. (2013). Organizational and supervisory justice effects on experienced threat during change: The moderating role of leader in-group representativeness. *Leadership Quarterly, 24,* 596–607.

39. Bass, B. M., & Avolio, B. J. (n.d.). *Multifactor leadership questionnaire: The benchmark measure of transformational leadership.* Retrieved from http://www.mindgarden.com/products/mlq.htm

40. Bycio, P., Hackett, R. D., & Allen, J. S. (1995). Further assessments of Bass's (1985) conceptualization of transformational and transactional leadership. *Journal of Applied Psychology, 80,* 468–478.

41. Carless, S. A., Wearing, A. J., & Mann, L. (2000). A short measure of transformational leadership. *Journal of Business and Psychology, 14,* 389–405.

42. Alimo-Metcalfe, B., & Alban-Metcalfe, R. J. (2001). The development of a new Transformational Leadership Questionnaire. *Journal of Occupational and Organizational Psychology, 74,* 1–27.

43. Podsakoff, P. M., MacKenzie, S. B., Moorman, R. H., & Fetter, R. (1990). Transformational leadership behaviors and their effects on followers' trust in leader, satisfaction, and organizational citizenship behaviors. *Leadership Quarterly, 1,* 107–142; Podsakoff, P. M., MacKenzie, S. B., & Bommer, W. H. (1996). Transformational leader behaviors and substitutes for leadership as determinants of employee satisfaction, commitment, trust, and organizational citizenship behaviors. *Journal of Management, 22,* 259–298.

44. Herold, D. M., Fedor, D. B., Caldwell, S., & Liu, Y. (2008). The effects of transformational and change leadership on employees' commitment to change: A multilevel study. *Journal of Applied Psychology, 93,* 1234–1248; Rubin, R. S., Munz, D. C., & Bommer, W. H. (2005). Leading from within: The effects of emotion recognition and personality on transformational leadership behavior. *Academy of Management Behavior, 48,* 845–858.

45. Helmreich, R. L., Sawin, L. L., & Carsrud, A. L. (1986). The honeymoon effect in job performance: Temporal increases in the predictive power of achievement motivation. *Journal of Applied Psychology, 71*, 185–188.
46. Helmreich, R. L., Sawin, L. L., & Carsrud, A. L. (1986). The honeymoon effect in job performance: Temporal increases in the predictive power of achievement motivation. *Journal of Applied Psychology, 71*, 185–188.
47. Boswell, W. R., Boudreau, J. W., & Tichy, J. (2005). The relationship between employee job change and job satisfaction: The honeymoon-hangover effect. *Academy of Management Journal, 48*, 889–909.

CHAPTER 5

Are Leaders Born or Made?

We live, learn, and work in environments where leaders and leadership are ubiquitous, and we have all likely encountered the extremes of leadership: Those wonderful leaders who elevate, respect, and develop us, and those leaders who sadly demean, humiliate, and belittle us. In trying to make sense of the extremes of leadership, most people have probably asked themselves—and others—whether leaders are born or made? Indeed, the extent to which we are absorbed by this issue can be gauged by submitting the question "Are leaders born or made?" to a search on google.com; doing so produced 37,100,000 results in 0.14 seconds![i]

Whether leadership is born or made is an issue about which most people have an opinion, often a very strong opinion. Even Shakespeare weighed in on the issue with his unforgettable observation in *Twelfth Night* that "Some are born great, some achieve greatness, and some have greatness thrust upon them." Perhaps we should not be surprised at how widespread opinions are on this issue. B.F. Skinner, one of the most influential and controversial psychologists of the 20th century, suggested some 40 years ago that we all stand "in awe of the inexplicable."[1] And what could be more seemingly inexplicable than some of the greatest leaders of the 20th century, be it Nelson Mandela, Mahatma Ghandi, or Mother Theresa, or some of their most destructive counterparts, such as Hitler, Pol Pot, or Stalin? When faced with big questions (such as explaining seemingly inexplicable leadership abilities), we seek "big" answers, and many people, psychologists included, believe that extraordinary leadership must surely be the gift of good genes, rather than something that can be learned.

i. Accessed on February 17, 2013.

All of this is exemplified in attempts to make sense of Nelson Mandela's leadership. Commenting on the enormity of his leadership, noted organizational scholar Rosabeth Moss Kanter observed that "There are very few people in the world who could have done what he did. I mean 27 years in prison, and coming out and repairing a troubled nation and forgiving his enemies. He's off the charts when it comes to leadership." In response to the question "Are leaders born or made?" Kanter went further, saying, "I think Nelson Mandela in South Africa had to be a natural leader.... I think you probably have to be born Mandela."[2] And Rosabeth Moss Kanter is not alone in these beliefs. After meeting Mandela, Roy Anderson, an industrialist and CEO of several large companies in South Africa during the 1990s, observed that "His charisma goes way beyond people respecting what he stands for and the sacrifices he has made," adding his voice to the familiar refrain that this "must be something he was born with."[3]

But to believe that genetic factors alone can fully explain the emergence and development of Mandela's leadership is to ignore the critical role that his early childhood socialization played in his later development—a common tendency among many biographers whose focus was primarily on Mandela's life *after* he ascended to leadership positions in the African National Congress (ANC) as a young man in the 1950s.[4] In doing so, they cast no light on his early family life, his teenage years, or his experiences as a university student. Rather than accepting that his early socialization was irrelevant to his subsequent leadership, a closer examination suggests the opposite is closer to the truth.

Nonetheless, understanding the influence of family and environmental factors in Mandela's early life on his later leadership is complicated by several factors. First, there is a reasonable fear that being able to understand any early influences might in some way minimize the magic of Mandela's leadership, but there need be no such concerns. Instead, understanding the roots of Mandela's leadership will remind us of the pervasive importance of early family socialization and adverse experiences in the development of leadership (e.g., parental alcoholism in the case of Bill Clinton's leadership, the early death of the father, as in the cases of Mandela, Franklin Delano Roosevelt, and Nixon, to name just a few, or the early death of Eleanor Roosevelt's father and four-year-old brother). Second, retrospectively understanding the leadership roots of anyone who has achieved iconic or mythical status is challenging, because we ascribe our own needs, dreams, and fears onto the iconic leader, all of which complicates the search for an objective understanding.

From scholars who have given serious attention to Mandela's early life, one thing is clear: While most rural Black children in South Africa lived lives of privation, this was not to be Mandela's plight. From a very early age, Mandela led a life of relative privilege. Mandela's father, Henry Gadla, was comfortable financially, at least relative to others in his community. Mandela was a member of the royal family of the ruling Thembu clan in the Transkei,[5] and after his father's death from tuberculosis when he was 10 years old,[6] Mandela was accepted as a ward of the Regent of the Thembu, and a companion to the Regent's son. As a child, Mandela was afforded the unusual opportunity of attending elite Methodist elementary schools, where he was eventually made a prefect in his boarding school—a position of considerable status, responsibility, and authority. Mandela also attended Healdtown, a prestigious Wesleyan secondary school. Some six decades later, former school friends remembered him for his magnanimity. These extraordinary opportunities for a rural, Black person in South Africa became more pronounced upon graduation from high school, when Mandela enrolled at Fort Hare University, "one of an intake of around 50 black Southern Africans"[7] in the year in which he enrolled. To understand what all this meant in South Africa in the early 1940s, recall that most young Black men grew up on farms or near cities, and precious few would have even attempted, let alone completed, secondary education.

It was at Fort Hare University that Mandela became politicized,[8] meeting many of the people with whom he would subsequently be politically involved. The influence of Fort Hare University in Mandela's leadership development becomes increasingly evident when we learn that this university was home to other African students who subsequently achieved the ultimate leadership positions in their own countries after independence from their colonial power: Presidents Kenneth Kaunda of Zambia, Robert Mugabe of Zimbabwe, Yusuf Lule of Uganda, and Julius Nyere of Tanzania; and Prime Minister of Botswana, Sir Seretse Khama.[9] Add to this the list of students who would subsequently become the leaders of the anti-apartheid movement in South Africa (e.g., Chris Hani, Rev. Allen Hendrickse, Govan Mbeki, Raymond Mhlaba, Robert Sobukwe, and Oliver Tambo), and it is clear that Mandela would have found himself in the midst of an extraordinarily dynamic environment at an especially impressionable time of his life.

The early political power of the regent was such that when Mandela later arrived in Johannesburg as a young man in the 1940s after leaving Fort Hare University, he immediately obtained a valued job working for the gold mines. He also met Walter Sisulu, who later became Secretary General and Deputy President of the ANC. By Mandela's own admission, Sisulu had a profound influence on his development.[10] During the mid-1940s, Mandela served as an articled law clerk in Johannesburg before eventually qualifying as a lawyer at a time—1946—when the South African census could identify only 18 African lawyers and 13 articled clerks. From a social perspective, Mandela's early encounters with the White community were unusually positive—including with his employers and mentors, Lazar Sidelsky and Nat Bregman. In fact, from his schooldays on, Mandela had the unusual opportunity of observing both Black and White role models, including situations in which Black teachers defied White authority. Clearly, then, Mandela's early life was replete with situations in which he saw others challenge authority and did so himself, and he both witnessed and practiced leadership. Thus, we begin to see that Mandela's subsequent leadership was likely a function of many different influences: genetic influences which should certainly not be discounted, early family adversity with the death of his father, a supportive family environment, early emergence as a leader in elementary school, and a rich political environment at a time when he was most amenable to political influence. Just how important experiences like this might be for the development of leadership will become clear throughout this chapter.

While intriguing, a single case study, even one as fascinating as Nelson Mandela, cannot unravel the complex roles of environmental and genetic factors in the emergence of leadership. So what do the results of scientific studies tell us? Fortunately, this issue has captured the attention of the research community and resulted in some imaginative and rigorous research studies. Before going any further, however, an important clarification is in order: Whether studies show that leaders are "born" or "made" is not just of theoretical interest, but may also have important practical implications for leaders' motivation. If the dominant belief is that individuals are born with the ability to lead, any subsequent success might simply be ascribed to luck. If that is the case, those not lucky enough to have been born with the gift of leadership could justifiably absolve themselves of blame for any failures, which would be viewed as beyond their control. That being the case, it would make little sense for these leaders to work hard at improving their leadership skills if they believed that leadership ability is a fixed or immutable trait. In contrast, believing that leadership can be learned and improved through one's own efforts would likely leave leaders inspired to work enthusiastically on their leadership behaviors. Clearly, whether leaders believe that leadership is learned or inherited can have significant effects on their motivation to lead.

Before turning to the scientific literature, perhaps it is appropriate to conclude this section by noting that even Mandela has an opinion on the nature-vs.-nurture debate. In his autobiography, Mandela tells us, "Nurture, rather than nature, is the primary moulder of personality."[11] But could it be that both nature and nurture interact to influence leadership? What does research teach us?

ENVIRONMENTAL INFLUENCES ON LEADERSHIP DEVELOPMENT

An initial understanding that one's early family environment might influence subsequent leadership derived indirectly from adolescents' first occupational choices. In the early 1930s, Erland Nelson reported on a survey of 321 college students, the results of which showed that fathers' occupations significantly

influenced their children's career choices.[12] What would probably not be surprising today is that any similarity between fathers' occupations and their
children's career choice was substantially stronger if only the choices of sons
were considered, because a girl's choice of career was socially restricted at that
time. The presence of gender differences in parental influences on children's
occupational choices has been replicated consistently in studies since then,
including in very large samples outside of the United States (e.g., in India),
thereby excluding the possibility that the phenomenon is specific to a North
American context. The lesson learned from this research is that the family
environments to which we are exposed early on affect subsequent occupational development, choices, and behaviors. Might these findings have any
bearing on our understanding of the emergence of leadership?

At about the same time that Nelson reported the findings from his study,
noted social scientist Emory Borgadus offered two observations on the importance of family influences for leadership development. First, Borgadus noticed
that the leadership development of several famous politicians, for example,
William E. Gladstone, Robert E. Lee, Woodrow Wilson, Benjamin Franklin,
and George Washington, had all been influenced through stimulating associations and interactions with their parents.[13] At the same time, and seemingly
arguing the opposite case, Borgadus reported that the early death of a parent forced children to assume responsibilities that could enhance leadership
development, all of which raise the possibility that early family socialization
affects the subsequent development of leadership.

Early Adversity

Accepting the general importance of early socialization in children's development, one early stream of research accorded special importance to the role
of early adversity. Anecdotally, it is clear that not all children are necessarily
affected negatively by early adversity in the long term, nor are all children
who suffer early adversity affected in the same way (just as not all children
who grow up in privileged circumstances benefit equally). Instead, some children seem to be unaffected by early adversity, and some suffer long-term consequences. But remarkably, some children rebound, or literally use the early
adversity to propel themselves onto a successful life course.[ii]

Why might early adversity facilitate later leadership? Borgadus had already
noted in 1934 that upon the death of a parent, children often assumed new
responsibilities that encouraged leadership development. To support this, he

---

ii. Psychologists now speak of post-traumatic growth, which reflects the positive
changes that can occur as a result of successfully navigating through extremely traumatic events and circumstances.

quoted renowned sociologist and social activist Beatrice Webb: "The death of my mother revolutionized my life. From being a subordinate, carrying out directions, ... I became a principal, a person in authority, determining not only my own but other people's conduct" (p. 88). Presidential scholar Doris Kearns Goodwin suggests that Eleanor Roosevelt's experience of ongoing disappointments by her father, and then his early death and that of her four-year-old brother, was the source of a "legacy" of "resilient strength" (p. 95).[14] In a similar vein, noted leadership scholar Warren Bennis[15] speculated that what characterizes individuals who successfully overcome early setbacks is their ability to find meaning in their adversity. Research findings support these comments.

One of the first large-scale studies of the effects of early exposure to adversity was conducted by Glen Elder, and was based on his access to the Oakland Growth Study, which provided a unique database that was briefly mentioned in Chapter 4.[16] For this particular study, data were collected on the psychological, social, and physical development of 167 children, starting initially in 1931 when they were all in fifth grade, continuing annually until 1939, with follow-up interviews conducted in the 1950s, in 1972, and again in 1982. This unusually rich dataset allowed for fascinating insights into the long-term effects of early experiences of hardship.[17] Among a host of interesting findings generated by this study, one was especially relevant for understanding the effects of early adversity on subsequent development. Adolescents whose fathers became unemployed during the Great Depression showed significantly *better* adjustment later on in life—their school performance was enhanced, they were more likely to enter the university, and were more satisfied with their work, their marriages, and their lives—than their counterparts whose fathers did not become unemployed during this same period. Elder suggested that this occurred because successfully navigating through a stressful, complex, and precarious adolescence taught invaluable lessons that accelerated later development. The importance of transforming early adversity into success experiences for subsequent learning is evident.

Charles Cox and Cary Cooper conducted what might be the only specific study on the effects of early adversity on leadership role occupancy.[18] They interviewed 45 CEOs, each of whom headed an organization with more than 1,000 employees. Eight of the 45 CEOs had experienced the death of their father before they themselves were 16 years old; the parents of one CEO had separated before he was 5 years old; and 10 of the participants were separated from their parents at an early age (either as a result of evacuation in World War II or because they attended boarding school). Thus, fully 19 of the 45 CEOs had experienced adversity in the form of some separation from at least one of their parents. From the interviews, the researchers realized that the development of a sense of self-sufficiency was a major factor in their interviewees' socialization, and that the most plausible factor motivating this self-sufficiency was their sense of early loss. Intriguingly, Cox and Cooper also noticed that despite the objective loss, and the sense of isolation and loneliness which forced these children to learn to rely on their own resources at an early age, as CEOs they retrospectively viewed their childhood as normal and happy. Thus, consistent with Elder's "downward extension hypothesis," Cox and Cooper speculated that it is not the objective loss that affects subsequent leadership development, but how the loss affected early coping and successful experiences in assuming responsibility. Nonetheless, while respecting the difficulty of gaining the cooperation of busy CEOs of large organizations to participate in interviews, the findings from this study need to be interpreted cautiously because of the relatively small sample size and rudimentary statistical analyses.

At first glance, the study by Weng-Dong Li, Richard Arvey, and Zhaoli Song on leader role occupancy and advancement might seem to have little to do with the effects of adversity, but one finding from their research is particularly instructive.[19] Using an unusually large sample of 1,747 employed individuals from the National Longitudinal Survey of Youth[20] over a 10-year period, they examined the effects of early family socioeconomic status on later leader emergence and advancement for men and women separately. While their findings showed that higher family socioeconomic status was weakly but positively associated with increases in leader advancement for men, the opposite was true for women. Specifically, early exposure to high family socioeconomic status had a negative effect on women's leadership advancement—the higher the family socioeconomic status, the lower the likelihood of later leadership advancement. In explaining these results, Li and colleagues suggest that the pressures on adolescents in relatively privileged homes to consistently perform at very high levels might make it more likely that females shy away from risky situations, and this would include leadership advancement. The lessons from this research coincide with those from Cox and Cooper's study on early adversity: Adolescent males who successfully confront the particular pressures inherent in privileged families might acquire invaluable skills and experience that stand them in good stead for subsequent development in general, and leadership in particular. The fact that adolescent women might be less willing to place themselves in similar situations will be explored further in Chapter 8.

The obvious fascination with children who navigate successfully through early adversity and their counterparts who do not heightens interest in the broad question of parental influences on children's leadership development. It is to studies of this nature that we now turn our attention.

Parental Influences

Just why would parent–child interactions influence children's later leadership development? Bass, whose foundational influence on our understanding of organizational leadership is evident throughout this book, noted in his 1960 book *Leadership, Psychology and Organizational Behavior*[21] that the scientific study of child development had already demonstrated the significance of the home environment in the development of children's "initiative; resourcefulness; self-reliance" (p. 195). Bass noted further that children who were lucky enough to receive opportunities for decision-making and independence from their parents were "more likely to transfer these successful responses to . . . activities with other children, to school, and to adolescent and adult situations in later life" (p. 196).

Perhaps the earliest formal research study directly investigating parental influences on children's leadership development was conducted in 1961 by renowned developmental psychologist Urie Bronfenbrenner.[22] Extending Bass' observations, Bronfenbrenner argued that consistent with the emphasis within psychology at the time on problem behaviors, the idea that parents negatively influence the socialization of their children was well accepted. What was less well understood, and what intrigued Bronfenbrenner, was the possibility that parents might also exert *positive* effects on their children's development. For his study, Bronfenbrenner randomly selected 10th-grade boys and girls from a school in upstate New York, and used a detailed questionnaire to ask the children about 20 facets of child–parent relationships—10 positive (e.g., parental affection, protectiveness, affiliative companionship) and 10 negative (e.g., parental neglect, physical punishment and threat, deprivation of privilege or property). Adding to the breadth of the study, two independent teachers separately rated the leadership behaviors of each of the children in the study.

What was learned from this early study? First, as we would now expect with the benefit of hindsight, both negative parenting (e.g., expressive rejection and neglect) and uninvolved parenting (e.g., parental absence) had negative effects on children's leadership (as rated by their teachers). In addition, constructive parent–child interactions (e.g., parenting that involved displays of affection, nurturance, companionship) were associated with more positive ratings of the children's leadership by their teachers. Second, and more intriguingly, there were significant gender differences in the pattern of results: Negative effects on children's leadership were more pronounced when parents and children were of the same sex, and were more likely to occur for daughters than for sons. Given these findings, one might think that the results of Bronfenbrenner's study would have captured the attention of leadership and child development researchers, producing a considerable body of research on the topic. This was not to happen, however, and the question of family influences on leadership emergence seemed to escape researchers' attention for most of the next three decades.

Consistent with developments in leadership theories from the 1960s on, the next generation of research on parental influences focused on specific types of child leadership behaviors. Motivated by the early theorizing of John Bowlby about the nature and consequences of parent–child attachment, Annette Towler was especially interested in the influence of specific parental attachment styles on children's charismatic leadership development.[23] Towler also speculated that higher levels of parental control (which would result in few opportunities for autonomy, responsibility, and mastery experiences for children[24]) would inhibit the development of their leadership.

Like Bronfenbrenner, Towler avoided asking university students themselves about their leadership because of the possibility of obtaining biased answers. Instead, the 81 introductory university students who participated in Towler's study first completed surveys on their parents' attachment styles and then engaged in a team activity. After that, each student's charismatic leadership behaviors were rated by all their team members. The results of this study highlight the parental factors involved in the development of adolescents' leadership. First and foremost, a secure parental attachment style (with both parents) was associated with students' use of charismatic leadership behaviors in the team task. Second, higher levels of parents' psychological control was indeed associated with lower levels of adolescents' charismatic leadership. However, like other studies showing gender differences, only fathers' control negatively influenced children's charismatic leadership; mothers' control did not. The results of Towler's study gain added importance because leadership ratings were based on performance on an actual task as rated by peers, and research being conducted at about the same time showed that secure attachment style was related to higher levels of charismatic leadership among military cadets.[25]

As interesting as the findings of these studies might be, one factor limiting the extent to which they explain the effects of parents' leadership and parenting behaviors is that they do not rely on parents' own reports of their behaviors; instead they ask children or adolescents about their parents' behavior. This could be a concern, because asking people to recollect how they were raised might seem like an invitation for subjective beliefs to creep in and bias the results. However, we need not be too concerned. Anecdotally, most parents (and children) will confirm that it is not the objective quality of parent–child interactions that drives children's behavior, but rather what children remember about parent–child interactions, and scientific findings confirm this. For example, our research on the effects of parenting (in this case, parents' job insecurity) on different aspects of children's behavior all yield the same basic finding:[26] Asking parents directly about their own behaviors and experiences provides less useful information for understanding children's behaviors than finding out how children perceived their parents' behaviors and experiences. There is every reason to suspect that this would hold true for understanding the development of children's leadership, with support for this notion coming from Sandra Hartman and Jeff Harris' study of 195 university students.[27]

They showed that students' reports of their own leadership (consideration structure) were more highly related to their *perceptions* of their parents' leadership behaviors (consideration structure) than were parents' reports of their own leadership (consideration structure).

Aside from finding that perceptions of parents' leadership are more influential than parents' actual leadership, several other lessons emerged from Hartman and Harris' research. First, students' perception of parents' consideration structure influenced their own consideration structure, but perceptions of parents' more task-focused initiation structure did not influence students' task focus. One possible explanation for this difference is that children's *leadership* behaviors are influenced by their parents, but their task-focused behaviors, which reflect managerial more than leadership skills, are not. Second, parental influences on children's leadership are specific, with little evidence of crossover effects. In other words, parents' actual or perceived consideration had little effect on children's initiation structure. Likewise, parents' initiation orientation had little effect on children's consideration behaviors. Finally, there were again important gender differences: Sons were more influenced than daughters, and fathers tended to be more influential than mothers.

Together with my colleagues Anthea Zacharatos and Kevin Kelloway, we were also interested in the effects of mothers' and fathers' parenting behaviors on adolescents' leadership behavior.[28] In a variation from earlier studies, however, we asked adolescents to report on their parents' behaviors in terms of the four dimensions of transformational leadership described earlier, and then obtained data on 112 adolescents' leadership from three different sources: the adolescents themselves, several of their peers, and their sports team coaches, which allowed for a more rigorous accounting of adolescents' early leadership. Both male and female adolescents' perceptions of their fathers' transformational parenting behaviors predicted their own leadership behaviors within the sports context. However, a gender effect again emerged as adolescents' perceptions of their mothers' leadership behaviors did not influence their leadership behaviors.

The studies discussed above were all interested in family influences on leadership behaviors. In contrast, Bruce Avolio, Maria Rotundo, and Fred Walumbwa[29] were interested in leadership role occupancy and the unique role of authoritative parenting behaviors (e.g., being consistent, rewarding positive behaviors, being warm and considerate),[30] which are positive in nature and different from authoritarian behaviors (e.g., being controlling and unsupportive). They used advanced statistical techniques to remove any possible effects of genetic influences and personality factors and showed that authoritative (but not authoritarian) parenting was indeed positively associated with subsequent leadership role occupancy. However, the effects of authoritative parenting on leader emergence turned out to be even more complex. Avolio and his colleagues also showed that authoritative parenting was associated with lower levels of adolescents' involvement in modest and serious rule-breaking behaviors, each of which predicted leadership role occupancy very differently. Modest rule breaking (which did not involve violations of the law) had a positive influence on subsequent leadership role occupancy, probably because constructively confronting the status quo relatively early in life, which would likely be encouraged, guided, and supported by authoritative parents, have positive socialization lessons for the long term. In contrast, serious rule breaking (which involved criminal activities such as theft, involvement with drugs) had a negative effect on subsequent leadership role occupancy, perhaps because involvement in serious rule breaking at the same age involves negative peer influences during impressionable years and might exert equally long-term, but negative, effects.

Thus, despite protests from many adolescents that their parents have no positive influence on them, the results of these studies show clearly that notwithstanding any adolescent arguments, parents influence children's subsequent leadership. But what of other adult role models?

Nonparental Influences

All of the studies considered so far operate as if parents were the only adults who influence the development of their children's leadership. Of course, this is simply not the case. Other adults also influence the emergence of leadership in children, especially as the children enter adolescence and encounter new adult role models and new peer relationships, as we showed in our study on parental influence on the emergence of adolescents' transformational leadership.[31] A full appreciation of the early and diverse influences on leadership development that children encounter thus requires that we look beyond their parents. In doing so, we should be mindful that the effects of different adult models do not occur in isolation but rather interact with each other. Any studies that examine the influence of multiple different role models acting simultaneously on children will be most informative.

The idea that multiple adult models influence children simultaneously is hardly novel. Borgadus had already speculated about the influence of teachers, elderly neighbors, and other family members on children's leadership development some 80 years ago, and today, parents know this, educators thrive on this, and psychological theories[32] emphasize this. Thus, it is more than a little surprising that only one study has focused on the simultaneous effects of different adult models' transformational parenting behaviors on children. Over the period of a full season, Sean Tucker and his colleagues[33] studied the effects of parents' and coaches' transformational leadership behaviors on the on-ice aggression of early teenage boys in two different ice hockey leagues. They showed that when the potential influence of parents and coaches was considered together, only coaches' transformational behaviors influenced teenagers' on-ice aggression; parents' transformational leadership behaviors did not. While not directly relevant to children's leadership behaviors and potentially limited to adolescents, not younger children, Tucker and colleagues' results can guide our understanding of the broad range of adult influences on adolescents' leadership development. A comprehensive understanding of the effects of adult role models on the development of children's leadership requires that researchers investigate the influence not just of parental models but of other potential role models as well (e.g., teachers, coaches, other family members, TV stars and characters), especially as children grow older and enter adolescence. This point is made more salient because Tucker and colleagues did not assume that the adult who most influenced the adolescent would be a parent. Instead, they asked the adolescent to select the adult who most influenced them—and not all chose a parent! Future research should investigate how these multiple adult role models influence leadership emergence or behavior simultaneously, or in some cases even compete with each other.

Before we move on to consider genetic influences on leadership development, we should note that Bronfenbrenner called our attention to the problem of what social scientists like to call "reverse causality," which pervades research on adult influences on children's leadership development. Within all the studies on parenting behaviors and children's leadership, the unstated assumption is that different parenting behaviors "cause" the development and emergence of children's leadership. However, common sense would dictate that the reverse is equally possible: Perhaps children who display positive leadership behaviors encourage and enable their parents to trust them more, use more positive and supportive parenting behaviors, and grant their children greater levels of initiative and independence. Alternatively, when children fail to display mastery, their parents may feel a need to impose further control—a phenomenon that finds some support in the child development literature[34] and in early workplace studies that will be considered in Chapter 10 showing that employees' performance levels affect their leaders' leadership behaviors.[35] While Bronfenbrenner offered a compelling explanation as to why this is *not* the case with the development of children's leadership, and this concern is limited to the studies that have used cross-sectional data collected at one point in time (see Chapter 4), we should not merely accept the primacy of parental influence over children's development—an idea that will resonate when considering the roles of followers in Chapter 10.

CONTRASTING ENVIRONMENTAL AND GENETIC INFLUENCES ON LEADERSHIP DEVELOPMENT

So far, we have considered environmental influences (especially parental role models) on children's leadership development. Research over the past decade, however, has gone beyond a sole focus on environmental influences and contrasted the *relative* influence of environmental *and* genetic influences on leadership emergence and leadership behavior. From these studies, we can also start to separate the role of genetic and socialization factors involved in the development of children's behaviors.

One of the most intriguing techniques for doing so emerged from a chance observation: In 1979, Thomas Bouchard, a psychologist at the University of Minnesota, read a newspaper article about a pair of identical twins who had been separated from each other since they were infants and had later been reunited. Upon meeting subsequently, the twins discovered that they shared amazing similarities that seemed to transcend coincidence: Although they had enjoyed no contact with each other at all, both had married women named Linda, and after they had each been divorced, had later remarried someone named Betty. And the similarities did not stop there. They both owned a dog named Toy, smoked the same brand of cigarettes, held the same kinds of jobs, were involved in the same hobbies and the same activities. Bouchard realized that this scenario presented the opportunity to isolate the effects of genetic effects on their behavior, as having been separated at infancy, these twins shared no environmental similarity. This led Bouchard to establish the now-famous Minnesota Study of Twins Reared Apart,[36] which has amassed a large database of identical twins who were reared apart since birth and were subsequently compared with identical twins who were reared together in their "normal" environments. To ensure methodological rigor, individuals who had been separated at birth underwent careful genetic screening to confirm that they were indeed identical twins before they were included in the data set.

Early indications that this technique could be useful in an organizational context emerged from a study investigating the contribution of environmental and genetic effects on job satisfaction.[37] Richard Arvey and his colleagues studied 34 identical twins who had been reared apart since birth and were part of the Minnesota Study of Twins Reared Apart. Participants in this study all completed the well-validated Minnesota Job Satisfaction Questionnaire, which provides information on intrinsic, extrinsic, and general job satisfaction. Even after statistically removing any effects of the characteristics of their current jobs, both genetic and environmental factors explained participants' intrinsic job satisfaction. While the authors could show that approximately 30% of the variation in job satisfaction was due to heritability, they did not isolate the specific amount attributed to environmental factors.

Despite its promise, several factors limit the potential for this methodology to separate the role of genetic and environmental factors in early childhood development, and thus its usefulness for our understanding of leadership development. For example, the extent to which the results are valid depends on both of the twins being separated at birth, or very soon afterward, and then being placed randomly in different environments. These are extraordinarily stringent criteria, and, not surprisingly, they are not always met. Instead, experience shows that the twins are sometimes only separated as late as approximately 18 months old. In addition, either one or both of the twins are often placed with a family member, thereby potentially weakening the lessons that might be learned. Accordingly, a variation of this technique was developed, in which relatively large samples of identical (monozygotic) and fraternal (dizygotic) twins who were reared together are contrasted, and it is within this framework that the roles of genetic and environmental factors in leadership role emergence, and leadership behavior, have been investigated.

Predicting Leader Role Occupancy

Arvey and his colleagues have conducted several ingenious studies that have added substantially to our understanding of leadership role occupancy. This includes how early in life they assumed such positions, whether individuals hold leadership positions or not, and how much responsibility is inherent in the position they hold. The researchers' interest in leadership role occupancy was motivated by the fact that holding a leadership role represents the very first step in the leadership process; issues of leaders' behavior and their success would follow later.

In the first of their studies, Arvey and colleagues' goal was two-fold: They were interested in (1) whether genetic factors directly predict the likelihood that someone will emerge as a leader and (2) whether personality mediates any effects of genetic effects on leadership emergence.[38] Several of the findings of their first study on 119 identical twins and 94 fraternal twins warrant attention. First, genetic factors did indeed predict leadership role occupancy directly. Second, genetic factors also influenced two personality variables, namely social potency and achievement. Although there was no definitive evidence that these personality variables directly affected leadership role occupancy, the authors argued that discounting this possibility is premature, and the issue awaits further investigation. Third, none of the environmental factors that the twins shared (e.g., family socioeconomic status) explained their emergence as leaders, but unshared environmental influences that were unique to each of the twins (e.g., differential parent–child interactions, work experiences) were critical in the development of leadership role occupancy.

Together with a different set of colleagues, Arvey conducted a follow-up study, because their first study had only included male participants; they focused exclusively on women's leadership emergence in their second study.[39] In doing so, Arvey et al. hoped that any understanding of gender differences in leadership emergence would be informed more by data than dogma, and they examined the effects of genetic factors, early family experiences, and later work experiences in their sample of 107 identical and 89 fraternal female twins. The results of this second study showed that genetic factors were as important in women's leadership role occupancy as they were with the male sample just discussed. Unexpectedly, however, family experiences did not predict leadership role occupancy, but this may have been because the range of family experiences included in the study was limited and nonspecific. Finally, like the earlier study on males, leader emergence or role occupancy was again explained by non-shared environmental experiences of the twins, suggesting that each of the twin's unique experience within the family environment remained a more powerful determinant of later leadership role occupancy than shared environmental characteristics.

These two studies compared the separate effects of genetic and environmental factors. Recent lessons from the study of behavioral genetics make it clear, however, that environmental and genetic factors interact in affecting subsequent behavior. As a result, Zhen Zhang, Remus Ilies, and Arvey[40] extended the earlier research by asking how three environmental factors experienced during adolescence (socioeconomic status, parental support, and parental conflict) might affect the way in which genetic factors influence leadership role occupancy. Their findings emphasize the importance of interactions between genetic and environmental factors: Any genetic effects on leadership role occupancy were much stronger for adolescents of lower socioeconomic status who experienced less parental support and witnessed more parental conflict. Stated somewhat differently, genetic influences on children's leadership emergence diminished in importance when adolescents experienced more positive and supportive family environments, suggesting that positive family environments may be sufficient to suppress the negative expression of any detrimental genetic effects.

A recent study by Jan-Emmanuel De Neve and his colleagues extends our understanding of genetic factors, by going beyond the traditional twin study paradigm.[41] They obtained their sample from the large-scale National Longitudinal Sample of Adolescent Health (the "Add Health" study)[42] that initially surveyed over 27,000 adolescents in the United States in 1994 and 1995. During the third wave of data collection for the Add Health study that took place in 2001 and 2002, information on genetic markers was collected for 2,574 people. These researchers then identified a sample of 432 identical and 440 fraternal twins who were still involved in the study during the fourth wave of data collection (which took place in 2008). Using the traditional twin study methodology, they first showed that genetic factors account for approximately 25% of the variation in leadership role occupancy. Using the genetic data, De Neve and his research team were then able to isolate a specific genotype that was associated with leadership role occupancy. While their results are strengthened because they managed to replicate the same effect using data from the Framingham Heart Study, which began in 1948,[43] the authors caution that we still do not know how the specific gene identified affects leadership role occupancy. For example, it could have a direct influence on role occupancy, but it might also affect the traits, skills, or attitudes that make role occupancy more likely.

These findings are of considerable practical and theoretical importance. From a pragmatic perspective, we have learned that early exposure to a positive social environment can lessen genetic influences on leadership role occupancy, reinforcing the importance of positive environmental experiences and parental role models. From a theoretical perspective, while both genetic and environmental factors play a role in leader role occupancy, and any explanations must take account of interactions between genetic and environmental influences, these studies still highlight the importance of unique environmental experiences.[44] One additional question is raised by these studies: Because the social influence of peers might well supersede that of their parents by the time children reach adolescence,[45] it would be intriguing to discover how nonfamilial socialization experiences during adolescence interact with genetic and family influences on leadership role occupancy.

Predicting Leadership Behaviors

All of the studies investigating the influence of environmental and genetic factors on the development of leadership discussed to this point focused on leadership role occupancy or emergence, that is, whether individuals achieve a leadership position or not. Gaining an understanding of why some people become leaders and others do not is obviously important and an integral question within leadership research. We need to go further, however. Just because genetic and environmental factors interact to predict who becomes a leader in the first instance does not help to explain leadership behaviors or success. While fewer studies exist on the genetic and environmental effects on leadership behaviors (perhaps because the fascination with whether leaders are born or made is inherently a question on leader emergence), some studies have addressed the genetic and environmental influences on leaders' behavior.

Andrew Johnson and his colleagues[46] used a large sample of 183 identical and 64 fraternal adult twins to investigate the effects of genetic and environmental factors on a broad range of transformational leadership behaviors. They went further than most studies on transformational leadership, which focus on an overall index of transformational leadership, and analyzed each of the four behaviors of transformational leadership separately. In addition, as noted in Chapter 1, the full-range model of transformational leadership theory also includes transactional leadership (i.e., contingent reward, management-by-exception, and laissez faire), which reflects management rather than leadership behaviors.[47] More often than not, these aspects are excluded from research on transformational leadership, presumably because they are less effective than transformational behaviors. However, the determinants of transactional leadership remain an interesting but largely unanswered question. Johnson and his colleagues also investigated the genetic and environmental determinants of these behaviors. They showed that while each of the four transformational leadership behaviors were heritable to some extent, the same was not generally the case for the transactional behaviors, which were largely environmentally determined. A follow-up study by Johnson and his team largely confirmed the role of genetic factors in transformational leadership.[48]

Although Sankalp Chatuverdi et al. did not directly contrast the relative effects of genetic and environmental factors, their study is interesting because it investigated how genetic factors and personality function together to predict transformational leadership.[49] Based on a sample of 107 identical and 89 fraternal twins from the Minnesota Twin Registry, their findings highlight a critical role for dispositional hope, which reflects individuals' ongoing beliefs that they can find and execute solutions to difficulties they encounter. Specifically, Chatuverdi and colleagues showed that genetic factors indirectly affected transformational leadership behaviors through the intervening effects of hope.

ARE *BAD* LEADERS BORN OR MADE?

To date, research on the effects of genetic factors and parents' behaviors has concentrated overwhelmingly on positive or desirable leadership behaviors in children. But, as is clear throughout this book, leadership behaviors can also be destructive, and how bad leadership develops is of at least equal importance. Simply because there is a cross-generational learning of positive leadership behaviors does not necessarily mean that destructive leadership behaviors would develop in the same way, for at least two reasons. First, there may be much to be learned about the development and display of destructive leadership from Albert Bandura's seminal research on how children learn aggression from role models.[50] In this classic study, observing aggressive adult models was sufficient for young children to learn the specific aggressive behaviors they had witnessed. However, mere exposure to aggressive models was not sufficient to explain whether children would then *act* aggressively. Instead, only when children witnessed the role models being rewarded for aggressive behavior were they likely to enact what they had seen. In contrast, when the children witnessed the adult model being punished for aggressive behavior, mimicry by the children became significantly less likely. What this suggests is that children might not simply imitate leaders who are negative role models, and whether they do so or not will depend on the consequences experienced by the role model. Second, as Hartman and Harris showed in their research, children are likely to learn positive leadership behaviors from their parents, but not necessarily task-focused or managerial skills. Thus, we cannot take for granted that poor parenting behaviors might influence children's leadership development, and this remains a critical question waiting to be explored by both organizational and child development researchers. Surprisingly, there seems to be only one recent study on this issue.

Christian Kiewitz and his collaborators suggested that there is a link between the extent of parental undermining (i.e., nonphysical abuse involving verbal criticism, insults, silent treatment, negative interactions) experienced as a child and later abusive supervision.[51] Consistent with Bandura's social learning theory, these researchers speculated that regular exposure to verbal aggression and undermining by parents that is seen as acceptable and goes unchallenged will be learned by young children and likely repeated as adults.[52] Moreover, because enactment of the aggression is seen as an acceptable means of resolving conflicts, subsequent performance of similar nonphysical abusive behaviors are likely to extend beyond the initial context in which they were learned, including to the workplace. Several important and intriguing findings emerged from their research. First, across two different samples, being undermined by their parents was significantly associated with the greater use of abusive supervision many years later. This finding is all the more credible, as the authors did not rely solely on supervisors' own retrospective recollections of their personal experiences with parental undermining, which may be faulty or biased. Instead, in their second study, siblings of the supervisors provided the ratings of parental undermining.

The second finding from this research may be even more important, as the researchers showed that this effect was not inevitable! In both samples, self-control was an important buffer, such that experiencing early parental undermining was not associated with later abusive supervision for supervisors who enjoyed higher levels of self-control. The implications of this last finding are enormous. We need to be careful not to slip into explanations that favor environmental determinism, that is, explanations inferring that family influences on later leadership behaviors are inevitable. As Kiewitz and his team's findings make clear, leaders can exercise self-control behaviors to ensure that early negative influences are lessened.

Thus, there are now some data from which we can conclude that adverse family experiences can play a role in the later emergence of destructive leadership behaviors, thus pointing further to the broad influence of family experiences on the development of leadership. At the same time, this study only investigated the effects of parental undermining, and future research should contrast the relative effects of family experiences and genetic factors in generating later destructive leadership. These researchers' findings also reveal the need to isolate the role of genetic, family, and environmental factors in the development of other negative leadership behaviors, such as unethical leadership on the one hand, or laissez-faire leadership on the other. Findings from different areas suggest that this might be a promising avenue for future research. For example, twin studies have long shown that genetic factors are implicated in the development of aggression,[53] and experiencing punitive parenting predicts interactional aggression in adult life.[54]

LOOKING FORWARD

The next decade has the potential to be one in which significant progress is made in understanding the development of leadership. One of the most rapid advances in the social sciences in the past two decades has been the growth of social neuroscience, which broadly represents the intersection of the social, biological, and genetic sciences and neuroscience.[55] One important influence on the development of this new body of knowledge has been social scientists' increasing access to functional magnetic reasoning imagery (fMRI), traditionally the domain of neuroscientists. A study by Jamil Zaki and his colleagues, which focused on supplementing social information on empathic ability with information about its neural bases,[56] illustrates the potential for understanding leadership development. Using fMRI technology, these researchers located two specific regions of the brain that can be used to differentiate between individuals capable of empathic accuracy, which is central to high-quality leadership, and those who were empathically inaccurate. In a different study, undergraduates in two separate experiments participated in a game in which they received rewards varying in terms of perceived fairness; the situation was made even more interesting because some of the rewards were unfair but financially desirable.[57] Functional MRI techniques showed that preferences for fairness and unfairness are located in different regions of the brain, as was the decision to accept unfair but profitable outcomes. The results of these studies on empathy and fairness might hold important implications for our study of leadership. Empathic ability underlies successful leadership,[58] and fairness preferences might tell us a lot about leaders' behaviors and how followers might respond to their leaders. In time, these same imaging techniques might be useful in isolating the neural underpinnings of other core leadership attributes, such as dignity, optimism, humility, and resilience.[59]

Advances in neuroscientific understanding of leadership would be limited if they were dependent on a particular technology such as fMRI equipment, which is still costly and requires advanced skills for interpreting results. In this regard, Pierre Balthazard and his co-researchers' study is noteworthy. They performed power spectral analyses using resting, eyes-closed electroencephalograms (EEGs) on 200 individuals who worked as leaders in a variety of different contexts (e.g., education, military, health care, banking, engineering, finance, and the nonprofit sector).[60] Other individuals (invariably their peers or subordinates) provided ratings of their transformational leadership, which the researchers showed could be correctly classified using neural imaging. Transformational leaders were significantly more likely to have activity in the prefrontal and frontal lobe areas of the brain, which are implicated in planning activities and the ability to anticipate future events, dealing with one's own and others' emotions in challenging circumstances, and understanding new and unusual situations. Successful performance of these behaviors is a hallmark of any form of high-quality leadership.

De Neve and colleagues[61] have already demonstrated that with the major strides made in the field of molecular genetics, it possible that we may soon be able to identify specific genes associated with leadership emergence and behavior. This is confirmed by Avi Caspi and colleagues' large-scale prospective study.[62] Based on data from the Dunedin Multidisciplinary Health and Development Study,[63] they showed that while in general children exposed to maltreatment between the ages of 3 and 11 years of age are much more likely to engage in later criminal behaviors, those who had a specific genotype were less likely to develop antisocial behaviors. One lesson from this research is that genes operate in such a way as to not only leave people more vulnerable, for example, to diseases, but in some cases to protect people from environmental threats.

The authors then used the same large sample[64] to show that individuals who had experienced a traumatic life event and who had what might euphemistically be called a "resilience" gene were far less likely to develop major depression than their counterparts who had experienced a traumatic life event but in whom the same genotype was lacking. A critical observation also emerged from these findings that will help guide our expectations of what the results of such molecular genetic studies might contribute to an understanding of leadership. Specifically, the presence or absence of the resilience gene by itself had no effect on major depression; it only exerted its protective effects in the presence of prior traumatic life events, resulting in it being referred to as the "resilience" gene.[65] This observation is very important, as it shows that findings from the field of social neuroscience clearly do not support the notion of genetic determinism, in which genes alone predict social behaviors. Any advances in understanding leadership development are most likely to emerge from the search for interactions between environmental and genetic factors. More specifically, the presence of the resilience gene may ultimately help explain why some people who encounter early adversity go on to enjoy leadership success, while others do not.

A major question that remains is what, if any, are the practical implications of the findings derived from social neuroscience and molecular genetics. While this critical issue will be discussed in more detail in the final chapter, it would be premature to apply any lessons to organizational practices (e.g., leadership selection) before considering what might well turn out to be an ethical and practical quagmire.

CONCLUSION

Whether leadership is born or made is a question that has intrigued people for centuries, with answers driven primarily by ideology. This question has attracted increasing interest from social scientists over the last 10 years, and we now know enough to provide an evidenced-based answer to the question: The family environment, the non-family environment, and genetic factors all influence who attains a leadership position within an organization in the first place and, subsequently, how they behave as leaders. Gaining a comprehensive understanding of the joint roles of genetic and environmental factors will continue to fascinate researchers, and using the traditional methods of behavioral research together with the new techniques of neuroscience and molecular genetics will help expand this understanding and deliver rich new insights regarding an intriguing and important question. Given that both environmental and genetic factors contribute to leadership emergence and leadership behaviors, the question of whether leadership behaviors can be taught—a question of profound practical importance—looms large, and is the subject of the next chapter.

SUGGESTED READING

Lodge, T. (2006). *Mandela: A critical life*. New York: Oxford University Press.
Shane, S. (2010). *Born entrepreneurs, born leaders: How your genes affect your work life*. New York: Oxford University Press.
Wead, D. (2005). *The raising of a president: The mothers and fathers of our nation's leaders*. New York: Atria Books.

NOTES

1. Skinner, B. F. (1972). *Beyond freedom and dignity*. New York: Bantam Books.
2. Kanter, R. M. (2007, November 5). Are leaders born or made? Retrieved from http://bigthink.com/videos/are-leaders-born-or-made
3. Nelson Mandela's lesson in leadership (2004, December 24). *South Africa: Financial Mail*, Special Souvenir Edition (p. 44).
4. Lodge, T. (2006). *Mandela: A critical life*. New York: Oxford University Press.
5. Tambo, I. (1965). Introduction. In N. Mandela, *No easy walk to freedom*. London: Heinemann Books, p. x.
6. There is some inconsistency as to how old Mandela was said to be when his father died. While many place his birth date as 1918, and the year of his father's death as 1928, Mandela's lifetime confidant, Oliver Tambo, maintained he was 12 when his father died.

7. Lodge, T. (2006). *Mandela: A critical life.* Oxford, UK: Oxford University Press.
8. Benson, M. (1986). *Nelson Mandela.* London: Penguin.
9. Ledgard, J. M. (2011, February 13). Revolution from within. *New York Times Book Review*, p. 16.
10. The Mandela tapes. CBC Radio. Retrieved from http://www.cbc.ca/ideas/themandelatapes/
11. Lodge, T. (2006). *Mandela: A critical life.* Oxford, UK: Oxford University Press, p. 1.
12. Nelson, E. (1939). Fathers' occupations and student vocational choices. *School and Society, 30*, 572–576.
13. Borgadus, E. S. (1934). *Leaders and leadership.* New York: Appleton-Century Crofts.
14. Goodwin, D. K. (1994). *No ordinary time.* New York: Simon & Shuster.
15. Bennis, W. (2004). *On becoming a leader.* Boston: Addison-Wesley.
16. Elder, G. H. (1974). *Children of the Great Depression.* Chicago: University of Chicago Press.
17. Elder, G. H. (2003). *Longitudinal studies and the life course, the 1960s and 1970s.* Paper prepared for the 75th Anniversary of the Institute of Human Development, University of California, Berkeley. Retrieved from http://www.unc.edu/~elder/presentations/Longitudinal_studies_and_the_life_course.html
18. Cox, C. J., & Cooper, C. L. (1989). The making of the British CEO: Childhood, work experience, personality, and management style. *Academy of Management Executive, 3*, 353–358.
19. Li, W-D., Arvey, R. D., & Song, Z. (2011). The influence of general mental ability, self-esteem and family socioeconomic status on leadership role occupancy and leader advancement: The moderating role of gender. *Leadership Quarterly, 22*, 520–534.
20. U.S. Deaprtment of Labor, Bureau of Labor Statistics. National longitudinal survey of youth. Retrieved from http://www.bls.gov/nls/
21. Bass, B. M. (1960). *Leadership, psychology, and organizational behavior.* New York: Harper & Brothers.
22. Bronfenbrenner, U. (1961). Some familial antecedents of responsibility and leadership in adolescents. In L. Petrullo & B. M. Bass (Eds.) *Leadership and interpersonal behavior* (pp. 239–271). New York: Holt, Rinehart and Winston.
23. Towler, A. (2005). Charismatic leadership development: Role of attachment style and parental psychological control. *Journal of Leadership and Organizational Studies, 11*(4), 15–25.
24. Moorman, E. A., & Pomeranz, E. M. (2008). The role of mothers' control in children's mastery orientation: A time frame analysis. *Journal of Family Psychology, 22*, 734–741.
25. Popper, M., Mayseless, O., & Castelnovo, O. (2000). Transformational leadership and attachment. *Leadership Quarterly, 11*, 267–289.
26. Barling, J., Zacharatos, A., & Hepburn, C. G. (1999). Parents' job insecurity affects children's academic performance through cognitive difficulties. *Journal of Applied Psychology, 84*, 437–444.
27. Hartman, S. J., & Harris, O. J. (1992). The role of parental influence on leadership. *Journal of Social Psychology, 132*, 153–167.
28. Zacharatos, A., Barling, J., & Kelloway, E. K. (2000). Development and effects of transformational leadership in adolescents. *Leadership Quarterly, 11*, 211–226.
29. Avolio, B. J., Rotundo, M., & Walumbwa, F. O. (2009). Early life experiences as determinants of leadership role occupancy: The importance of parental influence and rule breaking behavior. *Leadership Quarterly, 20*, 329–342.
30. Baumrind, D. (1991). The influence of parenting style on adolescent competence and substance use. *Journal of Early Adolescence, 11*, 56–95.

31. Zacharatos, A., Barling, J., & Kelloway, E. K. (2000). Development and effects of transformational leadership in adolescents. *Leadership Quarterly, 11*, 211–226.
32. Harris, J. R. (1995). Where is the child's environment? A group socialization theory of development. *Psychological Review, 102*, 458–489.
33. Tucker, S., Turner, N., Barling, J., & McEvoy, M. (2010). Transformational leadership and children's aggression in team settings: A short-term longitudinal study. *Leadership Quarterly, 21*, 389–399.
34. Moorman, E. A., & Pomeranz, E. M. (2008). The role of mothers' control in children's mastery orientation: A time frame analysis. *Journal of Family Psychology, 22*, 734–741.
35. Farris, G. F., & Lim, F. G. (1969). Effects of performance on leadership, cohesiveness, influence, satisfaction, and subsequent performance. *Journal of Applied Psychology, 53*, 490–497.
36. Bouchard, T. J., Lykken, D. T., McGue, M., Segal, N. L., & Tellegen, A. (1990). Sources of psychological differences: the Minnesota Study of Twins Reared Apart. *Science, 250*(4978), 223–228.
37. Arvey, R. D., Bouchard, T. J., Segal, N. L., & Abraham, L. M. (1989). Job satisfaction: Environmental and genetic components. *Journal of Applied Psychology, 74*, 187–192.
38. Arvey, R. D., Rotundo, M., Johnson, W., Zhang, Z., & McGue, M. (2006). The determinants of leadership role occupancy: Genetic and personality factors. *Leadership Quarterly, 17*, 1–20.
39. Arvey, R. D., Zhang, Z., Avolio, B. J., & Krueger, R. F. (2007). Developmental and genetic determinants of leadership role occupancy among women. *Journal of Applied Psychology, 92*, 693–706.
40. Zhang, Z., Illies, R., & Arvey, R. D. (2009). Beyond genetic explanations for leadership: The moderating role of the social environment. *Organizational Behavior and Human Decision Processes, 110*, 118–128.
41. De Neve, J. E., Mikhaylov, S., Dawes, C. T., Christakis, N. A., & Fowler, J. H. (2013). Born to lead? A twin design and genetic association study of leadership role occupancy. *Leadership Quarterly, 24*, 45–60.
42. National Longitudinal Study of Adolescent Health (Add Health). University of North Carolina Population Cetner. Retrieved from http://www.cpc.unc.edu/projects/addhealth
43. Framingham Heart Study. Retrieved from http://www.framinghamheartstudy.org/
44. Li, W-D., Arvey, R. D., Zhang, Z., & Song, Z. (2012). Do leadership role occupancy and transformational leadership share the same genetic and environmental influences? *Leadership Quarterly, 23*, 233–243.
45. Harris, J. R. (1995). Where is the child's environment? A group socialization theory of development. *Psychological Review, 102*, 458–489.
46. Johnson, A. M., Vernon, P. A., McCarthy, J. M., Molson, M., Harris, J. A., & Jang, K. L. (1998). Nature *vs* nurture: Are leaders born or made? A behavior genetic investigation of leadership style. *Twin Research, 1*, 216–223.
47. Barling, J., et al. (2010). Leadership. In S. Zedeck (Ed.), *Handbook of industrial and organizational psychology* (Vol. 1, pp. 180–243). Washington, DC: American Psychological Association.
48. Johnson, A. M., Vernon, P. A., Harris, J. A., & Jang, K. L. (2004). A behavior genetic investigation of the relationship between leadership and personality. *Twin Research, 7*, 27–32.

49. Chatuverdi, S., Arvey, R. D., Zhang, Z., & Christoforou, P. T. (2011). Genetic underpinnings of transformational leadership: The mediating role of dispositional hope. *Journal of Leadership and Organizational Studies, 18,* 469–479.
50. Bandura, A. (1965). Influence of models' reinforcement contingencies on the acquisition of imitative response. *Journal of Personality and Social Psychology, 1,* 589-595.
51. Kiewitz, C., Restubog, S. L. D., Zagenczyk, T. J., Schott, K. D., Garcia, P. R. J. M., & Tang, R. L. (2012). Sins of the parents: Self-control as a buffer between supervisors' previous experience of family undermining and subordinates' perceptions of abusive supervision. *Leadership Quarterly, 23,* 869–882.
52. Bandura, A. (1973). *Aggression: A social learning analysis.* Upper Saddle River, NJ: Prentice Hall.
53. Tackett, J. L., Waldman, I. D., & Lahey, B. B. (2009). Etiology and measurement of relational aggression: A multi-informant behavior genetic investigation. *Journal of Abnormal Psychology, 118,* 722–733.
54. Dodge, K. A., Bates, J. E., & Pettit, G. S. (1990, December). Mechanisms in the cycle of violence. *Science, 250,* 1678–1683.
55. Cacioppo. J. T., et al. (2007). Social neuroscience: Progress and implications for mental health. *Perspectives on Psychological Science, 2,* 99–123.
56. Zaki, J., Weber, J., Bolger, N., & Ochsner, K. (2009). The neural bases of empathic accuracy. *Proceedings of the National Academy of Sciences, 106(27),* 11382–11387.
57. Tabibnia, G., Satpute, A. B., & Lieberman, M. D. (2008). The sunny side of fairness: Preference for fairness activates reward circuitry (and disregarding unfairness activates self-control circuitry). *Psychological Science, 19,* 339–347.
58. Kellett, J. B., Humphrey, R. H., & Sleeth, R. G. (2006). Empathy and the emergence of task and relations leaders. *Leadership Quarterly, 17,* 146–162.
59. Peterson, S. J., Bathazard, P. A., Waldman, D. A., & Thatcher, R. W. (2008). Are the brains of optimistic, hopeful, confident and resilient leaders different? *Organizational Dynamics, 37,* 342–353.
60. Balthazard, P. A., Waldman, D. A., Thatcher, R. W., & Hannah, S. T. (2012). Differentiating transformational and non-transformational leaders on the basis of neurological imaging. *Leadership Quarterly, 23,* 244–258.
61. De Neve, J. E., Mikhaylov, S., Dawes, C. T., Christakis, N. A., & Fowler, J. H. (2013). Born to lead? A twin design and genetic association study of leadership role occupancy. *Leadership Quarterly, 24,* 45–60.
62. Caspi, A., McLay, J., Moffitt, T. E., Mill, J., Martin, J., Craig, I. W., Taylor, A., & Poulton, R. (1992). Role of genotype in the cycle of violence in maltreated children. *Science, 297,* 851–853.
63. Silva, P. A., & Stanton, W. (1997). *From child to adult: The Dunedin Multidisciplinary Health and Development Study.* New York: Oxford University Press.
64. Caspi, A., Sugden, K., Moffitt, T. E., Taylor, A., Craig, I. W...., & Poulton, R. (2003). Influence of life stress on depression: Moderation by a polymorphism in the 5-HTT gene. *Science, 301,* 386–389.
65. Bazelton, E. (2008). A question of resilience. *New York Times Magazine.* Retrieved from http://www.nytimes.com/2006/04/30/magazine/30abuse.html?pagewanted=all&_r=0

CHAPTER 6

Can Leadership Be Taught?

Leadership Interventions in Organizations

Individuals learn about leadership from a variety of sources and at various stages of their lifespan. As we saw in the previous chapter, individuals start to learn about leadership at a very early age—from the way in which their parents interact with them, the expectations their parents hold for them, and the rules that they establish for them. Subsequently they learn about leadership from other adult models, including family members, sports coaches, teachers, and TV characters. They also learn about leadership from the behaviors of their peers. The earliest formal experiences that children and adolescents have to practice leadership themselves is as captains of sports teams, chairs of cultural clubs, and supervisors in part-time jobs, all of which play a formative role in what they learn about leadership.[1] Most of this early learning takes place vicariously, and much of it is implicit. In this chapter, we deal with one critical source of learning about leadership that occurs later in the lifespan, namely through deliberate and planned interventions conducted within and by organizations. Such interventions are by no means new. As but one example, Ronald Lippitt was recommending the use of an "at-the-elbow" (p. 286) strategy as early as 1943,[2] in which a trainer accompanies a leader around the workplace, reinforcing positive leadership behaviors but also noting errors and mistakes.

There is now a multitude of organizational interventions devoted to developing leadership behaviors, and more than enough evaluations, which together make it possible to answer the question of whether leadership skills can be taught through organizational interventions. However, the fact that the leadership interventions that have been evaluated have varied substantially in terms of the approaches or theories that were tested, the intensity of the intervention, the outcomes that were used in the evaluations, and the relative methodological rigor imposed make it somewhat difficult to draw comparisons across the diverse studies.

Irrespective of these variations, what these interventions hold in common is that they are formal, planned initiatives that invariably take place over a specified period of time, involve a group of participants (who could be from the same or different organizations), and can occur either on- or off-site. As such, leadership interventions differ from other attempts to change or enhance leadership, such as executive coaching and mentoring, which are of variable or unspecified duration and occur within a one-on-one relationship. In addition, formal leadership development initiatives differ from management development programs in that they are typically more complex, less focused on a specific job,[3] and more inspirational, relational, and ethical in their focus.

We will return to an evaluation of leadership interventions shortly. Thereafter, we will consider what might be done to strengthen leadership interventions and draw upon lessons from decades of research on behavioral change within psychotherapy. In the meantime, given the extent to which interventions differ with respect to their methodological rigor, we first ask, what would constitute a sufficiently rigorous test of any intervention?

HOW DO WE KNOW IF AN INTERVENTION WAS EFFECTIVE?

Probably the most simple, quick, and cost-effective way of evaluating the success of any leadership intervention is to ask leaders at the completion of the program whether they feel they have learned anything, and this certainly does happen. However, this approach is fraught with so many problems as to render any findings uninterpretable. One major reason for this is the phenomenon of "cognitive dissonance," introduced by psychologists decades ago, which suggests that people try to maintain a consistency between what they do and what they say. Thus, if a busy leader spent some time away from work attending a leadership intervention or devoted considerable financial resources to secure attendance, she or he would be more likely afterward to say that it was time well spent—simply to justify the involvement. As a result, self-reports by participants would probably overestimate the success of any programs, especially if the participants are only reporting on their satisfaction with the program. David Terpstra's early research indicated how this might occur.[4] He evaluated the effectiveness of 52 organization development initiatives and showed clearly that more favorable results were much more likely to emerge from less rigorous (i.e., more subjective) evaluations.

Instead, several characteristics would need to be present in evaluations of the intervention to produce findings that allow for reasonable inferences. First, the group that receives the leadership intervention needs to be compared to a similar group that receives no intervention. At a minimum, this would provide some confidence that it was the leadership training that accounted for any outcomes. However, there are significant ethical and practical problems with denying people the opportunity to receive effective leadership training, thus it may no longer be acceptable to have a comparison group that is denied access to the training. Instead, intervention groups (that receive the optimal, experimental training) might be compared with groups receiving standard interventions currently offered, a practice that might yield valuable lessons. For example, by doing just this, Taly Dvir and her co-researchers were able to show that transformational leadership training was superior to traditional leadership training used by the organization in terms of critical outcomes.[5] This approach enabled the researchers to provide more practically useful information—not just whether the experimental training is better than no training at all, but whether it is better than what is the best currently available training.

Second, it is not enough to know that the group receiving the optimal leadership training differed from a group receiving no leadership training or the standard training following the intervention, as it is always possible that such differences existed before the intervention. Hence, assessments should also be obtained from the different groups before any intervention even starts. Third, because of the limitations of relying solely on self-reported learning or satisfaction mentioned earlier, a rigorous evaluation should include data from other sources, be it from the leaders, peers, or followers, or "objective" data (e.g., supervisors' performance evaluations, or sales data). Fourth, while this cannot always be accomplished in everyday organizational settings, an optimal evaluation would assign participants randomly to the intervention and comparison groups, or pre-existing groups would be assigned randomly to interventions.[6] Although practical constraints within organizations make such random assignment difficult, doing so certainly helps in making valid inferences about the effectiveness of the training. Thus, the strongest inferences about training effectiveness will come from those situations in which there is an appropriate comparison group, and in which measures of the different outcomes are obtained both before and after the training and not just from the participants themselves. Where possible, assignment to the training or nontraining groups should be on a random basis.

EFFECTIVENESS OF LEADERSHIP DEVELOPMENT INTERVENTIONS

Research on leadership development interventions can be separated into two different categories: those that take place in a laboratory setting, and those that are conducted in field studies. Laboratory research takes place in tightly controlled conditions, often uses college students as participants, and focuses on short-term outcomes. In addition, researchers conducting laboratory-based (or "experimental") studies are frequently interested in whether a specific intervention has a specific effect. Field studies usually take place where the participants—actual members of the group and organization—conduct their work, or at special facilities that cater to leadership interventions, and target broader leadership skills and longer term outcomes. Leadership interventions that take place in field settings are more likely to focus on the breadth or generalizability of any effects of the leadership training. Because of the wide differences in these two different types of studies, we will consider them separately. But much of our focus will be on field studies, the lessons of which are more immediate and have direct relevance to organizations.

Laboratory Studies

Perhaps the major issue from our perspective is whether it is possible to train individuals to perform credibly in the role of leaders in laboratory studies. After all, if you can teach leadership to an actor fulfilling a role, you should be able to train a leader whose motivation is likely much higher. Jane Howell and Peter Frost conducted a laboratory study to assess whether charismatic leadership would influence how individuals perform on a decision-making task.[7] Their study needed individuals to be trained to take on the leader role and closely follow a script; Howell and Frost provided detailed information in their report on the training regimen used. They carefully selected two actresses after auditions with 30 professional actors and actresses on the basis of factors such as their ability to portray three different leadership styles (charismatic, considerate, and structuring styles), their acting experience, and physical similarity to each other. The two "leaders" who were selected then received 30 hours of training. As part of the training, they were given a specific description of the different leadership behaviors, and they watched a demonstration of the emotional and verbal features inherent in each of the three leadership styles. The actors then had the opportunity to role-play the leadership behaviors that were videotaped, and they received feedback from the role-playing exercise. This is consistent with the process followed in many leadership training programs. At no stage did the two actresses know the purpose of the study, as this could bias their performance in favor of one of the three leadership styles. Rigorous statistical evaluations were then conducted that showed that the trained actors successfully portrayed considerate, structuring, and charismatic leadership behaviors, and the authors were able to conclude from their study that charismatic leadership was generally more effective than either of the other two styles.

A second study was reported by Shelley Kirkpatrick and Ed Locke.[8] Like Howell and Frost, they used professional actors to portray three core aspects of charismatic leader behavior. Unlike Howell and Frost, however, they deliberately selected one male and one female professional actor after an audition, both of whom received more than 30 hours of training over a five-week period.

In all other respects, Kirkpatrick and Locke followed the same procedures and precautions (e.g., actors were not told of the purpose of the study) that were used by Howell and Frost. Again, once trained, the actors successfully enacted the leadership behaviors they had been taught. The results of these two studies show that it is possible to train inexperienced people in positive leadership behaviors in approximately 30 hours.

Subsequent research confirms that it is also possible to train an actor to behave like a destructive leader. Like the two studies just mentioned, Amy Christie, Nick Turner, and I paid a professional actor to portray a pseudo-transformational leader—as will be seen in Chapter 9, this is someone whose behavior is dominated by self-interest but is highly inspirational, suppresses any independent thought by employees, and shows no concern for employees' needs.[9] Training for the actor consisted of an initial tutorial about the nature of transformational and pseudo-transformational leadership, and laissez-faire non-leadership. The actor read additional materials about these three leadership behaviors and then role-played with the researchers, after which he performed the three behaviors in front of a group of knowledgeable observers who provided feedback for improvement, and then in front of a group of individuals unfamiliar with the three styles. (Parenthetically, the actor was also taught successfully to portray transformational leadership.)

Importantly, all of the procedures involved in training the actors in these three studies would be considered routine within leadership development research. And yet the total amount of time required was minimal (a mere 20 hours at most in the study by Amy Christie, Nick Turner, and myself) to successfully learn several different types of leadership behavior—namely structuring, consideration, charismatic, transformational, and pseudo-transformational leadership behaviors. Together, these three studies—which typify other similar laboratory-based leadership development initiatives—provide confidence that leadership can be developed through deliberate initiatives, and that this can be accomplished relatively economically. The relative efficiency with which the actors can be trained is significant: If you can train an actor to behave like a leader within a relatively short time period and in a rigidly controlled social environment, what might be possible with experienced organizational leaders whose motivation to change and to learn might be high?

Field Studies

As already noted, there is no shortage of evaluation studies. This can readily be appreciated from the most comprehensive quantitative review of leadership intervention effectiveness, reported by Bruce Avolio and his team of researchers in 2009, in which they identified no fewer than 200 independent interventions that qualified for their review.[10] Because of the comprehensive and recent nature of this particular review, much of this discussion on the impact of leadership interventions will be guided by their framework and their results. Wherever appropriate, however, lessons learned from other credible research will be included.

Are leadership interventions effective? The results of Avolio et al.'s research enables us to answer unequivocally: Yes, they are! Based on their meta-analysis of the 132 interventions that qualified for particular analysis (involving 11,552 intervention participants), they noted that we can be "95% confident that... the entire breadth of included studies... had at minimum a small positive effect on all outcomes" (pp. 772–773). A close reading of their results shows that this would have to be considered the most conservative interpretation, as many of the leadership interventions achieved substantially more powerful effects. On average, their analysis showed that participants in leadership development interventions were about 30% more likely than their counterparts who did not receive leadership training to achieve significantly better outcomes after the leadership training. To put this into perspective, effects of this magnitude in the social sciences would typically be regarded as very impressive.

Leadership interventions may well be effective, but a more nuanced and practical question is whether they are cost-effective. To answer this question, Avolio and his team examined the estimated costs of the training in order to calculate what they referred to as the *RODI*, or the return on *development* investment.[11] Costs included in their analysis were participants' salaries while they were in the program, productivity losses while individuals were involved in training (e.g., sales), and other expenditures associated with the intervention (e.g., instructor salary and materials expenses, as well as costs incurred if the program was delivered off-site, such as travel, room rentals, accommodation, and meals). Their comprehensive cost estimate also accounted for differential expenditures associated with delivering leadership training to senior vs. mid-level leaders. For example, they assumed that interventions for senior leaders would be targeted to smaller groups than those of mid-level leaders (30 vs. 100 participants, respectively), thereby increasing the cost of delivering the intervention.

Their findings yielded some important lessons about the utility of leadership interventions. When we consider interventions that can be judged to have had a moderate or strong effect, the RODI is clearly positive, with some returns being double the value of the initial investment. These findings highlight how critical it is to ensure that the interventions are carefully designed to include features most likely to ensure that they have strong and lasting effects. Much of the latter part of this chapter focuses on the nature of the factors that might be included to enhance the likelihood of success.

Another lesson that can be drawn from the RODI analysis conducted by Avolio and his team is that while leadership interventions in organizations are indeed effective (and cost-effective), leadership development initiatives vary considerably in terms of content, mode of delivery, and so forth. The fact that there is considerable variability in their effectiveness suggests that there may be a host of systematic factors embedded in the programs that can explain the variation in outcomes in leadership development initiatives. Some of these factors include the theory underlying the intervention, the nature of the outcome being studied, the type of organization, the gender and level in the organization of the person receiving the intervention, and the setting in which the training took place. Researchers have addressed each of these issues, and there is some understanding of the extent to which these factors influence the outcome of leadership interventions.

Does the Theory Make a Difference?

Almost all leadership interventions are based to some extent on a specific, underlying theory. Might the theoretical foundation of the intervention influence the outcome? After all, the theory under study would directly influence the content of the training, the way in which participants come to think about leadership, and the leadership behaviors that are emphasized. Nonetheless, it would be difficult to analyze each and every theory separately given the number and range of theories. To cope with the range and multitude of different leadership theories that have been examined, Avolio and his colleagues classified them into three categories: "traditional," "newer," and "Pygmalion" theories. Traditional theories were those that were dominant until the end of the 1970s, such as the behavioral and contingency approaches to leadership. Newer theories included the most prevalent theories since the early 1980s, such as charismatic and transformational leadership. Pygmalion theories were those based around the idea of the self-fulfilling prophesy, which involves leaders holding strong and optimistic performance expectations about subordinates.

An interesting set of findings emerged from the analyses. First, and perhaps somewhat surprising given the amount of leadership research since the 1980s, both traditional and newer interventions exerted a moderate effect, but they did not differ from each other in terms of effectiveness. In addition, a close interpretation of the findings suggests that Pygmalion interventions were at least as effective as newer approaches, quite possibly more effective. Given the predominant focus on transformational leadership over the past few decades, how might we account for the finding that Pygmalion approaches might be more effective? Dov Eden, who more than anyone else is associated with defining and studying the leadership implications of the Pygmalion effect within leadership, has provided an answer to this question.[12] He suggests that the Pygmalion effect could be considered a core component of transformational leadership, as leaders might not be truly transformational if they do not engender self-fulfilling prophesies in their followers. Thus, the most effective form of leadership development seems to be transformational leadership training that explicitly includes a focus on self-fulfilling prophecies.

Does the Nature of the Outcome Make a Difference?

If there are fewer overall differences between the theoretical foundations of the interventions than we might have expected, might the nature of the outcome make a difference? In other words, is it possible that more change can be obtained on some outcomes than on others? Or that some leadership theories or behaviors will be more appropriate for some outcomes? Sufficient studies existed to allow Avolio and colleagues to draw inferences relating to affective (e.g., liking of the leader, trust in the leader, loyalty to the organization), behavioral (e.g., performance measures of behavior), and cognitive (e.g., idea generation) outcomes. What they found was that traditional interventions exerted stronger effects on behavioral outcomes than did newer or Pygmalion-type interventions, while newer and Pygmalion-type interventions exerted stronger effects on affective and cognitive outcomes than traditional outcomes. In addition, Pygmalion-type interventions exerted a greater effect on cognitive and behavioral outcomes than on affective outcomes.

The lesson learned from this set of analyses for designing future leadership interventions is potentially far-reaching. Because not all interventions influence all outcomes equally, the type of outcome in which specific organizations are most interested should be taken into account when considering which specific intervention might be implemented. Stated somewhat differently, just what the organization is hoping to achieve as a function of the leadership training should be a strong factor in dictating what specific training should be implemented. Given that corporate financial performance is a legitimate outcome of interest (see Chapter 2), the relative effectiveness of different leadership interventions in this context remains to be investigated.

Does the Type of Organization Make a Difference?

As we have already seen, context matters, and organizations differ substantively in important characteristics (e.g., their mission, hierarchical structure, age, size). Might the nature of the organization influence the effectiveness of leadership interventions? While only a broad categorization of for-profit, not-for-profit, and military organizations was feasible in Avolio et al.'s research, statistically significant and practically important differences did emerge. First, the effects of leadership interventions were substantially greater in not-for profit than in for-profit organizations. This replicates Kevin Lowe, Galen Kroeck, and Nagaraj Sivasubramaniam's earlier findings on the relative effectiveness of transformational leadership in public- vs. private-sector organizations.[13] One possible reason for this difference is that the style of leadership emphasized within the newer approaches (e.g., transformational, inspirational, relational, ethical) might be most suited to the culture of not-for-profit organizations, a culture that is more likely to respect and reward high-quality relationships, collegiality, mutual trust and fairness, and employee input.

Avolio and his team extended their analysis of the effectiveness of leadership interventions in for-profit and not-for-profit organizations to military organizations. Perhaps contrary to widely held stereotypes about the pervasiveness of a "command-and-control" management style in the military, they showed that leadership interventions in military organizations were at least as effective as those in not-for-profit organizations, and were substantially more effective than interventions conducted within for-profit organizations. While no definitive reasons can be offered for this finding, it has been noted in the Schumpeter column of *The Economist* that high-performing military organizations now specialize in leadership training, be it through routinizing everyday learning from experience or taking a far-sighted approach to leadership development by focusing not just on the next leadership opportunity but regularly developing leadership with an eye on "two rungs up."[14] In addition, the fundamental importance placed on leadership at all levels of military organizations and the dangerous contexts in which much of their work takes place might leave their leaders more receptive to leadership interventions and more supportive of individuals' attempts to change their leadership behaviors following interventions. Taken together, one implication from these findings is that we need to move beyond stereotypes and accept that private-sector organizations might have a lot to learn from leadership in military organizations.[15]

Going beyond the research by Avolio et al., one study indicates that leadership behaviors can be taught within the educational context. This is important, because confidence that leadership can be taught would increase if it turns out that that this is true across different contexts. Together with Mark Beauchamp and our colleagues, we introduced the notion of transformational teaching,[16] which reflects the specific application of the principles of transformational leadership to the behaviors of school teachers. Transformational teaching is predicated on the notion that within the educational context, teachers are leaders whose primary role is to motivate and elevate their students. Working within the framework of transformational teaching, we conducted a rigorous and extensive study to assess (a) whether teachers can be taught to use the four behaviors inherent in transformational leadership, and if indeed they can, (b) whether their newly learned behaviors would have any effects on students' behaviors.[17] Transformational teacher training consisted of a one-day eight-hour session, and the teacher-participants were provided with a package of relevant readings as a booster session two months later. The evaluation confirmed that transformational teaching could be taught, and newly learned transformational teaching behaviors influenced pupils' motivation.

Does the Leader's Organizational Position Make a Difference?

Who benefits most from leadership interventions—senior, middle, or lower level management? Avolio et al. contrasted the effects of leadership interventions on leaders within these different positions in organizations, and their findings were initially surprising. Leadership interventions were significantly more effective for lower level than for middle- or senior-level counterparts. Avolio and colleagues speculate that one reason for this might be that the degree of complexity facing leaders who are higher in the organizational hierarchy makes it difficult for interventions to be designed and delivered that fulfill all of their complex needs. Nonetheless, the fact that leadership interventions exert greater effects on lower level leaders in no way diminishes their importance. After all, it is precisely those leaders at lower levels in the organization whose jobs require significantly more frequent interactions with their followers, often on a daily basis.

Gender of Leader and Follower

As is evident throughout this book, gender is a significant issue in all aspects of leadership. One possible reflection of this is that men and women respond differently to leadership development initiatives. Working with a different group of colleagues, Avolio focused separately on gender effects in leadership development.[18] Their meta-analyses showed that when the focus of the training was restricted to development initiatives alone, women benefitted more from leadership training than did their male counterparts. Replicating earlier findings, there was also some evidence that the pattern of results again differed depending on which outcomes were studied. Specifically, men may benefit more from interventions when the outcomes are behavioral, whereas women benefit more when the outcomes are cognitively based (e.g., the way in which information is processed).

Thus, taken together, we end this section with a positive conclusion from a very large body of research: Leadership interventions can indeed change leadership behaviors and exert beneficial effects for organizations and their employees. Moreover, leadership development initiatives more than recoup the direct and indirect costs associated with their delivery. Nonetheless, there is much still to be learned, and vast possibilities remain for enhancing the effectiveness of leadership interventions, which would in turn strengthen any return on development investment.

RENEWING LEADERSHIP INTERVENTIONS

Research on leadership interventions has now arrived at a crossroad. If the goal is to generate a body of knowledge about leadership interventions that is theoretically founded and evidenced based, and benefits the largest possible audience of leaders and organizations, do we continue in the same direction? Or might significant benefits accrue from considering a meaningful change in direction for research on leadership interventions? I suggest that continuing down the same route in which we investigate, for example, whether a leadership intervention is better than a no-treatment control condition is unlikely to provide a justifiable return on the considerable investment that such intervention research requires. Instead, to appreciate what might be possible, both the understanding and benefits of leadership interventions could be advanced by learning from the field of psychotherapy, which also focuses on achieving substantial behavioral change.

Almost 50 years ago, Gordon Paul challenged (and arguably changed) the field of psychotherapy when he asked, "How much of which psychotherapy by whom is most effective for which patient with what type of problem?" (p. 111).[19] The time is ripe to extend Paul's challenge to leadership intervention research and ask, "How much of which leadership intervention offered by whom is most effective for which leaders with what type of challenge?"

Of course, there are crucial differences between psychotherapy and leadership interventions. For example, the empirically based body of knowledge on psychotherapy vastly exceeds that on leadership interventions; and the intended outcomes differ across the two endeavors. Moreover, providing psychotherapy is regulated in most jurisdictions, while implementing leadership interventions is subject only to the whims of the free market. In addition, psychotherapy is frequently conducted one a one-on-one basis, whereas leadership interventions most likely take place with one (or more) trainers and a group of participants. Finally, psychotherapy research has been as concerned with psychological and contextual factors that occur during therapy as it has with the effectiveness or outcome of the therapy. In contrast, there has been virtually no research conducted on similar contextual factors in leadership intervention research, despite the potential to enhance the effectiveness of leadership interventions.

There are several reasons for these latter differences, one of which is especially relevant here. To some extent, research on psychotherapy focused first on outcomes or effectiveness; interest in process issues tended to follow once effectiveness was established. Given that the effectiveness of leadership interventions has now largely been established,[20] leadership intervention research and practice is now ready to include and learn from many of these same process issues.

Before going any further, an important caveat should be mentioned: Any suggestion that leadership interventions might be enhanced by lessons from psychotherapy research in no way implies that leadership interventions should involve or mimic psychotherapy, nor that leaders necessarily need psychotherapy. Instead, as will be seen, psychotherapy process research will be invaluable in helping to identifying process factors in leadership interventions that might well enhance the effectiveness of leadership intervention.

BRINGING PROCESS FACTORS INTO LEADERSHIP INTERVENTIONS

For ease of understanding, this discussion is categorized in a way that reflects the stages of an intervention. Thus, we will first consider issues pertinent to the period before the intervention takes place, then while the intervention is in progress, and last, after the formal intervention has been completed.

Before the Leadership Intervention
Preselecting Individuals for Leadership Interventions

Findings within psychotherapy support the importance of preselecting participants for leadership development initiatives. First, individuals whose initial psychological distress is highest are most likely to benefit from workplace stress management programs.[21] Second, court-mandated treatment, for example for interpartner violence, does not necessarily reduce subsequent interpartner violence;[22] this points to the importance of being psychologically ready for change. Third, pretreatment patient characteristics (e.g., treatment expectations, past experiences with therapy) significantly influence how effective psychotherapy might be.[23] Fourth, early exit from psychotherapy can result from not being ready for therapy in the first place.[24]

Selecting individuals for leadership positions has long attracted the attention of researchers and practitioners,[25] and a similar focus on preselecting individuals who are most likely to be psychologically equipped to benefit from leadership interventions may be of value, but it presents something of a dilemma. It would be optimal if all leaders and potential leaders could be offered equal opportunities to participate in development initiatives. But participants in leadership interventions vary considerably in their motivation to learn,[26] their "readiness" for change, and the extent to which they might benefit from any training.[27] Aside from the fact that those whose overall readiness or motivation is low are less likely to benefit from participating in a leadership intervention and will consume scarce organizational resources with little prospect of any return on investment, they may even negatively affect other participants during the leadership training (or not even complete the training), thereby indirectly affecting the overall potential effectiveness of the initiative. Leadership scholar David Day goes so far as to openly call this scenario a waste of "valuable resources, both in terms of time and money" (p. 569).[28] Yet involvement in developmental opportunities is often mandated by the organization without any systematic attention to participants' psychological readiness. Despite this, the goal should not be to exclude people from leadership development opportunities who might not yet be psychologically ready. After all, these may be the individuals who most need the intervention. Instead, the goal should be to make it more likely that they will be in a position to benefit if and when they are offered the opportunity to participate in leadership development initiatives.[29]

Preselecting Organizations for Interventions

It is not just individual participants who need to be ready for the opportunity and ready for change.[30] It is equally important that trainees' own leaders and peers embrace any leadership changes that occur.[31] One actual example of this derives from my own personal experiences conducting leadership training. Upon starting a two-day, off-site leadership intervention with senior leaders of an international mining organization, the CEO chose to be present to introduce the program. In a highly unusual move, he then joined the group for the next two days as an active group member, personally showing his support for the initiative and visibly improving participants' mood and motivation. In contrast, we frequently hear from participants about the frustration of trying to change following leadership interventions and encountering active attempts to sabotage change not just from their followers but from their peers and senior management as well. Pointing to the role of organizational readiness, Bruce Avolio and Fred Luthans note how organizations can nurture the process by reinforcing employees' willingness to assume responsibility for their own leadership development.[32]

Thus, preselection for leadership development is a delicate and important issue, but one that can no longer be ignored. Any role for preselection would need to be confronted with great sensitivity and should not be limited to intervention participants alone. Instead, explicitly considering the extent to which organizations are ready to promote and support any leadership changes would likely enhance the effectiveness of the leadership training.

During the Leadership Intervention

Most of the significant psychotherapeutic issues that can inform leadership interventions take place during the treatment. These include the guiding role of theory, "nonspecific" factors in the intervention, questions as to whether some individuals might benefit more from the intervention, and whether there is a "dose-dependent" relationship between the intensity of the intervention and any outcomes.

Is There a Guiding Role for Theory?

By and large, we all have our favorite explanations for phenomena about which we care deeply. Leadership researchers and practitioners are surely no different, favoring particular explanations (or theories) of the nature of leadership, which in turn influence leadership intervention research. Even the best studies typically consist of one favored intervention (whether based on transformational leadership, LMX, or whatever) that is contrasted with a group that receives no intervention.[33] Less often, the favored intervention is contrasted with an eclectic intervention[34] or a wait-list[i] control group.[35]

Turning to research on psychotherapy for guidance on what questions leadership intervention research might ask, we see a rich tradition spanning several decades in which psychotherapeutic treatments based on very different theories were directly compared *with each other*, rather than only with a control group.[36] One immediate lesson from this approach would be to change the question typically asked in leadership intervention research, away from whether a particular leadership intervention is more effective than no intervention at all, and instead contrast the comparative effectiveness of different theoretically based interventions (e.g., transformational leadership vs. LMX vs. the current approach used by the organization). Following Paul, this would further answer the question of *which* leadership intervention is most effective.

It would be premature to guess which leadership theories might receive the most support from a research endeavor such as this. With only very few exceptions, there is no meaningful comparative leadership intervention research. However, some guidance emerges from psychotherapy research, where clinicians from sometimes radically opposing perspectives have had to

---

i. Evaluating the effects of any intervention requires, at minimum, a comparison with people who do not receive the intervention. At times, however, it is neither feasible nor ethically acceptable to deny people access to the intervention for reasons of experimental rigor. In such cases, a "wait-list control group" can be used; it consists of individuals who cannot receive the favored intervention yet, often because of resource issues, but whose scores on the outcome of interest can be used for comparison purposes before they participate in the intervention.

reconcile themselves to the fact that their treatments might be equally effective. For example, we now know that once the researchers' commitment to particular theories is excluded, behavioral therapies and pharmacotherapy (i.e., medication) are often equally effective in the treatment of depression.[37] Different psychotherapies might also be equally effective, a situation that has not changed over time with enhanced research methods.[38] Turning the focus back to leadership, this was certainly the case in the research I conducted with Kevin Kelloway and Jane Helleur:[39] Transformational leadership training and traditional goal-setting were equally beneficial in terms of outcome effectiveness. Nonetheless, important theoretical and practical questions will be answered even if research suggests that there are no "winners" in terms of leadership theories.

In making this suggestion, however, a cautionary note is in order: Researchers can become so partial to their own favorite theory that they endlessly seek to validate its superiority. One scientific case study indicates how this understandable process might be avoided. For several years, findings from Gary Latham and Miriam Erez's separate research programs on goal-setting consistently produced different findings. They eventually joined together with a third ("neutral") researcher[40] and jointly designed a series of studies that all three agreed beforehand would constitute a fair test of the reasons for the inconsistent findings. Following a similar process, which Daniel Kahneman[41] has referred to as "adversarial collaboration," might well help leadership intervention researchers avoid years of unproductive collaboration.

Nonspecific Factors in Leadership Interventions

A major lesson from psychotherapy research is that the actual therapy is only one of the many causes of behavioral change, and there is a substantial body of research focusing on what are referred to as the "nonspecific factors" in therapy that are critical for positive outcomes. In contrast, leadership intervention research has proceeded as if the intervention is the only operative factor accounting for any subsequent behavioral change. In psychotherapy research, many of the "nonspecific factors" have been clearly identified, two of which (the nature and quality of the therapeutic relationship, and the setting in which the therapy takes place)[42] could be relevant to leadership interventions.

Relationship Between Presenter and Participant

The therapist–patient relationship is critical from the earliest stages of treatment, often forming the core of the first few therapeutic sessions, well before any explicit treatment techniques are introduced. As one example, it is not uncommon for 50% of the total treatment effectiveness in the cognitive-behavioral treatment of depression to emerge in the first few weeks of therapy.[43] Moreover, this early change predicts the total amount of change that will occur following treatment,[44] and the importance of the relationship between therapist and patient is apparent.[45] Despite this knowledge, relationship factors between presenter and participants in leadership interventions have yet to be considered directly.

Technological necessities might also affect the presenter–participant relationship, and experiences from psychotherapy point to what might be an exciting, frequent, and controversial opportunity for extending the reach of leadership development initiatives in the near future. Starting several years ago, and expanding steadily since, a group of psychoanalysts led by Elise Snyder have been conducting psychodynamic therapy electronically via Skype with patients in China.[46] While controversial even among some psychotherapists, it does not take a leap of the imagination to see that leadership development initiatives will undoubtedly be offered virtually to widely dispersed participants in the not-too-distant future, in turn challenging the nature of the presenter–participant relationship. As was the case in offering psychoanalytic therapy from the United States to patients in China, sometimes the choice might be between conducting leadership interventions virtually (e.g., via Skype) or not at all. At that point, nonspecific factors (e.g., transfer of training, setting factors, the extent to which trainers and participants are comfortable and familiar with the technologies used in distributed training) will likely affect outcome effectiveness and need to be confronted in leadership development research.

In addition to relationship factors, psychotherapy research has also identified therapist and patient characteristics that contribute to post-therapy change. Even after the initial severity of the presenting problem is accounted for, some estimates suggest that 5% of the variation in therapeutic effectiveness is attributable to therapist characteristics[47] such as the therapist's ethnicity,[48] gender, experience, qualifications, and amount of supervision received.[49] A separate body of literature points to patient characteristics (e.g., gender, expectations of treatment outcome, ego strength, resilience) that affect treatment outcome.[50]

Participant and presenter characteristics might be equally important in explaining the effectiveness of leadership interventions. Avolio and colleagues' meta-analysis showed that women were more responsive to leadership interventions than men,[51] and this difference was even larger if the intervention was conducted in a field rather than laboratory setting. Similarly, the match between presenter and participant gender might be important, as children learn more about leadership from parents of the same gender as themselves (see Chapter 5),[52] and female political leaders influence adolescent girls' career aspirations more than those of adolescent boys.[53]

Psychotherapy almost inevitably occurs in settings (e.g., therapists' offices, hospitals, university clinics) that are very different from the context in which any meaningful change takes place. Accordingly, psychotherapy research has focused on factors that facilitate "transfer of treatment" from clinic to field settings, for more than half a century.[54]

While systematic data are scarce, it is reasonable to assume that many leadership interventions are also conducted off- rather than on-site, with off-site interventions more likely for participants who hold more senior organizational positions.[55] This is not simply a question of a major status differential in organizations,[56] whereby those with more status enjoy more luxurious training surroundings. If that were the case, the context in which the leadership development occurs would be of little or no importance. However, the context becomes a significant issue in that the transfer of lessons learned during the intervention to the workplace becomes more complex as differences between the training setting and daily work context become bigger.

Several broad features influence the extent to which transfer of training might be achieved,[57] all of which might be significant in enhancing the effectiveness of leadership interventions. The first feature reflects the extent to which opportunities exist during the training for feedback, practice, and overlearning (i.e., practice continues even after the behavior has been learned), all of which contribute to the successful transfer of training. Second, the likelihood that leadership behavior changes will extend back to the workplace increase when participants' motivation to learn and change and their self-efficacy for change are high, and when they are open to new experiences. Participants who show higher commitment to the organization and who see the intervention as useful for themselves and their careers are also more likely to make positive efforts to extend the leadership lessons learned to their own workplaces.[58]

A third set of characteristics concerns the workplace context. Participants in leadership interventions need opportunities to practice what they have learned upon their return to their workplaces. It would make little sense to teach new leadership skills if participants did not have the opportunity to use them relatively soon thereafter. The extent to which the organization's culture supports such practice will be critical in successful transfer of training.

Might Some Participants Benefit More from Leadership Interventions than Others?

There is always variability, sometimes considerable, in the extent to which participants change following the same intervention. Given this, the challenge is whether we can predict which individuals are most likely to benefit significantly from leadership training, and as we move forward, whether there might be some benefit to matching specific individuals to specific types of intervention (e.g., LMX, transformational leadership) or modes (e.g., off-site vs. on-site, electronically mediated vs. face-to-face) of interventions.

Aside from suggestions about the potential for preselecting participants for interventions, and findings suggesting that women are generally more responsive to leadership development initiatives than men,[59] the available literature on leadership interventions offers very little guidance on this issue. One study, however, focused specifically on whether some individuals might benefit more from involvement in leadership development initiatives, namely after-event reviews, which help people evaluate their experiences in a critical and orderly manner, than others.[60] After-event reviews, which are commonplace in the military,[61] had a positive effect on changes in leadership behaviors. These benefits were magnified for individuals who were open to the experience, conscientious, and generally emotionally stable, and who had a greater source of experiences to draw from prior to after-event review training.

Similar to the situation with psychological counseling,[62] the purpose of identifying which participants are more likely to benefit from leadership interventions is not to isolate and exclude certain individuals from developmental opportunities. Instead, the intent is to maximize the effectiveness of leadership interventions by matching individuals to the intervention opportunities that they are most likely to benefit from. This aim is especially important, because participation in leadership development training occurs infrequently for most individuals, thus the need to maximize such opportunities when they exist is magnified.

"Dose-Dependence": How Much Leadership Training Is Necessary or Optimal?

Is there a dose-dependent relationship between the amount of leadership training and change achieved? Stated somewhat differently, can we say, "the more training the better"? Lessons from psychotherapy research suggest that seemingly intuitive answers to this question might be misleading. In psychotherapy, research shows that we need not expect a 1:1 or linear relationship between the amount of psychotherapy provided and the amount of subsequent behavioral change. For example, while most outcome research on one-to-one approaches to treating depression involves 16 to 20 sessions, it is possible to achieve statistically significant effects that are maintained for three months after only five, two-hour sessions.[63] As the authors of this particular study noted, the practical utility of these effects are also far-reaching. They estimated the savings to participants in the brief therapy at 38–50% in session costs and 70% in travel costs, plus potential reductions in child care costs, all of which could increase participants' motivation to participate. Similarly, as noted earlier, many of the effects of treatment for depression occur very early in the therapy, which suggests that there may be an early breakpoint beyond which there are diminishing returns from any additional therapy.

In contrast, it is not unusual to find leadership interventions lasting three days,[64] five days,[65] more than a month,[66] sometimes even between 1 and 12 months.[67] Yet one study by John Antonakis, Marika Fenley, and Sue Liechti showed that charisma could be taught to middle managers in a Swiss organization in a five-hour training session that was followed by a one-hour telephone conversation in which a personalized leadership plan was developed.[68] A second intervention by the same research team with MBA students in Switzerland that provided 20 hours of leadership training resulted in only marginal increases in intervention effectiveness, suggesting that the additional 15 hours of training brought diminishing benefits.

Just how much training is *needed* to achieve the desired and sufficient changes is of tremendous theoretical, practical, and financial significance. The broader question of what it takes to achieve stable behavioral change has bedeviled researchers and theoreticians, psychotherapists, management, and parents for many decades, and providing some answers from the field of leadership would be invaluable. Practically, understanding just how intensive the intervention needs to be would help management understand what investment is required to make an organizational difference. Based on current available data, the benefits of leadership interventions exceed the investments required.[69] However, this conclusion was based on the amount of leadership training actually offered. Different and potentially more optimistic conclusions might be appropriate if they were based on the minimal amount of treatment *required* to achieve the changes.

Whether there is a dose-dependent relationship between the amount of leadership training received and the effectiveness of the intervention remains an unanswered but important question, and opens exciting opportunities for increasing organizations' RODI. This is an issue of practical efficiency, one to which we might expect organizational decision-makers to respond enthusiastically.

Relapse Prevention

Within the therapeutic environment, difficulties in maintaining behavioral gains after the completion of therapy are considered normal, and lapses are viewed as predictable. At the same time, maintenance is held to be too important to take for granted, thus the principles of relapse prevention are incorporated into many therapeutic initiatives, such as treatment for substance abuse disorders, depression, obesity, obsessive-compulsive disorders, panic disorder, bipolar disorder, and even schizophrenia.[70] If the principles of relapse prevention can be effective in the face of such profound behavioral problems, there is every reason to believe that they might be equally effective in maintaining behavioral gains following leadership interventions. Given that relapse prevention initiatives have also been successful in facilitating coping following job loss[71] and enhance the likelihood of successful transfer of training in military instructors,[72] relapse prevention might be equally beneficial for leadership development initiatives.

Accepting post-intervention lapses in no way suggests that the leadership development initiative failed. Rather, these lapses should be viewed as predictable, a transitional phase,[73] and an opportunity to reinforce maintenance of any leadership changes. Recognizing the factors that are likely to lead to a lapse is the first step in prevention. Research has shown that there are critical proximal or situational factors, as well as more stable, distal factors,[74] all of which are relevant to the maintenance of changes following leadership interventions. From a leadership perspective, the proximal or immediate factors might include interpersonal conflicts at work, negative moods (anger, anxiety, depression), and encountering unpredictable events. Research on the role of bad moods may be especially instructive for leaders' relapse prevention, because the buildup of negative moods in the hours before a lapse are far more consequential than chronically high levels of anxiety, anger, or depression.[75] Three distal (or stable) factors that would make lapses more likely are a general lack of self-awareness regarding emotions or moods, stress, and a lack of social support—whether work-related or not.[76] Importantly, these proximal and distal factors can interact with each other. For example, stressors at home might result in buildups of negative moods after arriving at work, together increasing the likelihood of relapse.

Developing and practicing a specific plan to confront these proximal and distal threats[77] could optimally be incorporated as a regular part of leadership interventions. The lesson for organizational practitioners is clear: Just like psychotherapists, we, too, should expect that many individuals who have changed their leadership behaviors will inevitably experience lapses that do not reflect a failure of the initial training. Decades of research now suggest, however, that relapse can be prevented, and the principles of relapse prevention ought to be included in leadership interventions.

Post-Intervention

Psychotherapy research has shown that what happens *after* the formal treatment is completed has a significant effect on how long any behavioral gains are maintained. Maintenance of behavioral changes has been a major target of psychotherapy psychology, with studies showing that maintenance is possible, sometimes for up to five years following treatment[78] or longer.[79] Within the organizational realm, leadership changes have been maintained for as long as six months.[80],[81] One earlier study showed that the benefits of leadership training that had been apparent at 6 months were no longer apparent 17 months following treatment,[82] leaving open the questions of when any effects of a training program might dissipate. But very few intervention studies even discuss when any positive effects might dissipate. Still, maintenance of any changes is critical: It would avail little to see initial positive behavioral changes if participants soon reverted to their former leadership behaviors.

Booster Sessions

Post-therapy booster sessions have long been a staple part of many therapeutic endeavors, and research findings consistently highlight their role in the maintenance of behavioral gains.[83] Even minimal post-treatment contact, for example via telephone and mail (in a pre-Internet era), was sufficient to significantly improve maintenance of post-treatment behavioral gains.[84] In sharp contrast, most leadership interventions described in the literature make no mention at all of any post-intervention "booster" sessions conducted after the formal intervention is completed. One study that did so showed that, following five hours of group-based leadership training, as little as a one-hour personalized telephone conversation could be sufficient.[85] Like Eden et al.,[86] we have frequently heard from our participants that some form of booster session, even minimal contact between presenters and participants, would be very useful for maintaining post-intervention changes. The effectiveness of leadership interventions can no doubt be improved through the use of post-intervention booster sessions, especially in situations where some level of "skill decay" is predictable,[87] and would go a long way in providing the emotional, informational, and instrumental support leaders need to maintain any behavioral gains.

CONCLUSION

People learn about leadership in many different ways, and this includes formal, structured leadership interventions offered by their organizations. The results of numerous evaluations leads to the reassuring conclusion that leadership behaviors can be taught, and that these interventions are cost-effective.[88] Future advances in leadership effectiveness are now likely to result from organizational scientists asking a new set of questions, many of which can be guided by successful lessons learned from decades of psychotherapy research. As a result, we can look forward with some optimism to meaningful advancements in intervention effectiveness in the years to come.

SUGGESTED READING

Avolio, B. J. (1999). *Full leadership development*. Thousand Oaks, CA: SAGE
     Publications.
Murphy, S. E., & Riggio, R. E. (2003). (Eds.) *The future of leadership development*.
     Mahwah, NJ: Lawrence Erlbaum.
Sosik, J. J., & Jung, D. I. (2010). *Full range leadership development: Pathways for people,
     profit, and planet*. New York: Taylor & Francis.

NOTES

1. Bass, B. M., & Bass, R. (2008). *The Bass handbook of leadership: Theory, research
   and managerial applications* (4th ed). New York: Free Press.
2. Lippitt, R. (1943). The psychodrama in leadership training. *Sociometry, 6*(3),
   286–292.
3. Salas, E., Tannenbaum, S. I., Kraiger, K., & Smith-Jentsch, K. A. (2012). The
   science of training and development in organizations: What matters in practice.
   Psychological Science, 13, 74–101.
4. Terpstra, D. E. (1981). Relationship between methodological rigor and reported
   outcomes in organization development evaluation research. *Journal of Applied
   Psychology, 66*, 541–543.
5. Dvir, T., Eden, D., Avolio, B. J., & Shamir, B. (2002). Impact of transformational
   leadership on follower development and performance: A field experiment.
   Academy of Management Journal, 45, 735–744.
6. Shadish, W. R. Cook, T. D., & Campbell, D. T. (2002). *Experimental and
   quasi-experimental designs for generalized causal experiments*. New York: Houghton
   Mifflin.
7. Howell, J. M., & Frost, P. J. (1989). A laboratory study of charismatic leadership.
   Organizational Behavior and Human Decision Processes, 43, 243–299.
8. Kirkpatrick, S. A., & Locke, E. A. (1996). Direct and indirect effects of three core
   charismatic leadership components on performance and attitudes. *Journal of
   Applied Psychology, 81,* 36–51.
9. Christie, A., Barling, J. A., & Turner, N. (2011). Pseudo-transformational leadership: Model specification and outcomes. *Journal of Applied Social Psychology, 41*,
   2943–2984.
10. Avolio, B. J., Reichard, R. J., Hannah, S. T., Walumbwa, F. O., & Chan, A. (2009).
    A meta-analytic review of leadership impact research: Experimental and
    quasi-experimental studies. *Leadership Quarterly, 20*, 764–784.
11. Avolio, B. J., Avey, J. B., & Quisenberry, D. (2010). Estimating return on leader-
    ship development investment. *Leadership Quarterly, 21*, 633–644.
12. Avolio, B. J., Reichard, R. J., Hannah, S. T., Walumbwa, F. O., & Chan, A. (2009).
    A meta-analytic review of leadership impact research: Experimental and
    quasi-experimental studies. *Leadership Quarterly, 20*, 779.
13. Lowe, K. B., Kroeck, K. G., & Sivasubramaniam, N. (1996). Effectiveness cor-
    relates of transformational and transactional leadership: A meta-analytic review
    of the MLQ literature. *Leadership Quarterly, 7*, 385–425.
14. Schumpeter. (2013, February 16). How to make a killing. *The Economist*, 65.
15. Schumpeter. (2013, February 16). How to make a killing. *The Economist*, 65.

16. Beauchamp, M. R., Barling, J., Li, Z., Morton, K. L., Keith, S. E., & Zumbo, B. D. (2010). Development and psychometric properties of the Transformational Teaching Questionnaire. *Journal of Health Psychology, 15*, 1123–1134.

17. Beauchamp, M. R., Barling, J., & Morton, K. (2011) Transformational teaching and adolescent self-determined motivation, self-efficacy, and intentions to engage in leisure time physical activity: A randomized controlled pilot trial. *Applied Psychology: Health and Well-Being, 3*, 127–150.

18. Avolio, B. J., Mhatre, K., Norman, S. M., & Lester, P. (2009). The moderating effect of gender on leadership intervention impact: An exploratory review. *Journal of Leadership and Organizational Studies, 15*, 325–341.

19. Paul, G. L. (1967). Outcome research in psychotherapy. *Journal of Consulting Psychology, 31*, 109–118.

20. Avolio, B. J., Reichard, R. J., Hannah, S. T., Walumbwa, F. O., & Chan, A. (2009). A meta-analytic review of leadership impact research: Experimental and quasi-experimental studies. *Leadership Quarterly, 20*, 764–784.

21. Flaxman, P. E., & Bond, F. W. (2010). Worksite stress management training: Moderated effects and clinical significance. *Journal of Occupational Health Psychology, 15*, 347–358.

22. Rosenfeld, B. D. (1992). Court-ordered treatment for spouse abuse. *Clinical Psychology Review,12*, 205–226.

23. Howard, K. I., Moras, K., Brill, P. L., Martinovich Z., & Lutz, W. (1996). Evaluation of psychotherapy: Efficacy, effectiveness, and patient progress. *American Psychologist, 51*, 1059–1064.

24. Cartwright, R., Lloyd, S., & Wicklund, J. (1980). Identifying early dropouts from psychotherapy. *Psychotherapy: Theory, Research and Practice, 17*, 263–267.

25. Cohn, J., & Moran, J. (2011). *Why are we so bad at picking good leaders?* San Francisco: Joseey-Bass.

26. Salas, E., Tannenbaum, S.I., Kraiger, K., & Smith-Jentsch, K. A. (2012). The science of training and development in organizations: What matters in practice. *Psychological Science, 13*, 74–101.

27. Harris, M. J., & Fleischman, E. A. (1955). Human relations training and the stability of leadership patterns. *Journal of Applied Psychology, 39*, 20–25.

28. Day, D. V. (2011). Integrating perspectives on longitudinal investigation of leader development: From childhood through adulthood. *Leadership Quarterly, 22*, 561–571.

29. Avolio, B. J., & Hannah, S. T. (2008). Developmental readiness: Accelerating leadership development. *Consulting Psychology Journal: Practice and Research, 4*, 331–347.

30. Johns, G. (2006). The essential impact of context on organizational behavior. *Academy of Management Review, 31*, 386–408.

31. Clark, C. S., Dobbins, G. H., & Ladd, R. T. (1993). Exploratory field study of training motivation. *Group and Organization Management, 18*, 292–307.

32. Avolio, B. J., & Luthans, F. (2006). *The high impact leader: Moments matter in accelerating authentic leadership development.* New York: McGraw-Hill.

33. Avolio, B. J., Reichard, R. J., Hannah, S. T., Walumbwa, F. O., & Chan, A. (2009). A meta-analytic review of leadership impact research: Experimental and quasi-experimental studies. *Leadership Quarterly, 20*, 764–784.

34. Dvir, T., Eden, D., Avolio, B. J., & Shamir, B. (2002). Impact of transformational leadership on follower development and performance: A field experiment. *Academy of Management Journal, 45*, 735–744.

35. Barling, J., Kelloway, E. K., & Weber, T. (1996). Effects of transformational leadership training on attitudinal and financial outcomes: A field experiment. *Journal of Applied Psychology, 81,* 827–832.

36. Strupp, H. H., & Howard, K. I. (1992). A brief history of psychotherapy research. In D. K. Freedheim, H. J., Freudenberger, J. W., Kessler, J. W., et al. (Eds.), *History of psychotherapy: A century of change* (pp. 309–334). Washington, DC: American Psychological Association.

37. Robinson, L. A., Berman, J. S., & Neimeyer, R. A. (1990). Psychotherapy for the treatment of depression: A comprehensive review of controlled outcome research. *Psychological Bulletin, 108,* 30–49.

38. Wampold, B. E., & Brown, G. S. (2005). Estimating variability in outcomes attributable to therapists: A naturalistic study of outcomes in managed care. *Journal of Consulting and Clinical Psychology, 73,* 914–923.

39. Kelloway, E. K., Barling, J., & Helleur, J. (2000). Enhancing transformational leadership: The roles of training and feedback. *Leadership and Organization Development Journal, 21,* 145–149.

40. Latham, G. P., Erez, M., & Locke, E. A. (1988). Resolving scientific disputes by the joint design of crucial experiments by the antagonists: Application to the Erez-Latham dispute regarding participation in goal setting. *Journal of Applied Psychology, 73,* 753–772.

41. Kahneman, D. (2007). Daniel Kahneman. In G. Lindzey & W. M. Runyan (Eds.), *A history of psychology in autobiography* (Vol. IX, pp. 155–197). Washington, DC: Amerian Psychological Association.

42. Frank, J. D. (1982). Therapeutic components shared by all psychotherapies. In J. H. Harvey & M. M. Parks (Eds), *Psychotherapy research and behavior change* (pp. 5–37). Washington, DC: American Psychological Association.

43. Howard, K. I., Kopta, S. M., Krause, M. S., & Orlinsky, D. E. (1986). The dose–effect relationship in psychotherapy. *American Psychologist, 41,* 159–164.

44. Ilardi, S. S., & Craighead, W. E. (1994). The role of nonspecific factors in cognitive-behavior therapy for depression. *Clinical Psychology: Science and Practice, 1,* 138–156.

45. Wampold, B. E. (2001). *The great psychotherapy debate: Models, methods, and findings.* Mahwah, NJ: Lawrence Erlbaum.

46. Osnos, E. (2011). Meet Dr. Freud: Does psychoanalysis have a future in an authoritarian state? *New Yorker,* January 10, 54–52.

47. Wampold, B. E., & Brown, G. S. (2005). Estimating variability in outcomes attributable to therapists: A naturalistic study of outcomes in managed care. *Journal of Consulting and Clinical Psychology, 73,* 914–923.

48. Imel, Z. E., Baldwin, S., Atkins, D. C., Owen, J., Baarseth, T., & Wampold, B. E. (2011). Racial/ethnic disparities in therapist effectiveness: A conceptualization and initial study of cultural competence. *Journal of Counseling Psychology, 58,* 290–298.

49. Elkin, I. (1999). A major dilemma in psychotherapy outcome research: Disentangling therapists from therapies. *Clinical Psychology: Science and Practice, 6,* 10–32.

50. Piper, W. E., Ogrodniczuk, J. S., Joyce, A. S., & Weideman, R. (2011). In W. E. Piper, J. S. Ogrodniczuk, A. S. Joyce, & R. Weideman (Eds.), *Short-term group therapies for complicated grief: Two research-based models* (pp. 107–144). Washington, DC: American Psychological Association.

51. Avolio, B. J., Mhatre, K., Norman, S. M., & Lester, P. (2009). The moderating effect of gender on leadership intervention impact: An exploratory review. *Journal of Leadership and Organizational Studies, 15*, 325–341.

52. Bronfenbrenner, U. (1961). Some familial antecedents of responsibility and leadership in adolescents. In L. Petrullo & B. M. Bass (Eds.), *Leadership and interpersonal behavior* (pp. 239–271). New York: Holt, Rinehart and Winston.

53. Beaman, L., Duflo, E., Pande, R., & Topalova, P. (2012). Female leadership raises aspirations and educational attainment for girls: A policy experiment in India. *Science, 335*, 582–586.

54. Margaret, A. (1950). Generalization in successful psychotherapy. *Journal of Consulting Psychology, 14,* 64–70.

55. Avolio, B. J., Reichard, R. J., Hannah, S. T., Walumbwa, F. O., & Chan, A. (2009). A meta-analytic review of leadership impact research: Experimental and quasi-experimental studies. *Leadership Quarterly, 20*, 764–784.

56. Pfeffer, J. (1998). Seven practices of successful organizations. *California Management Review, 40*(2), 96–124.

57. Burke, L. A., & Hutchins, H. M. (2007). Training transfer: An integrative literature review. *Human Resource Development Review, 6*, 263–296.

58. Salas, E., Tannenbaum, S. I., Kraiger, K., & Smith-Jentsch, K. A. (2012). The science of training and development in organizations: What matters in practice. *Psychological Science, 13*, 74–101.

59. Avolio, B. J., Mhatre, K., Norman, S. M., & Lester, P. (2009). The moderating effect of gender on leadership intervention impact: An exploratory review. *Journal of Leadership and Organizational Studies, 15*, 325–341.

60. DeRue, D. S., Nahrgang, J. D., Hollenbeck, J. R., Workman, K. (2012). A quasi-experimental study of after-event reviews and leadership development. *Journal of Applied Psychology, 97*, 997–1015.

61. Schumpeter. (2013, February 16). How to make a killing. *The Economist*, 65.

62. Cartwright, R., Lloyd, S., & Wicklund, J. (1980). Identifying early drop-outs from psychotherapy. *Psychotherapy: Theory, Research and Practice, 17*, 263–267.

63. Cohen, S., O'Leary, K. D., & Foran, H. (2011). A randomized clinical trial of a brief, problem-focused couple therapy for depression. *Behavior Therapy, 41*, 433–446.

64. Eden, D., Geller, D., Gewirtz, A., Gordon-Terner, R., Inbar, I., Liberman, M., Pass, Y., Salomon-Segev, I., & Shalit, M. (2000). Implanting Pygmalion leadership style through workshop training: Seven field experiments. *Leadership Quarterly, 11*, 171–210.

65. Dvir, T., Eden, D., Avolio, B. J., & Shamir, B. (2002). Impact of transformational leadership on follower development and performance: A field experiment. *Academy of Management Journal, 45*, 735–744.

66. Avolio, B. J., et al. (2005). Executive summary: 100-year review of leadership intervention research—Briefings report 2004-01, Gallup Leadership Institute, Kravis Leadership Institute. *Leadership Review, 5*(Winter), 7–13.

67. Avolio, B. J., et al. (2005). Executive summary: 100-year review of leadership intervention research—Briefings report 2004-01, Gallup Leadership Institute, Kravis Leadership Institute. *Leadership Review, 5*(Winter), 7–13.

68. Antonakis, J., Fenley, M., & Liechti, S. (2011). Can charisma be taught? Tests of two interventions. *Academy of Management Learning and Education, 10*, 374–396.

69. Avolio, B. J., Reichard, R. J., Hannah, S. T., Walumbwa, F. O., & Chan, A. (2009). A meta-analytic review of leadership impact research: Experimental and quasi-experimental studies. *Leadership Quarterly, 20*, 764–784.

70. Witkiewitz, K., & Marlatt, G. E. (2004). Relapse prevention for alcohol and drug problems: That was Zen, this is Tao. *American Psychologist, 59*, 224–235.

71. Caplan, R. D., Vinokur, A. D., Price, R. H., & van Ryn, M. (1989). Job seeking, reemployment, and mental health: A randomized field experiment in coping with job loss. *Journal of Applied Psychology, 74*, 759–769.

72. Tziner, A., Haccoun, R. R., & Kadish, A. (1991). Personal and situational characteristics influencing the effectiveness of transfer of training improvement strategies. *Journal of Occupational Psychology, 64*, 167–117.

73. Marlatt, G. A., & George, W. H. (1984). Relapse prevention: Introduction and overview of the model. *British Journal of Addiction, 79*, 261–273; Moos, R. H. (1980). Depressed patients' life contexts, amount of treatment, and treatment outcome. *Journal of Nervous and Mental Disease, 178*, 105–112.

74. Witkiewitz, K., & Marlatt, G. E. (2004). Relapse prevention for alcohol and drug problems: That was Zen, this is Tao. *American Psychologist, 59*, 224–235.

75. Shiffman, S., & Waters, A. J. (2004). Negative affect and smoking lapses: A prospective analysis. *Journal of Consulting and Clinical Psychology, 72*, 192–201.

76. Witkiewitz, K., & Marlatt, G. E. (2004). Relapse prevention for alcohol and drug problems: That was Zen, this is Tao. *American Psychologist, 59*, 224–235.

77. Marlatt, G. A., & George, W. H. (1984). Relapse prevention: Introduction and overview of the model. *British Journal of Addiction, 79*, 261–273.

78. Beidel, D. C., Turner, S. M., & Young, B. J. (2006). Social effectiveness therapy for children: Five years later. *Behavior Therapy, 37*, 416–425.

79. Saavedra, L. M., Silverman, W. K., Morgan-Lopez, A. A., & Kurtines, W. M. (2010). Cognitive behavioral treatment for childhood anxiety disorders: Long-term effects on anxiety and secondary disorders in young adulthood. *Journal of Child Psychology and Psychiatry, 41*, 924–934.

80. Dvir, T., Eden, D., Avolio, B. J., & Shamir, B. (2002). Impact of transformational leadership on follower development and performance: A field experiment. *Academy of Management Journal, 45*, 735–744.

81. Leister, A., Borden, D., & Fiedler, F. E. (1977). Validation of contingency model leadership training: Leader match. *Academy of Management Journal, 20*, 464–470.

82. Carron, T. J. (1964). Human relations training and attitude change: A vector analysis. *Human Relations, 17*, 403–424.

83. Whisman, M. A. (1990). The efficacy of booster maintenance sessions in behaviour therapy: Review and methodological critique. *Clinical Psychology Review, 10*, 155–170.

84. Perri, M. G., Shapiro, R. M., Ludwig, W. W., Twentyman, C. T., & McAdoo, W. G. (1984). Maintenance strategies for the treatment of obesity: An evaluation of relapse prevention training and posttreatment contact by mail and telephone. *Journal of Consulting and Clinical Psychology, 52*, 404–413.

85. Antonakis, J., Fenley, M., & Liechti, S. (2011). Can charisma be taught? Tests of two interventions. *Academy of Management Learning and Education, 10*, 374–396.

86. Eden, D., Geller, D., Gewirtz, A., Gordon-Terner, R., Inbar, I., Liberman, M., Pass, Y., Salomon-Segev, I., & Shalit, M. (2000). Implanting Pygmalion leadership style through workshop training: Seven field experiments. *Leadership Quarterly, 11*, 171–210.
87. Salas, E., Tannenbaum, S. I., Kraiger, K., & Smith-Jentsch, K. A. (2012). The science of training and development in organizations: What matters in practice. *Psychological Science, 13*, 74–101.
88. Avolio, B. J., Avey, J. B., & Quisenberry, D. (2010). Estimating return on leadership development investment. *Leadership Quarterly, 21*, 633–644.

CHAPTER 7
Leadership in Different Contexts

Our primary focus throughout this book is on leadership within and of traditional work organizations. Yet leadership is also central within other types of organizations and contexts, including labor unions, military organizations, the political sphere, schools, and sports teams. Parallels have even been drawn between the roles, responsibilities, and behaviors involved in transformational leadership and parenting,[1] with leadership theories recently being applied empirically to understanding parenting behaviors.[2] Each of these contexts boasts its own vibrant and ongoing literature on leadership. In this chapter, we examine each of these different literatures to understand (a) whether what we learn from research in each of these specific contexts might benefit our understanding and the effectiveness of leadership in traditional work organizations, and (b) if the lessons learned from traditional work organizations could have lessons for leadership in any of these contexts.

LABOR UNIONS

"Unions are fascinating organizations,"[3] and whether we are ideologically disposed toward or against labor unions, Bert Klandermans' comment rings true. Understanding leadership within unions is no less fascinating for a variety of reasons. First, as Klandermans continued in this perceptive quote, despite unprecedented attacks against unions over the past three decades, "contrary to what the prophets of doom will have us believe, they will not disappear in the near future." Just as leadership is one of the key factors in how organizations respond when they are under threat or decline, the quality of leadership will play some role in determining whether Klandermans turns out to be correct or not. What we already know is that the responses of organizational and union leaders are sometimes remarkably similar—for example, arranging mergers to increase their prominence and strength in the industry.[4]

Second, unions are democratic organizations in which leaders at virtually all levels of the organization are elected by a vote of those whom they will represent, and this democratic ethos is invariably enshrined in the union's constitution. When unions stray from this core value, judicial courts have stepped in and enforced supervised elections.[5] Unions and regular work organizations are fundamentally different in this respect—very few employees will ever have the luxury of electing their supervisors. To the extent that leadership processes and outcomes between labor and work organizations are similar, given the different contexts, greater confidence can be placed in the particular leadership theory.

The third reason for our interest in union leadership is that behavioral research conducted on union leadership has invariably focused on shop stewards, putting the spotlight on leadership at the lowest levels of labor organizations. As was apparent in Chapter 4, this parallels research on traditional work organizations, where almost half of all workplace research targets leadership at the lower levels of the organization. The positional equivalence of the two leadership roles might make any of lessons drawn from shop stewards' leadership more relevant to supervisors, and vice versa.

Last, several characteristics unique to labor unions increase our interest in union leadership for its own sake. First, irrespective of their organizational levels (e.g., shop steward vs. union president), union leaders wield very little formal authority or power. As a result, their influence on union effectiveness provides an unusual opportunity to understand the nature and effects of leadership uncontaminated by the benefits of formal power. Second, despite the stereotype of local union leaders as activists, socialists, or Marxists bent on advancing the goals of the union and harming management, most shop stewards in North America agree to take on this role out of a sense of obligation because no one else was interested in contesting an election for the role.[6] Thus shop stewards are often reluctant leaders and provide an opportunity to understand leadership when the motivation to lead is often low. The third characteristic unique to unions is that some trade union leaders have wielded wider social power and responsibilities, perhaps seen most vividly in their roles in overthrowing repressive governments in communist Poland and apartheid South Africa. Thus gaining a more complete understanding of union leadership becomes even more important.[7]

Against this backdrop, we address two questions concerning leadership and labor unions. First, what are the effects of union stewards on union members, especially new union members? Second, given that the predominant leadership model in behavioral research of union leadership has been transformational leadership, do the effects of transformational leadership extend to the union context?

Unions and union leaders have long attracted interest from researchers and the public. As but one example of the fact that research on union leadership is hardly new, Raymond van Zeist was interested in the effects of empathy on union business agents some 60 years ago. What makes van Zeist's research remarkable is that while leaders' empathy is now a popular topic of conversation and research, that was certainly not the case when this study was conducted six decades ago.[8] For his study, van Zeist interviewed 64 business agents of AFL-affiliated unions in the building trades in Chicago. Presaging findings of recent leadership research, van Zeist showed that empathy in business union agents was significantly correlated with several outcomes that would be critical to the success of a union, including the recruitment of new members, the ability to impose rules and regulations and resolve disputes and grievances, and, ultimately, the likelihood of winning the union election. While such early findings in the union context are interesting, more recent studies are characterized by much larger samples, broader questions, and greater methodological sophistication, allowing for greater confidence in any lessons derived from their findings.

In a study led by Kevin Kelloway, we were interested in the different ways in which shop stewards' transformational leadership influences union members' voluntarily participation in union-related activities.[9] Our interest in members' participation in union activities was sparked by the central role of members' voluntary engagement in union activities to ensure both union democracy and union effectiveness. This study included two different samples of members of a large government union in Canada. The first comprised 210 clerical and maintenance employees, and the second consisted of 150 guards and rehabilitation staff employed in a correctional facility. Shop stewards' transformational leadership also influenced different aspects of commitment to the union (namely attitudinal loyalty, feelings of responsibility to the union, and a willingness to work for the union), which in turn affected members' participation in the union. These indirect effects mimic the effects of transformational leadership across different contexts (see Chapter 3).

Tove Hammer, Mahmut Bayazit, and David Wazeter turned their attention to local union presidents and the effects of their leadership on members' commitment and participation.[10] Their large-scale study took place within school teacher unions, included 326 local union presidents, and over 4,000 unionized school teachers, and focused on external (e.g., developing external support for teachers and education) and internal leadership (e.g., consulting and communicating with union members). Both internal and external leadership influenced how effective members thought their union was with respect to wage and non-wage issues, wage equity, and procedural fairness. In addition, internal leadership was associated with members' loyalty to the union. In turn, the perception that the union was instrumental in resolving non-wage issues such as job security and ensuring wage equity and procedural fairness predicted the likelihood that union members would participate in union activities.

Socializing Union Members

Socializing new members into the organization in a way that ensures a smooth transition and integration is critical to any organizations' success, including labor organizations, and several studies point to the role of leadership in this process. Clive Fullagar, Don McCoy, and Carla Shull surveyed 71 electrical apprentices, all of whom were recent members of the same union, and investigated the role of transformational leadership on subsequent union socialization.[11] Intriguingly, higher levels of transformational leadership in journeymen mentors was associated with their greater involvement in union socialization activities, such as talking to apprentices about the union and explaining the goals of the union. In turn, the extent to which apprentices were exposed to these socialization activities was directly associated with subsequent loyalty to the union.

A different study on newcomer socialization provides a more nuanced view of the link between transformational leadership and union socialization. Together with a different set of colleagues, Fullagar and these colleagues distinguished between institutional and individual socialization techniques.[12] Within the union context, institutional socialization includes the length of the formal orientation meeting, the amount of printed materials distributed to new members, and the number of topics covered in the formal session. In contrast, individual socialization reflects shop steward activities, such as personally inviting new members to attend a union meeting, personally introducing new members to their union officials, and personally supporting and encouraging new members. Using a large sample of almost 600 members in their first year of membership with one specific union, union stewards high in charisma (a combination of idealized influence and inspirational motivation) and individualized consideration were more likely to engage in individual socialization tactics. In turn, individual socialization was associated with positive attitudes toward the union. In contrast, stewards' charisma and individualized consideration were not associated with institutional socialization in any way, and institutional socialization was not associated with attitudes toward the union.

From this body of research on leadership roles of shop stewards and union presidents several broad conclusions can be made. First, labor unions parallel work organizations in the extent to which leadership plays a role in meeting both interpersonal and organizational objectives. Second, the role of leaders at all levels of the organization is again emphasized. Third, the importance of indirect effects of leadership is not limited to traditional work organizations. Finally, because of the unique nature of labor organizations, confidence in the effects of transformational leadership is strengthened.

MILITARY ORGANIZATIONS

Most organizational leadership takes place in relatively routine, if not mundane, circumstances. In contrast, leadership in military contexts sometimes occurs in the most extreme situations—situations fraught with danger, fear, and excitement on the one hand, and boredom, loneliness, and sleep deprivation on the other. Some organizational leaders will occasionally find themselves in dire situations, as happened on September 11, 2001, or in the aftermath of disasters such as Hurricane Katrina.[13] Other leaders whose work involves public safety (e.g., law enforcement, firefighting, emergency medical personnel) encounter extreme situations as a regular part of their jobs. Extreme contexts sometimes elicit heroic behaviors from leaders,[14] as well as both morally exemplary and morally reprehensible conduct, all of which offer powerful lessons for leadership in traditional work organizations. Gaining an appreciation of leadership in such situations is important if we are to optimize the likelihood of successful outcomes. Leadership within military contexts offers an opportunity to learn about leadership in extreme contexts.

Given the history and ubiquity of warfare, there is a long and extensive tradition of research on military leadership—so much so that a full and comprehensive review of all the research on military leadership is simply not possible within this review. Not surprisingly, much research was conducted in the military during World War II, an example of which is the study by Stanley Williams and Harold Leavitt.[15] They initially surveyed candidate officers in 1944 two and five weeks after the officers entered Marine Corps training. A little while later, they had access to data on the leadership performance of 100 of these individuals in actual combat in the Iwo Jima and Okinawa campaigns. Williams and Leavitt used their data to show that fellow recruits' earlier opinions of these individuals' leadership abilities predicted the quality of their subsequent leadership performance in extreme situations. While researchers today might justifiably point to ambiguities in the questions asked in the survey and question the basic nature of the statistical analyses as limiting factors in generating knowledge, the serious interest in military leadership by early researchers is evident. What should also be noted is that a primary emphasis of leadership research during World War II concentrated on improving the selection of military leaders.

Support for the utility of organizational leadership theories would be strengthened if their findings could be generalized to the military context; and several studies provide the opportunity to test whether they indeed do so. In one study, Bass and his team studied 72 light infantry platoons in the U.S. Army that were participating in combat simulation exercises.[16] For this study, the researchers were able to obtain reports of the transformational and transactional leadership ratings of both direct, proximal (sergeant), and indirect, distal (platoon leaders, typically second lieutenants) leaders. Platoons' performance was rated by expert observers following the two-week simulation exercise. Several of the findings from this study warrant attention. First, direct, proximal leaders' (i.e., one's own sergeant's) transformational and transactional leadership behaviors exerted significant effects on platoon cohesion and performance. In contrast, indirect, distal leaders' (i.e., the sergeant's leader) transformational leadership was effective, but their transactional leadership was not. The probable reason for this is that indirect leaders do not exert direct authority or management responsibility over platoon members, nullifying the importance of any behaviors that would be based on more formal sources of power. Second, contrary to the widespread belief that passive and avoidant leadership might simply be ineffective, it was far more likely to result in negative effects. While this phenomenon is now seen consistently in research across different domains,[17] at the time this study was conducted such negative findings associated with passive leadership were somewhat novel. Finally, transformational leadership was again shown to exert both direct effects on performance and indirect effects through team cohesion.

A study by Taly Dvir and her co-researchers yielded findings in a military context that have important implications for our understanding of organizational leadership. They conducted their study among Israeli infantry platoons[18] and investigated performance measures that are unique to a military context. Importantly, their study also compared transformational with eclectic (or traditional) leadership training. What did they find? First, infantry soldiers with transformational leaders outperformed those whose leaders received the training normally offered in the organization with respect to written and practical knowledge of light weapons and speed on an obstacle course. This is important, because while there is much research showing that receiving leadership training is better than receiving no leadership training at all (see Chapter 6), Dvir and her colleagues showed that receiving transformational leadership was also more effective than what might be regarded as traditional (or "eclectic") leadership. Second, these findings reinforce the notion that leadership behaviors can be taught and that the newly learned leadership behaviors will influence subordinates. Finally, because they conducted their study within the Israeli military, their findings lend additional support to the cross-cultural or cross-national validity of transformational leadership theory. This study is particularly important, as it remains one of the few leadership studies that directly compares two different leadership theories or approaches.

Several conclusions can be drawn from this research on leadership in military contexts. First, the old stereotype that the best of military leadership is characterized by a "command-and-control" leadership style is simply no longer valid. If anything, traditional work organizations might have a lot to learn from modern military leadership, which in many respects epitomizes new-genre leadership.[19] Second, despite the remarkable differences in demands and context (e.g., hierarchy, task, amount of training) between military and work organizations, these representative studies support the validity of leadership theories in general, and transformational leadership in particular. Finally, there is a very substantial body of research on military leadership. However, a closer examination shows that much of the published research does not focus on leadership during actual military missions, which does limit to some extent what can be learned from this context.

POLITICAL LEADERSHIP

The public interest in leadership is perhaps nowhere as strong as on the behavior of our political leaders, and this is readily understandable. As we have learned throughout history, political leaders have the power to exert a substantial and long-lasting influence over the quality of people's lives—both positively and negatively. It makes sense, therefore, that we would want to continuously monitor what our political leaders do, and understand why they do what they do. As a result, a defining attribute differentiating modern political leadership from traditional organizational leadership is the transparency and scrutiny that political leaders must endure, which would be totally foreign to those in profit-oriented organizations. Parenthetically, it is not just this transparency that leaves political leaders' behavior more amenable to scrutiny by researchers. The ultimate outcomes of political leadership in a democratic framework, namely vote counts, are also perfectly transparent—and their validity is often vouched for by independent observers and monitors, making this an attractive situation for researchers.

We examine two issues that, while not unique to political leadership, are more amenable to research because of the transparency inherent in the political context: the nature and effects of charisma and transformational leadership, and leaders' physical and mental illnesses.

Charisma and Transformational Leadership

Understanding charisma in the political context might provide interesting insights for traditional work organizations, for several reasons. First, within work organizations, separating the effects of personal power (leadership) from the formal power associated with a management position is not always easy. Within the political realm, however, personal power is of greater importance than formal power. In fact, the ability to influence others derives almost exclusively from behaviors such as charisma (though leaders sometimes attempt to influence voting behavior through programs or initiatives that benefit constituents), and political leaders have little access to formal sources of power. Second, unlike leadership in work organizations, the effects of political leadership are invariably unequivocal: People either vote for or against the leader in question, providing an ideal outcome for researchers. Third, influencing large groups of individuals is a precondition of effective political leadership, which may have salient lessons for team leadership.

One set of studies provides a very clear perspective on the roles of transformational leadership and charisma in presidential voting. Rajnandini Pillai and Ethlyn Williams conducted two studies investigating charisma and transformational leadership in the 1996 and 2000 presidential elections in the United States. Going beyond other studies focusing on the outcome of elections, they first showed that across both time periods and both successful and unsuccessful candidates (Bill Clinton and Bob Dole in 1996, and George W. Bush and Al Gore in 2000), perceptions of the candidate's transformational leadership and charisma predicted not just *how* people voted but *whether* they voted in the first place.[20] Pillai and her team extended these findings in their study of the 2000 U.S. elections,[21] showing that perceptions of the candidates' empathy, proactivity, and need for achievement predicted whether the leader was seen as charismatic and transformational. Their findings also enabled them to show *why* leadership perceptions predicted voting behavior. Specifically, political leaders who were perceived as more transformational or more charismatic were trusted more, and it was the higher levels of trust that predicted the decision to vote for or against a candidate. Importantly, a similar pattern of findings emerged in a separate study of Israeli voting preferences in 1992,[22] pointing to the robust nature of these findings across cultures or countries. Taken together, these findings provide added confirmation that charisma predicts leadership success *and* failure, and substantiate the indirect effects of leadership.

Research on political leadership goes further, examining the effects of charisma during periods of significant crisis (see Chapter 3). What makes crisis situations so interesting is that they are of sufficient severity to cause extensive physical damage and personal injury or loss of life, but only occur infrequently. In addition, they often occur suddenly, and there may be ambiguity about their cause, but it is generally agreed that resolution must come swiftly.[23] Opportunities for personal control in crisis situations are also limited. Much of the available research focuses on national crises and political leadership.

It has long been held as axiomatic that during times of crisis, followers' need for charismatic leadership grows—in Bass' insightful observation, followers become "charisma hungry,"[24] and strong support for this notion derives from very different sources. In a series of analyses, Michelle Bligh, Jeffrey Kohles, and James Meindl analyzed President George Bush's speeches before and after the crisis of September 11, 2001.[25] They were able to show that the content of the president's speeches did indeed change, with an increased emphasis after 9/11 on themes reflecting charisma, such as collective action, a link between the past and the present, identification with the follower, morality of the leader's cause, tangible references within speeches, and action-orientation. These changes were described in media reports of his speeches, which influenced the way in which President Bush was perceived, as well as polling data.

In a separate study, Stewart McCann's analysis of 40 U.S. presidential elections between 1824 and 1984 showed that charismatic leaders were more likely to win, and by a higher margin of victory, when the social, political, and economic threat during the year of the election was higher.[26] While no definitive answers to this question are possible, might this help explain why Barack Obama won the 2008 presidential election—at a time when the American economy was in free-fall, and employment numbers were plummeting? And could this help explain his re-election in 2012?

Despite these findings, the link between crisis and charisma is by no means inevitable. When performance is viewed as below expectations during a crisis, leaders may bear the costs for the poor performance;[27] people will look elsewhere for charismatic leadership. This partially explains why even members of his own party deserted Neville Chamberlain, making an unpopular but charismatic Winston Churchill prime minister in 1940.[28] Similarly, if this occurs in less extreme circumstances when there is a possibility for a change in leadership—such as an election, motivation for a change may increase.[29] Michelle Bligh, Jeffrey Kohles, and Rajnandini Pillai studied the Californian recall election in 2003,[30] and their results confirmed these earlier findings. The incumbent (Gray Davis) was perceived as significantly less charismatic than either of his challengers, and the outside challenger (Arnold Schwarzenegger) was perceived as more charismatic than the challenger (Cruz Bustamante) from the same party as the current governor. In this case, the more charismatic candidate won.

This same crisis-charisma effect emerges in tightly controlled laboratory conditions. As part of a series of studies conducted in the Netherlands, Ernestine Gordijn and Diederik Stapel showed that undergraduate participants who were reminded of the terrorist attacks of 2001 and 2004 in the United States and Madrid, respectively, and told that repeat attacks in the Netherlands were plausible, scored significantly higher on the personal need for the visionary aspect of charismatic leadership.[31] Gordijn and Stapel also showed in separate studies that by experimentally creating a sense of mortality and terror, participants in their studies were more likely to be influenced by a charismatic leader, supporting Bass' earlier observation of how people become charisma hungry in crises. Two studies in the United States showed similar results. Creating a stress-provoking crisis in a laboratory situation resulted in perceptions by followers of higher levels of charisma among their leaders, and experimentally simulating the conditions of a terrorist attack prior to the 2004 elections increased ratings of President Bush's charisma.[32]

While so much of the research on political leadership has investigated presidential charisma, Harold Zullow and Martin Seligman examined how leaders' pessimistic rumination was associated with electoral defeat.[33] Their interest in presidential candidates' pessimistic rumination emerged because it signals depression in candidates, during a situation in which most voters look to their leaders for optimism and hope. To study this, they coded nomination acceptance speeches for all Republican and Democratic candidates during two separate periods, 1900 to 1944, and 1948 to 1984. Zullow and Seligman showed that the candidates whose acceptance speeches contained more pessimistic rumination lost 9 of the 12 earlier elections, and 9 of the 10 elections between 1948 and 1984. More pessimistic rumination in the acceptance speech also predicted the margin of defeat, such that greater pessimism was associated with a larger electoral defeat. Greater confidence can be placed in these findings because the influence of two external factors known to affect the outcome of presidential elections—how well the candidate was doing in the polls at the time of the convention and, most importantly, whether the candidate was the incumbent or not—were removed statistically in these analyses. Zullow and Seligman offer three reasons why depressive rumination affects voting outcomes: Candidates with higher depressive rumination scores are less active on the campaign trail; they are less likeable interpersonally when they interact with potential voters; and they are less hopeful than their optimistic counterparts. Each of these traits is relevant to leadership in work organizations.

Leaders' Physical and Mental Health

In years gone by, it was possible—perhaps even easy—for political leaders to hide from personal scrutiny of any kind. As a result, significant physical and psychological illnesses experienced by important world leaders went unreported, if not unnoticed. Ironically, at least partially because of the power of the political leader, the nature of their illnesses was sometimes kept not just from the public but from the leader as well, as was the case when the Shah of Iran initially contracted cancer. When the Shah was eventually made aware of the diagnosis, medical terminology was used (e.g., he was told he suffering from Waldenstrom's disease) that made very little sense to a layperson, or to the Shah himself.[34] Despite the political power of political leaders, or perhaps because of it, the public has now demanded and won the right to greater transparency of their leaders in many countries, as a result of which issues previously left invisible are now amenable to research.

Several authors have now started to examine the physical and mental health of leaders throughout the 20th century, culminating in Rose McDermott's *Presidential Leadership, Illness, and Decision Making*[35] and David Owen's appropriately titled book *In Sickness and in Power*.[36] McDermott analyses case studies of Woodrow Wilson, Franklin D. Roosevelt, John F Kennedy, Richard Nixon, and the Shah of Iran. David Owen takes a broader perspective and focuses on leaders such as Anthony Eden, Francois Mitterand, and the Shah of Iran, and more recent leaders such as George W. Bush and Tony Blair. If anything, Owen's perspectives on the effects of mental illness might be especially rich given his background. Not only is he a qualified clinical neurologist and psychiatrist, but having served as Foreign Secretary in the British government between 1977 and 1979 and one of the European Union negotiators with Bosnia in 1993, Owen is unusually well-qualified for the task of understanding the realities of leaders' physical and mental health.

McDermott presents the complex ways in which significant physical illness can affect leadership decision-making and behavior. Facing significant illness, the time left for leaders to accomplish their vision is shortened. Concerned about achieving their vision and cementing their legacy, their sense of time urgency is heightened, shifts in values and priorities can occur, and their focus becomes more inward. Revealing the complicated ways in which illness might affect leader behavior, significant illness can result in depression but also in unusual levels of compassion and empathy. For example, President Roosevelt's personal experience with polio helped him understand others' needs, and was likely one factor in promoting the social programs of the New Deal. McDermott also points to the death of President Kennedy's infant son Patrick as a major factor in the development of the field of neonatology.

When the window into political leaders' personal lives is opened, we see that they are by no means immune from the physical and mental maladies that afflict us all. In terms of physical illness, the Shah of Iran suffered from lymphoma in the latter years of his tenure; Woodrow Wilson suffered several strokes; Franklin D. Roosevelt had polio and heart disease; Dwight Eisenhower was hospitalized for seven weeks following a heart attack in September 1955;[37] and both Harry Truman and Eisenhower almost died from childhood diseases.[38] John F. Kennedy suffered from persistent digestive problems, a variation of Addison's disease, and chronic back pain as a result of an earlier injury, and took several different medications: anti-anxiety (Librium), pain (codeine, Demerol), and sleeping pills (barbiturates); stimulants (Ritalin); and hormones—often on a daily basis.[39] During the height of the Cuban Missile

Crisis, Kennedy was taking antispasmodic medications to combat his colitis, antibiotics to treat a urinary tract infection, as well as hydrocortisone, testosterone, and salt tablets to battle his adrenal problems and enhance his energy levels. John F. Kennedy's battles with illness were such that he was read the last rites no fewer than four times in his life![40] Clearly, the assumption that all leaders are physically healthy is simply not sustainable.

There has also been concern about leaders' mental health. Many commentators point to Richard Nixon's narcissism and possible borderline personality disorder, Winston Churchill's experience with depression (his "black dog") and his dependence on alcohol, and Lyndon Johnson's depression. A more rigorous scientific analysis has identified 10 American presidents who suffered significant psychopathology while in office (e.g., Nixon's alcohol abuse, LBJ's bipolar disorder, Coolidge and Hoover's major depressive disorders, and Woodrow Wilson's anxiety and depressive disorders). While the particulars of his many illnesses may not be certain, Hitler was reported to be taking 88 medications when Germany invaded the Soviet Union.[41] To believe that none of these leaders' physical or mental illnesses affected their performance in any way—either negatively or positively—is to challenge credulity. Making the role of leaders' mental illness even more complex is the case of the indefatigable Eleanor Roosevelt. While she periodically suffered significant bouts of depression, she used it as a motivation for work, saying, "If I feel depressed...I go to work. Work is always an antidote for depression" (p. 280).[42]

Given his personal and research-based knowledge of the psychology of political leaders, David Owen has proposed a specific syndrome that he argues is unique to political leadership: the "hubris personality syndrome."[43] The core characteristics of the hubris syndrome (e.g., "predisposition to actions that enhance one's own well-being," "disproportionate concern about self-image," "propensity to speak in the third person") grow stronger as the individual is in power for greater periods of time. Owen identified dictators (Stalin, Hitler, Mao, Pol Pot, Idi Amin, and Robert Mugabe) and democratically elected world leaders (Lloyd George, Margaret Thatcher, George W. Bush, and Tony Blair) who manifested the hubris syndrome. Importantly, the hubris symptom cannot overlap with other existing mental illnesses. As a result, Owen argues, neither Franklin Roosevelt nor Lyndon Johnson could be diagnosed as having had a hubristic personality, as they retrospectively received diagnoses of depression. Similarly, Richard Nixon suffered from alcoholism toward the end of his presidency, again precluding a diagnosis of hubris. Owen also argues that Kennedy did not suffer from hubris syndrome—his cynicism and humor excluded that diagnosis, and Kennedy's self-control also would have prevented development of the hubris symptom.

Effectively, hubris is offered by Owen as an independent syndrome in its own right. But in order to justify the term "syndrome," it would need to occur across different organizational types, not just be evident among political leaders. Nathan Hiller and Donald Hambrick[44] extended thinking about hubris and related syndromes such as narcissism and overconfidence to their research on organizational executives. They suggested that core self-evaluations, which comprise four independent personality dimensions— self-esteem, self efficacy, locus of control, and emotional stability[45]— provide a basis for understanding hubris. Specifically, they argue that hubris reflects very high levels of all these four dimensions, or what they call "hyper core self-evaluations." While the exact nature and effects of hubris, or hyper core self-evaluations, await rigorous scrutiny, a platform for thinking about hubris among leaders now exists.

With its elevated sense of self-importance, hubris bears some similarity with the concept of narcissism, and we have already seen the complex effects of CEO narcissism. Recall that the effects are neither uniformly bad nor uniformly good. Instead, narcissistic CEOs are likely to behave in ways that draw attention to themselves and produce more extremes in financial company performance—both their wins and their losses are greater than those of their less narcissistic counterparts. Research has also focused on the effects of CEO hubris. In one study of almost 3,000 CEOs, an unobtrusive measure of hubris was again used and was indicated when the CEO's report of the company's financial performance exceeded the actual objective performance of the organization.[46] The results of this study, which took place among a range of manufacturing companies in China, showed a significant link between CEO hubris and company risk-taking, which was reflected in decisions to invest in innovative, high-technology initiatives. A similar finding emerged from a study of 106 acquisitions of organizations in the United States in which payment for the targeted organization exceeded $100 million.[47] Not only did hubristic CEOs pay a premium to complete the acquisition, but this effect was again stronger when their discretion was higher.

Must mental illness or personality disorders detract from the ability to provide high-quality leadership? The cases of political leaders described above would suggest not, and Eleanor Roosevelt's resilience in the face of hardship provides one example. Nassir Ghaemi, a psychiatrist at Tufts University in Boston, goes even further, with his provocative hypothesis that some exposure to mental illness leaves individuals better suited to the demands of leadership during troubled times.[48] Before dismissing the hypothesis out of hand, Ghaemi's explains that mental illness leaves people with higher levels of resilience, realism, empathy, and creativity, all of which could form the foundation for higher quality leadership in troubled times. While these ideas await close scientific attention, they highlight the need for us to understand the role of physical and mental illness in the development and performance of leadership. Blithely assuming that all leaders are in full, good health, or that physical or mental health has no consequences on leaders' performance, is simply no longer appropriate.

The physical and mental health of our leaders has broad social and policy implications. From a policy perspective, if leaders' illnesses do indeed affect their own behavior or the well-being of the organizations they lead, one might question whether policies or laws ought to be in place to ensure that any necessary information about leaders' physical and mental illnesses are publicly available. Certainly in the United States, voters demand and receive information about the health of national political candidates. Access to similar information might be especially relevant in publicly traded organizations, where investors have a need and a right to know about all factors that affect the performance of the organization.

SCHOOLS

The success of our schools is critical to the long-term development of children and the healthy functioning of communities and societies. Not surprisingly, therefore, there is an extensive body of research investigating leadership among senior educational administrators, school principals, and teachers. There has been less focus on how teachers' in-class performance is affected by the leadership they are exposed to and how this might in turn affect their students' performance. We will examine these two issues, not only because of their intrinsic interest but also because they highlight a unique outcome of leadership, namely children's performance. We will also consider a novel initiative in which transformational leadership workshops are being provided for teachers, after which rigorous evaluations are being undertaken of the success of these workshops in terms of their effects on the students' attitudes and performance.

Transformational Leadership Among Senior Administrators and School Principals

Within the school context, individuals at different levels of authority (e.g., teachers, principals) could exert direct or indirect effects on students' attitudes and performance in their regular daily interactions. Teachers interact with their students far more frequently and intensively than is the case in most supervisor–follower relationships, but school principals have the opportunity to affect students' attitudes and performance indirectly, through their influence on teachers. This is important: While many people are inclined to think that students either have a "good" or a "bad" teacher—in other words, that teaching quality is a characteristic inherent within the teacher—teachers are as affected by the quality of leadership as employees in profit-oriented organizations. Faced with wonderful leadership by school principals (or department heads), teachers will be inspired to superior performance, but confronted with destructive or passive/avoidant leaders, teachers are likely to feel angry or apathetic, with predictable effects on teaching quality.

The effects of principals' transformational and transactional leadership have been investigated. One lesson from these studies is that, mimicking other organizations, principal's and head teachers' transformational leadership is associated with a variety of important attitudes among teachers, including job satisfaction,[49] voluntary citizenship behaviors,[50] commitment to their jobs and intent to remain as a teacher, collective teacher efficacy (i.e., the belief that teachers can be effective),[51] and commitment to the school's mission, to their professional community, and to school reform.[52] In some studies, both transformational and transactional leadership were studied, with transformational leadership exerting stronger effects than transactional leadership on teachers. All these findings were obtained from samples in very different countries (e.g., Canada, Israel, Tanzania, and the Netherlands), again showing that the effects of transformational leadership are consistent across contexts, whether they are schools or countries.[53]

In what remains one of the most in-depth and influential studies on this topic, William Koh, Richard Steers, and James Terborg conducted an extensive investigation on the influence of school principals' transformational leadership on teachers' citizenship, commitment, and satisfaction, and in turn, how these teachers influenced children's academic performance.[54] Their study included principals from no fewer than 89 elementary schools in Singapore, 1,690 teachers randomly selected within each school, and their pupils. Similar to studies on traditional work organizations, these researchers showed that principals' transformational leadership predicted teachers' commitment to the school, satisfaction with the principal, and organizational citizenship behaviors (i.e., willingness to help the school in ways that were not formally required of the teacher). In turn, while principals' transformational leadership had no direct effect on students' academic performance, indirect effects that would be predictable emerged, as teachers' commitment, satisfaction, and citizenship behaviors directly affected students' academic performance. These findings are interesting, as they demonstrate how principals' transformational leadership indirectly influences children's grade performance. This supports the extensive reach of transformational leadership given that its effects emerge within the school context and across national boundaries.

Developing Transformational Teaching

Mark Beauchamp at the University of British Columbia is leading a project that shifts the research focus, by investigating whether teachers manifest transformational behaviors, whether these behaviors can be taught, and how they affect children's motivation and performance. The purpose of his and his colleagues' first study was to confirm that the four transformational leadership behaviors are indeed exhibited by teachers. In addition, because physical education teachers have the potential to make a lasting effect on schoolchildren's health, and because more than half of North American schoolchildren are too sedentary for their own physical good, they focused on preadolescent children's physical activity in their initial study.[55] Based on results from eight focus groups and in-depth interviews with 18 teenage students, they found that teachers do indeed enact the four transformational components.

With respect to idealized influence, for example, one student remarked that "He's [the teacher] the kind of guy that can take a joke and give a joke, but at the same time he has the respect of the class so we know when to take him seriously and that's why we like him" (p. 254). Students were also motivated by teachers' inspirational motivation. As one student commented, "You kind of get carried away by him, because he's really into it. He likes it, so it helps you to kind of go with him, because he has energy and you're kind of 'okay, he's really into it. It must be fun, let's try it out'" (p. 250). Just how individualized consideration might influence children's activity levels is evident from one student who commented, "Ms. G. did influence my positive attitude towards PE because she was my first PE teacher in high school and really gave me her support [following an injury] and at the end of the year she gave me a little card that said 'thanks for your participation and good luck in future years'" (p. 252). In turn, each of these three transformational behaviors was associated with higher levels of students' physical activity. Ironically, however, despite the school context, intellectual stimulation was used less frequently than the other transformational behaviors, and students offered examples of the negative effects of its absence. One student observed, for example, that it would be important for teachers to "allow students to bring more ideas to class" (p. 251).

Having shown that at least three of the four transformational leadership components were reflected in teachers' behaviors, Mark Beauchamp, myself, and our team[56] took this a step further by asking whether it would be possible to extend the practice of transformational leadership interventions with organizational leaders and teach the four transformational leadership behaviors to teachers. We first acknowledged that the absence of an acceptable measure of transformational teaching hinders any research on this topic (e.g., any rigorous evaluation of transformational teaching workshops). We conducted several studies that resulted in a short, readable, reliable, and valid questionnaire of teachers' transformational behaviors that can be completed by large numbers of adolescents and made it freely available in our article (see Table 7.1). Just as importantly, we showed in results from this questionnaire that students who evaluated their teachers as higher on transformational teaching were again significantly more likely to manifest higher levels of self-determined motivation and positive affect.

Table 7.1. ITEMS FROM THE TRANSFORMATIONAL TEACHING
QUESTIONNAIRE

Idealized Influence

Acts as a person that I look up to

Treats me in a way that builds my respect

Talks about his or her personal values

Behaves as someone I can trust

Inspirational Motivation

Demonstrates that he or she believes in me

Is enthusiastic about what I am capable of achieving

Motivates me to try my hardest

Is optimistic about what I can accomplish

Intellectual Stimulation

Creates lessons that really encourage me to think

Provides me with tasks and challenges that get me to think in different ways

Gets me to question my own and others' ideas

Encourages me to look at issues from different sides

Individualized Consideration

Shows that she or he cares about me

Tries to know every student in the class

Tries to help students who might be struggling

Recognizes the needs and abilities of each student in the class

If the transformational teaching model is to be of practical value, it must be possible to work with teachers and help them develop transformational teaching skills, and these newly learned skills should then influence children's behaviors. Working with Mark Beauchamp and Katie Morton, we designed a one-day intervention for high school physical education teachers.[57] In a randomized field study (that appropriately had a wait-list control group and measures that took place immediately after the intervention and again several months later), teachers were assigned either to participate in a one-day transformational teaching development program or to be a member of a wait-list control group (which received the same training after the study was completed, but served as a control group in the interim). The findings showed that the development initiative was successful: Transformational teaching behaviors were enhanced significantly by the training, as rated by students and the teachers. In turn, changes in transformational teaching influenced preadolescent children's motivation for physical activity and their self-efficacy that they could do so effectively, both of which are typically obstacles to their involvement in actual physical activity.[58]

Society is preoccupied with athletes and sports performance. One consequence of this is the abundance of performance data available at both the player and team level[59] —a richness of data that is simply not accessible to leadership researchers in most regular work contexts. What this collection of data has done is to provide researchers with some wonderful opportunities to test their theories. There are now empirical studies within the sports context with diverse disciplines such as economics, labor relations, and psychology. Some organizational topics (e.g., pay and performance[60]) have received attention within the sports context, and the sports context could well advance our understanding of leadership, because different sports parallel different aspects of organizational life. For example, basketball, soccer, and field and ice hockey mimic fast-paced teams that demand high levels of cooperation and interdependence from their members; professional golf requires a high-quality, dyadic relationship between golfer and caddy; and football mirrors the need for strategy, control, and precise coordination between departments.[61] Research focusing on leadership within the sports context enables us to address two unrelated leadership questions: First, how does transformational leadership influence individual and/or team performance? Second, what are the effects of a sudden change in leadership?

Transformational Leadership and Sports Performance

Aside from what it tells us about the effects of different forms of leadership, Bill Curtis, Ronald Smith, and Frank Smoll's 1979 study, "Scrutinizing the Skipper,"[62] confirms that when we become absorbed by the latest scientific findings, we run the risk of ignoring older "gems." Curtis and his colleagues studied the effects of coaches' leadership behaviors on young boys aged 8 to 15, not only in terms of wins and losses, but also on these children's attitudes to their team and to baseball. To appreciate the contribution of their early research, it should be noted that they conducted their study before the advent of new-genre leadership theories. They took a broad perspective of leadership behaviors, focusing on leaders' responses to (a) desirable performance (e.g., through verbal or nonverbal rewards), (b) mistakes (e.g., by encouraging the player, instructing the player on technical issues, ignoring the mistake, or a negative reaction), and (c) misbehavior (e.g., taking action to restore the status quo). Curtis and his colleagues used team perceptions and coach self-ratings of these leadership behaviors, as well as observations by trained observers, and collected data across two separate years (1976 and 1977)—a comprehensive approach that would still be the envy of current researchers.

Several findings of this early study were truly interesting. First, the most frequent coaching behaviors used were technical instruction, encouragement, and rewards. Punitive control techniques and efforts to maintain control were the least frequently used leadership behaviors. Second, the use of punitive and control-oriented techniques were not random. Instead, coaches were more likely to respond negatively and punitively to player mistakes and misbehaviors in losing teams, but it remains unclear whether this was because negative leadership causes mistakes and misbehaviors or whether mistakes and misbehaviors "cause" negative and punitive leadership (and this will be discussed further in Chapter 9). In contrast, team perceptions of more positive leadership behaviors were associated with more positive attitudes to the team and to baseball, and to the likelihood of winning.

Bass and Riggio's full-range model of leadership includes both transformational and transactional leadership—basic management behaviors such as ensuring that individuals had sufficient instruction and training, and providing positive feedback to enhance clarity.[63] One study investigated the effects of these management behaviors on role clarity among individuals involved in team sports.[64] Higher levels of transactional leadership were associated with greater role clarity—but only for team players who were not considered good enough to command a position on the starting rotation (there were no significant effects of transactional leadership among starters). Possible reasons for this differential effect are that players in the starting lineup might have already enjoyed higher levels of clarity, or might have received more attention and training from the coach in the first instance, resulting in greater levels of clarity. Regardless, the findings remain important, as role clarity is consistently associated with higher levels of performance and health.[65]

Far more of the research in this area has focused on transformational leadership.[66] In the same way that school principal and head teachers' transformational leadership is associated with teachers' satisfaction and commitment, university athletic directors' transformational leadership is associated with sports coaches' satisfaction with leadership and satisfaction with their own jobs. In addition to the United States, this effect has also been seen in Canada[67] and Malaysia,[68] reinforcing the breadth of effects of transformational leadership. Alison Doherty and Karen Danylchuk's study provides two additional findings relevant to transformational leadership theory in the sports context.[69] First, the augmentation effect discussed earlier, which hypothesizes that transformational leadership exerts important effects beyond those of transactional leadership, was supported in their study. Second, like research on transformational leadership in general, passive leadership was associated with lower satisfaction with leadership and lower beliefs that the leader is effective.[70]

Finally, two studies investigated the effects of transformational leadership on sports performance. Both of these showed that transformational leadership exerted positive effects, but there were important differences between the studies. The first of these two studies focused on university athletes, and like other studies mentioned earlier, any effects of transformational leadership on sports performance were indirect. In this case they were mediated by players' intrinsic motivation.[71] The second of the two studies also yielded a link between transformational leadership and sport performance,[72] but extends our understanding in two ways. First, this study focused on the effects of adolescents' peer leadership, highlighting the breadth of transformational leadership effects. Second, athletes' skill was controlled for, thereby excluding the possibility that any findings could be attributed to peers' skill rather than leadership.

Effects of Changes in Leadership

An issue that occurs frequently in organizations, but which we only briefly touched on in considering the sudden death of a CEO in Chapter 2, is the effect of a change in leadership on individual, team, or organizational performance. While the effects of managerial and leadership changes have intrigued some researchers for decades—as is evident in the early debate between Oscar Grusky[73] and William Gamson and Norman Scotch[74] on the effects of changes in managers on team performance—the amount of current research on leadership changes would seem to be inversely related to its frequency, if not also to its importance.

One likely reason is that this is a difficult issue to study. Changes in leadership are invariably not made publicly known before they occur, given practical organizational constraints such as the need for confidentiality and the speed with which leadership changes often occur. The sports context allows for research on coach and managerial changes, however, because coaching changes are transparent, and longitudinal or archival performance data on individuals and teams are readily available. Thus, most studies that have been conducted occur within a single sport, implicitly controlling for critical external factors (e.g., organizational size, structure, goals).

Coaches can depart during a season or between seasons, and research has addressed this distinction for decades, with consistent findings.[i] Across several different sports (basketball, ice hockey, and soccer), and at both the amateur

---

i It is important to note that different terms are used in different countries for the same function. For example, within the context of U.K. soccer, the person primarily responsible for a team's performance is referred to as the manager. In U.S. basketball, the same person is the coach. Whatever the term used for the particular sport, the focus here is on the individual most directly responsible for the team's performance, typically evidenced by the person who has primary responsibility for making decisions (strategic, staffing) during games.

and professional levels,[75] changes that occur during the season tend to be disruptive and are usually accompanied by demonstrable short-term *decreases* in overall performance upon the arrival of the new coach. This is ironic, as mid-season leadership changes often occur during performance crises, when there is an immediate need to turn performance problems around. What this means is that new coaches typically arrive after a period of poor performance, and their immediate strategic priority is to staunch any losses. Ruud Koning's study of professional soccer in the Netherlands confirms that this is indeed the case, as defensive skills improved after a coach was fired, but offensive skills did not.[76] In contrast, changes in the coach or manager that occur between seasons do not exert negative effects, likely because between-season changes allow for organizational planning, building functional relationships, and team development. In addition, coach or manager changes between season often give the new incumbent sufficient time for preparation and for developing new relationships. Successful professional basketball coaches Red Auerbach and Pat Riley have both discussed this phenomenon in their respective autobiographies.[77]

What lessons might be learned by traditional work organizations from these findings? Perhaps the decision of *when* to replace current leaders is just as critical as the decision *whether* to replace the leader. While a change in leadership might often seem like an attractive option, if not a necessity, when things are not going well, organizational decision makers may be advised to consider whether a new leader would have the opportunity for planning and development that would parallel any between-season change in leadership. If changes are made mid-stream, it would perhaps be realistic to assume that the new leader will initially act defensively, and performance problems—the manifest reason for the change—may not be staunched in the short term. Regardless, more heed should be paid to Koning's question of whether firing coaches occurs too frequently, given the relatively modest benefits seen in the aftermath and what this might mean for organizational practice.

Further questions need to be answered before we have a comprehensive understanding of the effects of leadership changes. Team and individual performance will be influenced not just by when and whether changes are made, but also by the quality of leadership before the change occurred. Incumbent leaders leave organizations for different reasons, perhaps most prominently because they were doing poorly and were fired. However, the decision to depart could also be made by the leader or coach because their performance was superior, and thus they were head-hunted by rival organizations; because of retirement; or because of external factors beyond their control, all of which would create a different context for the new leader.

One final issue about changes in leadership warrants attention. When managers or head coaches are fired or resign or retire, their closest advisors and trusted assistants sometimes go with them. Oscar Grusky set out to study this phenomenon more than 40 years ago, using a carefully designed laboratory study with university students as the research participants.[78] All managers worked on a task with two assistants, and after doing so for three, six-minute periods, they were informed that, consistent with normal business practice, they were being transferred to a new unit to expand their experience (i.e., they were not fired). Half the managers were allowed to choose one of the assistant managers to go with them on the new assignment, while the other half went alone. Managers then continued on the tasks for five more periods, during which their interactions with others were carefully monitored by trained external raters. Grusky found that transferring with an ally resulted in a speedier and more positive adjustment and in better communication with an ally. At the same time, Grusky also cautioned that the same special relationship that resulted in these benefits could also breed resentment in the new context. To ensure that they retain any benefits of transferring with an ally, managers should proceed with caution.

CONCLUSION

Throughout this chapter we have extended the focus beyond traditional work organizations and examined leadership in several different work-related contexts. In doing so, we reinforced the robustness of some of the major findings on organizational leadership (e.g., the indirect effects of transformational leadership on performance, the augmentation effect). At the same time, novel issues related to organizational leadership (e.g., leaders' physical and mental health, effects of transitions between leaders and the timing of such transitions) pose new questions in the search for a more complete understanding of organizational leadership.

SUGGESTED READING

Barling, J., Fullagar, C., & Kelloway, E. K. (1992). *The union and its members: A psychological approach*. New York: Oxford University Press (see especially Chapter 6, pp. 125–149).
Ghaemi, N. (2011). *A first-rate madness: Uncovering the links between leadership and mental illness*. New York: Penguin.
Jackson, P., & Delehanty, H. (2013). *Eleven rings: The soul of success*. New York: Penguin Books.
McDermott, R. (2006). *Presidential leadership, illness and decision making*. New York: Cambridge University Press.
Owen, D. (2012). *The hubris syndrome: Bush, Blair and the intoxication of power*. London: Methuen & Co.

NOTES

1. Popper, M., & Mayseless, O. (2003). Back to basics: Applying a parenting perspective to transformational leadership. *Leadership Quarterly, 14,* 41–65.
2. Morton, K. L., Barling, J., Rhodes, R. E., Masse, L., Zumbo, B. D., & Beauchamp, M. R. (2010). Extending transformational leadership theory to parenting and adolescent health behaviors: An integrative and theoretical review. *Health Psychology Review, 4,* 128–157.
3. Klandermans, B. (1986). Psychology and trade union participation: Joining, acting, quitting. *Journal of Occupational Psychology, 59,* 189–204.
4. Chaison, G. N. (1996). *Union mergers in hard times: The view from five countries.* Ithaca, NY: Cornell University Press.
5. Teamsters for a Democratic Union (n.d.) Winning the fight for democracy (TDU history: the 1980s). Retrieved from http://www.tdu.org/node/755
6. McCarthy, W. E. J., & Parker, S. R. (1968). Research papers 1. The role of shop stewards in British industrial relations: A survey of existing information and research. London: Royal Commission on Trade Unions and Employers' Associations; Schuler, T., & Robertson, D. (1983). How representatives allocate their time: Shop steward activity and membership contact. *British Journal of Industrial Relations, 21,* 330–342; Strauss, G., & Sayles, L. R. (1953). Occupation and the selection of local union officers. *American Journal of Sociology, 58,* 585–591.
7. For a more comprehensive review of union leadership, see Barling, J., Fullagar, C., & Kelloway, E. K. (1992). *The union and its members: A psychological approach* (pp. 125-149) New York: Oxford University Press.
8. Van Zeist, R. H. (1952). Empathy test scores of union leaders. *Journal of Applied Psychology, 36,* 293–295.
9. Kelloway, E. K., & Barling, J. (1993). Members' participation in local union activities: Measurement, prediction and replication. *Journal of Applied Psychology, 78,* 262–279.
10. Hammer, T. H., Bayazit, M., & Wazeter, D. L. (2009). Union leadership and member attitudes: A multi-level analysis. *Journal of Applied Psychology, 94,* 392–410.
11. Fullagar, C., McCoy, D., & Shull, C. (1992). The socialization of union loyalty. *Journal of Organizational Behavior, 13,* 13–26.
12. Fullagar, C., Clark, P., Gallagher, D., & Gordon, M. E. (1994). A model of the antecedents of early union commitment: The role of socialization experiences and steward characteristics. *Journal of Organizational Behavior, 15,* 517–533.
13. Dutton, J. E., Frost, J. P., Worline, M. C., et al. (2002). Leading in times of trauma. *Harvard Business Review, 80*(1), 55–61.
14. Wansink, B., Payne, C. R., & van Ittersum, K. (2008). Profiling the heroic leader: Empirical lessons from combat-decorated veterans of World War II. *Leadership Quarterly, 19,* 547–555.
15. Williams, S. B., & Leavitt, H. J. (1947). Group opinion as a predictor of military leadership. *Journal of Consulting Psychology, 11,* 283–291.
16. Bass, B. M., Avolio, B. J., Jung, D. I., & Berson, Y. (2003). Predicting unit performance by assessing transformational and transactional leadership. *Journal of Applied Psychology, 88,* 207–218.
17. Bass, B. M., Avolio, B. J., Jung, D. I., & Berson, Y. (2003). Predicting unit performance by assessing transformational and transactional leadership. *Journal of Applied Psychology, 88,* 207–218; Kelloway, E. K., Mullen, J., & Francis, L. (2006).

Divergent effects of transformational and passive leadership on employee safety. *Journal of Occupational Health Psychology, 11*, 76–86.

18. Dvir, T., Eden, D., Avolio, B. J., & Shamir, B. (2002). Impact of transformational leadership on follower development and performance: A field experiment. *Academy of Management Journal, 45*, 735–744.

19. Schumpeter. (2013, February 16). How to make a killing. *The Economist*, 65.

20. Pillai, R., & Williams, E. A. (1998). Does leadership matter in the political arena? Voter perceptions of candidates' transformational and charismatic leadership and the 1996 U.S. presidential vote. *Leadership Quarterly, 9*, 397–416.

21. Pillai, R., Williams, E. A., Lowe, K. B., & Jung, D. I. (2003). Personality, transformational leadership, trust, and the 2000 U.S. presidential vote. *Leadership Quarterly, 14*, 161–192.

22. Shamir, B. M. (1994). Ideological position, leaders' charisma and voting preferences—personal vs. partisan elections. *Political Behavior, 16*, 265–287.

23. Pearson, C. M., & Clair, J. A. (1998). Reframing crisis management. *Academy of Management Review, 23*, 59–76.

24. Bass, B. M. (1990). *Bass and Stogdill's handbook of leadership: Theory, research and managerial implications* (3rd ed). New York: Free Press.

25. Bligh, M. C., Kohles, J. C., & Meindl, J. R. (2004). Charisma under crisis: Presidential leadership, rhetoric, and media responses before and after the September 11th terrorist attacks. *Leadership Quarterly, 15*, 211–239; Bligh, M. C., Kohles, J. C., & Meindl, J. R. (2004). Charting the language of leadership: A methodological investigation of President Bush and the crisis of 9/11. *Journal of Applied Psychology, 89*, 562–572.

26. McCann, S. J. H. (1997). Threatening times and the election of charismatic U.S. presidents: With and without FDR. *Journal of Social Psychology, 131*, 393–400.

27. Meindl, J. R., et al. (1985). The romance of leadership. *Administrative Science Quarterly, 30*, 78–102.

28. Olson, L. (2007). *Troublesome young men: The rebels who brought Churchill to power and helped save England*. New York: Farrar, Straus & Giroux.

29. Shamir, B., & Howell, J. (1999). Organizational and contextual influences on the emergence and effectiveness of charismatic leadership. *Leadership Quarterly, 10*, 257–283.

30. Bligh, M. C., Kohles, J. C., & Pillai, R. (2005). Crisis and charisma in the California recall election. *Leadership, 1*, 323–352.

31. Gordijn, E. H., & Stapel, D. A. (2008). When controversial leaders are effective: The influence of terror on the need for vision and impact of mixed messages. *European Journal of Social Psychology, 38*, 389–411.

32. See Halverston, S., Murphy, E., & Riggio, E. E. (2004). Charismatic leadership in crisis situations: A laboratory investigation of stress and crisis. *Small Group Research, 35*, 495–514; Merolla, J. L., Ramos, J. M., & Zechmeister, E. J. (2006). Crisis, charisma and consequences: Evidence from the 2004 U.S. presidential election. *Journal of Politics, 69*, 30–42, respectively.

33. Zullow, H. M., & Seligman, M. E. P. (1990). Pessimistic rumination predicts defeat of presidential candidates, 1900 to 1984. *Psychological Inquiry, 1*, 52–51.

34. Owen, D. (2003). Diseased, demented, depressed: serious illness in heads of state. *QJM: An International Journal of Medicine, 96*, 325–336.

35. McDermott, R. (2008). *Presidential leadership, illness and decision making*. New York: Cambridge University Press.

36. Owen, D. (2007). *In sickness and in power*. New York: Methuen.
37. Freidel, F., & Sidey, H. (2006). *The presidents of the United States*. Retrieved from http://www.whitehouse.gov/about/presidents/dwightdeisenhower
38. Gibbs, N., & Duffy, M. (2012). *The president's club: Inside the world's most exclusive fraternity*. New York: Simon & Shuster.
39. Altman, L. K., & Purdum, T. S. (2002, November 17). In J.F.K. file, hidden illness, pain and pills. *New York Times*. Retrieved from http://www.latinamericanstudies.org/bay-of-pigs/kennedy-pills.htm; Dallek, R. (2003). *An unfinished life: John F. Kennedy, 1917–1963*. New York: Little Brown.
40. Gibbs, N., & Duffy, M. (2012). *The president's club: Inside the world's most exclusive fraternity*. New York: Simon & Shuster.
41. Beevor, A. (2012). At home with Hitler. *New York Review of Books,* April 26, 27–28.
42. Goodwin, D. K. (1969). *No ordinary time*. New York: Simon & Shuster.
43. Owen, D. (2006). Hubris and nemesis in heads of government. *Journal of the Royal Society of Medicine, 99*, 548–551; Owen, D. (2008). Hubris syndrome. *Clinical Medicine, 8*, 428–432.
44. Hiller, N. J., & Hambrick, D. C. (2005). Conceptualizing executive hubris: The role of (hyper-) core self-evaluations in strategic decision-making. *Strategic Decision-Making, 26*, 297–319.
45. Judge, T. A., & Bono, J. E. (2001). Relationship of core self-evaluation traits—self esteem, generalized self-efficacy, locus of control, and emotional stability—with job satisfaction and job performance: A meta-analysis. *Journal of Applied Psychology, 86*, 80–92.
46. Li, J., & Tang, Y. (2010). CEO hubris and firm risk taking in China: The moderating role of managerial discretion. *Academy of Management Journal, 53*, 45–68.
47. Hayward, M. L. A., & Hambrick, D. C. (1997). Explaining the premiums paid for large acquisitions: Evidence of CEO hubris. *Administrative Science Quarterly, 42*, 103–127.
48. Ghaemi, N. (2011). *A first-rate madness: Uncovering the links between leadership and mental illness*. New York: Penguin.
49. Bolger, R. (2001). The influence of leadership style on teacher job satisfaction. *Educational Administration Quarterly, 37*, 662–683.
50. Geijsel, F., Sleegers, P., Leithwood, K., & Jantzi, D. (2002). Transformational leadership effects on teachers' commitment and effort toward school reform. *Journal of Educational Administration, 41*, 228–256.
51. Ross, J. A., & Gray, P. (2006). Transformational leadership and teacher commitment to organizational values: The mediating effects of collective teacher efficacy. *School Effectiveness and Improvement, 17*(2), 179–199.
52. Ross, J. A., & Gray, P. (2006). Transformational leadership and teacher commitment to organizational values: The mediating effects of collective teacher efficacy. *School Effectiveness and Improvement, 17*(2), 179–199.
53. Nguni, S., Sleegers, P., & Denessen, E. (2006). Transformational and transactional leadership effects on teachers' job satisfaction, organizational commitment, and organizational citizenship behavior in primary schools: The Tanzanian case. *School Effectiveness and Improvement, 17*(2), 145–177.
54. Koh, W. L., Steers, R. M., & Terborg, J. R. (1995). The effects of transformational leadership on teacher attitudes and student performance in Singapore. *Journal of Organizational Behavior, 16*, 319–333.

55. Morton, K. L., Keith, S. E., & Beauchamp, M. R. (2010). Transformational teaching and physical activity: A new paradigm for adolescent health promotion? *Journal of Health Psychology, 15*, 248–257.

56. Beauchamp, M. R., Barling, J., Li, Z., Morton, K. L., Keith, S. E., & Zumbo, B. D. (2010). Development and psychometric properties of the transformational teaching questionnaire. *Journal of Health Psychology, 15*, 1123–1134.

57. Beauchamp, M. R., Barling, J., & Morton, K. (2011). Transformational teaching and adolescent self-determined motivation, self-efficacy, and intentions to engage in leisure time physical activity: A randomized controlled pilot trial. *Applied Psychology: Health and Well-Being, 3*, 127–150.

58. Beauchamp, M. R., Barling, J., & Morton, K. (2011). Transformational teaching and adolescent self-determined motivation, self-efficacy, and intentions to engage in leisure time physical activity: A randomized controlled pilot trial. *Applied Psychology: Health and Well-Being, 3*, 127–150.

59. Bennett, J. (Ed.) (1998). *Statistics in sport.* London: Arnold Publishing.

60. Bloom, M. (1999). The performance effects of pay dispersion on individuals and organizations. *Academy of Management Journal, 42*, 25–40.

61. Wolfe, R. A., Wieck, K. E., Usher, J. M., Terborg, J. R., Poppo, L., Murrell, A. J., et al. (2005). Sports and organizational studies: Exploring synergy. *Journal of Management Inquiry, 14*, 182–210.

62. Curtis, B., Smith, R. E., & Smoll, F. L. (1979). Scrutinizing the skipper: A study of leadership behavior in the dugout. *Journal of Applied Psychology, 64*, 391–400.

63. Bass, B. M., & Riggio, R. E. (2006). *Transformational leadership* (2nd ed.). Mahwah, NJ: Lawrence Erlbaum.

64. Beauchamp, M. R., Bray, S. R., Eys, M. A., & Carron, A. V. (2005). Leadership behaviors and multidimensional role ambiguity perceptions in team sports. *Small Group Research, 36*, 5–20.

65. Beehr, T.A., & Glazer, S. (2005). Organizational role stress. In J. Barling, E. K. Kelloway, & M. R. Frone (Eds.), *Handbook of work stress* (pp. 7–33). Thousand Oaks, CA: SAGE Publications.

66. Hoption, C., Phelan, J., & Barling, J. (2007). Transformational leadership in sport. In M. R. Beauchamp & M. A. Eys (Eds.) *Group dynamics in exercise and sport psychology: Contemporary themes* (pp. 45–60). New York: Routledge.

67. Doherty, A. J., & Danylchuk, K. E. (1996). Transformational and transactional leadership in interuniversity athletics management. *Journal of Sport Management, 10*, 292–309.

68. Yusof, A., & Mohd Shah, P. (2008). Transformational leadership and leadership substitutes in sports: Implications on coaches' job satisfaction. *International Bulletin of Business Administration, 3*, 17–29.

69. Doherty, A. J., & Danylchuk, K. E. (1996). Transformational and transactional leadership in interuniversity athletics management. *Journal of Sport Management, 10*, 292–309.

70. Judge, T. A., & Piccolo, R. F. (2004). Transformational and transactional leadership: A meta-analytic test of their relative validity. *Journal of Applied Psychology, 89*, 755–768; Kelloway, E. K., Muller, J., & Francis, L. (2006). Divergent effects of transformational and passive leadership on employee safety. *Journal of Occupational Health Psychology, 11*, 76–86.

71. Charbonneau, D., Barling, J., & Kelloway, E. K. (2001). Transformational leadership and sports performance: The mediating role of intrinsic motivation. *Journal of Applied Social Psychology, 31*, 1521–1534.

72. Zacharatos, A., Barling, J., & Kelloway, E. K. (2000). Development and effects of transformational leadership in adolescents. *Leadership Quarterly, 11*, 211–226.
73. Grusky, O. (1963). Managerial succession and organizational effectiveness. *American Journal of Sociology, 69*, 21–31.
74. Gamson, W. A., & Scotch, N. A. (1964). Scapegoating in baseball. *American Journal of Sociology, 69*, 69–72.
75. Dobson, S., & Goddard, J. (2011). *The economics of football* (2nd ed.) Cambridge, UK: Cambridge University Press.
76. Koning, R. H. (2003). An econometric evaluation of the firing of coach on team performance. *Applied Economics, 35*, 555–564.
77. Auerbach, R. (with Joe Fitzgerald). (1977). *Red Auerbach: An autobiography.* New York: Putnam's Sons; Riley, P. (1993). *The winner within.* New York: Putnam's Sons.
78. Grusky, O. (1963). Managerial succession and organizational effectiveness. *American Journal of Sociology, 69*, 21–31.

CHAPTER 8
Gender and Leadership

O f all the hot-button issues in leadership—and there are more than a few—perhaps none generate as much passion, and perhaps as little logic, as gender. Are women underrepresented in the ranks of organizational leadership? Are women's leadership abilities compromised because of family responsibilities? Do men make better leaders than women? A meaningful evaluation of socially charged questions such as these must be guided by the highest quality data rather than steadfast adherence to dogma. Fortunately, there is an abundance of scientific data from which to make reasoned judgments. In addition to governmental bodies in different countries charged with maintaining relevant data on this issue (e.g., Statistics Canada, Bureau of Labor Statistics in the United States) and peer-reviewed academic research, there are several private organizations such as Catalyst (established in 1962 to promote "the unused capacities of educated women who want to combine family and work"[1]) that make data available to researchers, policy makers, and the general public from which valuable lessons can be learned. It is to these credible sources that we turn for answers in this chapter.

Throughout this book, leader emergence (or role occupancy), leader behavior, and leader effectiveness have been differentiated wherever appropriate and again provide an ideal structure for our discussion of the broad question of gender and leadership. After addressing these three aspects of leadership, the chapter will end with a discussion of workplace interventions and legislative initiatives designed to move toward gender equality in organizational leadership.

LEADER EMERGENCE AND LEADER PREFERENCES

Before we address issues related to gender and leadership behavior or gender and leadership effectiveness, we need to establish how likely it is that women will emerge as leaders in the first place. Analysis of the extent to which men and women are represented in leadership positions within organizations provides some important lessons. One inescapable conclusion is that women are *still* underrepresented in leadership positions in organizations. This claim is appropriate because historically, women have simply not been welcomed into the upper echelons of organizations. Going back to 1972, only one Fortune 1000 company had a female CEO, with the legendary Katharine Graham heading the *Washington Post*. This changed when Marion O. Sandler assumed the role of CEO of Golden West Financial Corporation, in 1976, but we had to wait more than 10 years before the Warnaco Group appointed Linda Wachner as CEO, in 1987. A second point is that there has been some progress over the past few decades—but not much! By 2013, only 21 (4.2%) Fortune 500 companies were headed by a female CEO. The situation for Fortune 1000 organizations was no better: 45 of the Fortune 1000 companies (4.5%) had female CEOs (see Figure 8.1). This imbalance is reflected further with respect to underrepresentation of women on governance boards (discussed in greater detail at the end of this chapter).[2] Third, most of the available data examining gender and leader role occupancy focus on leaders at the highest echelons of organizations. While this precludes an understanding of the leadership situation throughout organizations, it does point to the fact women remain severely underrepresented in the most powerful organizational positions.

The data demonstrating that men and women are still not equally represented in leadership positions at all levels of the organization are by no means the end of the story—in fact, these data are just the beginning of a much more

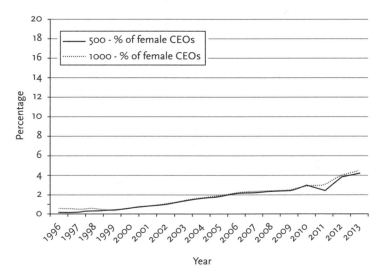

Figure 8.1
Percentage of women CEOs in Fortune 500 and Fortune 1000 companies, 1996–2013.

complex story. As will soon become apparent, despite these wide discrepancies, there are more subtle gender-based differences in leader role occupancy. Meta-analyses conducted by Alice Eagly and her colleagues will help unravel the results from a very large body of research.

Leader Role Emergence

Research investigating gender and leadership role occupancy has attracted attention for about 60 years. Indeed, Alice Eagly and Steven Karau identified no fewer than 75 laboratory and field studies on gender and leader emergence conducted between 1956 and 1988.[3] In order to make sense of this vast body of research, they limited their analyses to leader emergence in small groups that initially had no leader. Moreover, instead of focusing only on whether individuals emerged as leaders, they took a more nuanced view and studied leader emergence in different types of leadership roles (e.g., task vs. relationship oriented), in different leadership tasks (e.g., high or low in complexity; stereotypically masculine or feminine), and the context in which the data were collected (e.g., field settings or laboratory experiments). Their overall findings revealed a bias of moderate strength against women emerging as leaders in general. Further analyses indicated strongly that more nuanced interpretations were appropriate. For example, while men were more likely to occupy task-based and general leadership positions than women, women were more likely to hold leadership roles focused on social leadership. Further, women were also more likely to emerge as leaders when the tasks were high in social complexity and when groups were large (with men more likely to emerge as leaders of small groups), likely because social complexity increases as groups become larger.

Eagly and Karau also reported on a meta-analysis of the available laboratory studies, which were categorized according to whether the tasks took place in 20 minutes or less, lasted more than 20 minutes in a single session, or required participants to return for more than one session. This categorization enabled an interesting analysis of gender differences in leader emergence over time. The results of these analyses are certainly thought-provoking. In small groups, men were initially more likely to emerge as leaders than women, but women were more likely to emerge as leaders in situations where social interaction between participants increased over time. One explanation for these findings is that as participants gain additional information over time, decisions concerning whom to choose as leader are less dependent on gender stereotypes and more likely to be guided by objective evidence.

Two observations from these findings should be highlighted. First, even though the tendency to emerge as a leader was dependent on the situation, men remain more likely overall to emerge as leaders than women. Second, taken together, these findings suggest that there is not a simple undifferentiated preference for males, or a bias against females, emerging as leaders. Instead, not all leadership positions are perceived as equal, and men are disproportionately favored for those leadership positions perceived to be task-oriented (and hence more "masculine"), whereas female leaders were preferred for "feminine" tasks, which are perceived to be of lower status and attract lower compensation compared to male tasks. As a result, the notion that what we confront is not just a preference for male leaders but rather a bias against women leaders needs to be considered.

Despite this assessment, there may be some cause for optimism from two separate findings in Eagly and Karau's analyses. First, they analyzed all studies on gender and leader emergence between 1956 and 1988 and showed that across all studies during this time period, there was a statistically significant trend toward *less* discrimination against women leaders over time. Second, there was some evidence that younger individuals expressed less discrimination against women leaders than their older counterparts. While this paints a positive picture of the potential for continuing change over time, the studies being analyzed did not extend past 1988. Since then, there have been widespread social and economic changes, as well as some legislative initiatives advancing the role of women in the workplace. Thus more analyses are needed to guide judgments as to whether discrimination against female leaders persists.

The Glass Cliff

The conventional way in which gender and leader emergence has been understood is through the extent to which females attain leadership positions in the organization in the first place. But are there any situations in which females are preferred over men for leadership positions, over and above those already identified? The answer to this question is yes there are, but paradoxically, they again demonstrate a bias against female leaders.

In the first of a fascinating series of studies of gender and leadership, Michelle Ryan and Alex Haslam went beyond the familiar "glass ceiling"[i] and coined the term "glass cliff"[4] to describe the findings of their study of FTSE 100 companies in the United Kingdom in 2003. What they found was that women were significantly more likely than men to be appointed to the board of directors of companies that had witnessed a decline in performance over

---

i. The "glass ceiling" refers to barriers and difficulties that women encounter in rising to the top of organizations. The "glass cliff" refers to the disproportionately difficult situations in which women find themselves once they have attained senior organizational positions, difficulties that may not have been apparent initially.

the previous months.[5] Since their initial research, numerous studies have shed additional light on the invidious "glass cliff" phenomenon. We now know, for example, that when women do attain executive positions, they tend to experience more stress, enjoy less autonomy and job satisfaction, and receive fewer rewards for the same level of production than do their male counterparts, thus limiting the subsequent likelihood of success and promotional possibilities.[6] Relatedly, women are significantly more likely to leave management positions than men, and when they do choose to leave the organization they have the same reasons that male leaders have—just more of them.[7]

Research findings also show that business leaders and graduate management students (who presumably should know better) tend to view women as more appropriate for leadership positions in failing organizations, with business leaders believing that the demands of failing organizations fit women's unique leadership style, which stereotypically involves more listening, caring, and interpersonal sensitivity.[8] Similarly, when people were asked to identify the ideal traits for a leader of a poorly performing division,[9] they were more likely to "think crisis—think female," and identify stereotypically feminine characteristics as being more appropriate (e.g., good people management). Taken together, these findings help to explain why women are more likely to be selected for leadership positions in failing situations.

Additional support for the existence of the glass cliff has emerged from a very different study by Ryan, Haslam, and Tom Postmes.[10] After reading an online news report about the glass cliff in the business and political section of the BBC Web site, respondents answered questions about the glass cliff and why they believed it existed. The results are revealing, if not disturbing. Women believed that other women would be more likely to be appointed to precarious positions. At the same time, men also believed that other men would be appointed to precarious positions as well—despite this being inconsistent with actual practice. Thus, while women were aware of the bias inherent in the glass cliff phenomenon, men either were not aware of this bias or would not acknowledge it. In addition, women were more likely than men to see the glass cliff phenomenon as a problem, as unfair, and as a function of sexism. Comments from a male and female respondent in this study aptly reflect the overall findings. A female professional remarked, "I think when a cushy job comes up, the old boys' network set-up means that men select their friends for the position. When none of their chums want the job, it gets given to the woman" (p. 189). In contrast, a male middle manager suggested, "Maybe they're the best candidate at the time for the role? Whether they're male or female shouldn't come into it. Just their ability to do the job" (p. 192).

The glass cliff phenomenon is not restricted to work organizations; the same bias against women leaders extends to the political sphere. Again reflecting on the proportion of men and women in leadership positions, as of 2013, astonishingly few women (22.5%) had been elected to parliament in the

United Kingdom,[11] the Canadian parliament (24.6%),[12] and the U.S. House of Representatives (18%) and Senate (20%).[13] And these numbers are not atypical. David Hough notes that Britain ranks in the middle of the 27 European Union Countries in terms of female representation (15/27), and only slightly better (65th) when compared with 190 countries with a parliamentary system.[14] Together with their colleague Clara Kulich, Ryan and Haslam took a novel approach to understanding this phenomenon, focusing on electoral districts in which candidates competed in the 2005 general election in the United Kingdom.[15] They showed that even when women were nominated as candidates, it was most likely to be in competitions for significantly more precarious seats. This trend was most pronounced in the Conservative Party, in which women were nominated in districts where the rival Labour Party had a stranglehold, such that a victory by the female candidate would require an almost unheard of swing of 26% in the electoral vote.

A corollary of the glass cliff is the suggestion that female leaders are more likely to fall from grace than their male counterparts; in other words, the standards for holding onto their positions are more rigorous for women leaders. This is supported by research showing that when faced with poor employee performance, male leaders are more likely to find themselves on probation rather than being fired. In contrast, for female leaders, being fired was a more likely consequence for poor performance than being placed on probation.[16]

These findings are important because, like other studies discussed in this chapter, they reinforce the fact that the bias against women leaders is nuanced. It is not gender alone, but the way in which a leaders' gender interacts with characteristics of the organization, the task, and the leadership role that result in bias against women becoming leaders in the first instance—and retaining that position thereafter. Research investigating the glass cliff phenomenon now shows that we also need to consider the organization's prior financial performance, to understand fully any bias inherent in decisions regarding the selection of senior leaders in organizations.

Investors and the Emergence of Female Leaders

The research findings discussed so far point to a bias against installing female leaders by individuals *within* the organization. There could also be a bias against selecting female leaders among individuals outside of the organization, in particular, individuals with sufficient power to influence internal organizational decisions. The investor community has the power to influence senior selection decisions—and they do. As a result, whether investors believe that women leaders add the same value to the organization as do male leaders becomes a critical question. If board members are held accountable for the market value of the organization, they might be reluctant to hire a female CEO if the they believe that the decision would affect investor confidence in the organization's future, and hence in its market value.

Adding to this challenging situation for investors, selection of a new CEO usually occurs at a time of uncertainty, when poor-performing CEOs are being replaced, high-performing CEOs are leaving voluntarily, or the change is sudden and unexpected (e.g., illness or sudden death of the current CEO). This makes for an interesting context in which to investigate prejudice against female CEOs, as the speed with which the market responds reduces the possibility that a rational evaluation of the benefits of the specific leader has taken place. Instead, any immediate response of the stock market to the announcement of a female CEO is more likely to be guided by the most visible characteristics—such as gender—increasing the possibility of reactive unconscious prejudice.

Several studies have investigated how the stock market responds to the announcement that a woman has been appointed to the position of CEO. Peggy Lee and Erika James studied several different aspects of 2,555 announcements of a new CEO (and their top-management teams) in publicly traded companies between 1990 and 2000.[17] As they had predicted, there was a bias against women CEOs, inasmuch as stock market reactions to the announcement of female CEOs were significantly more negative than announcements about male CEOs over the same time period. Because media writers choose the tone of their stories conveying such news, their role is pivotal in the subsequent judgments of the shareholder community. Thus, Lee and James also examined whether any bias existed in media stories about new CEOs, and their results again identified a significant bias against female leaders. Their textual analysis showed that reports of the new CEO emphasized the CEO's gender, but only if the CEO was a woman. For female CEOs, reference to their gender was the third most important theme in the story, but for the group of male CEOs, it was the 64th most important theme! Lee and James extended their analysis and showed that references to family were also significantly more prominent in media reports about female CEOs than those about male CEOs (ranked 9th vs. 53rd, respectively). Differences in the extent to which family is discussed in these stories are also important, as this topic perpetuates stereotypes that women devote more time to family responsibilities than their male counterparts, thereby seeming to justify the bias against hiring female leaders and potentially influencing selection decisions.

Two additional findings from Lee and James' study warrant attention. First, the negative stock market response to the appointment of female CEOs was greater than the negative response to the appointment of females to top management. Presumably, the more consequential the role, the less women are perceived to be likely to fill the role successfully, and the greater the bias. Second, the stock market response to women from within the organization assuming the position of CEO was significantly less negative than for the appointment of female CEOs from outside of the organization. The probable reason for this is that in the case of female insiders, investors assume that the newly appointed female CEO has more relevant experience and more specific information about the organization and the industry at her disposal. Thus, investors are less likely to resort to unfounded stereotypes when they have access to more information, or they believe the decisions to be less critical to organizational functioning.

Further understanding of the bias against female leaders derives from a different study on stock market responses to the announcement of women's selection into senior organizational positions, between 1991 and 2006.[18] Alison Cook and Christy Glass' analyses showed no overall negative effects on stock market value following the appointment of senior female leaders. However, similar to the results of Eagly and Karau's meta-analysis,[19] the stock market responded positively to announcements of women assuming top-level positions in stereotypically female-dominated organizations, and responded negatively when women assumed top-level positions in stereotypically male-dominated organizations. Reinforcing conclusions about the existence of a gender bias against appointing female CEOs, negative responses did not emerge in Glass and Cook's analyses to the appointment of male CEOs to male- or female-dominated organizations.

Gender Bias and the Motivation to Lead

Men are more likely to be appointed to leadership positions than women—especially in male-dominated industries, organizations, or occupations, or over tasks perceived as masculine. Any understanding of why fewer women are in leadership positions would remain incomplete, however, if we did not go further and highlight the insidious psychological and self-perpetuating effects of this bias. Women clearly see this bias operating, as was evident from the study by Ryan, Haslam, and Postmes mentioned earlier,[20] and as a result, some women become less interested in assuming leadership positions in organizations. Understanding how this bias can affect women's motivation to lead, and what psychologists refer to as "stereotype threat," will help to explain this.

As women survey their prospects for promotion and notice the obstacles that must be overcome because of their gender, their motivation to manage or to lead might become negatively affected. In a recent study conducted in the United States and Spain, male and female participants (all of whom were non-leaders) were asked to imagine themselves assuming a mid-management, top-level, or CEO position, either in an auto manufacturing or clothing manufacturing organization.[21] Replicating earlier findings showing the importance of the gendered nature of the task,[22] males were more likely to envisage themselves as leaders in the auto manufacturing organization, and females were more likely to see themselves as leaders of the clothing manufacturing organization. In addition, both males and females viewed the prospect of becoming CEO of either of these organizations positively—but women saw this as very unlikely to actually happen. Thus, young girls see their future selves in organizations as confronting discrimination, for example, when they see themselves as deserving less pay than young boys for the same work.[23] Faced with such obstacles, which are not relevant for their male counterparts, at least some women's motivation to lead might be diminished.

This is not the only way in which women's motivation to lead might be compromised. Psychologists have noted how "stereotype threat"—the corrosive effects of being concerned that one might "live up" to the negative stereotypes held about one's group identity—can adversely affect personal aspirations. The classic laboratory study that launched the research on stereotype threat was conducted by Claude Steele and Joshua Aronson, and showed that simply asking African Americans to think of their social identities before performing a verbal task negatively affected their performance on that task.[24] Similarly, young girls reminded of the negative stereotype about females' gender and math performance before a math test perform more poorly on that test than do young boys.[25] Additional support for this negative effect comes from a study conducted in Germany which showed that young women were more likely to attribute their failure on a computer task to their lack of skills, while men were more likely to attribute the cause of any failure to computer problems.[26]

Extending these findings to the leadership context, we now know that stereotype threat influences women's aspirations for leadership positions. In research conducted in Canada, women (but not men) who viewed gender-stereotypic TV commercials that made no reference to leadership (e.g., a female college student daydreaming about being a homecoming queen), subsequently chose to avoid a leadership position of higher status in favor of taking on a lower-status, problem-solving role that had no leadership responsibilities.[27] As a result, stereotype threat can limit women's motivation and self-confidence to lead. The Economist points to research conducted by Hewlett-Packard which illustrates the effects of stereotype threat in practice. This research showed that men are willing to apply for positions if they believe they have at least 60% of the job requirements, whereas women only tend to apply for positions when they believe that they are perfectly suited (i.e., meet 100% of the job requirements).[28] In the extent to which this is true of leadership positions, stereotype threat could harm women's motivation to lead and contribute further to the underrepresentation of female leaders in work organizations.

To conclude this section, a large body of research shows that there is still a preference for male leaders, or more likely a bias against women leaders. As a result, women are less likely than their male counterparts to emerge as leaders, find themselves in the upper echelons of organizations, and even retain their positions of leadership. When they are selected for senior leadership positions, it may well be in more precarious situations where there is a lowered likelihood of success. All of these factors might contribute to negatively affecting some women's motivation to lead in the first instance. The existence of such a bias, however, tells us nothing about gender differences in actual leadership behaviors, and it is to this issue that we now turn.

LEADERSHIP BEHAVIOR

Whether there are differences in the leadership behaviors of men and women is a critical issue. If males do behave in ways that are more suited to organizational leadership compared to their female counterparts, perhaps the preference for male leaders could be justified by some people? Alternatively, if women lead in ways that are more aligned with organizational effectiveness, the folly of any bias against women leaders would be exposed.

Why might we even expect gender differences in leadership behaviors? Perhaps the most logical reason to expect gender differences in leadership behaviors are socialization differences between the sexes that start at infancy. For example, parents in one study described their newborn daughters as more feminine, and their infant sons as stronger.[29] Add to this the early expectations of what constitutes appropriate gender-role behavior (e.g., from preschool caregivers) and evidence that in play groups, very young boys and girls engage in different social and interpersonal behaviors for which they are differentially rewarded.[30] It should not be surprising, therefore, that researchers had already widely accepted that meaningful gender differences existed in social skills and behaviors by the mid-1980s. Alice Eagly and Blair Johnson summarized what was known when they concluded in 1990 that "Women as a group, when compared with men as a group, can be described as friendly, pleasant, interested in other people, expressive, and socially sensitive" (p. 235).[31] If this is the case, it would not be unreasonable to expect that by the time men and women emerge as organizational leaders, they bring with them to the workplace a different set of social skills, interests, and behaviors that will be reflected in how any leadership behaviors are expressed.

More recently, Shelley Taylor and her colleagues have indirectly bolstered the argument for gender differences in leadership behaviors. In a major challenge to conventional wisdom, they argued that the well-known "fight-or-flight" response to stress may be gendered and most characteristic of male behavior under stress. In its place, they contend, under stress, females would be more disposed to "tend and befriend."[32] In developing this idea, Taylor and her coauthors point out that we have long known that there are major gender differences in behaviors such as aggression but have been slow to study differences in behaviors such as affiliation with the same intensity.[33] When such research has been conducted, gender-based differences do emerge. For example, research conducted by Stanley Schachter in the 1950s showed that when stressed, women prefer to affiliate with others, while men do not.[34] Given the stress that male and female leaders experience at work (e.g., external pressure, time deadlines, financial restraints, interpersonal conflicts), any differential tendency toward fight-or-flight or tend-and-befriend might affect the expression of many leadership behaviors, such as autocratic vs. participative behaviors, task vs. relationship orientation, and the tendency toward passive or laissez-faire leadership on the one hand, or the emotional support that characterizes individualized consideration on the other.

Social pressures on leaders might further magnify gender differences in leadership behaviors. As noted earlier in this chapter, leadership continues to be viewed as masculine, with male leaders engaging in agentic behaviors more than their female counterparts.[35] When women do enact gender-incongruent agentic-type behaviors, not only are they are evaluated less positively than male leaders,[36] but they are likely to be punished in any number of formal (e.g., failure to obtain deserved promotions, pay discrimination, poor performance evaluations) or informal (e.g., ostracism, disrespect) ways, what Alice Eagly and Linda Carli refer to as a classic "double bind" situation.[37] Providing support for this notion, Madeline Heilman and her colleagues showed that when women succeeded in stereotypically male endeavors (e.g., becoming Assistant Vice President of Human Resources in the Financial Planning Division), they were liked less and their competence was questioned.[38] Similar effects did not emerge when women were seen to be successful in roles that were congruent with gender-role stereotypes, in this case becoming Assistant Vice President of Human Resources with responsibilities for employee assistance.

The question of what happens when women violate gender-role expectations was studied further by Madeline Heilman and Julie Chen, who focused on the consequences of engaging in voluntary helping behaviors in the workplace.[39] In an article appropriately entitled "Same Behavior, Different Consequences," Heilman and Chen showed that men were rated more favorably than women and were more likely to be recommended for a promotion, pay increase, and involvement in a valued project if they helped another employee in a difficult situation. In contrast, women did not benefit in the same way from the same voluntary helping behaviors, which were seen as consistent with their gender role and hence required rather than optional.

Jennifer Berdahl's research shows just how pervasive the informal punishment for women's success can be.[40] Based on a laboratory study and three surveys conducted in the United States, Berdahl dismissed the notion that sexual harassment is primarily a function of sexual desire. Instead, her research showed that women she referred to as "uppity" women (i.e., women who were more dominant, aggressive, and assertive) and who deviated from gender-role expectations were punished for these deviations and became significantly more likely to be the target of gender and sexual harassment than women who mirror stereotypically feminine characteristics (e.g., attractiveness). Thus, given the substantial formal and informal punishments for out-of-role behaviors, women leaders themselves might decide to suppress any expression of agentic leadership behavior. Everyday organizational reality may make it less likely that women would behave in an agentic manner, increasing differences in the behaviors of men and women leaders in organizations.

But what do empirical studies tell us about gender and leadership behaviors? Fortunately, there are countless studies from which evidenced-based conclusions can be justified. Some studies (usually those conducted earlier) focused on gender differences in democratic and task-oriented leadership, with later studies focusing more on transformational and transactional leadership. Our discussion will address these separately. Two large-scale meta-analytic investigations are particularly instructive.

Democratic, Autocratic, and Task-Oriented Leadership

The first of these two large-scale meta-analyses was based on 162 studies conducted between 1961 and 1987. Its authors examined whether there were gender differences in task-oriented, interpersonally oriented, or democratic vs. autocratic leadership styles.[41] The first interesting finding was that the expression of these three leadership behaviors differed in a way that was consistent with gender-role stereotypes. Specifically, men tended to be more task-oriented and more autocratic, while female leaders were more relationship-oriented and more democratic. Any gender differences were most pronounced on the democratic vs. autocratic leadership dimensions. As was the case with analyses for leader emergence, however, overall conclusions such as these conceal more interesting nuances in the findings.

Eagly and Johnson delved further into these studies and found support for the notion that in some situations, women voluntarily suppress male-oriented leadership behaviors. Specifically, although women's leadership styles were more interpersonal and democratic than men's, any such differences became *less* pronounced when women were leading groups with a greater proportion of males. Thus, gender differences in these leadership styles do exist, but are suppressed by women when selection procedures and socialization practices (e.g., informal punishments) ensure that expectations for appropriate and adequate leadership performance are conveyed and obeyed. Female leaders pay a price for being in gender-incongruent situations in which their leadership and gender-based roles conflict with each other.

Another finding from this meta-analysis warrants attention. As was the case with the research on gender and leader role emergence, the nature of the task performed affects gendered expressions of leadership. Despite the perception that task-oriented leadership is a male prerogative, female leaders remained more task-oriented than their male counterparts in situations where the leader role was seen as more appropriate for women, or perceived as needing interpersonal skills for successful task completion. Again, therefore, while predictable gender differences exist in the expression of task, interpersonal, and democratic vs. autocratic leadership styles, contextual factors (e.g., the nature of the organization, task) could motivate women to suppress the expression of agentic leadership behaviors.

Transformational, Transactional, and Laissez-Faire Leadership

As is evident throughout this book, transformational leadership has attracted a disproportionate share of scientific attention, and this is no less the case in analyses of the effects of gender and leadership. As a result, we can ask whether we might expect to find differences between male and female leaders in terms of their transformational, transactional, and laissez-faire behaviors. More than a decade after the meta-analysis just discussed, Alice Eagly, Mary Johannesen-Schmidt, and Marloes van Engen turned their attention to gender differences in transformational, transactional, and laissez-faire leadership behaviors and conducted another meta-analytic study.[42]

Eagly and her colleagues suggested that we could expect gender differences because transformational leadership de-emphasizes hierarchy and the notion of command-and-control, and because women are socialized in a way that emphasizes communal behaviors, which would then predispose women toward greater expression of the four transformational leadership behaviors. For example, going beyond one's own needs for the benefit of the organization and its members (the hallmark of idealized influence and inspirational motivation) is consistent with a communal rather than agentic orientation. Similarly, the emphasis on high-quality relationships that characterizes individualized consideration might again be more consistent with the way in which women are socialized.

In general, the findings from the 45 studies conducted between 1985 and 2002 confirmed the existence of gender differences. As a group, women leaders scored higher on all four components of transformational leadership (idealized influence, inspirational motivation, intellectual stimulation, and individualized consideration) and contingent reward. In contrast, male leaders as a group scored higher on management-by-exception and laissez-faire behaviors, though conclusions from these findings should be tempered somewhat, as there were fewer studies investigating these components. These findings can be considered robust for several reasons. First, unlike prior analyses already discussed, there were very few exceptions to this pattern of results.

Second, recall from Chapter 2 that transformational leadership is associated with more positive employee and organizational outcomes, while laissez-faire leadership is associated with adverse outcomes. Nonetheless, in interpreting the meaning of these findings, it should be noted that the magnitude of the gender differences in transformational and transactional leadership across the 45 studies was modest. However, as the authors note, even modest differences can have meaningful effects on organizational success when repeated over many individuals and situations.

Several aspects of the finding that, on average, women leaders displayed more transformational leadership than their male counterparts, while male leaders displayed more management-by-exception and laissez faire behaviors than female leaders, warrant mention. First, the largest difference of the four transformational leadership components emerged for individualized consideration, which seems consistent with young girls' early gender-role socialization. Second, Eagly and colleagues' analyses showed that over the period for which data were available for this meta-analysis (1985–2002), the tendency for women leaders to enact more transformational leadership than their male counterparts *increased*. One possible explanation for this is that as the proportion of female leaders increased during this same period (see Figure 8.1), it became a little less risky for female leaders to deviate from gender-role and organizational expectations.

A third aspect worth mentioning is that, limiting the analyses to data collected in Canada and the United States, the female advantage in transformational leadership was greater in Canada than in the United States, and this is consistent with findings from the multi-country GLOBE leadership project. The relatively individualistic nature of the United States[43] compared with the more collectivist nature within Canada likely means that expression of the more communally based transformational leadership overall, and by women leaders specifically, is more likely to be accepted in Canada, accounting for the greater advantage for female transformational leaders in Canada.

Other more recent studies have probed even further and add to our understanding of gender differences in transformational leadership. One study by Claartje Vinkenburg, van Engen, Eagly, and Johannesen-Schmidt examined the consequences of gender stereotypes about transformational leadership.[44] In their first study of U.S. and Dutch employees (most of whom had managerial experience), participants' stereotypes regarding gender differences in the four transformational leadership behaviors, contingent reward, and laissez-faire leadership styles were accurate. With one exception (i.e., inspirational motivation), these participants' stereotypes about gender differences in transformational and transactional leadership were consistent with the actual differences described above.

This first study details how people think male and female leaders *do* behave. Vinkenburg and her team took this further in a second study, in which they investigated how people believe female leaders *should* behave to warrant a promotion. Because some of the transformational components are perceived as more agentic (viz. idealized influence, inspirational motivation), and others like individualized consideration are more communal, they investigated whether the expression of transformational leadership behaviors perceived to be out-of-role might compromise women's quest for promotion. All four transformational leadership behaviors and contingent reward (but neither management-by-exception nor laissez-faire) behavior were seen as important for promotion, irrespective of leader gender, by the Dutch and American participants in their study, most of whom had managerial experience. Of the four transformational behaviors, inspirational motivation was viewed as most important for promotion, somewhat more so for men than for women. Individualized consideration was seen as most important for women's promotion. Thus, while recognizing the inherent conflict in roles and double burden placed on women leaders who must display the agentic behaviors of inspirational motivation and the communal behaviors of individualized consideration (while men need only to emphasize agentic inspiration), the researchers suggest that men seeking promotion need to show strength, whereas women seeking similar promotions would need to show both strength and sensitivity.[45]

Further evidence for the notion that female leaders are punished for out-of-role behaviors comes from intriguing research on physical attractiveness. There is consistent support for the notion that physically attractive people enjoy higher educational attainment (possibly because of larger social networks, more social support, and high expectations, which can set up a Pygmalion effect, discussed in Chapter 5) and, subsequently, greater career success.[46] However, the benefits of physical attractiveness for women in organizations do not extend to leadership. One study conducted in Germany showed that despite broad evidence for the positive benefits of physical attractiveness within organizations (e.g., greater earning capacity), physically attractive female leaders suffer negative consequences.[47] In this study, Susanne Braun, Claudia Peus, and Dieter Frey showed that followers expressed less trust in and loyalty toward attractive female transformational leaders than followers of unattractive female transformational leaders. In contrast, attractive male transformational leaders were rated more positively than unattractive male transformational leaders, providing support for the "beauty is beastly" effect.[48] Supporting this interpretation, similar effects did not emerge for transactional leadership. Thus, there is a subtle but significant bias against attractive female transformational leaders, whereas male transformational leaders accrue the benefits of physical attractiveness, again showing how female leaders are punished when they do not conform with gender-based stereotypes.

In concluding this discussion on gender differences and leadership styles and behaviors, a paradox emerges. While men are more likely to hold and retain positions of organizational leadership, women leaders as a whole are more likely to enact the leadership behaviors that lead to the outcomes that organizations seek. This does not mean that all female leaders exhibit the four transformational leadership behaviors more than their male counterparts, nor that all male leaders display management-by-exception and laissez-faire behaviors more than their female counterparts. Nonetheless, social biases and pressures leave women less likely to emerge as leaders and more likely to suppress the very leadership behaviors most associated with positive outcomes. This situation raises some very difficult questions for organizations, which will be considered later in this chapter.

LEADERSHIP EFFECTIVENESS

In our discussion thus far, we have found that women continue to face more barriers in assuming leadership roles in organizations, and their leadership style is more transformational than that of their male counterparts. To fully understand the intersection of gender on leadership, one more question needs to be asked, and that is whether there are any differences in the effectiveness of male and female leaders. As organizations search for the most effective leaders, this is a question of great practical importance. Any of three possible scenarios could prevail.

First, male leaders might be more effective than female leaders. One reason this might occur is explained by social role theory,[49] which suggests that people's behavior will conform to the way in which gender-role expectations are constructed in their groups and societies. This presents challenges for female leaders, who face different and a greater number of external pressures than male leaders, and are devalued (and punished) for exhibiting "out-of-role" behavior (i.e., perceived as more masculine).[50] Add to this the fact that women experience prejudice after assuming leadership positions. A frequently cited example of this is the continuing pay gap between male and female leaders holding equivalent positions, which is made all the more stressful for women leaders, as compensation for male executives is more directly contingent on performance than it is for female executives,[51] leaving them with a diminished sense of control. In addition, the stress experienced when one's gender and organizational roles conflict is associated with poorer health and compromised organizational performance.[52] As a result, women leaders likely confront a unique set of stressors not experienced by their male counterparts, all of which could impede their leadership effectiveness.

However, it is also possible that there are no differences in the effectiveness of male and female leaders. Underlying this proposition is what Eagly and Karau refer to as the structural position,[53] which holds that sufficient information regarding optimal leadership behaviors is available and conveyed to employees, minimizing other expectations that convey contrary or erroneous information. These explicit role prescriptions do not act in isolation and are bolstered by personal expectations about appropriate leadership behavior. Taken together, these formal and informal expectations would be sufficient to minimize any gender biases and prejudice against women leaders. In addition, it is also possible that women are more effective leaders, but because this capability threatens the gendered status quo, they are purposefully kept away from positions of power.

Finally, there is also good reason to believe that women might be more effective as leaders than men, an argument that rests ironically on the biases against selecting women leaders in the first place. Given all the pressures faced by female leaders, it is possible that only the most skilled women enter the selection competition[54] or survive the leadership selection process, which might not be as true for men. It is also possible that with the prevailing biases against women leaders, women who are less confident voluntarily remove themselves from the competition for a leadership position. Taken together, this would mean that only the more confident and skilled women become leaders. Also, given that, on average, women leaders display more transformational leadership behaviors than male leaders, and transformational leadership is consistently associated with an array of important organizational outcomes, women may well be more effective than male leaders.

Sufficient research has been conducted to enable an evidenced-based answer to the question of whether women or men are more effective leaders. An earlier meta-analysis conducted by Eagly, Karau, and Mona Makhijani[55] provides the basis for understanding the relative effectiveness of male and female leaders. At first glance, the results of this meta-analysis appear to suggest that there are no differences in the extent to which men and women are effective leaders. However, additional analyses highlight a more nuanced and interesting pattern of results, many of which are consistent with earlier findings regarding gender and leader emergence, and leader behavior.

First, differences in the effectiveness of male and female leaders were again dependent on contextual factors, the first of which was the outcome measure under consideration. Males were rated consistently as more effective when the leadership role was masculine in nature, while female leaders were rated as more effective when the leadership role was more feminine in nature. For example, male leaders were more effective in military organizations, where there is a long-standing preference for male leaders. In contrast, female leaders were more effective in the educational and public sectors and in social service organizations. Female leaders were also perceived to be more effective when the leadership role was judged as requiring interpersonal skills and cooperation. In contrast, male leaders were rated as more effective in line positions. Female leaders also performed better than male leaders in middle-management positions, which is consistent with the perception that line management is mostly task-oriented, while middle-management requires interpersonal skills to coordinate and motivate others to be effective. Finally, an important indicator of gendered workplace culture is the extent to which men predominate numerically over women. Male leaders were also rated as more effective than female leaders in male-dominated groups. Taken together, these findings strengthen the general conclusion that context is critical, and that there is a nuanced preference for male leaders and a bias against female leaders.

Within the psychological domain, numerous laboratory studies have been conducted evaluating the relative effectiveness of men and women leaders. A major benefit of these laboratory studies is their ability to control extraneous factors (e.g., leader age, experience) that could limit any conclusions from the research. Eagly, Makhijani, and Bruce Klonsky conducted a meta-analysis of the findings of 61 laboratory studies that focused on how leaders are evaluated.[56] Like the findings of the earlier meta-analysis, men were not uniformly rated more favorably. Instead, confirming the findings of earlier research, contextual factors such as the nature of the organization, leadership role, and task were again important in determining whether a bias emerged against female leaders. First, the nature of the organization influenced how female leaders were evaluated. Male leaders were evaluated more positively in organizations typically perceived as male-dominated, such as business, manufacturing, and athletic organizations. Second, confirming the notion that leadership itself is seen as being gender-typed, male leaders were rated more favorably than female leaders when the leadership style was perceived as (a) masculine more than feminine, (b) autocratic, and (c) occupied more typically by men.

In concluding this section, several points regarding differences in effectiveness between male and female leaders are appropriate. First, and of great practical significance, there are no overall differences in effectiveness. As Alice Eagly and her colleagues concluded on the basis of their 1995 meta-analysis,[57] "Female and male leaders did not differ in effectiveness. This finding is important in applied terms because it suggests that, despite barriers and possible handicaps in functioning as leaders, the women who actually serve as leaders...are in general succeeding as well as their male counterparts" (p. 137). Second, any differences that do emerge in the rated effectiveness of male and female leaders are the consequences of prejudices and stereotypes about gender and leadership in general, rather than any inherent sex-based differences in leadership effectiveness. As a result, any argument that organizations will compromise their potential for success by selecting female leaders simply cannot be sustained by the available data. In fact, the opposite is true: Organizations will continue to limit the size and quality of the available leadership talent pool until they free themselves of informal cultures, symbolic communications, and formal structures that discourage women from seeking or holding leadership positions for which they are qualified (and sometimes, more than qualified).[58]

DOES THE BIAS AGAINST FEMALE LEADERS PERSIST?

Most of the studies analyzed in the meta-analyses reviewed above were conducted before 2000, sometimes well before 2000. Given major social changes in many countries, the question of whether a similar bias persists today requires an answer. Several recent studies suggest that the bias continues. First, an online survey posted on the MSNBC Web site in 2011 in the United States inviting participants to "rate your boss" attracted an enormous response: Just over 60,000 participants completed the survey (51% of whom were males),[59] providing some very useful insights. Of those who indicated a gendered preference, male leaders were preferred by more than two-thirds of the respondents. Support for the notion that this lingering preference for male leaders constitutes prejudice against women leaders derives from two additional aspects of these findings. First, respondents preferred a male leader because they devalued women leaders. Second, and even more telling, the bias toward male leaders was strongest among respondents who reported that they had never worked for a female leader!

A separate study on the perceived suitability of men and women for different leadership roles provides additional support for the notion that the gender bias persists today. Geoffrey Ho reported on a laboratory study with Margaret Shih and Daniel Walters in 2012, in which they showed that male leaders were more likely to emerge when the task under completion was introduced as a "building project"; but when the identical project was presented as an "art project," females were more likely to emerge into a leadership position.[60] The conclusion that this reflects a bias is reinforced because the same pattern of gendered preferences again emerged with a separate group, in which the same task was described as either a "knot-tying task" or a "hair-braiding task."

Finally, in 2008, Madeline Heilman and Tyler Okimoto investigated whether there is a specific bias against mothers.[61] To do so, they devised an experiment in which their participants rated the perceived competence and commitment of job applicants who were described as either male or female, parents or not, and also provided recommendations as to whether the applicant should be hired for the position of "Assistant VP." Regardless of whether these ratings were completed by undergraduate psychology or full-time employees currently pursuing an MBA degree, both parents were rated as lower on future commitment and competence; this effect was markedly worse for mothers than for fathers. Not surprisingly, mothers were recommended for the position substantially less than fathers or non-parents. Importantly, this discrimination is even greater against pregnant women.[62] In suggesting that a bias still exists against women leaders, the findings from these studies provide support for the existence of what Joan Williams has referred to as "the maternal wall," the tendency for women's progression to be blocked either when they become pregnant, become mothers, or choose to work on some form of alternative work schedule.[63]

Thus, in answer to the question of whether the bias against women leaders persists today, we cannot avoid an affirmative answer. In the next section, we turn our attention to two broad initiatives to confront this bias against women leaders.

INTERVENTIONS FOR A GENDER-DIVERSE LEADERSHIP

What then can be done to overcome this bias against female leaders and leave organizations better equipped to confront the need for high-quality leadership? There is a plethora of suggested interventions in the literature,[64] so many that discussing them all is just not feasible. Instead, we will limit our discussion to the small proportion of interventions and initiatives that have been subjected to some research scrutiny. These include workplace initiatives (e.g., diversity training, family-friendly and human resource practices, and mentorship programs) and intriguing (and no doubt controversial) legislative initiatives.

Workplace Initiatives

Minimizing Stereotype Threat

Given that women may be disinclined to seek leadership positions in organizations in the first instance, initiatives are needed that overcome this early barrier to leadership entry. Potentially useful lessons on eliminating motivational disincentives to seek leadership positions derive from Paul Davies, Steven Spencer, and Claude Steele's research on stereotype threat.[65] As noted earlier, they first confirmed that women's aspirations for leadership suffer when they fear that any personal leadership failures would confirm stereotypes that women are less suited to leadership roles than men. These researchers followed this investigation with a separate study in which one group of participants was exposed to what the researchers called "identity safety," in an attempt to nullify these negative effects. The participants read a brief passage which emphasized strongly that despite much "controversy in psychology surrounding the issue of gender-based differences in leadership and problem-solving ability... our research has revealed absolutely no gender differences in either ability" (p. 281) on the task they were soon to complete.

All participants were then required to indicate whether they would prefer to assume the role of leader or problem-solver. Their findings demonstrated conclusively that any negative effects of stereotype threat on aspirations for the leadership role were "completely eliminated" (p. 283) when participants read the sentence quoted above. The lessons from these findings for management are potentially huge: Reinforcing a consistent finding throughout the book, small interventions might go a long way toward allaying fears or encouraging leadership aspirations among women in organizations. In addition, the notion that greater information can reduce stereotypes, including those against pregnant women in the workplace,[66] is supported. Thus, these findings beg the question of whether similar statements might be used in recruitment efforts to increase the quantity and quality of external female applicants for leadership positions.

Diversity Training

Diversity training is among the most frequently used initiatives by organizations to combat gender biases. It is often mandatory, at least for some individuals in the organization (e.g., those involved in hiring decisions). Estimates suggest that as many as two-thirds of U.S. organizations offer some form of diversity training,[67] with some researchers concerned that the sheer extent of diversity training in organizations exceeds the capacity of organizational practitioners to absorb all the lessons.[68]

One recent study is particularly useful in integrating the findings of prior research. Zachary Kalinoski and his team conducted a meta-analysis of 65 research articles involving 8,465 participants that had been published since the Civil Rights Act was passed in the United States in 1964.[69] Overall, they showed that diversity training was effective in changing attitudes, cognition, and skills. Specific features of their findings provide even more useful and encouraging information. First, while diversity training affected attitudes positively, the effects on participants' self-efficacy beliefs were even more pronounced, an important finding given that self-efficacy beliefs predict very diverse employee behaviors.[70] Second, the researchers showed that diversity training was most beneficial when it (a) provided participants greater opportunities for social interaction, (b) was delivered in person rather than via computer, and (c) took place for four hours or more over several days rather than in a single session. In addition, diversity training was more effective when delivered by the participants' direct supervisor rather than by an outsider (e.g., someone from Human Resources), presumably because it signaled that the organization attached greater importance to the training initiative. Third, contrary to concerns about the effectiveness of mandatory counseling,[71] mandatory and voluntary training were equally effective. This is important because involvement in diversity training is often a requirement associated with certain positions or roles. Fourth, there was some evidence that the effectiveness of diversity training has increased steadily over time. While these results are encouraging, research now needs to go beyond a focus on the effects of broad-based diversity training on attitudes, cognition, and skills, and examine whether and how gender-based diversity training influences all aspects related to female leadership.

Family-Friendly Initiatives

The fact that society still expects women to bear a disproportionate share of family responsibilities is often cited as a major obstacle to women acquiring leadership roles, remaining in them in the longer term, and competing on an equal footing with male leaders. Scholars and practitioners have acknowledged that this pattern may have impeded women's progress in organizations for decades. In the 1970s, Hall noted that men had the luxury of fulfilling their work and family roles sequentially; in other words, while they were at work, they would not be bothered by family demands. In contrast, society expected that women perform their work and family roles simultaneously; when women were at work, they were also required to take responsibility for any family demands. While differences in such expectations have diminished since then, women continue to bear an unfair and disproportionate share of family responsibilities, resulting in greater difficulties in working long hours[72] and in greater absence from work than their male counterparts.[73]

High-quality, on-site child care is frequently seen as an important initiative in this respect, and has a long history in workplaces. High-quality child care was available in the United States during World War II and even included full services for employees working night shifts. However, with the return of men from the war front and the exit of most women from the workplace, these facilities were soon disbanded.[74] Private-sector organizations implemented on-site child care programs to reduce the disproportionate burden on women, starting in the early 1970s, with the Stride Rite Corporation being the first organization to do so in the United States.[75] In the early 1980s, there was a remarkable increase in media and scholarly interest in what became known as work–family conflict,[76] and by the end of the 1980s and early 1990s, organizations had dramatically expanded family-friendly practices to include elder care programs, flexible work schedules, variations in the traditional workweek, such as compressed workweeks, and telecommuting.

There are now numerous studies investigating the benefits of various family-friendly initiatives, the results of which are consistently encouraging. These initiatives reduce the level of work–family conflict, especially for women,[77] and enhance employed mothers' well-being, which in turn has a positive effect on children's well-being.[78] But it is not just employees' and their families who benefit from these initiatives. Research investigating organizational-level effects of family-friendly practices started in earnest in the 1990s and have shown equally positive effects. For example, announcements in the *Wall Street Journal* between 1971 (the year in which the first on-site day care was established) and 1996 of a work–family program initiated by a Fortune 500 company were accompanied by an increase in share price on the day of the announcement,[79] presumably because such announcements signal that it is a well-run organization. Importantly, family-friendly workplace initiatives are also cost-effective; in other words, their implementation is associated with positive outcomes for employees, and they generally pay for themselves.[80] As a result, initiatives such as flex-time, child care, elder care, maternity leave, and job sharing are now commonplace.

To remove any stigma from these initiatives and promote their usage more broadly, there have been recent calls for such initiatives to be gender-free, to be available not only to female employees but to all organizational members.[81] Given their overall effectiveness, the remaining question is whether the general effects that accrue from family-friendly initiatives to employees in general extend to female leaders.

Mentorship Programs

Formal and informal mentorship programs have attracted considerable attention within organizations for several decades. The basic premise underlying mentorship programs is that extensive knowledge can be passed from mentor to mentee within the confines of a high-quality relationship in which the mentor is a trusted role model. Mentees might also benefit in terms of the social networks and political connections opened up by mentors. Mentorship has been shown to influence women's leadership emergence. Of a sample of 91 female university presidents at four-year, independent colleges in one study, most (56%) had primary mentors who had been instrumental in their own careers (including in their earlier career advancement) and had later encouraged them to seek the position of college president.[82] In addition, most of the college presidents themselves (64%) subsequently served as mentors to others. A separate study of 133 mentor–mentee dyads during a seven-month mentoring program showed that mentors' role modeling during the program was positively related to mentees' transformational leadership at the end of the program.[83]

Based on extensive research on mentorship programs in general, several evidence-based lessons targeting greater leader diversity can be drawn. First, the outcomes being targeted should be considered when determining the gender of the mentor. For example, higher compensation is more likely to result for women with male than with female mentors, but greater social capital is a more likely outcome when female leaders are paired with female (rather than male) mentors.[84] Second, greater benefits for leadership-based gender diversity are yielded when mentorship programs are integrated with succession planning.[85] A major lesson to be learned from this finding is that any gender diversity interventions targeted at influencing leadership will be optimized when they are integrated into the overall fabric of organizations' human resource initiatives. Finally, concerns have been raised about the so-called queen bee syndrome, according to which some women who have risen to the top of organizations might not make the most appropriate mentors.[86] More needs to be known about the appropriate selection of mentors.

Legislative Interventions

Because the lack of gender diversity in organizational leadership is not just a function of organizational forces but is a symptom of a wider social issue, some of the solutions to the problem will necessarily lie outside of specific organizational practices. Two very different examples of outside interventions, both of which involve setting targets for diversity to some extent, show much promise, but they also raise important and difficult questions.

Female Representation on Governance Boards

If we are to gain a meaningful appreciation of women in organizational leadership, we need to go beyond an understanding of the situation in work organization themselves and also focus on the gender composition of boards of directors. As will immediately become apparent, much remains to be accomplished with respect to gender equality on governance boards. As of 2011, approximately 14% of Fortune 1000 companies in the United States still had no female directors, and only 15% of all directors were female. Because this might be a somewhat optimistic picture, as the data are taken from top-ranked organizations, the authors of this report examined another 1,000 companies (with annual revenue between 500 million and three billion dollars): 30% of these large organizations had no female representation on their boards of directors at all.[87]

A deeper understanding of the underrepresentation of women on governance boards derives from two further findings. First, paralleling many of the findings mentioned earlier showing that context shapes the bias against women leaders, men are more likely than women to be members of governance boards' executive committees, while women are more likely to find themselves as members of public affairs committees.[88] Second, underrepresentation of women on governance boards is not limited to the United States; it is a global phenomenon. Despite progressive legislation and initiatives across many countries, males continue to dominate in terms of membership on boards of governance and in holding the position of chair of such boards.

Underrepresentation of women on governance boards is not simply an equity issue, as it has negative consequences for organizations. Siri Terjeson, Ruth Sealy, and Val Singh analyzed research reports in 400 publications in the organizational (e.g., leadership, finance, management, corporate governance, entrepreneurship) and social sciences (e.g., psychology, sociology, gender studies).[89] Their analyses showed that having a greater number of female board members was associated with having more female leaders at all different levels of the organization. In addition, women board members served as role models and mentors, opening up formerly unavailable networks for women throughout the organization, potentially influencing their motivation to lead and their retention by the organization. Terjeson and her colleagues also point to a more cooperative decision-making and civil culture within boardroom discussions that occurs when there are more female board members.

A separate study of corporate boards reinforces the importance of gender diversity among boards of directors.[90] In a set of findings that resonate throughout this chapter, Sabina Nielsen and Morten Heuse showed in their analysis of 201 Norwegian firms that greater gender diversity among the board was associated with heightened strategic control, but not operational control, within the organization. Other findings of note from this study are that board developmental activities (e.g., presence of socialization activities for new board members, and ongoing developmental programs and evaluations) were more likely to take place when board gender diversity was higher, and internal board conflict was lower when there was greater female representation. Both of these patterns predicted board effectiveness. Finally, a separate study of Fortune 1000 organizations showed that having three or more women board directors resulted in higher levels of corporate environmental responsibility.[91]

Faced with significant differences in board composition across countries, there is always the temptation to search for complex solutions, but this may be one situation where that would not be necessary. Within the past decade, many countries (e.g., Norway, Finland, Iceland, Spain, France, Italy, the Netherlands) have chosen to introduce legislation mandating female representation on governance boards.[92] The mandated targets differ across countries, as do the rewards or penalties for achieving or missing the target. In contrast, it would be politically imprudent to mandate female representation in some other countries (e.g., U.K., U.S.). Along similar lines, some countries have introduced legislation (e.g., India) that would motivate proactive organizations to institute changes ahead of the implementation. A third option has seen many countries opt for voluntary activities, such as requiring that

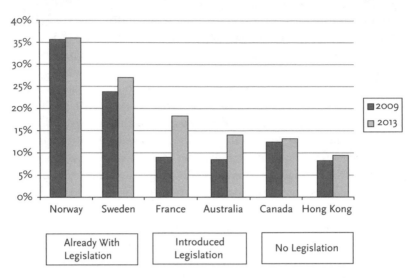

Figure 8.2
Percentage of women in the boardroom before and after legislation.

privately held organizations publicly disclose the gender composition of their boards, or that they have specific, public targets of greater gender diversity (e.g., Australia, Germany). Irrespective of the means of creating greater female board representation, the effect seems to be the same: As is evident from Figure 8.2, which categorizes countries in terms of the presence or absence of legislation mandating voluntary targets across a five-year period, an interventionist approach is effective in meeting the goals of greater diversity on governance boards. Intriguingly, some powerful organizations (e.g., the Ontario Teachers' Pension Fund) are beginning to push their regulatory agencies to mandate increased gender diversity, and make the point that this should be the first step toward broader diversity on boards more generally.[93]

Still, caution must be exercised to avoid negative unintended consequences from well-intentioned legislation. A lesson can be learned from the newly elected ANC government's Black Economic Empowerment initiative, implemented after 1994 to redress racial imbalance in the workplace. After mandating specific racial targets for corporate ownership and board representation, the same small group of highly qualified, politically connected individuals tended to find themselves in ownership and governance positions across many large organizations, so much so that four of the most prominent of these individuals—Cyril Ramaphosa, Tokyo Sexwale, Saki Macazoma, and Patrice Motsepe—became known as the "fab four." As a result, concern was raised that relatively few Black people benefitted from the well-intentioned legislation, paradoxically increasing rather than reducing social inequity.[94] While up-to-date data on the extent to which this same situation characterizes female representation on governance boards are not readily available, Douglas Branson counseled that some degree of caution is warranted.[95] Based on data from 2001 and 2005, he reported that there had been a large increase in the number of female "trophy directors"—people serving on four or more boards simultaneously.

A very different approach to legislative mandates has occurred in India. A fascinating study by Lori Bearman, Esther Duflo, and their colleagues provides valuable insights into what might be achieved through government-initiated programs.[96] In 1993, the Indian government embarked on a bold social experiment when they passed legislation imposing gender quotas requiring that women assume the position of head of the village council between 1998 and 2003. Making this situation even more inviting to researchers, the legislation only imposed gender quotas on some villages, and the quotas were imposed either once or twice during this time period. The researchers took advantage of the new context created and investigated the long-term effects of being exposed to female leadership models on 1,852 adolescent girls and 1,828 boys, and their mothers and fathers, in a random sample of 495 villages, between 2006 and 2007.

The findings from this study provide strong support for the effects of female role models, and what might be achieved through legislation. First and foremost, extensive exposure to female leader role models was associated with positive changes in adolescents' aspirations and behaviors. Specifically, imposing female role models on village councils increased adolescent girls' school attendance and desire to graduate from school. At the same time, adolescent girls' desire to become a housewife was reduced in the presence of female leadership role models. Second, even the fathers of these children were affected! Fathers in villages that were exposed to female leadership were significantly more likely to want their daughters to become village leaders than fathers who were not exposed to female leadership. Third, in villages that were never exposed to female leaders, parents had significantly higher career aspirations for their sons than for their daughters. However, these differences were markedly reduced when there was female leadership. Changes were a function of increases in daughters' aspirations and were not achieved through any decreases in sons' aspirations. Finally, adolescent girls exposed to female leadership reduced the amount of time spent involved in household chores. The importance of this finding should not be underestimated: Household chores are typically relegated to girls in developing societies, which likely inhibits their educational, occupational, and leadership aspirations and attainment.

One final aspect of this study must be mentioned. Concern is often expressed that installing leaders of minority groups through legislative requirements could create a backlash against the very people meant to benefit from the policy. As the authors of this study noted, however, the positive effects overwhelmed any possible backlash effects in this study. In fact, the legislated policy had no negative effects at all on the aspirations of those who did not benefit from the new policy.

To reiterate, this study is important because it confirms that bias against female leaders starts well before they enter the workplace. Even more importantly, the data showed pervasive beneficial effects of female role models—not just for adolescent girls, but for their fathers as well. None of these beneficial changes would have occurred, however, without the bold social legislative initiative introduced by the Indian government.

CONCLUSION

To conclude, after several decades of research, we now know that the bias against female leaders in organizations is subtle, and it persists. In general, when women contradict gender-role expectations in organizations, they are less likely to be selected for leadership positions. This bias continues if and when they do become leaders, when deviating from gender-role expectations is likely to be punished in formal and informal ways. This must be seen against the fact that there is no evidence that the quality of women's leadership behavior is any less than that of their male counterparts. The time for debate is over, and both social justice (e.g., ridding society of different forms of discrimination) and organizational functioning (e.g., expanding the pool of qualified leaders) demand that appropriate action be taken.

SUGGESTED READING

Eagly, A. H., & Carli, L. L. (2007). *Through the labyrinth: The truth about how women become leaders*. Boston: Harvard Business School Press.

Genovese, M. A., & Steckenrider, J. S. (2013). *Women as political leaders: Studies in gender and governing*. London: Routledge.

Kellerman, B., & Rhode, D. L. (Eds.). (2007). *Women and leadership: The state of the play and strategies for change*. San Francisco, CA: Jossey-Bass.

Klenke, K. (2011). *Women in leadership: Contextual dynamics and boundaries*. Bingley, UK: Emerald Group.

NOTES

1. Catalyst. http://www.catalyst.org/
2. Catalyst (2012). *Women in U.S. management*. Retrieved from www.catalyst.org/
3. Eagly, A. H., & Karau, S. J. (1991). Gender and the emergence of leaders: A meta-analysis. *Journal of Personality and Social Psychology, 60*, 685–710.
4. Ryan, M. K., & Haslam, S. A. (2005). The glass cliff: Implicit theories of leadership and gender and the precariousness of women's leadership positions. In

B. Schyns & J. R. Meindl (Eds.), *Implicit leadership theories: Essays and explorations* (pp. 137–160). Greenwich, CT: Information Age.

5. Ryan, M. K., & Haslam, S. A. (2005). The glass cliff: Evidence that women are over-represented in precarious leadership positions. *British Journal of Management, 16*, 81–90.

6. Haslam, S. A., & Ryan, M. K. (2008). The road to the glass cliff: Differences in the perceived suitability of men and women for leadership positions in succeeding and failing organizations. *Leadership Quarterly, 19*, 530–546.

7. Haslam, S. A., & Ryan, M. K. (2008). The road to the glass cliff: Differences in the perceived suitability of men and women for leadership positions in succeeding and failing organizations. *Leadership Quarterly, 19*, 530–546.

8. Haslam, S. A., & Ryan, M. K. (2008). The road to the glass cliff: Differences in the perceived suitability of men and women for leadership positions in succeeding and failing organizations. *Leadership Quarterly, 19*, 530–546.

9. Ryan, M. K., Haslam, S. A., Hersby, M. D., & Bongiorno, R. (2011). Think crisis-think female: The glass cliff and contextual variation in the think manager-think male stereotype. *Journal of Applied Psychology, 96*, 470–484.

10. Ryan, M. K., Haslam, S. A., & Postmes, T. (2007). Reactions to the glass cliff: Gender differences in the explanations for the precariousness of women's leadership positions. *Journal of Organizational Change Management, 20*(2), 182–197.

11. Hough, D. (2013). *Women in parliament and government*. London: House of Commons Library.

12. Brown, M. (2011). *Edging towards diversity: A statistical breakdown of Canada's 41st parliament, with comparison to the 40th parliament*. Ottawa: Public Policy Forum.

13. Manning, J. E. (2013). Membership of the 113th Congress: A profile. Washington, DC: Congressional Research Service. Retrieved from http://www.fas.org/sgp/crs/misc/R42964.pdf

14. Hough, D. (2013). *Women in parliament and government*. London: House of Commons Library.

15. Ryan, M. K., Haslam, S. A., & Kulich, C. (2010). Politics and the glass cliff: Evidence that women are preferentially selected to contest hard to-win seats. *Psychology of Women Quarterly, 34*, 56–64.

16. Eagly, A. H., Johannesen-Schmidt, M. C., & van Engen, M. I. (2003). Transformational, transactional, and laissez-faire leadership styles: A meta-analysis comparing women and men. *Psychological Bulletin, 129*, 569–591.

17. Lee, P. M., & James, E. H. (2007). She'-E-Os: Gender effects and investor reactions to the announcements of top executive appointments. *Strategic Management Journal, 28*, 227–241.

18. Cook, A., & Glass, C. (2011). Leadership change and shareholder value: How markets react to the appointments of women. *Human Resource Management, 50*, 501–519.

19. Eagly, A. H., & Karau, S. J. (1991). Gender and the emergence of leaders: A meta-analysis. *Journal of Personality and Social Psychology, 60*, 685–710.

20. Ryan, M. K., Haslam, S. A., & Postmes, T. (2007). Reactions to the glass cliff: Gender differences in the explanations for the precariousness of women's leadership positions. *Journal of Organizational Change Management, 20*(2), 182–197.

21. Killeen, L. A., López-Zafra, E., & Eagly, A. H. (2006). Envisioning oneself as a leader: Comparisons of women and men in Spain and the United States. *Psychology of Women Quarterly, 30*, 312–322.

22. Eagly, A. H., & Karau, S. J. (1991). Gender and the emergence of leaders: A meta-analysis. *Journal of Personality and Social Psychology, 60*, 685–710.

23. Desmarais, S., & Curtis, J. (1999). Gender differences in employment and income experiences among young people. In J. Barling & E. K. Kelloway (Eds.), *Young workers: Varieties of experiences* (pp. 59–88). Washington, DC: American Psychological Association.

24. Steele, C. M., & Aronson, J. (1995). Stereotype threat and the intellectual performance of African Americans. *Journal of Personality and Social Psychology, 69*, 797–811.

25. Spencer, S. J., Steele, C. M., & Quinn, D. M. (1999). Stereotype threat and women's math performance. *Journal of Experimental Social Psychology, 35*, 4–28.

26. Koch, S. C., Muller, S. M., & Sieverding, M. (2008). Women and computers: Effects of stereotype threat on attribution of failure. *Computers & Education, 51*, 1795–1803.

27. Davies, P. G., Spencer, S. J., Steele, C. M. (2005). Clearing the air: Safety moderates the effects of stereotype threat on women's leadership aspirations. *Journal of Personality and Social Psychology, 88*, 276–287.

28. The feminist mystique. (2013, March 16). *The Economist*, p. 82.

29. Karrakker, K. H., Vohel, D. A., & Lake, M. A. (1995). Parents' gender-stereotyped perceptions of newborns: The eye of the beholder revisited. *Sex Roles, 33*, 687–701.

30. Maccoby, E. E. (1988). Gender as a social category. *Developmental Psychology, 24*, 755–765.

31. Eagly, A. J., & Johnson, B. T. (1990). Gender and leadership style: A meta-analysis. *Psychological Bulletin, 108*, 233–256.

32. Taylor, S. E., Klein, L. C., Lewis, B. P., Gruenewald, T. L., Gurung, R. A. R., & Updegraff, J. A. (2000). Biobehavioral responses to stress in females: Tend-and-befriend, not fight-or-flight. *Psychological Review, 107*, 411–429.

33. Azar, B. (2000). A new stress paradigm for women. *Monitor on Psychology, 31*(7), 42–43.

34. Schachter, S. (1959). *The psychology of affiliation*. Palo Alto, CA: Stanford University Press.

35. Koenig, A. M., Eagly, A. H., Mitchell, A. A., & Ristikari, T. (2011). Are leader stereotypes masculine? A meta-analysis of three research paradigms. *Psychological Bulletin, 137*, 616–642.

36. Eagly, A. H., & Karau, S. J. (2002). Role congruity theory of prejudice toward female leaders. *Psychological Review, 109*, 573–598.

37. Eagly, A. H., & Carli, L. L. (2007). Women and the labyrinth of leadership. *Harvard Business Review, 85*(9), 62–71.

38. Heilman, M. E., Wallen, A. S., Fuchs, D., & Tamkins, M. M. (2004). Penalties for success: Reactions to women who succeed at male gender-typed tasks. *Journal of Applied Psychology, 89*, 416–427.

39. Heilman, M. E., & Chen, J. J. (2005). Same behavior, different consequences: Reactions to men's and women's altruistic citizenship behavior. *Journal of Applied Psychology, 90*, 431–441.

40. Berdahl, J. L. (2007). The sexual harassment of "uppity" women. *Journal of Applied Psychology, 92*, 425–437,

41. Eagly, A. H., & Johnson, B. T. (1990). Gender and leadership style: A meta-analysis. *Psychological Bulletin, 108*, 233–256.

42. Eagly, A. H., Johannesen-Schmidt, M. C., & van Engen, M. I. (2003). Transformational, transactional and laissez-faire leadership styles: A meta-analysis comparing women and men. *Psychological Bulletin, 129*, 569–591.

43. Triandis, H. C., Bontempo, R., Villareal, M. J., Asai, M., & Lucca, N. (1988). Individualism and collectivism: Cross-cultural perspectives on self-ingroup relationships. *Journal of Personality and Social Psychology, 54*, 323–338.

44. Vinkenburg, C. J., van Engen, M. L., Eagly, A. H., & Johannesen-Schmidt, M. C. (2011). An exploration of stereotypical beliefs about leadership styles: Is transformational leadership a route to women's promotion? *Leadership Quarterly, 22*, 10–21.

45. Johnson, S. K., Murphy, S. E., Zewdie, S., & Reichard, R. J. (2008). The strong, sensitive type: Effects of gender stereotypes and leadership prototypes on the evaluation of male and female leaders. *Organizational Behavior and Human Decision Processes, 106*, 39–60.

46. Judge, T. A., Hurst, C., & Simon, L. S. (2009). Does it pay to be smart, attractive, or confident (or all three)? Relationships among general mental ability, physical attractiveness, core self-evaluations, and income. *Journal of Applied Psychology, 94*, 742–755.

47. Braun, S., Peus, C., & Frey, D. (2012). Is beauty beastly? Gender-specific effects of leader attractiveness and leadership style on followers' trust and loyalty. *Zeitschrift für Psychologie, 220*(2), 98–108.

48. Heilman, M. E., & Saruwatari, L. R. (1979). When beauty is beastly: The effects of appearance and sex on evaluations of job candidates for managerial and nonmanagerial jobs. *Organizational Behavior and Human Performance, 23*, 360–372.

49. Eagly, A. H. (1987). *Sex differences in social behavior: A social role interpretation.* Mahwah, NJ: Lawrence Erlbaum.

50. Eagly, A. H., Makhijani, M. G., & Klonsky, B. G. (1992). Gender and the evaluation of leaders: A meta-analysis. *Psychological Bulletin, 111*, 3–22.

51. Kulich, C., Trojanowski, G., Ryan, M. K., Haslam, S. A., Renneborg, L. D. R. (2011). Who gets the carrot and who gets the stick? Evidence of gender disparities in executive remuneration. *Strategic Management Journal, 32*, 301–321.

52. Beehr, T. A. (2005). Organizational role stress. In J. Barling, E. K. Kelloway & M. Frone (Eds.), *Handbook of work stress* (pp. 7–33). Thousand Oaks, CA: SAGE Publications.

53. Eagly, A. H., & Karau, S. J. (2002). Role congruity theory of prejudice toward female leaders. *Psychological Review, 109*, 573–598.

54. The feminist mystique. (2013, March 16). *The Economist*, p. 82.

55. Eagly, A. H., Karau, S. J., & Makhijani, M. G. (1995). Gender and the effectiveness of leaders: A meta-analysis. *Psychological Bulletin, 117*, 125–145.

56. Eagly, A. H., Makhijani, M. G., & Klonsky, B. G. (1992). Gender and the evaluation of leaders: A meta-analysis. *Psychological Bulletin, 111*, 3–22.

57. Eagly, A. H., Karau, S. J., & Makhijani, M. G. (1995). Gender and the effectiveness of leaders: A meta-analysis. *Psychological Bulletin, 117*, 125–145.

58. The feminist mystique. (2013, March 16). *The Economist*, p. 82.

59. Elsesser, K. M., & Lever, J. (2011). Does gender bias against female leaders persist? Quantitative and qualitative data from a large-scale survey. *Sex Roles, 64,* 1555–1578.
60. Ho, G. C., Shih, M., & Walters, D. J. (2012). Labels and leaders: The influence of framing on leadership emergence. *Leadership Quarterly, 23,* 943–952.
61. Heilman, M. E., & Okimoto, T. G. (2008). Motherhood: A potential source of bias in employment decisions. *Journal of Applied Psychology, 93,* 189–198.
62. Hebl, M. R., King, E. B., Glick, P., Singletary, S. L., & Kazama, S. (2007). Hostile and benevolent reactions toward pregnant women: Complementary interpersonal punishments and rewards that maintain traditional roles. *Journal of Applied Psychology, 92,* 1499–1511.
63. Williams, J. C. (2001). *Unbending gender: Why work and family conflict and what to do about it.* Oxford, UK: Oxford University Press.
64. Eagly, A. H., & Carli, L. L. (2007). Women and the labyrinth of leadership. *Harvard Business Review, 85*(9), 62–71.
65. Davies, P. G., Spencer, S. J., & Steele, C. M. (2005). Clearing the air: Safety moderates the effects of stereotype threat on women's leadership aspirations. *Journal of Personality and Social Psychology, 88,* 276–287.
66. Hebl, M. R., King, E. B., Glick, P., Singletary, S. L., & Kazama, S. (2007). Hostile and benevolent reactions toward pregnant women: Complementary interpersonal punishments and rewards that maintain traditional roles. *Journal of Applied Psychology, 92,* 1499–1511.
67. Kulik, C. T., & Robertson, L. (2008). Diversity initiative effectiveness: What organizations can (and cannot) expect from diversity recruitment, diversity training, and informal mentoring programs. In A. P. Brief (Ed.), *Diversity at work* (pp. 265–317). Cambridge, UK: Cambridge University Press.
68. Pendry, L. F., Driscoll, D. M., & Field, S. C. T. (2007). Diversity training: Putting theory into practice. *Journal of Occupational and Organizational Psychology, 80,* 27–50.
69. Kalinoski, Z. T., Steele-Johnson, D., Peyton, E. J., Leas, K. A., Steinke, J., & Bowling, N. A. (2012) A meta-analytic evaluation of diversity training outcomes. *Journal of Organizational Behavior.* Retrieved from http://onlinelibrary.wiley.com/doi/10.1002/job.1839/abstract
70. Stajkovic, A. D., & Luthans, D. (1998). Self-efficacy and work-related performance: A meta-analysis. *Psychological Bulletin, 124,* 240–261.
71. Rosenfeld, B. D. (1992). Court-ordered treatment for spouse abuse. *Clinical Psychology Review, 12,* 205–226.
72. Eagly, A. H., & Carli, L. L. (2007). Women and the labyrinth of leadership. *Harvard Business Review, 85*(9), 62–71.
73. Smeby, L., Bruusgaard, D., & Claussen, B. (2009). Sickness absence: Could gender divide be explained by occupation, income, mental distress and health. *Scandinavian Journal of Public Health, 37,* 674–681.
74. Goodwin, D. K. (1994). *No ordinary time.* New York: Simon & Shuster.
75. Arthur, M. M., & Cook, A. (2004). Taking stock of work-family initiatives: How announcements of "family-friendly" human resource decisions affect shareholder value. *Industrial and Labor Relations Review, 57,* 599–613.
76. Barling, J. (1990). *Work, employment and family functioning.* Chichester, UK: John Wiley & Sons.
77. Hammer, L. B., Neal, M. B.,Newsom, J. T., Brockwood, K. J., & Colton, C. J. (2005). A longitudinal study of the effects of dual-earner couples' utilization

of family-friendly workplace supports on work and family outcomes. *Journal of Applied Psychology, 90,* 799–810.

78. Estes, S. E. (2004). How are family-responsive workplace arrangements family friendly? *The Sociological Quarterly, 45,* 637–661.

79. Arthur, M. M., & Cook, A. (2004). Taking stock of work-family initiatives: How announcements of "family-friendly" human resource decisions affect shareholder value. *Industrial and Labor Relations Review, 57,* 599–613.

80. Bloom, N., Kretschmer, T., & van Reenen, J. (2011). Are family-friendly workplace practices a valuable firm resource? *Strategic Management Journal, 32,* 343–367.

81. Stewart, J. (2012, October 9). The end of the "family-friendly" workplace. Retrieved from http://www.fastcompany.com/3001986/end-female-friendly-workplace

82. Brown, T. M. (2005). Mentorship and the female college president. *Sex Roles, 52,* 659–666.

83. Chun, J. U., Sosik, J. J., & Yun, N. Y. (2012). A longitudinal study of mentor and protégé outcomes of formal mentoring relationships. *Journal of Organizational Behavior, 33,* 1071–1094.

84. Ragins, B. R., & Cotton, J. L. (1999). Mentor functions and outcomes: A comparison of men and women in formal and informal mentoring relationships. *Journal of Applied Psychology, 84,* 529–550.

85. Virick, M., & Greer, C. R. (2012). Gender diversity in leadership succession: Preparing for the future. *Human Resource Management, 51,* 575–600.

86. Drexler, P. (2013, March 6). The tyranny of the queen bee. Retrieved from http://online.wsj.com/article/SB10001424127887323884304578328271526080496.html

87. CTP Partners (2012). Women on boards: Review and outlook. Retrieved from http://www.ctnet.com/uploadedFiles/Women-On-Boards_2012.pdf

88. Peterson, C. A., & Philpot, J. (2007). Women's roles on U.S. Fortune 500 boards: Director expertise and committee membership. *Journal of Business Ethics, 72*(2), 177–196.

89. Terjesen, S., Sealy, R., & Singh, V. (2009). Women directors on corporate boards: A review and research agenda. *Corporate Governance: An International Review, 17,* 320–337.

90. Nielsen, S., & Huse, M. (2010). The contribution of women on boards of directors: Going beyond the surface. *Corporate Governance: An International Review, 18,* 136–148.

91. Post, C., Rahman, N., & Rubow, E. (2011). Green governance: Board of directors' composition and environmental corporate social responsibility. *Business & Society, 50,* 189–223.

92. McFarland, J. (2012, November 26). Women's work. *Globe and Mail.* Retrieved from http://www.theglobeandmail.com/report-on-business/careers/management/board-games-2012/glacial-progress-of-women-on-canadas-boards-prompts-calls-for-reform/article5644350/

93. McFarland, J. (2013, October 7). Ontario teachers' pension plan wants OSC to force firms to add female directors. Retrieved from http://www.theglobeandmail.com/report-on-business/companies-should-have-3-women-directors-or-face-delisting-teachers/article14721742/

94. Southall, R. (2007). Ten propositions about black economic empowerment in South Africa. *Review of African Political Economy, 34,* 67–84; Tangri, R., &

Southall, R. (2008). The politics of black economic empowerment in South Africa. *Journal of Southern African Studies, 34*, 699–716.

95. Branson, D. M. (2007). *No seat at the table—How corporate governance and law keep women out the boardroom.* Retrieved from http://www.sfu.ca/~mfs2/ SUMMER%202010/SA%20101/ASSIGNMENT%202/fulltext.pdf.

96. Beaman, L., Duflo, E., Pande, R., & Topalova, P. (2012). Female leadership raises aspirations and educational attainment for girls: A policy experiment in India. *Science, 335*, 582–586.

CHAPTER 9

When Leadership Goes Awry

In virtually all the discussion of leadership so far, the spotlight has been on positive, or high-quality leadership. For example, we have focused on the nature of high-quality leadership, its effects, how it works, how it develops, and whether it can be taught. Organizations and the people they employ would be in a wonderful position if the story ended here. Sadly, as anyone who has spent any time in an organization will tell you, what is missing from this discussion is any consideration of negative, destructive, or poor leadership. To complete the story, this chapter now deals with bad leadership, focusing first on the many ways in which bad leadership is expressed, and then on its diverse and serious effects.

Before embarking on this discussion, a brief comment on terminology is warranted. While the term "destructive leadership" is used extensively here, it tells us only about the *consequences* of bad leadership and provides no information about the *nature* of bad leadership. Why is this problematic? It does not take a leap of faith to know that leaders sometimes engage in truly abhorrent behaviors—and get away with it, inasmuch as there are no negative consequences. But it should be the quality of the leadership behavior that defines its nature, not its consequences. Despite this caveat, I will still use the term "destructive leadership," to avoid confusion. We now turn to a consideration of what constitutes destructive leadership, and then consider the effects of such leadership.

THE NATURE OF DESTRUCTIVE LEADERSHIP

Most people have some understanding of what exactly destructive leadership is from their own personal experiences, be it through paid employment, their school career, or extracurricular sports. Add to this those who might not have experienced destructive leadership but were third-party witnesses, and it is likely that precious few people will have had no experience with bad leadership. Perhaps not surprisingly, therefore, bad leadership attracts considerable public attention, whether in movies such as *Swimming with Sharks* or *Bad Bosses*, Web sites such as http://reallybadboss.com/, or in the daily *Dilbert* cartoons by Scott Adams, a feature of many newspapers for two decades. But bad leadership comes in many different forms, some of which would be readily recognizable (e.g., abusive supervision), others perhaps not (e.g., laissez faire leadership). As an example of the latter, while many employees might sometimes wish they would see much less of their supervisors, recent research shows the damage that can be caused by passive styles of leadership, a topic to which we will turn later in the chapter. But first we will deal with the more visible forms of bad leadership.

Abusive Supervision

Some two decades ago, Blake Ashforth introduced the concept of the "petty tyrant"—the organizational leader "who lords his or her power over others."[1] Several characteristics of the petty tyrant were identified: They care little about their subordinates, whom they would demean and embarrass; have a dictatorial style of conflict resolution ("my way or the highway"); discourage personal initiative; and, perhaps most chillingly, engage in random punishment. In addition, their behavior is self-serving. All of these traits are seen vividly in the provocative e-mail sent by William Ernst, owner of QC Mart, a chain of convenience stores in Iowa and Illinois, to all employees (see Table 9.1). Despite the seemingly intriguing nature of "petty tyranny," the concept has attracted very little scientific attention, even though Ashforth's research showed that the personal and organizational consequences of tyrannical behavior are far from petty.[2]

Several years later, Bennett Tepper proposed the existence of a separate form of destructive leadership, namely "abusive supervision,"[3] which he defined as "the sustained display of hostile and nonverbal behaviors, excluding physical contact" (p. 178). Abusive supervision shares important similarities with abuse in intimate relationships (e.g., romantic partners, elderly relatives, or parent–child relationships). Thus, within the workplace, the abuse will be sustained rather than occur only once, and will likely only stop when either the supervisor or subordinate terminates the relationship or the perpetrator changes his or her behavior, which is unlikely, as few abusive supervisors would take responsibility for their behavior. Like the situation with intimate partner abuse, subordinates remain in the toxic relationship because they feel personally and/or economically powerless to confront the abusive supervisor or leave the relationship or organization. They may also feel that they have few if any employment alternatives available to them, which inadvertently

Table 9.1. PETTY TYRANNY AT MEANIE MART

The following is from a March 2011 memo sent to employees of QC Mart, a chain of convenience stores in Iowa and Illinois, by the company's owner, William Ernst. In May 2011, a judge ruled than an employee who quit in response to the memo was eligible for unemployment benefits.

NEW CONTEST—GUESS THE NEXT CASHIER WHO WILL BE FIRED!

To win our game, write on a piece of paper the name of the next cashier you believe will be fired. Write today's date, today's time, and your name. Seal it in an envelope and give it to the manager to put in my envelope.

Here's how the game will work: We are doubling our secret-shopper efforts, and your store will be visited during the day and at night several times a week. Secret shoppers will be looking for cashiers wearing a hat, talking on a cell phone, not wearing a QC Mart shirt, having someone hang around/behind the counter, and/or a personal car parked by the pumps after 7 P.M., among other things.

If the name on your envelope has the right answer, you will win $10 CASH. Only one winner per firing unless there are multiple right answers with the exact same name, date, and time. Once we fire the person, we will open all the envelopes, award the prize, and start the contest again.

And no fair picking Mike Miller from Rockingham. He was fired at around 11.30 A.M. today. Good luck!!!!!!!!!!

From *Harper's Magazine*, July 2012, p. 22.

reinforces the supervisor's power and abusive behaviors. Moreover, like intimate partner violence, abusive supervision does not occur all of the time. Instead, the abusive supervisor may cycle through periods of abuse, and even longer periods of normal behavior, thereby falsely raising subordinates' hopes that their supervisor's abuse is finally over. This pattern is important to recognize, because cycling between periods of considerate and abusive management has more negative effects on the victim than a consistent pattern of abusive supervision.[4] The precise nature of the behaviors involved in abusive supervision is evident from Tepper's frequently used questionnaire (see Table 9.2).

Why would leaders engage in such behavior? Despite the practical, organizational, and conceptual importance of this question, much more attention has been focused on the consequences of abusive supervision than on its antecedents and causes. Nonetheless, several studies have attempted to answer this question.

Perhaps the most plausible explanation for the emergence of abusive supervision is the "trickle down" effect. Simply stated, when leaders themselves experience abusive supervision at the hands of their own supervisors, they become more likely to enact the same behaviors against their own subordinates.[5] Thus, one's own experience of mistreatment might also result in behaving abusively indirectly. A different study by Tepper and his colleagues showed that leaders who were depressed as a function of their own experience of injustice in the workplace were also more likely to engage in abusive

Table 9.2. TEPPER'S (2000) ABUSIVE SUPERVISION QUESTIONNAIRE

My boss....

1. Ridicules me.
2. Tells me my thoughts or feelings are stupid.
3. Gives me the silent treatment.
4. Puts me down in front of others.
5. Invades my privacy.
6. Reminds me of my past mistakes and failures.
7. Doesn't give me credit for jobs requiring a lot of effort.
8. Blames me to save himself/herself embarrassment.
9. Breaks promises he/she makes
10. Expresses anger at me when he/she is mad for another reason.
11. Makes negative comments to me about others.
12. Is rude to me.
13. Does not allow me to interact with my coworkers.
14. Tells me I am incompetent.
15. Lies to me.

Each item is responded to on a five-point scale, where 1 = I cannot remember him or her ever using this behavior with me; 2 = He or she very seldom uses this behavior with me; 3 = He or she occasionally uses this behavior with me; 4 = He or she uses this behavior with me moderately; and 5 = He or she uses this behavior very often with me.
From Tepper, B. (2000). Consequences of abusive supervision. *Academy of Management Journal, 43,* 178–190.

supervision—but crucially, only against subordinates who appeared weak, vulnerable, and either unable or unwilling to defend themselves.[6] Depressed leaders were most likely to take out their frustrations on what seemed to be safe targets, and both these studies provide added support for the concept of displaced aggression.[7] A later study by Tepper and his colleagues showed that employees with lower performance are more likely to be targeted by abusive supervisors.[8]

Even though some answer is provided as to why leaders might engage in abusive styles of supervision, it is equally clear that not all leaders who are subjected to abusive supervision go on to be abusive to their own subordinates. Some use their negative experience as positive motivation to be the best leaders they can, which raises a much bigger question: What psychological and situational factors make some leaders fall into the trap of doing to others what was done unto them? And perhaps even more intriguingly, what makes it possible for others—though likely a smaller number—to translate their own worst experiences with leaders into positive lessons and motivation for themselves? The study by Christian Kiewitz and his colleagues that was discussed in Chapter 5 provides one answer to this question.[9] Recall that they showed that managers who had been undermined by their parents generally engaged in more abusive supervision themselves. However, managers who had higher levels of self-control did not respond to earlier experiences of parental undermining by engaging in abusive supervision.

In closing the discussion on abusive supervision, it is worth noting that the research conducted to date has all focused on face-to-face abusive interactions. Yet Celia Romm and Nava Pliskin's call for caution should give us pause for concern.[10] While e-mail was initially introduced as just one more office technology to enhance productivity, it has become one more medium through which abusive supervision can be transmitted, and the potential for abusive supervisory behaviors being enacted through new social media is very real (as demonstrated by the behavior of the owner of QC Mart portrayed in Table 9.1).

Interactional Injustice or Unfairness

Most people care deeply about just treatment from authorities. Just treatment may communicate status and value, whereas lack of justice may be a source of oppression, deprivation and distress.

Kivimäki et al. (2005, p. 2250)[11]

Why do people care so deeply about the way in which they are treated by those in positions of authority at work, and respond so negatively when they believe their treatment falls short of their expectations? Mika Kivimäki and his colleagues remind us in the quotation above that how people are treated by organizational leaders confirms whether they are valued or not. Being treated fairly means you are a person of value; being treated unfairly is demeaning and belittling. A second reason is that most people feel the need to believe that the world is just (or fair), and that, by and large, people ultimately get what they deserve.[12] According to the just-world theory, discomfort and distress emerge when bad things happen to good people, or stated differently, when either victims or witnesses of the mistreatment believe they deserved better. Finally, being treated fairly implies that you belong, while being treated unfairly signifies exclusion.

There is an extensive literature on fairness in the workplace. Clearly, people are concerned about "distributive fairness," in other words, people want to see that their inputs (time, effort, skills, loyalty) are matched by their organizations' outputs (in this case, salary and benefits). People are also concerned about fair procedures at work. For example, beyond being concerned about whether they are paid fairly, people are also concerned about how decisions about compensation are made. Perceptions of procedural fairness are enhanced when procedures are applied consistently across people and across time, any information used in decisions is accurate and unbiased, and, importantly, unfavorable decisions can be appealed.

Interpersonal unfairness goes beyond distributional and procedural issues and occurs when employees feel they have been treated disrespectfully or rudely, for example, by their leader. Being treated unjustly in interpersonal interactions could vary from experiencing impolite behavior all the way to being humiliated publicly. This could occur within organizations by denying employees access to the information they need to do their jobs adequately, or ensuring that they receive required information too late for it to be useful or that important details are omitted. Such treatment conveys a sense of distrust and disrespect. Importantly, interactional injustice has negative effects for organizations and their employees, and these effects are exacerbated in the presence of procedural or distributive injustice.[13]

Several aspects related to interpersonal injustice widen its negative effects. First, it is not just the direct victims of poor leadership who suffer the consequences. Instead, recent research shows that the circle of people affected by unjust leadership is wider than those directly targeted for mistreatment[14]—employees who experience the mistreatment vicariously (i.e., they see it happen) can also be negatively affected.[15] For example, Joel Brockner and colleagues' extensive research in the 1990s showed that when employees (survivors) watch their coworkers being laid off by managers, their organizational attitudes are also affected (e.g., loyalty to the organization, perceptions of justice, intentions to leave the organization).[16] Extending this research, we showed in a series of studies that when children witness their parents' job insecurity during times of high layoffs, their views of the workplace[17] and school performance[18] were negatively affected. Employees are not the only witnesses to bad leadership. Customers can also witness mistreatment with very negative consequences for the organization, including a reluctance to purchase the company's products in the future and reduced interest in being hired by the company.[19] The lessons to be learned from this research are that people care greatly about fair treatment from those in authority, and sometimes seek retribution when mistreatment occurs to themselves or others around them. A little mistreatment goes a long, long way, and those directly targeted by bad leadership are not the only ones affected.[20]

There is a second aspect related to interpersonal injustice having broader negative effects. As important as unfairness perceptions are to a host of outcomes of importance to successful organizational functioning, recent research has expanded our understanding by questioning the static vs. dynamic nature of justice perceptions. Together with Michael Sturman and Quinetta Roberson, John Hausknecht surveyed a group of more than 500 employees four times over a one-year period asking study participants about their work experiences each time.[21] Their findings showed that *changes* in feelings that one is being treated unfairly tell us much more about employees' long-term job dissatisfaction, organizational commitment, and intentions to leave the organization than do "end-state" or static injustice perceptions.[i] These findings suggest that because most of the research on perceived injustice focuses on static assessments, the consequences of perceived interpersonal injustice may be even more troublesome than currently realized.

Third, employees do not make judgements about their leaders' fair or unfair treatment of others in isolation. Instead, as the old adage confirms, your reputation precedes you in such situations. Based on a laboratory study, David Jones and Daniel Skarlicki[22] showed that what people hear about a leader, even in the absence of any personal experience with that leader, biases perceptions of how fair the leader is. In their study, hearing about a reputation for unfairness exerted more detrimental effects than hearing about a reputation for being fair, or hearing nothing at all. In an era in which employees can access so much information about current and future leaders electronically, the fact that a leader's prior reputation for fairness might cloud employees' own direct experiences is of considerable importance.

One final point warrants reiteration. While most of the research on unfair leadership has focused on negative outcomes, not all individuals respond negatively to mistreatment. Instead, some people respond to mistreatment with acts of forgiveness or attempts to reconcile or improve the organization.[23] Even in such circumstances, however, we would still be dealing with destructive leadership, which is defined by the nature of the initial behaviors, rather than whether there are negative consequences.

Unethical Behavior

No discussion of bad or destructive leadership could be complete without some consideration of unethical leadership. Some approaches to understanding ethical leadership were discussed in Chapter 1. Here we will consider three different approaches to unethical leadership behavior that focus on leaders' moral disengagement, pseudo-transformational leadership, or need for power.

Moral Disengagement

Perhaps the most influential psychologist of the twentieth century, Stanford University psychologist Albert Bandura, has devoted himself for several

---

i. What does this mean? Take two hypothetical people who obtain a score of 5 out of 10 on an imaginary scale measuring unfairness (with higher scores indicating more fairness). This study suggests that if a year earlier person A had a score of 9, but person B had a score of 2, person A would now likely be more dissatisfied and more inclined to leave the organization.

decades to understanding the psychological and situational mechanisms that enable people to engage in unethical conduct. Bandura's model of moral disengagement[24] is worthy of discussion for several reasons. First, most approaches to understanding moral conduct in organizations focus on the role of a single aspect of unethical leadership. In contrast, Bandura argues that predicting the decision to behave unethically is more complex, and he has specified the multiple conditions under which moral disengagement will occur. Second, Bandura's moral disengagement model has been shown to be successful in predicting unethical behavior and the pursuit of self-interest in many nonorganizational contexts. As one example among many, Bandura, Michael Osofsky, and Philip Zimbardo showed how disengaging oneself from the moral implications of one's decisions and behaviors enables individuals to justify their participation in carrying out the death penalty.[25] As one participant who was required to strap offenders' legs prior to execution told them (and perhaps himself), "I never pulled the trigger," he said, "I wasn't the executioner" (p. 385).

Bandura's model outlines three major psychological mechanisms that precede moral disengagement: how (a) the reprehensible conduct, (b) any detrimental effects, and (c) the victims are perceived. Bandura goes further, specifying the different behaviors that would result in these three major conditions. First, because people would not typically engage in behaviors they view as reprehensible or shameful, they need to change the way they see those behaviors. *Moral justification* is achieved by offering reasons for unethical behaviors that suggest they serve a higher purpose. In this sense, poor interpersonal mistreatment might be justified as necessary to achieve larger organizational goals that would benefit the collective. Thus, during difficult times, leaders might tell themselves and others that they mistreated others to ensure that the organization would survive. Second, *euphemistic labeling* involves changing one's language so that the questionable behavior is seen not as unacceptable but perhaps even as noble. For example, those involved in unethical behaviors might avoid the term "co-conspirators," elevating those involved with them to "team players."[26] A third way in which individuals change the way they see their own questionable behavior is through *advantageous comparisons*. Comparing one's own behavior with something that is unambiguously worse can make our own behavior seem benign and perhaps even benevolent.

Reframing how one views one's behavior would not be sufficient in itself to result in unethical conduct. Bandura argues further that individuals also need to disconnect any link in their own minds between their behaviors and its consequences, and two psychological mechanisms could facilitate this process. The classic example of *displacement of responsibility*—"I was just following orders" enables individuals to absolve themselves of any responsibility for their own actions. In addition, *displacement of responsibility* weakens moral self-control by enabling responsibility for the conduct to be shared with others.

If leaders can minimize or negate perceptions that their actions have harmed the victim, reprehensible behaviors would seem of minimal or even no consequence. *Distortion of consequences* is seen on a large scale in revisionist historians' attempts to question the number of people killed in genocidal activities. At the organizational level, for example, suggesting that one's subordinates enjoy being the target of inappropriate humor would exemplify distortion of consequences.

Finally, it is difficult to transgress against those we see as people with the same rights as ourselves. Individuals can disengage moral self-control by reframing the way in which they see the victims of their mistreatment. *Dehumanizing others* strips them of their human nature and responsibilities. Referring to Tutsis as "cockroaches" just prior to the genocide in Rwanda allowed Hutus to massacre Tutsis without feelings of responsibility or remorse. At the organizational level, viewing employees as "deserving recipients" rather than "unfortunate victims" of leaders' irascible moods or inconsistent behaviors would achieve the same purpose. Leaders can also achieve moral disengagement and absolve themselves of responsibility for their actions by *attributing blame* to the victims of mistreatment. Leaders' abusive behavior toward subordinates could be self-justified by arguing that subordinates brought the mistreatment upon themselves by their own actions, for example, because of poor job performance.

Several studies suggest that Bandura's model of moral disengagement can help explain morally questionable conduct by organizational leaders. In a series of case studies, Bandura, Gian-Vittorio Caprara, and Laszio Zsolnai examined four notorious organizational disasters, namely Bhopal in India, the Ford Pinto case, the Nestle case, and Three Mile Island in the United States, showing how components of the moral disengagement model helped to bring about each disaster.[27] For example, by casting blame on the Indian government and refusing any compensation for victims living in nearby shantytowns, Union Carbide engaged in displacement of responsibility and dehumanization, respectively, in the case of the Bhopal disaster. By continually arguing that they had followed U.S. safety regulations in the case of the hundreds of fatal crashes involving Ford Pintos, Ford continually displaced ethical responsibility away from their own actions. When Nestle faced mounting international criticism of the sales of infant formula in Third World countries, beginning in the 1970s, their strategy was to minimize or disregard any harmful consequences caused by their actions—including failing to tell the truth about post-marketing research they claimed had been completed. Finally, in the case of Three Mile Island, arguably the most significant disaster within the nuclear industry in the United States to date, displacement of responsibility was evident between the major stakeholders (namely the operators, manufacturer, and the Nuclear Regulatory Commission), for example, in attempts to displace responsibility by blaming "operator error."

What lessons can be learned from this discussion of the nature of unethical behavior in organizations? First, every step in Bandura's theory makes it clear that unethical behaviors follow an active and rational thought process. Second, paraphrasing Bandura,[28] given that most ethical transgressions in organizations are carried out by otherwise considerate leaders who understand the possible consequences of their actions, organizations cannot simply rely on individuals not to transgress ethics. Instead, organizations must institute systems that prevent leaders' personal pursuit of greed and self-interest. At a minimum, this requires instituting systems that ensure that people throughout the organization can question the legitimacy of any behaviors they see or orders they receive, without any fear of reprisal.[29]

Pseudo-Transformational Leadership

The story is told of a group of leadership scholars who gathered several decades ago at the University of Maryland to debate critical questions about leadership.[30] Included in the group were eminent leadership scholars Bernie Bass and James MacGregor Burns, and as so often happens in situations like this, the "Hitler problem" was raised. Could Hitler, and others of his ilk, be regarded as a transforming leader? Early in the discussion, Bass argued that he could, as he met the core criterion of bringing about major social change. After several days of vigorous debate, MacGregor Burns countered that, by definition, leadership had a core moral component and Hitler therefore could not be described as a "transformational leader" who inspires and influences others for the collective good. Bass then relented, and in resolving the long-standing debate, he offered the alternative term, "pseudo-transformational" leadership. Hitler was not a transformational leader, he was a pseudo-transformational leader who used those same inspirational abilities for self-gain.

Earlier attempts to describe the nature of pseudo-transformational leadership centered on leaders' moral character and ethical values.[31] This "character" approach is supported by research showing that Western leaders in the 20th century who were charismatic and constructive to their followers, as opposed to charismatic and detrimental, differed in terms of narcissism (defined as the extent to which they deliberately manipulated those they were leading for their own self-interest) and their personal need for power.[32] In recent attempts with my colleagues Amy Christie and Nick Turner, we have embedded pseudo-transformational leadership in the four components of transformational leadership.[33] Within this framework, important differences exist in how most of the transformational vs. pseudo-transformational leadership behaviors are manifested (see Table 9.3).

Idealized influence is manifest when leaders put others' interests before their own, and they are focused on the collective good. In contrast,

Table 9.3. COMPARISON OF TRANSFORMATIONAL,
PSEUDO-TRANSFORMATIONAL, AND LAISSEZ-FAIRE LEADERSHIP

Transformational Component	High or Low Levels		
	Transformational Leadership	Pseudo-Transformational Leadership	Laissez Faire
Idealized influence	High	Low	Low
Inspirational motivation	High	High	Low
Intellectual stimulation	High	Low	Low
Individualized consideration	High	Low	Low
Contingent reward	High	Low	Low
Management-by-exception	Low	High	Low
Laissez-faire	Low	Low	High

pseudo-transformational leaders are dominated by their own self-interest and seek to become personal idols rather than an instrument of change for the collective good. Because of their need to maximize self-interest at the expense of others, they are domineering and controlling to ensure followers' complete compliance with their own personal needs and agenda. As a result, pseudo-transformational leaders would not gain the respect typically earned by transformational leaders.

Intellectual stimulation involves encouraging followers to think for themselves, to question the reasons for personal and organizational actions, and to be critical. Motivated by their own self-interest, pseudo-transformational leaders can ill-afford subordinates who think for themselves and challenge their decisions, as the results could be personally disastrous. Thus, pseudo-transformational leaders will do whatever is needed to ensure that their subordinates do not think for themselves. Tactics to ensure this could include censoring, manipulating, and hiding opposing perspectives from their employees or punishing any challenging ideas—all to ensure obedience and compliance.[34]

Transformational leaders display individualized consideration when they listen to, care about, and support their followers. To pseudo-transformational leaders, however, followers' needs remain secondary to their own self-interest. Thus, employees are only valued if they can benefit the leaders' own needs and goals. Thus, unlike laissez-faire leaders who would be disinterested in their followers, pseudo-transformational leaders will focus on their followers' needs— but only if and when it suits themselves.

The one component of transformational leadership not yet mentioned is inspirational motivation, because there are no differences in the level of inspirational motivation between transformational and pseudo-transformational leaders. Both transformational and pseudo-transformational leaders effectively inspire others, for example, by expressing high levels of confidence in their employees, conveying an attractive vision of the future, and so on. It is for this reason that pseudo-transformational leadership can be so dangerous: What we are faced with initially are individuals who have an uncanny ability to inspire people—but for their own rather than the collectives' best interests.

With respect to transactional leadership, both transformational and pseudo-transformational leaders are skilled in managing others (i.e., contingent reward). Likewise, neither can be described as laissez-faire leaders. However, unlike transformational leaders, pseudo-transformational leaders engage in management-by-exception, keenly looking for and punishing behaviors that threaten their personal interests.

Initial research has supported the central tenets of pseudo-transformational leadership. We first conducted studies validating the core components of pseudo-transformational leadership. In one study of 611 Canadian executives, we focused only on the idealized influence and inspiration motivation components of transformational and pseudo-transformational leadership[35] and found that pseudo-transformational leadership (low idealized influence and high inspirational motivation) was associated with significantly higher levels of obedience to and dependence on authority, fear of the leader, and job insecurity (likely because their own jobs were perceived to be vulnerable if that was in the best interest of the leader). In addition, pseudo-transformational leaders were viewed as abusive. Amy Christie, Nick Turner, and I then conducted four more studies that validated the comprehensive model of pseudo-transformational leadership reflected in Table 9.3.[36]

Thus, the full-range model of leadership that includes both transformational and transactional leadership can be extended to explain unethical leadership. Learning a lesson from the development of knowledge about transformational leadership, where Bass' proposed model was soon followed by the Multifactor Leadership Questionnaire, which enabled research to flourish, further developments on pseudo-transformational leadership will be dependent on the availability of a usable and valid questionnaire of pseudo-transformational leadership.

"Power Corrupts, and Absolute Power Corrupts Absolutely"

With this statement, Lord Acton attributes responsibility for unethical leadership to the power embedded in situations, rather than in people, thoughts, or relationships.[ii] Thus, ethical transgressions would no longer be a function of

---

ii. In contrast, moral reasoning embeds ethical leadership within the leader's own thoughts, Gilligan's ethic of care places responsibility for ethical leadership within relationships, and pseudo-transformational leadership embeds unethical leadership within leaders' behaviors.

breakdowns in moral reasoning, ethical attitudes, or an ethic of care, but the power inherent in a situation. Early support for this notion emerged from several different sources. In the now-famous Stanford prison experiment,[37] student volunteers from Stanford University were randomly assigned to play the role either of a prison guard or a prisoner. Intriguingly, those allocated to play the role of prison guard started to abuse their new-found power so quickly that the experiment had to be stopped soon after it started! More recently, David Owen refers to the "intoxication of power" in analyzing how the leadership behavior of British Prime Minister Tony Blair and U.S. President George W. Bush was affected by the Iraq War.[38]

Some intriguing findings have emerged from research on how people respond both to holding power and to gaining power. In one study by Niro Sivanathan, Madan Pillutla, and Keith Murnighan, when individuals' power increased to the same level as that held by a different group for some time, they responded with greater self-interested demands following their gains in power than their counterparts who had consistently held the same levels of power over time.[39] Also interesting is the finding from this research that this effect was somewhat higher among American than Asian participants, suggesting that cultural nuances cannot be ignored. A second group of studies extended these findings, showing that individuals who hold power overestimated the amount of control they had over relevant outcomes,[40] potentially explaining the excessive behavior of leaders toward subordinates in some situations.

Leaders do not just experience gains in power, however; they also lose power frequently (e.g., cabinet members in government following cabinet reshuffles, following election losses, retirement, or being fired). What happens to those individuals who lose power in organizations is a question that has long intrigued social scientists and philosophers. For example, in his classic text, *On War*, Carl von Clausewitz made the fascinating suggestion that those who lose power, lose more than winners gain.[41] Thus, might the loss of power be more important for subsequent unethical behavior than being consistently powerless over time? In the study discussed above regarding power gains, Sivanathan and his colleagues also investigated power losses. Unlike the situation they found with power gain, participants in their research responded appropriately to losses in power, inasmuch as their expectations were more realistic, in other words, similar to others who had held that same level of power consistently.[42] While these findings are intriguing, more research is needed before we pronounce Clausewitz to have been incorrect.

Passive-Avoidant Leadership

Most leadership theories and research, and popular books on leadership, emphasize the active nature of leadership. Following this tradition, the discussion about bad or destructive leadership has focused uniformly on behaviors enacted by leaders. Stopping here would ignore a very passive side of leadership that has long been recognized. As one example, Robert Blake and Jane Mouton's managerial grid explicitly identified the nature and negative effects of passive management in their work 50 years ago.[43] Why, then, has passive leadership been so thoroughly ignored? One plausible reason is found in Bass and Riggio's discussion of laissez faire, which they described as the "most ineffective" (p. 8) of all leadership styles.[44] If laissez-faire leadership is ineffective, in other words doing nothing causes nothing to happen, why would it be either interesting or important?

Recent research makes it clear, however, that just doing nothing as a leader is not without its problems. There is now growing evidence that doing nothing can have significant negative consequences. For example, laissez-faire leadership results in diminished leadership effectiveness and greater follower dissatisfaction with leaders,[45] and lower safety consciousness on the part of employees, which is sufficient to compromise safety.[46] The neglect that characterizes laissez-faire leadership is also associated with employees experiencing ambiguity and conflict about their work roles, and creates a climate in which bullying can flourish.[47] Passive-avoidant leadership is also negatively associated with the learning climate in the organization. Hilda Hetland and her researchers showed that the more passive-avoidant the supervisor, the less employees believed that they had sufficient time to learn, and the less support employees provided to other team members.[48]

We are reminded from a separate study that the absence of high-quality leadership is not just the opposite of high-quality leadership. Joellyn Townsend, James Phillips, and Teri Elkins studied poor-quality leader–member exchange (LMX) relationships[49] and, as expected, showed that high-quality relationships were associated with positive outcomes, such as employee performance and citizenship behaviors. They then showed that poor-quality LMX relationships were not associated with these outcomes in any way. Instead, poor-quality LMX relationships predicted a different set of outcomes, namely retaliatory behavior from followers.

Two last thoughts on passive or laissez-faire leadership are in order. First, laissez faire is different from other forms of bad leadership discussed so far, all of which require active behaviors on the part of the leader. In contrast, laissez-faire leadership involves leaders doing very little, if anything. In this sense, laissez-faire leadership has been referred to as "poor" rather than "bad" or "destructive" leadership. Second, despite the negative consequences outlined above, and the fact that laissez-faire leadership has a formal place in the full model of transformational leadership, it remains little researched and even less understood. We need to know more about the nature, causes, and consequences of passive or laissez-faire leadership.

We end this discussion on the nature of destructive leadership with a comment on one aspect related to high-quality leadership. Irrespective of which aspect of high-quality leadership is being considered, it is invariably assumed that it has a *linear* (and positive) effect on the outcome of interest. What this means, for example, is that with increasing levels of whatever aspect of high-quality leadership is under consideration, there is a corresponding increase in levels of the outcome. However, this assumption is overly simplistic and potentially misleading. The effects of leadership are not necessarily linear. One study in particular, described below, shows all too well how this clouds our understanding of bad leadership.

Research findings have yielded a long-established, linear relationship between leaders' assertiveness on the one hand, and both leadership emergence and effectiveness on the other.[50] What this means is that as a leaders' assertiveness increases, so too does the likelihood of leadership effectiveness. But is it not possible that negative consequences could result from very high levels of leaders' assertiveness? One reason to believe this is the case is that the highest levels of assertiveness are typically associated with behaviors such as aggression, hostility, and dominance, which would be antithetical to high-quality leadership and hardly likely to foster the positive leader–follower relationships essential for high performance. In addition, discussions in the literature about the relationship between assertiveness and leadership have traditionally been driven by the "positive," or what Daniel Ames and Francis Flynn refer to as the factors that "make" rather than "break" leadership.[51] Ames and Flynn questioned all this in three different studies in the United States and showed that moderate levels of assertiveness were associated with an array of positive leader behaviors relevant to (a) motivation, influence, conflict, and teams; (b) leader effectiveness; and (c) predictions of future leader success. However, this was not the case for leaders who scored really high or really low on assertiveness. In both those cases, leaders' assertiveness (or lack thereof) was associated with poorer outcomes. Thus, ever-higher levels of leaders' assertiveness do not necessarily result in progressively higher quality leadership, and the notion of "too much of a good thing" applies to some aspects of leadership behavior. This phenomenon is supported indirectly by a study of 1,489 health care workers in the Netherlands showing that while moderate levels of workplace social support were associated with employee well-being, very high levels of workplace social support, including support from the senior nursing officer, were not.[52]

Ames and Flynn's research offers a very important lesson for understanding bad leadership: Specifically, bad leadership does not simply comprise a set of behaviors that are qualitatively distinct from high-quality or positive leadership. Instead, there are instances in which moderate levels of a particular aspect of leadership behavior are constructive and beneficial, but very high levels of the same behavior are most appropriately characterized as bad leadership.

CONSEQUENCES OF DESTRUCTIVE LEADERSHIP

You may not be able to stop the bullying, but you can make the bully's own life miserable or cause them to lose their own job or business. If you work closely enough with someone that they can bully you, then you are close enough to wreak havoc in their work or home life. If it is the owner/CEO, you can leak business secrets to competitors, send anonymous reports to OSHA or other regulatory agencies, start rumours, cause flat tires on company vehicles, crash computer networks, etc....Be creative, be careful, and remember they deserve it and you will feel better.

Posted by ed238yth, March 11, 2008, New York Times Blog

Several years ago, the *New York Times* wrote a story about research that my colleague Sandy Hershcovis and I had completed, comparing the effects of sexual harassment and workplace aggression.[53] The *New York Times* then opened up a blog, and invited readers to share their experiences. They certainly did not hold back! *Ed238yth* shared the above advice, and this comment just cannot be ignored. In graphic detail, it reminds us that bad leadership does not go unpunished; instead, the insult is returned—with interest! As malicious and vengeful as the suggestions in this comment are, they are primarily targeted against the organization—though Ed238yth also extends them somewhat to harming the leader's family life. The negative consequences of bad leadership go even further, however, and we now examine what empirical studies tell us about the organizational, health, and family consequences of bad leadership.

Organizational Consequences

"Payback Time!"

A consistent lesson from research is that employees tend not to remain passive when bearing the brunt of the worst forms of leadership. Instead, employees respond actively and in a target-specific manner to different forms of bad leadership, including interpersonal injustice from a supervisor.[54] This is shown amply in a study conducted by Jerald Greenberg across three different plants of a manufacturing organization in the automotive and aerospace industries in the U.S. Midwest.[55] Prior to the study, the parent organization had experienced the loss of two large manufacturing contracts. Rather than engage in layoffs, the organization chose to cut payroll by 15% for *all* employees for 10 weeks in the two plants directly affected by the loss of the contracts. A third plant also located in the Midwest experienced no layoffs, and no pay cuts. News of the pay cuts was delivered by a senior company executive differently in the two plants. In the first, which was called the "adequate explanation," news of the pay cuts was delivered to all employees in a way that was designed to convey respect and remorse. For example, the company vice president delivered the news in person, and then stayed for an hour afterward and answered all questions sensitively. In the second group, termed the "inadequate explanation," a company vice president delivered the same news about the pay cuts, but in a way that minimized any display of respect or remorse. For example, the meeting and question-and-answer session lasted only 15 minutes. In this way, the sensitivity of the news varied across the two groups, but they both received the same information and the identical pay cut for the same reason. Should any differences emerge between these two groups, they can clearly be tied to differences in interpersonal sensitivity rather than a loss in pay. (The third group was not made aware of what had transpired in the two other sites, and their working conditions were unaffected, in effect making them an ideal control group.)

The primary focus of this study was on whether any differences in theft emerged between the three groups during the 10 weeks in which the 15% pay cuts were in effect, and in a 10-week period after pay levels returned to normal. Clear inferences about the effects of the sensitivity of the pay cuts could be made, because the researcher also had data on patterns of employee theft for a period of 10 weeks before the announcement from the company's accounting department, which kept this information routinely. The results were dramatic, and can be seen in Figure 9.1. As expected, there were no differences in employee theft between the three groups prior to the announcement, but that was soon to change. During the period of pay cuts, theft almost doubled among employees in the adequate-explanation group, perhaps validating the notion that there is no good way for leaders to give bad news. The remarkable response, however, occurred among those in the inadequate-explanation group, where theft rose to levels about twice as high as those for the adequate-explanation group.

What happened within the 10 weeks after the pay cuts ended is equally surprising and important: In both these groups, theft resorted to its former levels, and there were no longer any differences between the three plants. The organizational lessons of these findings are massive. While it is often assumed that employee theft is a consequence of dishonest employees, the results of this study suggest that employee theft is also a direct consequence of feeling disrespected by one's leader and wanting to redress the perceived imbalance. Thus, employee theft—which many managers view as a major organizational problem, and is regarded as a "counterproductive behavior" by organizational scholars—may not always be seen by employees as morally reprehensible.

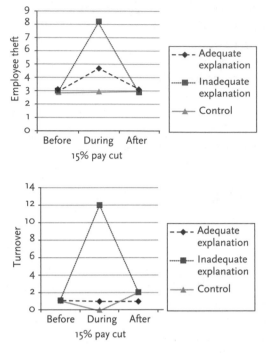

Figure 9.1
Effects of perceived injustice on employee theft and turnover.

Instead, employee theft is likely viewed by employees as "payback" for unacceptable treatment and therefore ethically justifiable in the face of disrespectful and exploitative employers; in terms of Bandura's theory of moral disengagement discussed earlier, this would involve a form of moral justification. This is supported in the title of a later research article on employee theft, by Greenberg, which yielded the same negative effects of mistreatment in a work context: "Stealing in the Name of Justice."[56] A second but equally important lesson from this research is that small deviations from acceptable leadership behavior can have enormous effects on employee behavior.

Payback can be extracted in different ways. A different study involved a group of over 1,000 employees in Michigan who had been identified by a company physician as suffering from repetitive motion injury. While we might expect that the severity, duration, and impairment resulting from the injury would be the only predictors of whether an individual chose to file a compensation claim, this was not the case.[57] Even after accounting for the severity of the injury, feeling that one had been poorly treated by one's supervisor was a significant factor in whether injured employees chose to file a compensation claim. Why this would be the case is adequately captured in the title of the article, "Claiming in the Name of Justice," and the lesson is unambiguous: Employees believe they are entitled to obtain some form of compensation for mistreatment by workplace supervisors, and they can be unusually creative in how they ensure that they receive what they deserve.

While these studies show the consequences of disrespect and mistreatment suffered by manufacturing employees by their leaders, how likely is it that individuals higher in the organization would respond in the same way? In early 2010, comedian Conan O'Brien suffered a major public humiliation at the hands of his employer, NBC, when his show was first moved to the most prized evening time slot, and then not long thereafter, relegated to a much less favorable time slot. Asked to explain how he intended to respond to the public humiliation and loss, Mr. O'Brien responded: "Everyone wants to know what my plans are. All I can say is I plan to keep putting on a great show night after night while stealing as many office supplies as humanly possible. I'm going to rob this place blind."[58] The pride in the quality of his work remained intact, but the need to respond to abysmal treatment by his leaders and resolve the perceived imbalance was as predictable as ever.

The lesson for organizations and leaders alike is clear: Employees expect to be treated fairly by their leaders, and when they are not, they will be motivated to re-establish what they see as an appropriate balance and view whatever actions they feel they must take as, quite literally, justifiable. However, bad leadership prompts employees to not just seek payback. There are numerous other responses open to employees, whether deliberate or not, that may have equally detrimental effects for the organization.

Organizational Withdrawal—When Times Are Tough, the Tough Get Going

One rational way of coping with bad leadership is to avoid the source of the mistreatment. Within the workplace, this could be achieved through different forms of withdrawal from work. One series of studies conducted by Hugo Westerlund, Anna Nyberg, and their associates documented how poor leadership is associated with higher absence levels. In one study on a very large sample of more than 12,500 forestry workers across Finland, Germany, and Sweden, low levels of what they termed "attentive managerial leadership" (e.g., leaders or supervisor do not consider the well-being of their employees or do not appreciate their subordinates' work) was associated with higher levels of sickness absence as a result of work fatigue.[59] Importantly, these findings are credible because the sickness absence was medically certified.[60]

The consequences of interpersonal mistreatment at the hands of a leader go deeper than temporary withdrawal from the workplace. Greenberg's study that was just discussed showing that employees respond to perceived interpersonal mistreatment did not stop at employee theft. Instead, because doing what one can to avoid the source of the mistreatment would be a rational way of coping, Greenberg also investigated whether perceived supervisory mistreatment might lead people to leave the organization. The effects on turnover were as immediate and dramatic as those on theft, and are graphically presented in Figure 9.1. While turnover remained negligible or unchanged in the control and, in this case, the adequate-explanation sites, an astonishing 12 of the 53 people in the inadequate-explanation group resigned during the 10-week pay-cut period! Clearly, there are some situations in which employees believe that their treatment is so unacceptable that they will not be willing to wait to see if the situation is rectified—they will just leave. Equally revealing is that as soon as the normal pay levels were reintroduced, turnover returned to its former levels, demonstrating again just how responsive people are to what they see is unjust treatment by their leaders. These findings are important: In a business environment where employee retention is a goal of many high-performing organizations, the extent of turnover experienced in the 10-week period by the group receiving inadequate explanation would simply be unsustainable. While no information was provided as to which employees chose to leave the organization, a common assumption is that high-performing employees who can more readily find other jobs elsewhere may be most likely to leave, aggravating any negative effects on the organization.

What lessons can be learned from the research on bad leadership and employee absence and turnover? First, one response when employees confront aversive situations in the workplace is to avoid the aversive conditions, whether on a short-term basis through absenteeism or permanently through turnover. Where the cause of the mistreatment is one's leader, avoiding the leader might in some cases mean choosing to absent oneself from the workplace. Second, facing what employees' themselves might see as extremely negative leadership—as might be the case in the pay cut study, employees might simply resign to avoid the toxic leadership.

An appropriate way of closing the discussion on employee withdrawal would be to remember how the story on comedian Conan O'Brien ended. Not only did O'Brien resign from NBC after negotiating a hefty settlement (reportedly worth $32.5 million[61]), he also made good on his threat to "rob the place blind," by taking his band and most of his staff with him.

Organizational Performance

Research studies consistently highlight the negative effects of bad leadership on employee attitudes (e.g., job satisfaction, organizational commitment) and job performance, and several lessons have emerged from this large body of research. First, in a meta-analysis of the effects of psychologically aggressive behaviors in the workplace, Sandy Hershcovis and I showed that such behaviors (e.g., bullying, incivility, undermining) exert consistent negative effects on job performance.[62] But our analyses went further and showed that these behaviors had significantly worse effects on job performance when perpetrated by leaders than by coworkers or outsiders (e.g., customers). The most plausible explanation for these findings is that employees have a greater expectation of being treated fairly and decently by their leaders than by their coworkers, and any departure from these expectations has significant negative effects.

Second, the broad-ranging negative consequences of mistreatment are evident from several other studies. In one example, team leaders' abusive supervision limited employees' creativity.[63] This same study also showed that when employees believed that their supervisors engaged in abusive behaviors in an effort to make employees work harder and enhance performance, the negative effects of abusive supervision were lessened somewhat. In contrast, when team members saw the abusive supervision as an attempt to hurt their feelings or damage their reputation, the effects of abusive supervision were magnified. Finally, David Prottas has extended our understanding of the range of negative leadership behaviors that can exact a toll on organizational performance.[64] Based on a large sample from the 2008 National Study of the Changing Workforce in the US, Prottas has shown that low levels of leaders' behavioral integrity predicts high levels of employees' moral distress (viz. "On my job, I have to do some things that really go against my conscience"), which in turn is associated with lower levels of job engagement.

What can be learned about the organizational consequences of bad leadership? Two lessons might be especially salient. First, while all the relevant research could not be presented here, the effects of bad leadership are sufficiently broad to include almost all aspects of performance that have been studied. Second, as will become more apparent, people are remarkably responsive to small deviations from what they consider to be the quality of leadership they deserve.

Physical and Psychological Health Consequences

One way of responding to bad leadership is to "fire back"[65] at the target. However, for a variety of reasons, individuals do not always feel that option is available to them. Sometimes, they personally absorb the mistreatment and are affected physically and psychologically.

"My Boss Makes Me Sick!"

How often have we heard employees uttering some version of this statement? Might there be any truth to statements such as this? Indirect answers to this question can be derived from two different streams of research.

In the first series of studies, Mika Kivimäki and his colleagues analyzed data from the Whitehall II study to assess whether supervisory behavior could predict new instances of heart disease over time.[66] A remarkable research undertaking, the Whitehall II study was established by Sir Michael Marmot in 1985,[67] and surveyed all public-sector office staff from 20 different departments in England who were aged between 35 and 55 during the first administration of the surveys. All participants first completed extensive surveys and underwent a comprehensive medical examination and were then followed up several more times. For this particular study, the researchers included 6,442 men who completed questionnaires about supervisory behavior between 1985 and 1988.[68] Assessments of coronary heart disease were then made from 1990 on. On average, cardiovascular disease was assessed just less than nine years after the quality of supervisory leadership was measured, which allows sufficient time for any health consequences to emerge.

Characteristic of all the research by the group responsible for the Whitehall II study, the researchers first controlled statistically for a slew of variables that might provide alternative explanations for their findings, including personal variables such as ethnicity, marital status, educational level, and employment level, and health status indicators such as cholesterol levels, body mass index (BMI), hypertension, smoking and alcohol consumption, and physical activity level. Even after doing so, perceived unfairness in the treatment received from their supervisors predicted the onset of new instances of heart disease. This finding is even more compelling, because the injustice experienced by participants did not rise to a level that most people would regard as especially harsh, suggesting again that people are remarkably sensitive to what they view as injustice or mistreatment by their supervisors. Specifically, the behaviors that reflected participants' perceptions of unjust treatment included not getting consistent or sufficient information from line supervisors, not being praised by a supervisor, being criticized unfairly, and not having a supervisor who is willing to listen to one's problems.

One possible limitation of this study is that only men were included. Might women respond differently to confronting negative leadership? Importantly, research has shown in different samples that interpersonal mistreatment at work exerts similar effects on women. For example, using a much smaller sample of 57 women working in an elder care facility in Finland, Marko Elovainio and colleagues showed that the risk for blood pressure problems was 3.8–5.8 times higher in employees who experienced mistreatment.[69]

Before turning our attention from physical illness, it is worth noting that the studies mentioned above were all conducted by the same researchers using the same large dataset (i.e., the Whitehall II study). A hallmark of scientific research is that findings are more credible when they are replicated by different researchers using different samples and different measures. In this respect, the research of Anna Nyberg and her colleagues is important.[70] Using a different sample (Swedish employees from the WOLF study[71]), they assessed whether what they referred to as managerial leadership (e.g., the extent to which the manager is considerate of the employee, provides clear goals, expectations, information, and feedback) predicted subsequent incidents of medically certified cases of ischemic heart disease (ISD). During the approximately nine years that the sample was followed after initial assessments were made, there were 74 new ISD incidents, showing that employees exposed to the poor managerial leadership were more likely to experience an ISD incident.

Finally, because findings gain greater weight when derived from different methodologies—and virtually all the research described above used survey data with large prospective samples—one further study warrants brief attention. Using a very creative research design, Nadia Wagar, George Fieldman, and Trevor Hussey studied employees who reported to different supervisors on different days. This approach can provide very valuable information, because each of the supervisors differed in the quality of their leadership, and the possibility that any results are a function of employees' personality could be discounted. What Wagar and her team showed was that employees' ambulatory systolic blood pressure was 15 mmHg higher on days they reported to a supervisor they perceived as unfair.[72]

"My Boss Is Driving Me to Drink!"

There is a long-standing[73] and vibrant research literature investigating the prevalence, causes, and consequences of employee drinking.[74] Examining that body of research will show that exposure to acute crises at work, such as the disaster of 9/11; having inadequate resources to fulfill one's task;[75] and exposure to chronically aversive workplace conditions (e.g., workplace stressors)[76] are associated with alcohol consumption at work. But do the available scientific data support widespread public beliefs about the role of leadership in employee alcohol consumption? Two large-scale studies, in two different countries, focusing on different manifestations of bad leadership, provide an answer to this question.

In one study, Peter Bamberger and Sam Bacharach[77] sampled almost 1,500 blue-collar workers in 10 different unions in the United States. They found that being exposed to abusive supervision was associated with problem drinking on the part of employees. Importantly, this effect is not limited to blue-collar workers, as other researchers have shown that discriminatory treatment, sexual harassment, and psychological humiliation at the hands of one's supervisor or leader also resulted in increased alcohol consumption among a group of physicians.[78]

Anne Kouvonen and her colleagues[79] analyzed this question further, using part of the extraordinarily large, prospective Finnish 10-Town cohort study that included all employees in 10 local governments. In what must be one of the largest projects of this nature ever attempted, tens of thousands of employees were surveyed during 2000–2001, and again in 2004, with 24,196 male and female employees eventually participating in both phases of this particular study. Both men and women who initially experienced supervisory unfairness had a significantly greater likelihood of being involved in heavy drinking at follow-up (i.e., they consumed at least 210 g. of heavy alcohol per week). These finding are especially credible, as Kouvonen and her team imposed rigorous statistical controls in their analyses. This meant that their findings could not be explained by participants' age, gender, marital status, and socioeconomic status, or by initial levels of work stress or psychological distress.

"My Boss Is Making Me Crazy!"

While "crazy" is undoubtedly a powerful and attention-grabbing word, the notion that workplace experiences have powerful effects on psychological and physical well-being is by no means new. Starting with trail-blazing researchers such as Arthur Kornhauser and Harry Levinson in the 1940s and 1950s, respectively, the link between workplace conditions and employee mental health is now the topic of much workplace research, and it has benefited greatly from scientific advances in understanding mental health and illness.

One of the largest studies to date again provides sufficient insight into this question. Jaana Ylipaavalniemi and her team chose to investigate whether a link exists between the quality of leadership and physician-diagnosed cases of depression.[80] They used a very large sample of more than 18,000 participants from the Finnish 10-Town Study, which was supplemented with just fewer than 5,000 participants from the Finnish Hospital Personnel Study. Initial assessment of employee perceptions of supervisors' procedural and interpersonal fairness was undertaken in 2000 and 2001. While most of the research on employees' psychological health is based on employees' own reports, the researchers also obtained physician-diagnosed depression of all participants in 2004. This mammoth undertaking ensured that their findings were more credible. After controlling for the possible effects of relevant demographic variables (e.g., age, gender, socioeconomic status), feeling that one's supervisor acted unfairly predicted subsequent diagnoses of depression by qualified physicians.

These findings show that active supervisory mistreatment can result in employee depression. But what is clear throughout the book is that passive leadership is not just ineffective, it too can yield negative results, for example on occupational safety. Might passive leadership also "drive employees crazy"? Töres Theorell and his colleagues used data obtained on 5,141 participants in 2008 and 20008 from the Swedish Longitudinal Occupational Survey of Health to investigate this question.[81] After again adjusting for demographic variables, passive leadership (what the authors of this study called "non-listening leadership") measured in 2006 predicted employee depression in 2008, extending the array of negative leadership behaviors that can affect employees' mental health.

Kick the Dog! When Bad Leadership "Hits Home"

An old adage used to explain organizational life is that when individuals are treated poorly by their leaders—people against whom retaliation would be inadvisable because of their status and power—they choose to let their frustrations out against those less powerful than themselves, the "kick the dog" phenomenon. In this instance, when employees cannot channel their frustration or anger against a leader because of fear of retaliation and punishment, they direct their anger against individuals over whom they feel they do have control, whether family members or subordinates. Often referred to in the literature as "displaced aggression," what is the empirical evidence for this phenomenon?

A study by Mary Bardes Mawritz and her co-researchers focused on subordinates as the powerless targets.[82] Findings from this study, which was conducted in the southeastern United States, showed that abusive manager behavior was associated with abusive behavior by their direct subordinates. In turn, the more these subordinates behaved abusively, the more likely it was that their own subordinates engaged in interpersonally deviant behaviors in the organization (e.g., saying hurtful things to others, behaving rudely to others, making sexist and/or racist jokes, deliberately embarrassing others). Because these researchers focused deliberately on reports from individuals working at different levels of the organization, support for what they call a "trickle down" phenomenon is convincing.

Several studies have now investigated whether experiencing poor-quality leadership spills over onto family members. Jenny Hoobler and Daniel Brass surveyed 210 supervisors in the United States, their subordinates, and the subordinates' family members (a spouse, partner, or child).[83] Each person in the triad answered different questionnaires. Supervisors reported on the extent to which they believed that the organization had not met their expectations, subordinates described the extent to which they experienced an abusive form of supervision, while family members reported on the extent to which family interactions were affected by the subordinates' work. The results of this study provide significant support for the "kick the dog" metaphor. To use the researchers own words, negative experiences "flow downhill" (p. 1125); supervisors holding negative beliefs that their own expectations were not fulfilled then engaged in greater levels of abusive supervision toward their direct reports, which spilled over into negative family interactions.

Dawn Carlson and her colleagues were also interested in the extent to which experiencing poor-quality leadership could spill over onto the family.[84] Their findings identify a different, less direct path through which bad leadership can affect other family members. In their research, 280 subordinates experiencing abusive supervision reported higher levels of tension in their relationship with their spouses or partners, which they attributed directly to their interactions with their leaders. In turn, the increased relationship tension negatively affected their spouse or partner's family satisfaction and family functioning. Evidence of this same phenomenon emerged in two separate samples in the Philippines.[85] Experiencing higher levels of abusive supervision was associated with greater psychological distress. In turn, the employed partner's psychological distress predicted the extent to which the spouse engaged in "undermining" behaviors (e.g., being critical, angry, or unpleasant).

After several decades of research, it is now widely accepted that work affects family, and family affects work. Most of this research focused on the consequences of conflict between work and family demands. This recent research shows just how pervasive negative leadership experiences are, in this case spilling over onto the family and affecting not just the romantic partner but children as well.

CONCLUDING THOUGHTS

Several salient lessons emerge from all this research. First, bad leadership need not rise to dramatic levels to exert its negative effects. People are remarkably sensitive to the way in which they are treated and mistreated! Second, the costs of bad leadership for the organization are enormous and include employee theft, absence, turnover, and lower job performance. In addition to the heavy toll on employees' psychological and physical well-being, any negative effects extend beyond employees personally exposed to bad leadership to their families through a trickle-down effect. Clearly, it is in the organization's best interests to do what it can to ensure that high-quality leadership pervades the organization, not bad leadership. Third, limiting our focus to "direct" targets will underestimate the prevalence and consequences of destructive or poor leadership. Those who witness the worst of leadership often suffer negative effects as well, and the reach of bad leadership should not be underestimated.

Finally, why does bad or destructive leadership exert such negative effects? While the reasons are many (see Chapter 3), it would be sufficient at this stage to revisit Kivimäki and colleagues' conclusion:[86] Bad leadership matters deeply to people because it conveys messages of disrespect and demeans people. And as Conan O'Brien's response to his perceived mistreatment reminds us, this is as true for celebrities earning millions of dollars each year as it is for manufacturing workers in the Midwest of the United States. Thus, extending the lessons learned earlier about how high-quality leadership "works" (see Figure 3.1), bad leadership and destructive leadership exert their negative effects by harming the way that people see themselves and their work, and by damaging the leader–follower relationship.

SUGGESTED READING

Babiak, P., & Hare, R.D. (2006). *Snakes in suits: When psychopaths go to work.* New York: Harper.

Kellerman, B. (2004). *Bad leadership: What it is, how it happens, why it matters.* Boston: Harvard Business School Press.

Lipman-Blumen, J. (2005). *The allure of toxic leaders: Why we follow destructive bosses and corrupt politicians—and how we can survive them.* New York: Oxford University Press.

Sutton, R.I. (2007). *The no asshole rule: Building a civilized workplace and surviving one that isn't.* New York: Warner Business Books.

NOTES

1. Ashforth, B. (1994). Petty tyranny in organizations. *Human Relations, 47*, 755–778.
2. Ashforth, B. (1997). Petty tyranny in organizations: A preliminary examination of antecedents and consequences. *Canadian Journal of Administrative Sciences, 14*, 126–140.
3. Tepper, B. (2000). Consequences of abusive supervision. *Academy of Management Journal, 43*, 178–190; Tepper, B. J. (2007). Abusive supervision in work organizations: Review, synthesis, and research agenda. *Journal of Management, 33*, 261–289.
4. Duffy, M. K., Ganster, D., & Pagon, M. (2002). Social undermining in the workplace. *Academy of Management Journal, 45*, 331–351.
5. Aryee, S., Chen, Z. X., Sun, L., & Debrah, Y. A. (2007). Antecedents and outcomes of abusive supervision: Test of a trickle-down model. *Journal of Applied Psychology, 92*, 191–201; Mawritz, M. B., Mayer, D. M., Hoobler, J. M., Wayne, S. J., & Marinova, S. V. (2012). A trickle-down model of abusive supervision. *Personnel Psychology, 65*, 325–357.
6. Tepper, B. J., Duffy, M. K., Henle, C. A., & Lambert, L. S. (2006). Procedural injustice, victim precipitation, and abusive supervision. *Personnel Psychology, 59*, 101–123.
7. Hoobler, J. M., & Brass, D. J. (2006). Abusive supervision and family undermining as displaced aggression. *Journal of Applied Psychology, 91*, 1125–1133.
8. Tepper, B. J., Moss, S. E., & Duffy, M. K. (2011). Predictors of abusive supervision: Supervisor perceptions of deep-level dissimilarity, relationship conflict, and subordinate performance. *Academy of Management Journal, 54*, 279–294.
9. Kiewitz, C., Restubog, S. L. D., Zagenczyk, T. J., Schott, K. D., Garcia, P. R. J. M., & Tang, R. L. (2012). Sins of the parents: Self-control as a buffer between

supervisors' previous experience of family undermining and subordinates' perceptions of abusive supervision. *Leadership Quarterly, 23*, 869–882.

10. Romm, C. T., & Pliskin, N. (1999). The office tyrant—social control through email. *Information Technology and People, 12*, 27–43.

11. Kivimäki, M., Ferrie, J. E., Brunner, E., Head, J., Shipley, M. J., et al. (2005). Justice at work and reduced risk of coronary heart disease among employees: The Whitehall II Study. *Archives of Internal Medicine, 165*, 2245–2251.

12. Lerner, M. J. (1980). *The belief in a just world: A fundamental delusion.* New York: Plenum.

13. Skarlicki, D. P., & Folger, R. (1997). Retaliation in the workplace: The roles of distributive, procedural, and interactional justice. *Journal of Applied Psychology, 82*, 434–443.

14. Miner-Rubino, K., & Cortina, L. M. (2007). Beyond targets: Consequences of vicarious exposure to misogyny at work. *Journal of Applied Psychology, 92*, 1254–1269.

15. Barling, J. (1996). The prediction, psychological experience and consequences of workplace violence. In G. VandenBos & E. G. Bulatao (Eds.), *Violence on the job: Identifying risks and developing solutions* (pp. 29–49). Washington, DC: American Psychological Association.

16. Brockner, J., & Wiesenfeld, B. (1993). Living on the edge (of social and organizational psychology): The effects of layoffs on those who remain. In J. K. Murnighan (Ed.), *Social psychology in organizations: Advances in theory and research* (pp. 119–140). Upper Saddle River, NJ: Prentice Hall.

17. Barling, J., Dupré, K., & Hepburn, C. G. (1998). Effects of parents' job insecurity on children's work beliefs and attitudes. *Journal of Applied Psychology, 83*, 112–118.

18. Barling, J., Zacharatos, A., & Hepburn, C. G. (1999). Parents' job insecurity affects children's academic performance through cognitive difficulties. *Journal of Applied Psychology, 84*, 437–444.

19. Skarlicki, D. P, Ellard, J. H, & Kelln, B. R. C. (1998). Third-party perceptions of a layoff: Procedural, derogation and retributive aspects of justice. *Journal of Applied Psychology, 83*, 119–127.

20. Rupp, D. E. (2011). An employee-centred model of organizational justice and social responsibility. *Organizational Psychology Review, 1*, 72–94.

21. Hausknecht, J. P., Sturman, M. C., & Roberson, Q. M. (2011). Justice as a dynamic construct: Effects of individual trajectories on distal work outcomes. *Journal of Applied Psychology, 96*, 872–880.

22. Jones, D. A., & Skarlicki, D. P. (2005). The effects of overhearing peers discuss an authority figure's reputation on reactions to subsequent treatment. *Journal of Social Psychology, 90*, 363–372.

23. Aquino, K., Tripp, T. M., & Bies, R. J. (2006). Getting even or moving on? Power, procedural justice, and types of offense as predictors of revenge, forgiveness, reconciliation and avoidance in organizations. *Journal of Applied Psychology, 91*, 653–668.

24. Bandura, A. (1991). Social cognitive theory of moral thought and action. In W. M. Kurtines & J. L. Gewirtz (Eds.), *Handbook of moral behavior and development: Theory, research and applications* (Vol. 1, pp. 71–129). Mahwah, NJ: Lawrence Erlbaum.

25. Osofsky, M. J., Bandura, A., & Zimbardo, P. G. (2005). The role of moral disengagement in the execution process. *Law and Human Behavior, 29*, 371–393.

26. Jackall, R. (1988). *Moral mazes: The world of corporate managers.* New York: Oxford University Press.

27. Bandura, A., Caprara, G., & Zsolnai, L. (2000). Corporate transgression through moral disengagement. *Journal of Human Values, 6,* 57–64.

28. Bandura, A. (1999). Moral disengagement in the perpetration of inhumanities. *Personality and Social Psychology Review, 3,* 193–209.

29. Beu, S. B., & Buckley, M. R. (2004). This is war: Hoe the politically astute achieve crimes of obedience through the use of moral disengagement. *Leadership Quarterly, 15,* 551–568.

30. Bass, B. M., & Riggio, R. E. (2006). *Transformational leadership* (2nd ed.) New York: Psychology Press.

31. Bass, B. M., & Steidleier, P. (1999). Ethics, characters and authentic transformational leadership behavior. *Leadership Quarterly, 10,* 181–217.

32. O'Connor, J., Mumford, M. D., Clifton, T. C., Gessner, T. L., & Connelly, M. S. (1995). Charismatic leaders and destructiveness: A historiometric study. *Leadership Quarterly, 6,* 529–555.

33. Barling, J., Christie, A., & Turner, N. (2007). Pseudo-transformational leadership: Towards the development and test of a model. *Journal of Business Ethics, 81,* 851–861; Christie, A., Barling, J., & Turner, M. (2011). Pseudo-transformational leadership: Model specification and outcomes. *Journal of Applied Social Psychology, 41,* 2943–298.

34. Bass, B. M., & Steidlmeier, P. (1999). Ethics, characters and authentic transformational leadership behavior. *Leadership Quarterly, 10,* 181–217.

35. Barling, J., Christie, A., & Turner, N. (2008) Pseudo-transformational leadership: Toward the development and test of a model. *Journal of Business Ethics, 81,* 851–861.

36. Christie, A., Barling, J. A., & Turner, N. (2011). Pseudo-transformational leadership: Model specification and outcomes. *Journal of Applied Social Psychology, 41,* 2943–2984.

37. Haney, C., Banks, C., & Zimbardo, P. (1973). Interpersonal dynamics in a simulated prison. *International Journal of Criminology and Penology, 1,* 69–97.

38. Owen, D. (2012). *The hubris syndrome: Bush, Blair and the intoxication of power.* London: Methuen.

39. Sivanathan, N., Pillutla, M. M., & Murnighan, K. (2008). Power gained, power lost. *Organizational Behavior and Human Decision Processes, 105,* 135–146.

40. Fast, N. J., Gruenfeld, D. H., Sivanathan, N., & Galinsky, A. D. (2009). Illusory control: A generative force begind power's far-reaching effects. *Psychological Science, 20,* 502–508.

41. Clausewitz, C. V. (1983). *On war* (transl. by Colonel J. J. Graham). London: N. Tuebner.

42. Sivanathan, N., Pillutla, M. M., & Murighan, K. (2008). Power gained, power lost. *Organizational Behavior and Human Decision Processes, 105,* 135–146.

43. Blake, R. R., & Mouton, J. S. (1964). *The managerial grid.* Houston, TX: Gulf Publishing Company.

44. Bass, B. M., & Riggio, R. E. (2006). *Transformational leadership* (2nd ed.) New York: Psychology Press.

45. Judge, T. A., & Piccolo, R. F. (2004). Transformational and transactional leadership: A meta-analytic test of their relative validity. *Journal of Applied Psychology, 89,* 755–768; Hinkin, T. R., & Schreisheim, C. A. (2008). An examination of "nonleadership": From laissez faire leadership to leader

reward omission and punishment omission. *Journal of Applied Psychology, 93,* 1234–1248.

46. Kelloway, E. K., Mullen, J., & Francis, L. (2006). Divergent effects of transformational and passive leadership on employee safety. *Journal of Occupational Health Psychology, 11,* 76–86.

47. Skogstad, A., Einarsen, S., Torsheim, R., Aasland, M. S., & Hetland, H. (2007). The destructiveness of laissez-faire leadership behavior. *Journal of Occupational Health Psychology, 12,* 80–92.

48. Hetland, H., Skogstad, A., Hetland, J., & Mikkelsen, A. (2011). Leadership and learning climate in a work setting. *European Psychologist, 16*(3), 163–173.

49. Townsend, J., Phillips, J. S., & Elkins, T. J. (2000). Employee retaliation: The neglected consequence of poor leader-member exchange relations. *Journal of Occupational Health Psychology, 5,* 457–463.

50. Lord, R. G., De Vader, C. L., & Alliger, G. M. (1986). A meta-analysis of the relationship between personality traits and leadership perceptions: An application of validity generalization procedures. *Journal of Applied Psychology, 71,* 402–410.

51. Ames, D. R., & Flynn, F. J. (2007). What breaks a leader: The curvilinear relation between assertiveness and leadership. *Journal of Personality and Social Psychology, 92,* 307–324.

52. De Jonge, J., & Schaufeli, W. B. (1988). Job characteristics and employee well-being: A test of Warr's Vitamin Model in health care workers using structural equation modelling. *Journal of Organizational Behavior, 19,* 387–407.

53. Hershcovis, M. S., & Barling, J. (2010). Comparing victim attributions and outcomes for workplace aggression and sexual harassment. *Journal of Applied Psychology, 95,* 874–888.

54. Hershcovis, S., Turner, N., Barling, J., Arnold, L., Dupré, K., Inness, M., Leblanc, M., & Sivanathan, N. (2007). Predicting workplace aggression: A meta-analytic approach. *Journal of Applied Psychology, 92,* 228–238.

55. Greenberg, J. (1990). Employee theft as a reaction to underpayment inequity: The hidden cost of pay cuts. *Journal of Applied Psychology, 75,* 561–568.

56. Greenberg, J. (1993). Stealing in the name of justice: Informational and interpersonal moderators of theft reactions to underpayment inequity. *Organizational Behavior and Human Decision Processes, 54,* 81–103.

57. Roberts, K., & Markel, K. S. (2001). Claiming in the name of justice: Organizational justice and the decision to file for Workplace Injury Compensation. *Journal of Occupational Health Psychology, 6,* 332–347.

58. Ryan, A. (2010, January 10). Conan rejects the NBC shuffle, hints he's poised to take a hike. *The Globe and Mail.* Retrieved from http://www.theglobeandmail.com/arts/conan-rejects-the-nbc-shuffle-hints-hes-poised-to-take-a-hike/article1207227/

59. Westerlund, H., Nyberg, A., Bernin, P., Hyde, M., Oxenstierna, G., Jäppinen, P., Väänänen, A., & Theorell, T. (2010). Managerial stress is associated with employee stress, health, and sickness absence independently of the demand-stress-control model. *Work, 37,* 71–79.

60. Kivimäki, M., Ferrie, J.E., Brunner, E., Head, J., Shipley, M. J., Vahtera, J., & Marmot, M. G. (2005). Justice at work and reduced risk of coronary heart disease among employees: The Whitehall II Study. *Archives of Internal Medicine, 165,* 2245–2251.

61. Carter, B. (2010, January 10). Fingers still pointing, NBC and O'Brien reach a deal. *New York Times.* Retrieved from http://www.nytimes.com/2010/01/22/

business/media/22conan.html?_r=0&adxnnl=1&adxnnlx=1369767776-GEN/
wn0S++vfxsuUOw84LQ

62. Hershcovis, M. S., & Barling, J. (2010). Toward a multi-foci approach to workplace aggression: A meta-analytic review of outcomes from different perpetrators. *Journal of Organizational Behavior, 31,* 24–44.

63. Liu, D., Liao, H., & Loi, R. (2012). The dark side of leadership: A three-level investigation of the cascading effect of abusive supervision on employee creativity. *Academy of Management Journal, 55,* 1187–1212.

64. Prottas, D. J. (2013). Relationships among employee perception of their manager's behavioral integrity, moral distress and employee attitudes and well-being. *Journal of Business Ethics, 113,* 51–60.

65. Fox, J. A., & Levin, J. (1994). Firing back: The growing threat of workplace homicide. *Annals of the American Academy of Political and Social Science, 536,* 16–30.

66. Kivimäki, M., Ferrie, J. E., Brunner, E., Head, J., Shipley, M. J., Vahtera, J., & Marmot, M. G. (2005). Justice at work and reduced risk of coronary heart disease among employees: The Whitehall II Study. *Archives of Internal Medicine, 165,* 2245–2251.

67. University College London Research Department of Epidemiology and Public Health. Whitehall II Study (Stress & Health Study). Retrieved from http://www.ucl.ac.uk/whitehallII

68. Kivimäki, M., Ferrie, J. E., Brunner, E., Head, J., Shipley, M. J., Vahtera, J., & Marmot, M. G. (2005). Justice at work and reduced risk of coronary heart disease among employees: The Whitehall II Study. *Archives of Internal Medicine, 165,* 2245–2251.

69. Elovainio, M., Kivimäki, M., Puttonen, S., Lindholm, H., Pohjonen, T., & Sinervo, T. (2006). Organisational injustice and impaired cardiovascular regulation. among female employees. *Occupational and Environmental Medicine, 63,* 141–144

70. Nyberg, A., Alfredsson, L., Theorell, T., Westerlund, H., Vahtera, J., & Kivimäki, M. (2009). Managerial leadership and ischaemic heart disease among employees: The Swedish WOLF study. *Occupational and Environmental Medicine, 66,* 51–55.

71. Job Stress Network (n.d.). The Wolf Project: Selected abstracts. http://www.workhealth.org/projects/hpwolf.html

72. Wagar, N., Fieldman, G., & Hussey, T. (2003). The effect of ambulatory blood pressure of working under favourably and unfavorably perceived supervisors. *Occupational and Environmental Medicine, 60,* 468–474.

73. Trice, H. M., & Roman, P. M. (1978). *Spirits and demons at work: alcohol and other drugs on the job.* Ithaca, NY: New York State School of Industrial and Labor Relations.

74. Frone, M. R. (2013). *Alcohol and illicit drug use in the workforce and workplace.* Washington, DC: American Psychological Association.

75. Bacharach, S. B., Bamberger, P. A., & Doveh, E. (2008). Firefighters, critical incidents, and drinking to cope: The adequacy of unit-level performance. *Journal of Applied Psychology. 93,* 155–169.

76. Frone, M. R. (2013). *Alcohol and illicit drug use in the workforce and workplace.* Washington, DC: American Psychological Association.

77. Bamberger, P. A., & Bacharach, S. B. (2006). Abusive supervision and subordinate problem drinking: Taking resistance, stress and subordinate personality into account. *Human Relations, 59,* 723–752.

78. Richman, J. A., Flaherty, J. A. & Rospenda, K. M. (1996). Perceived workplace harassment experiences and problem drinking among physicians: Broadening the stress/alienation paradigm. *Addiction, 91*, 391–403.
79. Kouvenen, A., Kivimäki, M., Elovainio, M., Väänänen, A., De Vogel, R., et al. (2008). Low organizational injustice and heavy drinking: A prospective cohort study. *Organizational and Environmental Medicine, 65*, 44–50.
80. Ylipaavalniemi, J., Kivimäki, M., Elovainio, M., Virtanen, M., Keltikangas-Järvinen, L., & Vahtera, J. (2005). Psychosocial work characteristics and incidence of newly diagnosed depression: A prospective cohort study of three different models. *Social Science and Medicine, 61*, 111–122.
81. Theorell, T., Nyberg, A., Leineweber, C., Magnusson Hanson, L. L., Oxenstierna, G., et al. (2012) Non-listening and self-centered leadership—relationships to socioeconomic conditions and employee mental health. *PLoS ONE 7*(9): e44119.
82. Mawritz, M. B., Mayer, D. M., Hoobler, J. M., Wayne, S. J., & Marinova, S. V. (2012). A trickle-down model of abusive supervision. *Personnel Psychology, 65*, 325–357.
83. Hoobler, J. M., & Brass, D. J. (2006). Abusive supervision and family undermining as displaced aggression. *Journal of Applied Psychology, 91*, 1125–1133.
84. Carlson, D. S., Ferguson, M., Perrewé, P. L., & Whitten, D. (2011). The fallout from abusive supervision: An examination of subordinates and their partners. *Personnel Psychology, 64*, 937–961.
85. Restubog, S. L. D., Scott, K. L., & Zagenczyk, T. J. (2011). When distress hits home: The role of contextual factors and psychological distress in predicting employees' responses to abusive supervision. *Journal of Applied Psychology, 96*, 713–729.
86. Kivimäki, M., Ferrie, J. E., Brunner, E., Head, J., Shipley, M. J., Vahtera, J., & Marmot, M. G. (2005). Justice at work and reduced risk of coronary heart disease among employees: The Whitehall II Study. *Archives of Internal Medicine, 165*, 2245–2251.

CHAPTER 10
Enough about Leadership
Let's Talk about Followership!

Not all corporate success is due to leadership.
R.E. Kelley (1988, p. 142)[1]

E ven a cursory glance at leadership theories over the past decade will show that organizational and leadership theories worship the role of leaders and ignore or denigrate the role of followers in understanding leadership and organizational success. This is evident in the titles of books on heroic leaders: *Indispensable,*[2] *Churchill: The Prophetic Statesman,*[3] and *The Last Lion.*[4] Intriguingly, *Troublesome Young Men*[5] is also a book about Winston Churchill, but tells the very different story of approximately 30 young parliamentarians without whose active support and efforts Churchill would not have been elevated to the position of prime minister in the first instance. Which books do we choose to read? Which stories do we remember?

The virtual worship of leadership is reflected equally in various media. Newspaper articles, TV shows, and movies about wonderful and dreadful political and organizational leadership abound, but it would be difficult indeed to find similar articles or movies that lionize followers to the same extent.

In contrast, consider the situation in a different social science discipline. The psychology of intimate relationships includes the study of the *dyadic* nature, causes, and consequences of romantic and marital relationships. Now imagine if the last 50 years of social science research devoted to understanding intimate relationships had focused almost exclusively on one of the partners alone (perhaps the husband), implicitly denying that the other partner had any role in the success of their relationship. How likely would we be to see the knowledge generated as credible or complete? Yet arguably, this is what has happened in the study of leadership, and the goal in this chapter is to highlight the inseparable role of followers in the leader–follower relationship. To achieve this goal, I will investigate four separate topics: conceptions about followership, leadership "in the eye of the beholder," leader and follower personality, and the influence of followers on leader behavior.

Before embarking on this discussion, one crucial point must be emphasized. Isolating and highlighting the role of followers in no way implies that leaders and leadership are of no importance within organizations. On the contrary, bringing followers and followership back into the equation will enable a more complete understanding of leadership, at the same time providing an opportunity to enhance leadership and organizational effectiveness.

CONCEPTIONS ABOUT FOLLOWERSHIP

Almost everyone has a view on what constitutes "ideal" or prototypical leadership, and these views start to form well before people encounter their first organizational leaders. As Tiffany Keller showed in her research,[6] for example, the parenting behaviors to which people are exposed early in their lives help shape later perceptions of what will be considered an ideal leadership style, or what is now known as implicit leadership theories. Given this, might people develop beliefs about what constitutes ideal followership behavior in the same way? The idea is not far-fetched. Consider a child about to embark on her or his first part-time job, be it as a babysitter, newspaper deliverer, minding tables at a restaurant, or working in a fast-food chain. It would not take a leap of imagination to believe that this child will arrive at the job having been counseled on the characteristics of an ideal employee: deferential, punctual, obedient, tidy, a good listener, and so forth.

As Augustine Agho's survey of 302 senior-level public- and private-sector executives in the United States shows, adults certainly have stereotypes of effective followership.[7] She found that senior-level executives ranked honesty/integrity, competence, dependability, loyalty, and supportiveness as the five most important characteristics of effective followers. In contrast, they ranked integrity/honesty, competence, forward looking, inspirational, and intelligence as the five most important attributes of successful leaders. While it is comforting to learn that honesty and integrity are ranked so highly for both leaders and followers, the passive roles attached to followers are emphasized in the other attributes (competence, dependability, loyalty and supportiveness). Given significant differences between lay people's notions of effective leadership vs. followership, recent studies investigating the nature and consequences of implicit followership beliefs tell an interesting story.

The Nature of Implicit Followership Theories

Two very different research projects highlight how people view ideal followership. In the first project, Thomas Sy conducted five separate studies that used a total of 1,362 participants. Across these different studies,[8] Sy showed that six different adjectives were generally believed to characterize followers and their behavior: industry, enthusiasm, good citizen, conformity, insubordination, and incompetence. Further analysis showed that these six characteristics could be accurately described by two dimensions, the first being prototypical (or positive) followership, comprising industry, enthusiasm, and good citizenship, with the second dimension comprising antiprototypical (or negative) followership, which was reflected by conformity, insubordination, and incompetence. Sy went further and showed that these two perceptions of followership are associated with significant outcomes. When leaders' views about followership were prototypical (or positive), they were positively and significantly associated with the extent to which followers trusted and liked their leaders and with the overall quality of the leader–follower relationship. In contrast, higher antiprototypical (or negative) scores were associated with lower trust and liking of the leader and a poorer quality of relationship between leader and follower.

Melissa Carsten and her colleagues took a different approach, and investigated people's perceptions of followership through in-depth interviews with 31 participants from a variety of different organizations and organizational levels in the United States and Canada.[9] Like Sy's study, Carsten and her team again found that perceptions about followership are best captured within several different categories. However, based on their interview data, the researchers suggest that followership is best described as passive, active, or proactive. Passive followership probably emerges from deep-rooted social traditions that value obedience to authority and reward those who hold senior hierarchical positions as knowledgeable and powerful. Individuals who hold an active perspective of followership still value obedience to authority, but would willingly take any opportunities for involvement that were available. In contrast, followers who hold a proactive perspective of followership see themselves as active and on an equal footing with their leaders. As a result, they would not wait for invitations to participate in decisions, but would actively create opportunities for themselves to do so.

Unlike Sy, who suggests that implicit followership theories revolve around two somewhat separate dimensions, Carsten and colleagues see a continuum extending from passive through to proactive followership. Irrespective of any such differences, what is far more important is that both approaches assume that implicit theories of followership hold important implications, and research findings support this.

Perhaps one of the first studies that shed some light on the effects of follower-ship was conducted more than two decades ago, in an attempt to understand a long-standing social problem: Why do so few people intervene in emergency situations in which someone is clearly in distress? For this study, undergraduate students who had volunteered to participate in a study were told that they were being placed in a four-person group[10] and that they would be assigned randomly as either the group's leader or one of the assistants. After the experiment had begun, all participants heard a person outside of their room calling for help, ostensibly choking. While the overwhelming majority (80%) of study participants who thought they were "leaders" left the room to provide some assistance, only 35% of those who believed that they were "assistants" did so. Clearly, thinking one holds a leadership role presupposes action. However, because this study was focused on providing help in emergencies, it does not speak directly to the effects of being labeled a "follower."

Several years after this study, David Day, Hock-Peng Sin, and Tina Chen extended this idea beyond the laboratory and investigated the effects on performance levels of being named as team captain in the National Hockey League (NHL) in the United States.[11] They collected data on all teams over a 10-year period, from which they compared player performance during seasons in which they were the team captain with performance during seasons when they were not. Because one of the major reasons that players would be elevated to team captain is the high quality of their performance in the previous year, Day and his colleagues controlled statistically for performance in the year prior to be selected as the team captain, adding to the credibility of their study. Their findings showed convincingly that players' performance was better in years in which they themselves were team captains than those in which they were not, and team captains performed better than other players. What both of these studies convey is that not being labeled as a leader tells people that they have little or no responsibility and, extending the lessons learned from previous chapters, they then respond accordingly.

Neither of these studies focused specifically on the term "follower." Acknowledging that the term "follower" conveys a stigma, Collette Hoption, Amy Christie, and I conducted two separate studies[12] to understand the specific consequences of being labeled a "follower." In both studies, we were interested in followers' own responses to this label. In the first study, undergraduate business student volunteers were led through an elaborate set of bogus "personality" tests that they had been led to believe would assess whether they were best suited in the long term to the role of "leader" or "follower." (There was also a control group for whom no label was given.) Based purely on random assignment, student volunteers were assigned the "leader" or the "follower" label. Two intriguing findings emerged. First, simply getting the students to believe that they were more suited to the "follower" label resulted in their scoring significantly lower than the "leaders" on a measure of positive affect (i.e., the extent to which they were generally interested, determined, able to concentrate, attentive, and active). Second, the lower positive affect that resulted from being labeled "follower" in turn resulted in a decrease in the extent to which that individual was willing to attend an early-morning or weekend meeting—the cooperative behaviors that would help one's group and organization to thrive. To appreciate the strength of the stigma surrounding the term "follower," the immediacy of any effects of being told one was likely to be a follower must be emphasized: Participants' affect and voluntary behaviors were affected immediately upon being labeled as a follower (or leader)!

This study, however, only tells us what happens when we explicitly give people the label of follower or leader. In organizational settings, the process is more subtle, and an equally salient and practical psychological question concerns the effects of labeling oneself as a follower. In a variation of our first study, we asked people who were employed on a part-time basis how they labeled themselves in their work roles (e.g., "Overall, I would say that my role in this job is that of a follower"). Labeling oneself as a follower again resulted in lower positive affect, which in turn resulted in less willingness to engage in voluntary activities to assist one's organization.

Two recent studies focus on the effects of more positive conceptions of followership. In the first, Melissa Carsten and Mary Uhl-Bien were interested in followers' beliefs about the "co-production of leadership"—the extent to which followers see themselves as partners in the leadership process, working together as co-equals to achieve higher levels of productivity.[13] Based on a large U.S. sample, 206 followers who endorsed a belief in the co-production of leadership were more likely to engage in upward communications with their leaders (e.g., voluntarily make recommendations about work-related issues) and, when appropriate, to constructively resist attempts by their supervisors to influence them. Findings such as these indirectly underline the importance of any negative effects associated with the follower label.

Paul Whitely, Thomas Sy, and Stefanie Johnson examined implicit followership theories from the perspective of the Pygmalion effect discussed earlier (see Chapter 6).[14] Both of these theories involve thoughts and expectations about followers' skills, motivation, and performance. Aside from positive or negative expectations, a major difference is that while the Pygmalion effect focuses on specific employees, implicit followership theories involve expectations about followers in general and, presumably, therefore, would be stable across different situations and different followers. Whitely and his team examined the effects of leaders' general views of followership on employee performance (as rated by a team member). Several important findings emerged from their study in 151 workgroup leaders and their followers in the United States. Replicating the Pygmalion effect, leaders' positive conceptions of followership strongly predicted their expectations about the performance of individual teams. In addition, leaders' positive views of followership were directly associated with (a) higher levels of liking of the leader by team members, and (b) higher quality leader–member exchanges, (c) both of which directly predicted followers' job performance.

One question that remains is whether any negative consequences invoked by the follower label might be circumvented by eliminating or avoiding this term altogether. While there is no evidenced-based answer to this question, it is unclear whether merely substituting other terms (e.g., "subordinate," "assistant," "worker") would make any difference. Nonetheless, in searching for an appropriate a term, perhaps a lesson can be learned from marital contexts, where individuals in the dyad are referred to as partners—conveying equal roles, rights, and responsibilities. A different option emerges from Whitely and colleagues' finding that leaders with less supervisory experience held stronger conceptions about followership. This suggests that early leadership training ought to focus explicitly on the predisposition to hold such conceptions about followership and the potentially negative consequences of the Golem effect (in which supervisors' lower expectations result in lower employee performance).[15] If the follower label has negative consequences because of what it conveys symbolically, one option open to leaders would be to ensure that their behaviors convey a different message, one that is more consistent with the proactive conception of followership identified by Carsten and her colleagues.[16]

"IN THE EYE OF THE BEHOLDER?"

One of the more memorable features of terrible crises, whether they be wars between great nations, or national crises such as the 9/11 attacks in the United States, is how someone almost inevitably steps forward to provide remarkable, charismatic leadership. Much has been written in this respect about U.S. President George W. Bush's leadership before, during, and after the 9/11 attacks.[17] Before the attacks, Bush's approval ratings had been languishing, with only 51% of Americans expressing satisfaction with his job performance as president. Yet just days after the attacks, with his iconic speech to the joint session of Congress on Thursday, September 20, 2011, and the image of the President standing on a pile of rubble at the site of the World Trade Center. arm-in-arm with a firefighter, his approval rating rose to 81%, the highest ever recorded by the Gallup poll organization, which had been conducting similar polling analyses since World War II.

Just how charismatic leaders seem to step to the fore in times of great crisis is even more apparent in the case of New York City Mayor Rudy Giuliani. Giuliani's mayoral performance prior to the attacks was nothing short of problematic.[18] He had unleashed racial tension by impugning the character of Amadou Diallo, a young, unarmed West African immigrant who had been shot in the back 41 times by four police officers at the door to his apartment in a case of mistaken identity.[19] Embarrassingly, in a public display of lack of empathy and respect, Giuliani announced at a press conference that he would be separating from his wife after an extramarital relationship—before telling his wife! And as the 9/11 Commission would subsequently show, significant decisions influenced by the Mayor before 9/11 (e.g., placing the New York City emergency command center at the World Trade Centre in 1997 despite arguments from the chiefs of the police and emergency management departments that it was a probable future target for terrorism given the earlier 1993 attacks; and choosing not to upgrade communication devices so that police and firefighter personnel could communicate directly after failures in the 1993 attack) negatively affected rescue efforts immediately after the 9/11 attacks and contributed to the enormous loss of life.[20] Despite the seemingly shocking nature of these actions, I do not mention them simply to impugn former Mayor Giuliani. Instead, these incidents will help to highlight the magnitude of the apparent changes in Giuliani's leadership during the crisis of 9/11.

Despite this negative public persona, Mayor Giuliani was soon to demonstrate a quality of leadership that transformed him from what Michael Powell called "a grouchy pol slip-sliding into irrelevancy"[21] to a leader who would be lionized across the world, and the subject of considerable discussion in leadership development courses in business schools. A few incidents are sufficient to illustrate his apparent change in leadership. Speaking at a press conference several hours after the two towers had collapsed, when people in New York were overwhelmed with fear, anxiety, and uncertainty, Giuliani showed optimism and a firm belief in people's ability to overcome the tragedy, saying: "Tomorrow New York is going to be here. And we're going to rebuild, and we're going to be stronger than we were before.... I want the people of New York to be an example to the rest of the country, and the rest of the world." Speaking at the same press conference, Giuliani was asked if he could estimate the number of people who had died that day, and his answer was full of empathy when he responded: "The number of casualties will be more than any of us can bear ultimately." In the days and weeks following the attacks, Giuliani then did what must have been exceptionally painful—attending funerals, sometimes five in a day, of people who had perished in the attacks. As each funeral ended, he again lifted the mourners, inviting them to say their final farewell with a standing ovation. What these three examples illustrate is the optimism, empathy, and ability to elevate others when in their darkest moments, all of which is characteristic of great leadership in crises.

Giuliani's leadership did not go unnoticed. By the end of 2001, he was awarded an Honorary Knighthood by Queen Elizabeth, and *Time Magazine* named him their 2001 Person of the Year, for "having more faith in us than we had in ourselves, for being brave when required and rude where appropriate and tender without being trite, for not sleeping and not quitting and not shrinking from the pain all around him."[22] He had become, as *Time Magazine* called him, the "Mayor of the World."

Examples of seemingly charismatic leaders rising to the top during times of great duress are not infrequent, and are epitomized in comments such as "Cometh the hour, cometh the man"[i]—often used to describe Winston Churchill's ascendancy in World War II and in the "great man" theory of leadership. But is it really possible to see so much change occur, and so quickly, in one leader? Could one leader, acting single-handedly, really act as the Mayor of the World—overnight? Or is there a different, more complex but more plausible explanation for such a visible and important phenomenon? The answer would appear to be yes. Although all of these examples tell compelling stories about charismatic leaders—which we all like to believe, especially during crises—they all share one common characteristic: They completely ignore the vital role of followers.

To begin to appreciate this leadership phenomenon though, recall Bass' observation that during times of great crisis, followers become "charisma hungry"[23] and display a "psychological receptiveness" for charismatic leadership. The fact that journalists are not immune from this hunger for or receptiveness to charisma adds considerably to our understanding of this phenomenon. Steve Rendell observed that "On September 11, 2001, with George W. Bush in hiding for much of the day, mainstream journalists were desperately looking for a man on horseback. For many, that man would be New York City Mayor Rudolph Giuliani."[24] Having found their charismatic leader, Giuliani would now feature prominently in their media stories, at the very least helping to create, reinforce, and perpetuate the image of a remarkable leadership transformation.

Leadership myths aside, there is now a growing body of theorizing and supportive research findings showing that we can no longer ignore the needs and behavior of followers during major crises. Indeed, until the roles of followers are fully appreciated, a realistic understanding of leadership emergence, behavior, and effectiveness during crises will remain beyond our grasp. Two separate literatures, focusing on mortality salience and the romance of leadership, will offer an alternative to the "great leader" phenomenon.

Mortality Salience

One characteristic of the worst crises (or natural disasters) is the threat (both existential and physical) that they pose to those caught up in the crisis,

---

i. The beguiling simplicity of this statement belies the complex story of Churchill's rise to power in World War II, masterfully told in Lynne Olson's (2007) *Troublesome Young Men: The Rebels who Brought Churchill to Power and Helped Save England.*

because crises of this magnitude remind people of their mortality. One way of coping with existential threats and thoughts about one's mortality is to coalesce around charismatic leaders, who help people cope by increasing the belief that they can get through the crisis and promoting feelings of being a valued member of the in-group. This effect is magnified when an existential threat is perceived as externally generated, as feelings of in-group identity and solidarity would be heightened and attributed to the actions of the charismatic leader. If this is indeed the case, Rudy Giuliani's leadership following the attacks of 9/11 must be explained, at least partially, not just by his actions, but by the overriding needs of people everywhere.

Several studies have investigated the effects of what psychologists like to call "mortality salience"—that is, subtle external reminders of the inevitability of one's mortality and its relevance to leadership. Fiorette Cohen and her associates conducted two separate studies after 9/11 that clarify the relationship between mortality salience and leadership perceptions. In their first study, which was appropriately titled "Fatal Attraction,"[25] the researchers used an experimental technique in which one group of participants was reminded of their inevitable mortality, while the second group was not exposed to thoughts of mortality salience at all. The effects of being reminded of one's potential mortality were then assessed on how participants responded to three different leadership styles—charismatic, relationship-oriented, and task-oriented leadership. As expected, enthusiasm for and evaluation of the charismatic leaders were significantly higher when participants were reminded of their mortality, but this was not the case for either of the other two leadership styles. In fact, there was lower enthusiasm for the relationship-oriented leader who emphasized the importance of personal responsibility. The researchers went further, and asked participants which of the three leaders they would vote for if an election took place. Once mortality salience had been induced, there was a massive increase (almost 800%) in votes for the charismatic leader. In contrast, being reminded of one's mortality produced no change in votes for the task-oriented leader and an unexpected decline in votes for the relationship-oriented leader.

Cohen and her colleagues then conducted a second study, in which they investigated actual voting preferences of registered voters for George W. Bush and John Kerry just prior to the 2004 U.S. presidential election.[26] To place this second study in context, the elections took place at a time when there were constant reminders to the public at large of their mortality, expressed most frequently through electioneering speeches and intermittent warnings about the need for heightened security. Against this backdrop, Cohen and her colleagues found that in psychologically nonthreatening situations where mortality salience was not an issue, study participants overwhelmingly preferred Senator John Kerry (by 4:1). When participants were reminded of the existential and physical threats around them, the tables were turned, with participants significantly expressing a preference for George W. Bush by more than 2:1.

Other research studies confirm that subtle reminders of death influence people's perceptions of leadership. First, merely providing people with subliminal stimuli associated with the attacks in 9/11 was sufficient to trigger thoughts of one's mortality, which in turn increased individuals' support for President Bush (but again, not for Senator John Kerry), and also for President Bush's policies regarding counterterrorism.[27] Second, mortality salience influenced what people regard as an effective leader.[28] A laboratory study showed that both men and women who were exposed to thoughts about mortality were more likely to see an effective leader as someone who was proactive, competitive, and confident, that is, more agentic, than those not exposed to mortality thoughts.

A separate study examined the effects of government-issued terror warnings on approval ratings of President Bush using an entirely different research methodology.[29] Robb Willer found 26 instances between February 1, 2001 and May 9, 2004 in which a government agency had declared that there was an increased threat of terrorism in the United States. During the same period, there were 44 Gallup opinion polls measuring presidential approval. Even after controlling for prior levels of approval of the President's performance, a terror warning issued in the previous week was associated with an average 2.75% increase in approval of President George W. Bush. Two aspects of these findings are especially worth noting. First, any positive effects of a terror warning were not limited to overall presidential approval ratings, but were also associated with better perceptions of the President's handling of the economy, pointing to the potential widespread effects of mortality salience. Second, any positive effects of mortality salience in this situation were short-lived, lasting no longer than a week. This has important practical implications, suggesting that any potential leadership opportunities of the more positive perceptions are time-limited.

Finally, the role of the media in the relationship between followers and leaders during crises cannot be ignored. We have already seen that journalists are equally susceptible to the need for charisma during crises[30] and likely convey this in their stories. However, if leaders come to believe the way in which they are portrayed, overconfidence or hubris might result, with negative consequences for their future behavior and for their followers.[31] Because there is no certainty that all leaders would act responsibly and ethically faced with employees or followers who are unusually receptive to charisma, safeguards may need to be considered. In this respect, Linda Simon and her coauthors showed that the effects of mortality salience can be limited if rational information is available to followers during major crises.[32] Notwithstanding any personal anguish they themselves are experiencing,[33] journalists have a role in ensuring that this occurs.

The Romance of Leadership

As humans, we are faced with many seemingly inexplicable situations, and we struggle to make sense of what is happening around us or even to us. Controversial behavioral psychologist B.F. Skinner best captured this predicament more than 40 years ago, when he observed, "We stand in awe of the inexplicable, and...we are likely to admire behavior more as we understand it less" (p. 53).[34] Whether in work organizations or the larger social environment, people are frequently confronted with events that appear to defy explanation: Managing the fall of the Soviet empire, overturning apartheid and installing a nonracial government, or even watching a city and country recover from the attacks of 9/11 all serve as perfect examples.

Just over a decade after Skinner's observation, James Meindl and his colleagues Sanford Ehrlich and Janet Dukerich set out to understand how people make sense of situations in which extremely high performance occurs.[35] The findings from their classic study revealed that people ascribe increasing prominence to leadership in explaining ever-higher levels of organizational performance, but leadership is also likely to be seen as the cause of poor organizational performance. Meindl and his colleagues then showed in a separate study that as people search for explanations for improvements or declines in their national economy, there is a greater interest in understanding leadership, and this was especially true for those involved in business. One additional aspect of their conclusions warrants special attention given earlier comments in this chapter. Like others subsequently,[36] they emphasized the critical role of the business media in advancing a romanticized view of leadership. Tellingly, what was totally absent in followers' understanding of the causes for high (or low) performance is any role that they themselves may have had, or any role that the situation may have played. Taking all these findings together, Meindl and his colleagues spoke of the "romance of leadership": the near-blind faith that followers place in the power of their leaders—sometimes despite all the existing evidence to the contrary.

Following Meindl, Ehrlich, and Dukerich's classic study, there has been a considerable body of research investigating the romance of leadership, so much so that Michelle Bligh, Jeffrey Kohles, and Rajnandini Pillai identified more than 100 articles in major management journals over the ensuing 25 years.[37] The results of these studies confirm the causal role people ascribe to leadership in comprehending organizational successes and failures and major social events. While it would obviously be impossible to tell the story of each of these studies, the romance of leadership has several broad implications worthy of discussion.

First, not all individuals romanticize leadership to the same extent. Instead, as Meindl made clear,[38] people differ meaningfully in the extent to which they are prone to romanticizing leadership. As a result, Meindl and his colleagues developed the Romance of Leadership questionnaire, which has been validated in different countries (Germany, the Netherlands, the United States).[39] Items in this questionnaire do not focus on any specific leader but instead on followers' perceptions of leadership in general and of the presumably important role of leadership in social situations. Analyses confirm that followers who obtain higher scores on the Romance of Leadership scale do indeed exaggerate their leaders' importance, for example, by overemphasizing information about their leaders rather than characteristics of the situation in making decisions.[40]

Second, leaders may come to romanticize their own leadership, a process that could be heightened by overly positive media coverage,[41] and positive feedback from other sources as well. Data from U.S.[42] and Australian business executives[43] support this, showing that leaders' estimates of their own transformational leadership are inflated. Third, while CEOs are romanticized in situations of unusually favorable performance, the corollary is not necessarily true: CEOs are more likely to escape accountability for organizational failures. Acknowledging that CEO and executive tenure is higher in successful organizations, Warren Boeker investigated the effects of poor organizational performance on CEO dismissal in the semiconductor industry between 1968 and 1989.[44] Dismissal of CEOs for poor performance does occur, but it is relatively infrequent. A more common phenomenon is that CEOs would not be dismissed for poor overall performance, but top managers were! The data from Bocker's study revealed 206 cases in which a member of the top management team, rather than the CEO, was dismissed, but only 77 situations in which a CEO but no top manager was dismissed. In fact, more powerful CEOs were more likely to hold onto their own positions, as they could shift any blame for poor performance onto members of top management.

The fourth implication of romanticizing leadership involves followers' arousal. In crises this is an important consideration: While not all crises result in thoughts of mortality, they are often sufficient to enhance physiological arousal (e.g., heart rate). Juan Carlos Pastor, Margarita Mayo, and Boas Shamir showed that in a state of high arousal, participants rated a charismatic leader as even more charismatic (compared with participants in a state of low arousal) but found no changes for leaders low in charisma.[45] Importantly, this effect was specific to charisma, as arousal had no effect at all on ratings of transactional leadership.

Fifth, when interpreting employee feedback within a 360-degree feedback exercise, it is assumed that subordinates provide objective information about their leaders' behaviors. The romance of leadership might suggest otherwise: Perhaps the information provided by followers tells us as much about the followers as about their leaders. At the very least, follower data in 360-degree exercises should be interpreted with caution during times of organizational success or turmoil, when the differential tendency to roman-ticize leadership might be at its highest. Relatedly, the conventional prac-tice in 360-degree feedback exercises is to aggregate all employees' reports. Doing so, however, would miss the opportunity to uncover important infor-mation about any differences or similarities in followers' perceptions of leaders' behaviors.

Finally, Meindl answered the question of why followers would willingly overemphasize the role of leadership in their attempts to understand com-plex social phenomena, in an article published posthumously, shortly after his passing in 2004.[46] He suggested that in seeking to reduce uncertainty and make sense of complex social and organizational phenomena that may signifi-cantly affect people's own well-being, a certain level of psychological comfort and a sense of security would result from a firm belief in leadership. In addition to these emotional benefits, there are also cognitive advantages.[47] Assigning responsibility for successful (or unsuccessful) company performance to just one cause (leadership) helps people make sense of the complex, multiple, and diverse causes that do exist. Paradoxically, however, as emotionally and cogni-tively comforting as the sole belief in leadership may be, it reduces the likeli-hood that we will eventually develop a sufficiently nuanced understanding of the real nature and effects of leadership.

GOING (WAY) BEYOND LEADERS' PERSONALITY

When researchers try to unlock the secrets of leadership, the possibility that leaders' personality is heavily implicated in leader emergence, leader-ship behaviors, and leadership success always looms large. In fact, the role of personality is one of the most frequently studied aspects within leadership. Before going any further, however, we need to delineate briefly what research-ers view as "personality," given that it is a topic burdened by the widely differ-ent meanings that people ascribe to it.

While many researchers have investigated the nature and meaning of per-sonality, Robert McCrae and Paul Costa are among the most recent research-ers credited with delineating what has come to be known as the "Big 5" personality dimensions:[48] openness to experience, conscientiousness, extra-version, agreeableness, and neuroticism (collectively known by the acronym OCEAN). Two important points must be highlighted, because much of the credible research on personality and leadership has been focused on the Big 5 personality dimensions. First, fully describing personality within these five dimensions does not mean that other personality characteristics (e.g., asser-tiveness or altruism) do not exist. Instead, more specific characteristics are subsumed within the Big 5, which are meant to reflect the highest level of personality. Second, the Big 5 is a system that describes personality among the regular population, rather than disorders of personality (e.g., borderline personality disorder).

While it is dangerous to try and encapsulate the vast body of research on leadership and personality in just a few sentences, several conclusions are justified from Timothy Judge and colleagues' extensive research on personality and leadership.[49] First, leaders' extraversion is the most consistent predictor of leadership emergence, leadership, and leadership effectiveness. Second, conscientiousness and openness to experience are also strongly associated with leadership, with conscientiousness strongly associated with leader emergence. This is not surprising, as conscientious employees would quickly come to the fore and be more likely to be promoted to a leadership position. Third, neither neuroticism nor agreeableness seemed to be meaningfully implicated in leadership.

Joyce Bono and Timothy Judge extended these analyses to investigate how leaders' personality was associated with transformational leadership in general, and its four dimensions more specifically.[50] Several conclusions can be drawn from their research. First, extraversion was again the most consistent personality correlate of transformational leadership and its four dimensions (but especially, idealized influence and inspirational motivation). Second, the correlations of the Big 5 personality dimensions with transactional leadership (contingent reward, management-by-exception, and passive leadership) were low enough to be of no practical meaning whatsoever. Third, taking these results together with those of Judge and colleagues' previous study,[51] personality is likely implicated more in leadership emergence than in the performance of transformational and transactional leadership behaviors.

The discussion so far reflects the enormous body of research on the link between leader personality and leader emergence, behavior, and effectiveness. The primary objective of this chapter is to take leader personality further, however, and to show how including follower personality, needs, and preferences together with those of their leaders will expand our understanding of leadership and increase leader effectiveness. This possibility is neither new nor far-fetched. As early as 1956, William Haythorn and his co-researchers demonstrated in a laboratory study that when authoritarian leaders were paired with authoritarian followers, they behaved in a more autocratic manner. In contrast, they behaved less autocratically when their followers were less authoritarian.[52] This led the researchers to conclude that "the behavior of leaders is, to a significant degree, a function of the attitudes or personality characteristics of the followers" (p. 218). More recently, we have seen that any effects of CEO charisma on organizational effectiveness are dependent on situational characteristics, specifically the extent of environmental uncertainty,[53] all of which suggests that leadership effectiveness is a function of more than just the leader.

Leaders' Extraversion

Susan Cain noted in a *New York Times* article that most people believe that extraversion is a necessary condition for leadership (even though they may not understand precisely what extraversion really is); in fact, she suggested that "culturally, we tend to associate leadership with extraversion."[54] Notwithstanding such conclusions, a close reading of the research shows that the magnitude of the relationship between leader extraversion and leader emergence or success is modest at best; there is probably a lot more to the story regarding leaders' extraversion!

Should we expect that extraversion provides an advantage for all leaders under all conditions? Are there perhaps no situations in which less extraversion manifested by leaders might be beneficial? After all, Ames and Flynn have shown that high levels of leader assertiveness can be counterproductive.[55] Consistent with the ideas discussed earlier of a more active role for followers in both the leader–follower relationship and in leadership effectiveness, Adam Grant, Francesca Gino, and David Hofmann reasoned that the extraversion advantage for leaders is dependent on followers' proactivity.[56] This intriguing idea is based on several assumptions. First, the notion that one leadership characteristic would be sufficient to account fully for leader effectiveness ignores the increasing complexity and uncertainty that characterizes current organizational reality. Second, the growing importance to organizational success of employee proactivity has become apparent over the past decade or so. Employees' proactive behaviors include spontaneously taking action to correct problems and offering advice up the hierarchy regarding work-related problems and issues.[57] But as Grant and his colleagues note, not all leaders are receptive to such behaviors from their employees. Central to the researchers' argument about extraverted leadership is the fact that both extraversion and proactivity involve a level of dominant and assertive behavior, while higher quality interpersonal interactions emerge when there is a balance (rather than a similarity) between characteristics such as dominance and assertiveness, or obedience and compliance. Intriguingly, going back to their 1956 study, Haythorn and his team found that follower satisfaction was higher when there was *dissimilarity* between leader and follower with respect to authoritarianism (although they acknowledged at that stage that they could not offer a satisfactory explanation).[58]

Thus, defying conventional wisdom about leader extraversion, Grant and his colleagues predicted that group performance would be highest when extraverted leaders were paired with less proactive employees, and proactive employees were paired with less extraverted leaders. They conducted two different studies, the first of which investigated 57 store leaders and 374 employees of a nationwide pizza delivery company in the United States. They showed that after controlling for aspects such as each store's proximity to a university campus, which can significantly influence profitability, extraverted leadership was indeed associated with higher store profits—but only when paired with *less* proactive employees. At the same time, store profitability was significantly *lower* when extraverted leaders were paired with proactive followers. The researchers then replicated these findings in a laboratory study that allowed for greater control of external factors that might have affected their findings.

The results of these two studies offer an important practical lesson. The seemingly counterproductive finding that extraverted leaders are less effective when paired with proactive employees in no way implies that employee proactivity should be discouraged. Instead, organizations and their leaders need to be aware of the possible negative consequences of any leader–follower personality differences. One way of achieving this awareness would be to ensure that leadership development programs deal explicitly with the realities of followership.

Leaders' Anger

Everyday work experience would confirm that leaders clearly differ in their displays of diverse emotions. Some leaders tend to display positive emotions such as happiness to influence the motivation and performance of their followers. When this happens, followers could infer that their behaviors and performance were optimal and be motivated to maintain or increase their efforts. Other leaders express more negative emotions—and use anger, for example, in an attempt to achieve the same goals. In these situations, leaders may believe that followers would assume that problems in their work performance had brought on the anger and be motivated to correct or improve their performance.

Some research studies have investigated the performance consequences of anger and positive emotions as leadership styles, and at first glance, the results of these studies seem somewhat contradictory. Expressions of leader anger and positive emotions have both been associated with positive team performance.[59] At the same time, negative emotions such as leader anger have been linked with lower ratings of leaders' effectiveness.[60] Seemingly inconsistent findings such as these typically do not discourage researchers. On the contrary, they almost invite researchers to delve deeper for the factors that account for any inconsistencies. In this case, psychological theory about emotions[61] would suggest that any effects of anger are at least partially dependent on recipients (i.e., followers), who would differ in the extent to which they see anger as acceptable in interpersonal interactions or not.

Gerben Van Kleef and his colleagues conducted two laboratory studies in the Netherlands to investigate how leaders' anger affects followers' motivation and team performance.[62] They used the Big 5 personality dimensions to help explain any effects of leaders' anger and included a focus on followers' agreeableness. Specifically, because agreeable people will prefer more amiable social interactions, performance should be lower when leaders express anger toward followers who themselves are high in agreeableness. Van Kleef et al.'s findings supported this notion. Across the two studies they conducted, motivation and performance were compromised when followers higher in agreeableness were teamed up with leaders higher in anger, but motivation and performance were higher when followers with higher levels of agreeableness were paired with leaders who expressed either happiness or no anger. These findings again point to the importance of understanding followers' personality if we wish to gain a full appreciation of leadership effectiveness.

Followers' Self-Construal

We seem to live in an era of apologies. Hardly a week goes by without some public apology for what might be regarded as a perceived or actual wrong-doing by an organization. Whether it is the CEO of Toyota apologizing for the recall following safety concerns with their vehicles (and embarrassingly being seen driving away from the press conference in a black Audi!),[63] the Apple CEO apologizing for problems with the mapping function in the iPhone,[64] or the CEO of Canadian company Maple Leaf Foods apologizing for *Listeria*-tainted meat that resulted in nine confirmed deaths,[65] it might appear that apologizing is now the normal course of action following transgressions. But this is not the case: Advice given to leaders as to whether to apologize or not is by no means consistent. On the one hand, leaders are advised that apologies are a prerequisite for high-quality leadership, and a first step in repairing relationships and restoring trust following transgressions.[66] The fact that Southwest Airlines has a staff member who writes letters of apology to disgruntled customers, and who is internally referred to as the Chief Apology Officer, is a vivid acknowledgement of what Southwest Airlines thinks of the power of an apology.[67] On the other hand, following Ralph Waldo Emerson, who famously said that "No sensible person ever made an apology," internal pressure is frequently placed on leaders not to apologize following any transgressions, invariably because of a fear of exposing their organizations to legal liability.[68]

Research now exists showing that apologies are associated with perceptions of higher, not lower, transformational leadership,[69] and with both leaders' and followers' well-being.[70] Ryan Fehr and Michelle Gelfand suggest, however, that to fully understand the possible effects of apologies, we also need to understand (a) that an apology means more than just saying you are sorry,[ii] and (b) that

ii. Most researchers would agree that a full apology would express remorse, display acceptance of responsibility for the action, show empathy, and offer some form of restitution and a plan of action to reduce the chances of the transgression re-occurring.

followers will receive the information contained in the apology differently.[71] They argue that we all construe ourselves in relation to others in three ways, namely as independent, relational or collective selves, which predispose us to respond differentially to information contained in an apology. Fehr and Gelfand hypothesize that individuals who emphasize their independence are more likely to respond to offers of compensation contained in the apology; those who highlight the relational components of the self will tend to respond more to empathy expressed in the apology; while those who emphasize the collective aspects of self will respond most favorably to leaders' acknowledgements that a violation of rules or of norms has occurred. They conducted two studies in the United States, both of which support the notion that a full appreciation of the effects of leaders' apologies on victims' willingness to forgive must include an understanding of follower characteristics. A practical lesson from their findings is that apologies with multiple, specific components increase the effectiveness of the apology, probably because it most matches what specific followers need to hear.

Followers' Belongingness Needs

Abraham Maslow's theory of self-actualization, or need hierarchy theory, remains a classic in psychological theorizing some 70 years after it was first proposed.[72] According to Maslow, all people ascend through a series of physical and psychological needs that are arranged in a fixed order, starting with the most basic physiological needs; moving on to safety and security, belongingness, and self-esteem needs; and culminating with the need for self-actualization. Individuals are only motivated by the next need in the hierarchy when they have satisfied the previous need level, which explains why most individuals never reach the pinnacle of self-actualization.[73] Maslow's theory gained considerable traction, with psychologists from widely disparate areas such as education, child development, personality, and clinical and even organizational psychology invoking his need hierarchy as an explanation of behavior. One of the core ideas in Maslow's theory still survives: Contemporary psychologists place considerable emphasis on people's need for belongingness as a fundamental human motivation or need,[74] which includes the need to trust others.[75] Thus followers' need for belongingness may affect how they respond to different leadership behaviors.

Scholars and practitioners alike have noted that fair treatment has become a significant issue in the past decade or so, and the question here is why fair treatment from a leader is viewed as so important.[76] One reason is that fair treatment conveys critical, relational information, namely that followers are valued and respected members of the group. In contrast, unfair treatment symbolically communicates disrespect and exclusion.[77] Studies conducted in the Netherlands and Germany show that the way in which people process and respond to fairness is dependent in part on their own levels of belonging-ness.[78] Specifically, individuals with higher needs for belongingness were more sensitive to, and processed information about, unfair treatment more care-fully. These findings also help to explain why other forms of bad leadership might have such harmful personal and physical effects.

Ilse Cornelis, Alain van Hiel, and David De Cremer have suggested that fol-lowers' needs for belongingness influence the extent to which their supervi-sors behave fairly, through a process of reciprocal, interpersonal attraction.[79] The rationale underlying this is that when followers express strong needs to belong to a certain group, they signal the group's high status and the desirabil-ity of membership of that group. Being the formal representative of a valued group in turn puts the leader in a valued position, making them more respon-sive to the importance of fairness in their interactions with followers with high needs for belongingness. Cornelis and her team validated this process with data from 139 supervisors and one of their subordinates.

Follower Personality and Preferences for Different Leadership Styles

If you were to read the leadership literature, you would be forgiven for believ-ing that there is something inherent in leadership that appeals equally to *all* followers, irrespective of followers' own needs, personality, and interests. The likelihood that this is true, however, is small at best, and Mark Erhart and Katherine Klein's earlier research confirms this.[80] Among a sample of 267 university students in the United States who were given the choice of three different leaders whom they would like to work for, 50% chose a relationship-oriented leader, 30% selected a charismatic leader, and only 20% chose a task-oriented leader. While their actual preferences will be discussed later, for now the lesson from these findings is clear: Followers do express idiosyncratic preferences. But do these preferences matter?

Several studies conducted in different countries illustrate how follower per-sonality and preferences influence leadership effectiveness. In the study just mentioned,[81] individuals who manifested stronger work values and who were low in security needs (e.g., job security) were more predisposed toward char-ismatic leaders. In contrast, individuals who were higher on security needs were more likely to be drawn to task-oriented leaders, while individuals who were more oriented toward extrinsic rewards (e.g., pay, benefits) that can be obtained through work were more likely to be drawn to relationship-oriented leaders. Any focus on task and relationship orientation should not be limited to leaders; followers can also be oriented toward tasks or relationships. One study on 108 U.S. Army personnel serving in Germany[82] showed that under conditions of a more positive leader–follower relationship, supervisor ratings of followers' job performance were higher for relationship-oriented followers.

In contrast, supervisor ratings of follower performance within a less favorable leader–follower relationship were higher for task-oriented followers.

Christiane Schoel and her colleagues further demonstrated the complex role of follower characteristics.[83] Acknowledging that most followers will prefer democratic rather than autocratic leaders, they were interested in isolating the psychological conditions under which followers would prefer autocratic leaders. They hypothesized that when faced with relative certainty, most followers would prefer a democratic style of leadership, and the results of their research supported this assumption.

These same authors also suggested that any preferences for autocratic leadership would emerge when followers faced uncertainty, because individuals who experienced unstable and low self-esteem (such that it could change almost daily dependent on external feedback) would prefer the certainty of autocratic leadership. In contrast, followers confronting uncertainty who experienced stable, high self-esteem would prefer democratic leadership because of their confidence that they could negotiate the uncertainty. Their suggestions were supported across four separate studies conducted in Germany, reinforcing the role of followership characteristics in understanding preferences for leadership.

A different way to understand followers' needs and preferences is through the strength of their attachment styles. British developmental psychologist John Bowlby[84] introduced attachment theory some five decades ago, which proposes that we all develop unique styles of relational attachment based on early infant and childhood experiences. These attachment styles are stable and continue into adulthood. Bowlby's theory has attracted considerable research within the developmental psychology community, and more recently has attracted the attention of organizational psychologists. In a study in Israel,[85] Alon Shalit, Micha Popper, and Dan Zakay investigated how a secure (e.g., follower finds it easy to establish close relationships) attachment style and an avoidant (e.g., followers experience discomfort in close relationships) attachment style predispose individuals to favor socialized or personalized charismatic leadership. Their findings again underscore the role of followership. Followers with a secure attachment style preferred a socialized charismatic leadership style, whereas their counterparts with an avoidant attachment style preferred the more personalized charismatic leadership style.

Finally, two studies focused on preferences for transformational and transactional leadership behaviors. In one study in Norway, Hilde Hetland, Gro Sandal, and Tom Johnsen turned the table on much of the research on personality and transformational leadership. Instead of focusing on leader personality, they investigated the influence of followers' personality on ratings of transformational and transactional leadership.[86] Unlike findings linking leaders' extraversion with leadership emergence, behaviors, and effectiveness,[87] Hetland and her team showed that followers' extraversion was not associated with a preference for transformational, transactional, or passive-avoidant leadership. Instead, higher levels of followers' agreeableness and lower levels of followers' neuroticism were associated with ratings of transformational leadership.

In another study investigating followers' personality, this time in a financial services company in Germany, Jörg Felfe and Birgit Schyns replicated the finding that followers' agreeableness was associated with their ratings of transformational leadership.[88] However, followers' extraversion was also associated with transformational leadership ratings, and followers high in neuroticism were less likely to see their leaders as high in individualized consideration. Thus, while some ambiguity remains about the role of followers' extraversion, follower characteristics do play a role in whether transformational leadership will be preferred by followers.

Finally, as workplaces become more diverse and inclusive, effective leadership will depend on the extent to which followers' unique needs are acknowledged and accommodated through leadership behaviors. This is amply illustrated in Alissa Parr, Sam Hunter, and Gina Logan's recent research, in which they investigated whether the four components of transformational leadership would be equally effective with employees with autism spectrum disorder (ASD).[89] Parr and her colleagues based their investigation on the premise that employees with ASD generally have higher levels of anxiety and greater difficulty in coping with leadership behaviors that increase change and uncertainty. Their findings again point to the importance of accounting for followers' needs, as they showed that the inspirational motivation component of transformational leadership did indeed increase these employees' anxiety, which in turn decreased their commitment to the organization. In contrast, individualized consideration was associated with lower levels of anxiety and had the strongest relationship with job performance of all the transformational leadership components.

Thus, leaders need to be aware of how their personality (and behavior) interacts with follower characteristics in influencing follower performance. Achieving this might require additional leadership training that highlights the benefits of complementarity (rather than similarity) in leader–follower characteristics and enhances leaders' emotional intelligence to help leaders be more perceptive about, and receptive to, followers' needs. In addition, findings from these studies are not just of academic interest. Follower characteristics will likely influence followers' choice of whom to work for in the first instance, and perhaps whether to continue working for them, or not.

CAN FOLLOWERS INFLUENCE LEADERSHIP BEHAVIOR?

The results of the studies discussed above all point in the same direction: A comprehensive understanding of the effectiveness of different leadership styles or behaviors requires that we consider attributes of the followers. But can we go a step further? Is there any evidence that followers directly influence the behaviors of their leaders? One response would have to be that there is very little research, given the importance of this question, probably because followers continue to be seen as passive and reactive, and leaders as proactive and primarily responsible for organizational outcomes. Nonetheless, some tentative, but intriguing, evidenced-based answers are possible.

What might be regarded as the first generation of studies on this topic were conducted within laboratory settings in the 1970s. Researchers asked directly whether the quality of followers' job performance affects leadership behavior. To investigate this, volunteers typically were placed in a contrived situation in which they would play the role of the leader. Unbeknownst to them, the performance of their "subordinates" was deliberately manipulated, such that some would be high-performing and some, low-performing subordinates. How the leaders responded was then investigated. In one such study in which the purpose of the experiment was cleverly disguised and participants truly believed that they had been hired to fulfill the role of a supervisor on an actual work task,[90] leaders who closely monitored poorly performing followers were more task-oriented (initiation structure) and less relationship-oriented (consideration structure). The opposite effects emerged for those who were leading high-performing followers. A separate study was conducted in a management simulation game.[91] Followers whose past performance was inadequate again predicted closeness of supervision, which included the use of punitive measures. At the same time, leaders allowed greater levels of decision-making for followers who had enjoyed high levels of previous performance. These findings were supported in other experiments, which provided two additional insights. First, one of the ways in which leaders respond to poor follower performance is to increase their emphasis on production. Second, leaders are more responsive to positive changes in employee performance than they are to negative changes.[92]

While these early laboratory studies enable us to infer that followers' performance does indeed influence leaders' behaviors, concerns emerge about the generalizability of the findings because of the laboratory-based nature of these studies. In addition, some of the leader behaviors might be more appropriately viewed as management (e.g., goal emphasis, work facilitation) behaviors[93] rather than leadership behaviors (e.g., charisma, vision). More recent studies have gone beyond the laboratory and have been conducted in organizations.

Some support for the idea that leader behaviors can be the result of external events rather than their cause derives from the study conducted by Judith Scully and her co-researchers in 56 technology companies in the United States.[94] Appropriately entitled "Tough Times Make Tough Bosses," their study showed that the firm's financial performance influenced CEO behavior.

Specifically, following poor financial performance, CEOs were more likely to enact what the authors referred to as the "strongman" role, issuing more instructions and commands, and a greater number of reprimands not directed at performance to members of the top management team. While not focused directly on followers, this study reinforces the notion that leadership behaviors are directly affected by events around them.

Turning to followers directly, a frequent practice within organizations is the implementation of upward feedback, in which employees have the opportunity to provide feedback to their leaders about their leadership behaviors. Within this context, Leanne Atwater, Paul Roush, and Allison Fischthal studied the effects of upward feedback on supervisors' leadership behavior among 978 student leaders and 1,232 followers in the U.S. Naval Academy.[95] After receiving feedback from followers, leadership behaviors improved significantly. However, these researchers showed that only *negative* feedback from followers subsequently improved leadership performance; positive feedback from followers did not change leadership behavior at all.

In addition to research findings showing that follower characteristics moderate leadership effectiveness, the few studies that are available suggest that followers influence their leaders' behaviors more directly. The theoretical implications of this are immense: These limited studies open up an important and intriguing avenue for why leaders behave in the way that they do. The practical implications of these findings are no less important: Organizations need to reassure employees that they can indeed influence leader behaviors (e.g., through upward feedback). Taken together, the results of these studies further emphasize the need to understand followers' roles in the leadership process more fully.

CONCLUSION

In grappling with what the findings on followership mean for the understanding and practice of organizational leadership, several implications loom large. First, there are no leaders so powerful that all organizational successes (or failures) should be attributed to them alone. Instead, leaders and followers act in concert in securing sought-after organizational objectives. Second, caution must be expressed not to let the pendulum swing all the way in the opposite direction, and blame followers for the moral excesses or organizational failures of leaders! Attributing primary blame to followers for the outrageous behaviors of infamous leaders like "Chainsaw Al" Dunlop (e.g., "it's the story of isolates and bystanders who were unwilling or unable to stop him from leading so poorly"; p. 91[96]) is to ignore the chilling effect and fear that leader behaviors can inculcate, often deliberately. Third, because performance is higher when leader and follower characteristics are appropriately matched, optimal leader selection may need to go beyond a sole focus on leader characteristics. Last, and most controversially, taking Pfeffer's advice that "the benefits of the performance of the many should not be awarded to the few"[97] would force a radical rethinking of the nature of leader and executive compensation.

Returning to the search for an explanation for the dissolution of the old Soviet empire, the fall of apartheid in South Africa, or the survival and renewal of New York following the attacks of 9/11, we now know that people attribute the successful resolution of these major national events to the remarkably charismatic leadership of people such as Gorbachev, Mandela, and Giuliani. But to do so demands that we ignore complex situational factors and the role of the citizenry. In the case of the dissolution of the Soviet empire, we would have to ignore decades of economic gloom, food shortages, and government oppression. Attributing the fall of apartheid to one person alone requires that we disregard decades of active resistance by South Africans who were ready for change, a successful economic and sports boycott, and world condemnation and isolation. Add to this the fact that for most of this period, the lionized Mandela was jailed and largely invisible to South Africans, as legislation prohibited any display of his picture or reproduction of his speeches or writings. Finally, attributing New York's recovery to Mayor Giuliani at the very least overlooks the legendary resilience of New Yorkers. Attributing successful (or unsuccessful) resolution of major social or organizational events to one leader is an understandable response, but flies in the face of evidence to the contrary.

A more nuanced and comprehensive understanding of leadership requires that we replace what Melissa Carsten and colleagues refer to as the "subordination of followership; the view that followers are largely ineffectual" (p. 546)[98] with Pastor and colleagues' "fire metaphor":[99] Leaders constitute the spark, followers the flammable material, and the situation the oxygen—and without an appropriate mix of all three components, nothing of much significance will ever happen!

SUGGESTED READING

Cain, S. (2012). *Quiet: The power of introverts in a world that can't stop talking.* New York: Random House.
Kellerman, B. (2008). *Followership: How followers are creating change and changing leaders.* Boston: Harvard Business School Press.
Olson, L. (2007). *Troublesome young men: The rebels who brought Churchill to power in 1940 and helped to save Britain.* New York: Farrar, Straus and Giroux.

NOTES

1. Kelley, R. E. (1988). In praise of followers. *Harvard Business Review, 76*(6), 142–148.

2. Mukunda, G. (2012). *Indispensable: When leaders really matter*. Boston: Harvard Business School Press.
3. Humes, J. C. (2012). *Churchill: The prophetic statesman*. New York: Perseus.
4. Manchester, W., & Reid, P. (2012). *The last lion: Winston Spencer Churchill: Defender of the realm, 1940–1965*. New York: Little, Brown.
5. Olson, L. (2007). *Troublesome young men: The rebels who brought Churchill to power and helped save England*. New York: Farrar, Straus and Giroux.
6. Keller, T. (1999). Images of the familiar: Individual differences and implicit leadership theories. *Leadership Quarterly, 10*, 589–607.
7. Agho, A. O. (2009). Perspectives of senior-level executives on effective followership and leadership. *Journal of Leadership and Organizational Studies, 16*(2), 159–166.
8. Sy, T. (2010). What do you think of followers? Examining the content, structure, and consequences of implicit followership theories. *Organizational Behavior and Human Decision Processes, 113*, 73–84.
9. Carsten, M. K., Uhl-Bien, M., West, B. J., Patera, J. L., & McGregor, R. (2010). Exploring social constructions of followership: A qualitative study. *Leadership Quarterly, 21*, 543–562.
10. Baumeister, R. F., Chesner, S. P., Senders, P. S., & Tice, D. M. (1988). Who's in charge here? Group leaders do lend help in emergencies. *Personality and Social Psychology Bulletin, 14*, 17–22.
11. Day, D. V., Sin, H. P., & Chen, T. T. (1994). Assessing the burdens of leadership: Effects of formal leadership roles on individual performance over time. *Personnel Psychology, 57*, 573–605.
12. Hoption, C., Christie, A., & Barling, J. (2012). Submitting to the follower label: Followership, positive affect and extra-role behavior. *Zeitschrift für Psychologie, 220*(4), 221–230.
13. Carsten, M. K., & Uhl-Bien, M. (2012). Follower beliefs in the co-production of leadership: Examining upward communication and the moderating role of context. *Zeitschrift für Psychologie, 220*(4), 210–220.
14. Whitely, P., Sy, T., & Johnson, S. K. (2012). Leaders' conceptions of followers: Implications for naturally occurring Pygmalion effects. *Leadership Quarterly, 23*, 822–834.
15. Babad, E. Y., Inbar, J., & Rosenthal, R. (1982). Pygmalion, Galatea, and the Golem: Investigations of biased and unbiased teachers. *Journal of Educational Psychology, 74*, 459–474.
16. Carsten, M. K., & Uhl-Bien, M. (2012). Follower beliefs in the co-production of leadership: Examining upward communication and the moderating role of context. *Zeitschrift für Psychologie, 220*(4), 210–220.
17. Bligh, M. C., Kohles, J. C., & Meindl, J. R. (2004). Charisma under crisis: Presidential leadership, rhetoric and media responses before and after the September 11th terrorist attack. *Leadership Quarterly, 15*, 211–239.
18. Powell, M. (2007, September 21). In 9/11 chaos, Giuliani forged a lasting image. *New York Times*. Retrieved from http://www.nytimes.com/2007/09/21/us/politics/21giuliani.html?_r=2&ref=thelongrun&pagewanted=all&
19. Kellerman, B. (2004). *Bad leadership: What it is, how it happens, why it matters*. Boston: Harvard Business School Press.
20. Barrett, W., & Collins, D. (2006). *Grand illusion: The untold story of Rudy Giuliani and 9/11*. New York: Harper Collins.

21. Powell, M. (2007, September 21). In 9/11 chaos, Giuliani forged a lasting image. *New York Times.* Retrieved from http://www.nytimes.com/2007/09/21/us/politics/21giuliani.html?_r=2&ref=thelongrun&pagewanted=all&.

22. Gibbs, N. (2001, December 31). Person of the year: Rudy Giuliani. *Time Magazine World.* Retrieved from http://www.time.com/time/magazine/article/0,9171,189808,00.html

23. Bass, B. M. (1990). *Bass and Stogdill's handbook of leadership: Theory, research and managerial applications* (3rd ed.). New York: Free Press.

24. Rendell, S. (May/June, 2007). The media's mayor: Mythologizing Giuliani and 9/11. FAIR: Fairness and Accuracy in Reporting. Retrieved from http://www.fair.org/index.php?page=3117

25. Cohen, F., Solomon, S., Maxfield, M., Pyszczynski, T., & Greenberg, J. (2004). Fatal attraction: The effects of mortality salience on evaluations of charismatic, task-oriented, and relationship-oriented leaders. *Psychological Science, 15,* 846–851.

26. Cohen, F., Ogilvie, D. M., Solomon, S., Greenberg, J., & Pyszczynski, T. (2005). American roulette: The effects of reminders of death on support for George W. Bush in the 2004 Presidential election. *Analyses of Social Issues and Public Policy, 5,* 177–187.

27. Landau, M. J., Solomon, S., Greenberg, J., Cohen, F., Pyszczynski, T., Arndt, J., Miller, C. H., Ogilvie, D. M., & Cook, A. (2004). Deliver us from evil: The effects of mortality salience and reminders of 9/11 on support for President George W. Bush. *Personality and Social Psychology Bulletin, 30,* 1136–1150.

28. Hoyt, C. L., Simon, S., & Innella, A. N. (2011). Taking a turn toward the masculine: The impact of mortality salience on implicit leadership theories. *Basic and Applied Social Psychology, 33,* 374–381.

29. Willer, R. (2004). The effects of government-issued terror warnings on presidential approval ratings. *Current Research in Social Psychology, 10*(1). Retreived from http://www.uiowa.edu/~grpproc/crisp/crisp.10.1.html

30. Rendell, S. (May/June, 2007). The media's mayor: Mythologizing Giuliani and 9/11. FAIR: Fairness and Accuracy in Reporting. Retrieved from http://www.fair.org/index.php?page=3117

31. Hayward, M. L. A., Rindova, V. P., & Pollock, T. G. (2004). Believing one's own press: The causes and consequences of CEO celebrity. *Strategic Management Journal, 25,* 637–653.

32. Simon, L., Greenberg, J., Harmon-Jones, E., Solomon, S., Pyszczynski, T., Arndt, J., & Abend, J. (1997). Terror management and cognitive-experiential-self theory: Evidence that terror management occurs in the experiential system. *Journal of Personality and Social Psychology, 72,* 1132–1146.

33. Feinstein, A. (2006). *Journalists under fire: The psychological hazards of covering war.* Baltimore, MD: Johns Hopkins University Press.

34. Skinner, B. F. (1971). *Beyond freedom and dignity.* New York: Knopf.

35. Meindl, J. R., Ehrlich, S. B., & Dukerich, J. M. (1985). The romance of leadership. *Administrative Science Quarterly, 30,* 78–102.

36. Hayward, M. L. A., Rindova, V. P., & Pollock, T. G. (2004). Believing one's own press: The causes and consequences of CEO celebrity. *Strategic Management Journal, 25,* 637–653.

37. Bligh, M. C., Kohles, J. C., & Pillai, R. (2011). Romancing leadership: Past, present and future. *Leadership Quarterly, 22,* 1058–1077.

38. Meindl, J. R. (1990). On leadership: An alternative to the conventional wisdom. *Research in Organizational Behavior, 12,* 159–203.
39. Schyns, B., Meindl, J. R., & Croon, M. A. (2007). The romance of leadership scale: Cross-cultural testing and refinement. *Leadership, 3,* 29–46.
40. Felfe, J., & Peterson, L. E. (2007). Romance of leadership and management decision making. *European Journal of Work and Organizational Psychology, 16,* 1–24.
41. Hayward, M. L. A., Rindova, V. P., Pollock, T. G. (2004). Believing one's own press: The causes and consequences of CEO celebrity. *Strategic Management Journal, 25,* 637–653.
42. Judge, T. A., LePine, J. A., & Rich, B. L. (2006). Loving yourself abundantly: Relationship of the narcissistic personality to self- and other perceptions of workplace deviance, leadership, and task and conceptual performance. *Journal of Applied Psychology, 91,* 762–776.
43. Gray, J. H., & Densten, I. L. (2007). How leaders woo followers in the romance of leadership. *Applied Psychology: An International Review, 56,* 558–581.
44. Boeker, W. (1992). Power and managerial dismissal: Scapegoating at the top. *Administrative Science Quarterly, 37,* 400–421.
45. Pastor, J. C., Mayo, M., & Shamir, B. (2007). Adding fuel to the fire: The impact of followers' arousal on ratings of charisma. *Journal of Applied Psychology, 92,* 1584–1596.
46. Meindl, J. R. (2004). The romance of teams: Is the honeymoon over? *Journal of Occupational and Organizational Psychology, 77,* 463–466.
47. Schyns, B., & Bligh, M. C. (2007). Introduction to the Special Issue on the Romance of Leadership—In memory of James R. Meindl. *Applied Psychology: An International Review, 56,* 501–504.
48. McCrae, R. R., & Costa, P. T. (1987). Validation of the five-factor model of personality across instruments and observers. *Journal of Personality and Social Psychology, 52,* 81–90.
49. Judge, T. A., Bono, J. E., Ilies, R., & Gerhardt, M. W. (2002). Personality and leadership: A qualitative and quantitative review. *Journal of Applied Psychology, 87,* 765–780.
50. Bono, J. E., & Judge, T. A. (2004). Personality and transformational and transactional leadership: A meta-analysis. *Journal of Applied Psychology, 89,* 901–910.
51. Judge, T. A., Bono, J. E., Ilies, R., & Gerhardt, M. W. (2002). Personality and leadership: A qualitative and quantitative review. *Journal of Applied Psychology, 87,* 765–780.
52. Haythorn, W., Couch, A., Haufner, D., Langham, P., & Carter, L. (1956). The effects of varying combinations of authoritarian and egalitarian leaders and followers. *Journal of Abnormal and Social Psychology, 53,* 210–219.
53. Waldman, D., Ramirez, G.G., House, R. J., & Puranam, P. (2001). Does influence matter? CEO leadership attributes and profitability under conditions of perceived environmental uncertainty. *Academy of Management Journal, 44,* 134–143.
54. Cain, S. (2012, September 15). Must great leaders be gregarious? *New York Times.* Retrieved from http://www.nytimes.com/2012/09/16/opinion/sunday/introverts-make-great-leaders-too.html
55. Ames, D. R., & Flynn, F. J. (2007). What breaks a leader: The curvilinear relation between assertiveness and leadership. *Journal of Personality and Social Psychology, 92,* 307–324.

56. Grant, A. M., Gino, F., & Hofmann, D. A. (2011). Reversing the extraverted leadership advantage: The role of employee proactivity. *Academy of Management Journal, 54*, 528–550.

57. Parker, S. K., Bindl, U. K., & Strauss, K. (2010). Making things happen: A model of proactive motivation. *Journal of Management, 36*, 827–856.

58. Haythorn, W., Couch, A., Haufner, D., Langham, P., & Carter, L. (1956). The effects of varying combinations of authoritarian and egalitarian leaders and followers. *Journal of Abnormal and Social Psychology, 53*, 210–219.

59. Sy, T., Côté, S., & Saavedra, R. (2005). The contagious leader: Impact of the leader's mood on the mood of group members, group affective tone, and group processes. *Journal of Applied Psychology, 90*, 295–305.

60. Glomb, T. M., & Hulin, C. L. (1997). Anger and gender effects in observed supervisor–subordinate dyadic interactions. *Organizational Behavior and Human Decision Processes, 72*, 281–307.

61. Van Kleef, G. A., De Dreu, C. K. W., & Manstead, A. S. R. (2010). An interpersonal approach to emotion in social decision making: The emotions as social information model. In M. P. Zanna (Ed.), *Advances in experimental social psychology* (Vol. 42, pp. 45–96). San Diego: Academic Press.

62. Van Kleef, G. A., Homan, A. C., Beersma, B., & van Knippenberg, D. (2010). On angry leaders and agreeable followers: How leaders' emotions and followers' personalities shape motivation and team performance. *Psychological Science, 21*, 1827–1824.

63. Ross, B. (2010, January 29). Toyota CEO apologizes to his customers: 'I am deeply sorry.' *ABC News*. Retrieved from http://abcnews.go.com/Blotter/ toyota-ceo-apologizes-deeply/story?id=9700622

64. Tsukayama, H. (2012, September 28). Apple CEO Tim Cook apologizes for Maps app. *Washington Post*. Retrieved from http://articles.washingtonpost. com/2012-09-28/business/35496114_1_mapquest-and-waze-apple-m aps-google-maps

65. Maple Leaf apology. Uploaded August 25, 2008. *YouTube*. Retrieved from http:// www.youtube.com/watch?v=cSrazdNo55U

66. Blanchard, K., & McBride, M. (2003). *The one minute apology*. New York: Harper Collins; Lazare, A. (2004). *On apology*. Oxford, UK: Oxford University Press.

67. Bailey, J. (2007, March 18). Airlines learn to fly on a wing and an apology. *New York Times*. Retrieved from http://www.nytimes.com/2007/03/18/ business/18sorry.html?pagewanted=all&_r=0

68. Wilson, T. (2011, February 7). The best legal advice is often an apology. *Globe and Mail*. Retrieved from http://www.theglobeandmail.com/report-on-business/ small-business/sb-growth/day-to-day/the-best-legal-advice-is-often-an-apology/ article626797/

69. Tucker, S., Turner, N., Barling, J., Reid, E. M., & Elving, C. (2006). Apologies and transformational leadership. *Journal of Business Ethics, 63*, 195–207.

70. Byrne, A., Barling, J., & Dupre, K. (2013). Leader apologies and employee and leader well-being. *Journal of Business Ethics*. DOI: 10.1007/ s10551-013-1685-3

71. Fehr, R., & Gelfand, M. (2010). When apologies work: How matching apology components to victims' self-construals facilitates forgiveness. *Organizational Behavior and Human Performance, 113*, 37–50.

72. Kremer, W., & Hammond, C. (2013, August 31). Abraham Maslow and the pyramid that beguiled business. *BBC News*. Retrieved from http://www.bbc.co.uk/news/magazine-23902918
73. Maslow, A. H. (1943). A theory of human motivation. *Psychological Review, 50*, 370–396.
74. Baumeister, R. F., & Leary, M. R. (1995). The need to belong: Desire for interpersonal attachments as a fundamental human motivation. *Psychological Bulletin, 117*, 497–529.
75. Fiske, S. T. (2004). *Social beings: A core motives approach to social psychology*. Chichester, UK: John Wiley & Sons.
76. Brockner, J. (2006). Why it's so hard to be fair. *Harvard Business Review, 84*(3), 122–129.
77. Kivimäki, M., Ferrie, J. E., Brunner, E., Head, J., Shipley, M. J., et al. (2005). Justice at work and reduced risk of coronary heart disease among employees: The Whitehall II Study. *Archives of Internal Medicine, 165*, 2245–2251.
78. De Cremer, D., & Blader, S. L. (2006). Why do people care about procedural fairness? The importance of belongingness in responding and attending to procedures. *European Journal of Social Psychology, 36*, 211–228.
79. Cornelis, I., van Hiel, A., & De Cremer, D. (2012). The effects of followers' belongingness needs on leaders' procedural fairness enactment. *Journal of Personnel Psychology, 11*, 31–39.
80. Erhart, M. G., & Klein, K. J. (2001). Predicting followers' preferences for charismatic leadership: The influence of follower values and personality. *Leadership Quarterly, 12*, 153–179.
81. Erhart, M. G., & Klein, K. J. (2001). Predicting followers' preferences for charismatic leadership: The influence of follower values and personality. *Leadership Quarterly, 12*, 153–179.
82. Miller, R. L., Butler, J., & Cosentino, C. J. (2004). Followership effectiveness: An extension of Fiedler's contingency model. *Leadership and Organization Development Journal, 25*, 362–368.
83. Schoel, C., Bluemke, M., Mueller, P., & Stahlberg, D. (2011). When autocratic leaders become an option—Uncertainty and self-esteem predict implicit leadership preferences. *Journal of Personality and Social Psychology, 101*, 521–540.
84. Bowlby, J. (1969). *Attachment and loss: Vol. 1: Attachment*. New York: Basic Books.
85. Shalit, A., Popper, M., & Zakay, D. (2010). Followers' attachment styles and their preferences for social or for personal charismatic leaders. *Leadership and Organization Development Journal, 31*, 458–472.
86. Hetland, H., Sandal, G. M., & Johnsen, T. B. (2008). Followers' personality and leadership. *Journal of Leadership and Organizational Studies, 14*, 322–331.
87. Bono, J. E., & Judge, T. A. (2004). Personality and transformational and transactional leadership: A meta-analysis. *Journal of Applied Psychology, 89*, 901–910; Judge, T. A., Bono, J. E., Ilies, R., & Gerhardt, M. W. (2002). Personality and leadership: A qualitative and quantitative review. *Journal of Applied Psychology, 87*, 765–780.
88. Felfe, J., & Schyns, B. (2010). Followers' personality and the perception of transformational leadership: Further evidence for the similarity hypothesis. *British Journal of Management, 21*, 393–410.
89. Parr, A. D., Hunter, S. T., & Ligon, G. S. (2013). Questioning the universal applicability of transformational leadership: Examining employees with autism spectrum disorder. *Leadership Quarterly, 24*, 608–622.

90. Lowin, A., & Craig, J. R. (1968). The influence of level of performance on managerial style: An experimental object-lesson in the ambiguity of correlational data. *Organizational Behavior and Human Performance, 3*, 440–458.
91. Farris, G. F., & Lim, F. G. (1969). Effects of performance on leadership, cohesiveness, influence, satisfaction, and subsequent performance. *Journal of Applied Psychology, 53*, 490–497.
92. Barrow, J. C. (1976). Worker performance and task complexity as causal determinants of leader behavior style and flexibility. *Journal of Applied Psychology, 53*, 433–440.
93. Farris, G. F., & Lim, F. G. (1969). Effects of performance on leadership, cohesiveness, influence, satisfaction, and subsequent performance. *Journal of Applied Psychology, 53*, 490–497.
94. Scully, J. A., Sims, H. P., Olian, J. D., Schnell, E. R., & Smith, K. A. (1994). Tough times make tough bosses: A meso analysis of CEO leader behavior. *Leadership Quarterly, 5*, 59–83.
95. Atwater, L., Rousch, P., & Fischthal, A. (1995). The influence of upward feedback on self- and follower ratings of leadership. *Personnel Psychology, 48*, 35–59.
96. Kellerman, B. (2007). What every leader needs to know about followers. *Harvard Business Review*, December, 84–91.
97. Pfeffer, J. (1998). *The human equation: Building profits by putting people first.* Boston: Harvard Business School Press.
98. Carsten, M. K., Uhl-Bien, M., West, B. J., Patera, J. L., & McGregor, R. (2010). Exploring social constructions of followership: A qualitative study. *Leadership Quarterly, 21*, 543–562.
99. Pastor, J. C., Mayo, M., & Shamir, B. (2007). Adding fuel to the fire: The impact of followers' arousal on ratings of charisma. *Journal of Applied Psychology, 92*, 1584–1596.

CHAPTER 11

Leading into the Future

We have seen throughout this book that leadership has positive effects on important employee and organizational outcomes, how this occurs, that leadership can be taught, and that formal initiatives to do so within organizations are cost-effective. The importance of leadership is strengthened by extensive findings showing that destructive and poor leadership have negative personal, family, and organizational effects. In this chapter, we turn our attention to some issues that we are both likely to see addressed and that perhaps should be addressed in future research. We also consider where we will need to tread cautiously if we are to continue to capitalize on decades of research and strengthen the likelihood of leadership success. We will close the chapter by considering what all of this means for everyday leadership behaviors.

LEADERSHIP SELECTION

By now, you have no doubt realized what has not been covered elsewhere in the book,[i] and that is the whole area of leadership selection. One reason for its exclusion could be that the topic is simply not pertinent to a book of this nature; clearly, that is not the case. Another possibility is that organizations already excel in the way in which they go about leadership selection, thus any discussion of the topic would be redundant. Again, this is not so, leaving Jeffrey Cohn and Jay Moran to ask in the title of their book on leader selection, *Why Are We Bad at Picking Good Leaders?*.[1] So why, then, not focus intensively on leadership selection? The answer is that despite its importance for organizational effectiveness, organizational researchers have not turned their

---

i. Especially if you read the heading immediately preceding this sentence!

attention to leadership selection with the same persistence and ingenuity that have characterized their efforts elsewhere. Thus, a robust, evidence-based foundation on the topic has not been developed.

Paradoxically, one of the earliest topics that industrial psychologists addressed was selection, or as it was frequently referred to at the time, "vocational classification."[2] Much of this earlier research occurred during World War II when placing the right person in the right position was often a life-or-death decision, and the criteria on which decisions were based were mostly what we would now regard as "hard" skills. In contrast, as we saw in Chapter 1, all new-genre leadership theories revolve around "soft" skills, and successful leadership selection requires that organizations be able to target those soft skills deemed most necessary and hardest to change.[3]

Making leadership selection even more complicated is the fact that, as we move up the organizational hierarchy, a different set of procedures and criteria are often invoked. For example, leadership selection decisions for supervisory or middle-management positions typically rely on "experts" with specific training or expertise related to selection. But this is not necessarily the case with senior-management and CEO positions, where responsibility for selection is more likely to be held by members of governing boards, who might have a financial stake in the process and the outcome, or they could be influenced by external consultants, who themselves have a financial stake in the outcome.

A case in point is the celebrated elevation of Marissa Meyer to the position of CEO of Yahoo in 2012, a decision that captured the attention of the media, investors, and the lay public alike. After holding his position for only four months, Yahoo's then-CEO, Scott Thompson, became embroiled in a very difficult situation in the spring of 2012, with public claims that his CV had been significantly embellished. With attention already focused intensely on Yahoo because of its poor financial performance, the very public firing of former CEO Carol Bartz only eight months earlier, and concerns about Yahoo's ability to innovate, Thompson euphemistically "left the company."[4]

Marissa Meyer was soon announced as the new CEO, a decision in which Yahoo board member and major shareholder Daniel Loeb played a very significant role.[5] What the selection of Marissa Meyer makes abundantly clear is that a different process and set of criteria are used by a different group in the selection of CEOs and senior executives, a process that is saturated in politics rather than science. This may be a lost opportunity, as research suggests that traditional selection techniques might be able to identify leadership skills. Jo Silvester and Christina Dykes studied the selection of parliamentary candidates in the United Kingdom and showed that information gathered on critical thinking skills and competence from standard structured interviews that formed part of a traditional selection process using an assessment center and job analysis[6] predicted the change in vote from the 2001 to the 2005 general election in the United Kingdom for 106 Conservative Party candidates.[ii]

Where does this leave us? Certainly no closer to an evidenced-based protocol for leadership selection, especially executive leadership selection, but perhaps more aware of the enormity of the issue. If as is often claimed, approximately 40% of all executive leadership selection decisions result in failure in their first 18 months on the job,[7] the need for an evidenced-based body of knowledge that can guide leadership selection into the future could not be more urgent.

LEADERSHIP TRAINING AND DEVELOPMENT

Practical pressures to develop, strengthen, and maintain high-quality leadership have resulted in innumerable attempts to do so, using a variety of different techniques and programs (e.g., formal training, coaching, mentoring). Earlier in this book, peer-reviewed and published research evaluating the effectiveness of formal leadership development initiatives that used rigorous and interpretable experimental methods was presented. The results of this research are both comforting and unsettling—comforting inasmuch as we can conclude broadly from Chapter 6 that leadership development initiatives are effective, and cost-effective too, but unsettling because it is also clear that we can, and need, to do so much more.

Notwithstanding the extensive research on leadership training and development, one aspect that is not covered is how individuals are typically selected to participate in these leadership development initiatives in the first place. As noted by others,[8] and consistent with my own experience conducting leadership development workshops, what invariably happens is that high-quality leaders who are loyal organizational members are selected by their organizations to attend leadership workshops. At a very superficial level, one might like to argue that this makes perfect sense: Leadership development programs are costly, so why would organizations allocate considerable training resources to leaders who might be less committed and more likely to leave the organization, taking any newly learned skills with them? No less importantly, why would or should organizations allocate their scarce resources to poor performers who may not benefit from the developmental opportunity?

This argument can be questioned on the basis of scientific findings. Though seemingly counterintuitive, the more organizations invest in their members, the more likely they are to stay. George Benson, David Feingold, and Susan

---

ii. Parenthetically, despite the underrepresentation of female candidates in the 2005 election, these authors also showed that there were no gender differences in critical thinking skills or general competence.

Mohrman investigated the effects of a retention program in a large, high-tech manufacturing company in the United States, in which employees were fully reimbursed for tuition expenses incurred for completing a degree or professional development program, and even received a bonus upon completion.[9] What happened then is most revealing. Attaining a graduate degree was predictably associated with higher turnover rates because it created additional opportunities. However, turnover was reduced where the company invested fully in the people who had attained the new skills, with the largest retention effect for those who had attained new skills and were then promoted and hence had the opportunity to use the new skills. The lesson is clear: Investing in people signifies that they are important and that they belong. They will become more attached to organizations that invest in their leadership development and provide opportunities and discretion to use their newly acquired skills, and more motivated to do what they can in the pursuit of high performance.

Contrast this with the prevailing way of thinking about leadership development in so many organizations, where attending leadership development initiatives is invariably a reward for good leadership, rather than an opportunity to improve leadership. Worsening this situation, leadership training is invariably only offered *after* becoming a leader, not beforehand, clearly revealing the risk-averse attitude of most organizations to investing in leadership development.[iii] What is called for is nothing less than a total change in the approach to leadership development, and appropriate lessons might again be gleaned from high-functioning military organizations, in which leaders are trained well before they are ever allowed to enter the theater of battle.[10] When the consequences of leadership directly affect the life and death of followers, training takes place first. Given the effects of leadership on employee injuries and occupational safety, their physical health and mental illness (see Chapter 3), why would traditional work organizations pursue a different path?

At the very least, after selection decisions have been made, but prior to assuming their role, newly selected leaders should have access to leadership development initiatives. Waiting for individuals to be selected for their first leadership role, and then providing them with developmental opportunities, is still a case of "too little, too late." Ensuring that the organizational need for leadership is met requires that the appropriate talent pool be identified, developed, expanded, and nurtured long before people are ever allowed to step into the role. Organizations cannot meet this burden alone, and societies concerned about their future have a role to play in expanding the overall pool of leadership talent required for their own social and economic well-being.

iii. I have thought long and hard about this issue, and cannot think of another work role in which organizations would only offer job training to people long after starting in that role, and then primarily to those individuals already showing that they can do the job!

Opportunities that go well beyond work organizations and are available well before adulthood—perhaps even integrated into regular school curricula—will undoubtedly serve the greatest good. As DeAlton Partridge argued about adolescent experiences in schools, "there should be ample opportunity for...individuals who have potential leadership qualities to exercise these qualities in a way which will equip them to be of better service to humanity"[11]—but he said this in 1935. Whether at the organizational or wider social level, insisting on the one hand that leaders matter while on the other refusing to invest in their development is simply no longer defensible.

The advent of Internet technologies and their accessibility in all corners of the world now offer exciting opportunities to extend the reach of leadership development initiatives to meet the needs of many more people in ways and places that previously would have been unthinkable. Again we can learn from the field of psychotherapy,[12] where people can now successfully receive computer-aided therapy for some psychological disorders in the comfort of their own home,[13] or as we saw in Chapter 6, psychoanalysts in New York provide ongoing therapy to patients in China via Skype.[14] Opportunities for spreading the benefits of leadership development are at a point where the major limitations will be the presenter's creativity and openness to change. Webinars delivered through videoconferencing or booster sessions conducted on smart phones are already possible. Ironically, many of these technologies will enable leadership development interventions to be personalized in ways that are incompatible with delivery in larger groups. It does not take much to predict that the future of leadership development initiatives will look very different from the past.

LEADERSHIP AND FOLLOWERSHIP

Despite incredible strides in understanding leadership since the focus on new-genre leadership approaches, we still have a long way to go before we even approach optimal leadership effectiveness. One opportunity for enhancing leadership effectiveness is through embracing the role of followership. This is not a call for more research on the motivators and demotivators of employee performance. There is already a long-standing, deep, and extensive body of research on employee motivation and performance that is at least as large as the existing research on leadership[15]. Instead, what we need is an understanding of the leader–follower relationship, and how follower characteristics add to and sometimes detract from leadership effectiveness. Stated somewhat differently, it is time to realize that leaders cannot do it all themselves, and probably never have, and act upon this realization.

The organizational study by Adam Grant, Francesca Gino, and David Hofmann provides striking evidence for this.[16] As already discussed, they have demonstrated that despite long-held beliefs, leaders' extraversion by itself was not sufficient to account for sales performance or revenue generated in pizza franchises. Instead, extraverted leaders were more effective when they worked together with less proactive employees; when teamed with proactive employees, they were less effective than introverted leaders paired with proactive employees. An example of this from the world of politics is the leadership of President Barack Obama (who himself is reputed to be an introverted leader[17]). While manifesting the same behaviors to all Americans, his leadership is clearly accepted, respected, and trusted by about half the population, but not by the other half.[iv] Is there something in his leadership that results in the admiration of so many, but certainly not all? Alternatively, might the most appropriate explanation for this reside more in follower characteristics such as political viewpoint, age, race, and gender, to name a few as voting patterns would suggest? The lesson to be learned from these different examples is wide-ranging: There may be no natural benefits accruing to extraverted leadership, and in the same way, introverted leadership is not necessarily harmful. Instead, both extraverted and introverted leadership might be equally effective—when matched together with the appropriate followers.

Explicitly incorporating the role of followers into the way we think about leadership will have vast implications for fundamental organizational practices that are often based on long-held beliefs and stereotypes, namely, leader and executive compensation, and leader selection. If leader success is somewhat dependent on followers, what might this mean for executive compensation? At the same time, if leader extraversion alone does not account for success, but interacts with follower characteristics to do so, how might this influence leader (or follower) selection? As daunting as these questions might be, excellent organizations did not get that way by shying away from the most difficult issues and will likely be the first to embrace the new challenge.

GENDER AND LEADERSHIP: THE TIP OF AN ICEBERG?

How do we best make sense of what we now know about gender and leadership? After many years of knowing that a problem exists, women and men are still not equally represented in leadership positions throughout organizations. Further, the higher one goes in the organizational hierarchy, up to and including CEOs, board members, and board chairs, the worse it gets! At the same time, there has been some change over the past few decades, and we now understand *why* the gender disparity in leadership still exists.

iv. To be more exact, 65,455,010 (51% of eligible voters) Americans expressed approval of his leadership in November 2012, while 60,771,703 (47%) did not!

At one level, the persistence of a preference for male leaders, and a bias against female leaders, should not be a shock to anyone. Consistent with an open-systems perspective, Daniel Katz and Robert Kahn argued as early as 1966 that organizations functioned within a larger social context of which they were a part,[18] and the gender composition of organizational hierarchies mimics that of the larger social environment, where equal gender representation remains elusive. As was seen in Chapter 8, women remain significantly underrepresented as elected members of parliament in Canada and the United Kingdom, in Congress and the Senate in the United States, and as CEOs and members of governance boards across many different countries.

One issue not considered earlier is whether women leaders are alone in experiencing such discrimination in the workplace. What about members of other visible minorities in the workplace? Do they face a similar form of discrimination with respect to leadership emergence, behavior, or effectiveness? While there seems to be very little research from which to draw conclusions, the available data suggest that women are not alone in the discrimination encountered in the workplace. One series of studies by Timothy Judge and Daniel Cable concluded that "height...continues to be a factor in terms of promotions" (p. 438).[19] More recently, these same two researchers focused on weight in their research in Germany and the United States, and found complex indications of prejudice. For males, irrespective of any positive health consequence of being thin, earnings are higher for heavier men, other factors held constant. In contrast, when women match what Judge and Cable refer to as the "improbably thin female" ideal portrayed in the media, they are rewarded with the highest earnings in both countries.[20] Finally, Elizabeth Deitch and her team turned their attention to racial discrimination in three separate studies in the United States, and they showed that Black people experience what they referred to as everyday mistreatment and discrimination (e.g., not receiving assignments needed for promotion, having their work performance evaluated unfairly, not receiving the information needed to do the job properly), which resulted in lower job satisfaction and well-being.[21] Given the existence of discrimination in organizations based on diverse characteristics, there is every reason to believe that discrimination would also be encountered by members of other visible groups seeking leadership opportunities within organizations.

Complicating matters is the fact that these different characteristics do not act in isolation. Research has provided support for the notion of "double jeopardy," such that minority women experience the most sexual harassment.[22] As one example of double jeopardy, Sonia Ghumman and Anne Marie Ryan conducted an ingenious study on discrimination against religious women wearing a hijab that covered their hair, ears, neck, and chest.[23] These researchers had women volunteers enter local retail stores and restaurants near shopping malls in the U.S. Midwest. In some situations, the volunteers wore the full hijab, in others, not at all. In all other respects, they were dressed identically. Their findings clearly isolated the presence of both formal (women wearing hijabs received fewer requests to complete job applications and fewer call-backs) and informal discrimination (these same women perceived a greater level of negativity and lower level of interest). These findings are important, as they demonstrate that under some conditions, prejudice against women in the workplace in general, and women seeking or holding leadership positions in particular, may be deeper than that portrayed already. Extending Ghumman and Ryan's findings, what might happen if a woman wearing a full hijab applied for a leadership position in one of these same organizations?

Several separate imperatives point to the need for immediate change. At one level, denying anyone an equal opportunity to assume a leadership position and then denying equal treatment as a leader on the basis of characteristics other those demonstrably relevant to performance in the position are ethically unacceptable and legally questionable. At a different level, continuing this mindless discrimination will limit the available leadership talent pool for no valid reason, depriving organizations of access to people with the motivation and skills required to enact high-quality leadership behaviors.

NEUROSCIENCE, GENETICS, AND THE BIOLOGY OF LEADERSHIP: THE RACE IS ON

Unquestionably, among the most exciting advances made by psychological researchers over the past several years is the discovery of genetic, biological, and neurological causes of behavior. Implications of these findings within the organizational realm should not be underestimated. Consider one early example: Until the end of the 1980s, the consensual definition of job satisfaction (or dissatisfaction) was of a "pleasurable or positive emotional state resulting from the appraisal of one's job or job experience" (p. 1300),[24] that is, a response to environmental conditions. Arvey and his colleagues then showed that such explanations are incomplete. Using a sample of identical twins who had been reared apart, they demonstrated that job satisfaction cannot just be explained by the job alone.[25] Instead, a significant portion of people's job (dis)satisfaction is dispositional, a finding confirmed by other research showing that removing some people from dissatisfying work environments did not diminish their job dissatisfaction.[26]

Fast forward 25 years, and research is now showing how leadership emergence is a function of complex genetic–environmental interactions. Add to this the fact that genetic factors account for approximately 30% of the variation in leadership development (see Chapter 5), and organizations and their leaders are faced with the question of what this all means. Rather than inferring from these findings that genetic factors place absolute limits on who will or will not emerge as leaders or succeed as leaders (which implies a genetic determinism), most leadership scholars would interpret these findings to mean that organizations and their leaders must appreciate that while leadership development initiatives can result in changes in leader behaviors, in some cases even the leaders most motivated to learn and to change may be somewhat frustrated in their attempts. Humility is called for in realizing that there are some things beyond our control.

At the same time, new discoveries about the influence of genetic, biological, and neurological factors on leadership development and behavior are moving forward, with increases in technological sophistication spreading excitement about a possible neuroscience of leadership. Against this exciting backdrop, some caution needs to be exercised. One reason for caution is that whenever a new research area is embraced so enthusiastically, we may simply be riding the crest of a fad. But this is unlikely to be the case, given how new neuroscientific discoveries are already changing the practice of medicine. Instead, the bigger concern derives not from the near-certainty that we will witness important discoveries in the biological, genetic, and neurological bases of leadership over the next decade, but from how this new knowledge might be used. Given the intense competitive environment in which organizations exist, and the constant need for innovation and sometimes for a "quick fix," are we headed for an era in which X-rays, functional MRIs, and genetic testing are used for leadership selection? Will we see a pill to "correct" introverted leadership, or surgeries to reduce abusive leadership?

These new discoveries will bring with them enormous and unpredictable scientific, ethical, and legal implications regarding their application to the practice of leadership, implications that are so broad-reaching that they will go beyond the boundaries of organizations and probably involve policy makers, labor unions, and the public. While this is no way is meant to be a red light that discourages or stops scientific progress, it should be taken as a flashing yellow light to proceed with the utmost caution. The time is ripe to take a deep collective breath and think wisely about where we are headed, and why, before we find ourselves in the midst of a "brave new world" of leadership.

"FROM LEADERSHIP THEORY TO LEADERSHIP BEHAVIORS" REVISITED

Having considered the enormous literature on the nature, development, and consequences of organizational leadership, perhaps the most appropriate way in which to end this book is to ask what all this means for any individual leader. In this last section, we consider the implications from many of the theoretical nuances for everyday leaders' leadership behaviors. A valid point of departure for such a discussion would be to refer to research conducted since the 1980s, as a result of which we now understand *how* leadership works. Simply stated, organizational leadership typically does not exert direct and immediate effects on any needed outcomes. Instead, as we saw in Chapter 3, any effects of leadership are most likely to be indirect and more often than not, delayed. This insight has several very meaningful lessons.

Directly Targeting the Outcome Is Futile

One critical lesson for the way in which leaders behave is the futility of directly targeting outcomes of interest (e.g., employee sales performance, customer service quality, corporate performance). Instead, these same outcomes will be achieved when leaders behave in ways that change how employees think and feel about themselves (e.g., self-efficacy beliefs), their leaders (e.g., trust in their leader), and their own work experiences (e.g., how meaningful their work is). In this sense, effective leadership is not about relentlessly targeting the desired outcomes but about creating the personal (e.g., self-efficacy), interpersonal (e.g., trust), and contextual conditions (e.g., moderators) within which employees will willingly strive toward superior performance.

Patience Is a Virtue?

A second major lesson to be learned from indirect effects of leadership is that we should not expect leadership to exert immediate effects on intended outcomes. If anything, leaders should be counseled to expect delayed effects. Thus, leaders need to do what they can to influence the core mediators that influence the outcomes of interest (see Figure 3.1)—and then be ready to show much patience while the process gets under way.

Leaders, Not Saints

Developing everyday leadership behaviors from theories with titles as lofty as "transformational leadership," "servant leadership," or "authentic leadership" is nothing short of intimidating! Despite this, the search for what this means for everyday leader behaviors should be very reassuring. Even the very best of leaders do not do everything! Bass and Riggio make this clear in their standard text on transformational leadership, when they say that transformational leaders "behave in ways to achieve superior results by employing *one or more* of the four core components of transformational leadership"[27] (p. 5, italics added). This is reinforced over and over when we conduct leadership interventions with executives. Like many others, I start by asking participants to think about the best leaders they have ever had, and then they tell us what it is that these people did that made them the best leader. Invariably an extensive list of wonderful leadership behaviors is produced by the group.[28] If you then ask how many of these wonderful leaders did "everything," you will be met with silence. Even the best leaders do not do everything, indeed could not do everything. Instead, what our participants tell us is that each one of these leaders excels at no more than a few of the behaviors identified.

When we go further with our participants, another leadership lesson emerges: Not only do the best leaders not do everything, but they also make mistakes in their leadership behaviors! And they are not alone. In an article in *The Guardian,* celebrating Nelson Mandela's 90th birthday in 2008, Adam Roberts proudly proclaimed, "But Mandela is not perfect," adding later that his "imperfections are real."[29] Graça Machel, Mandela's wife, enthusiastically agreed about Mandela's mistakes, as did Archbishop Desmond Tutu. Also agreeing with them was none other than Mandela himself, who would remind anyone who would listen that "I am not a saint, unless you think of a saint as a sinner who keeps on trying."

What differentiates wonderful and less-than-wonderful leaders is not whether they make mistakes or not, but what they do afterward. What we continually hear from participants in our workshops is that all they want from their leaders following most transgressions is an apology. Intriguingly, apologies are not forthcoming, probably because of organizational concerns about legal liability and leaders' own apprehensions about appearing to be weak in the eyes of their followers, despite the fact that leaders who offer an apology are viewed as more transformational, not less.[30] The benefits of apologies do not stop there. More recent research that I conducted with Alyson Byrne and Kate Dupré even shows that apologies enhance employees' well-being—and leaders' well-being as well (likely because of the authentic pride associated with having done the right thing).[31]

Despite the belief by many leaders that they need to display wonderful leadership all the time, it is worth remembering that this is neither possible nor necessary. One reason that this is not possible is that leaders are not physically co-located with their followers most of the time; in the globalized workplace, leaders may not even be in the same country as their followers. Add to this the fact that employees would likely be totally overwhelmed by a leader who, for example, was empathic or inspirational all the time. The challenge is not whether you can sustain high-quality leadership all the time—but whether you can ensure that you do it at the right time. Employees do not hold their leaders accountable for what they cannot do, but will certainly do so for what their leaders could have done but chose not to do.

The everyday opportunity from all of this is to remember that it is the smallest things that leaders do at the right times that can have very meaningful outcomes, and to act on it. This is more than amply demonstrated by Adam Grant and Francesca Gino's research that was discussed in Chapter 3.[32] In their research, simply being told, "Thank you so much! I am really grateful" in an otherwise ordinary e-mail was enough to motivate more voluntary helping behavior—in one case, this small expression of gratitude more than doubled the willingness to help on a voluntary task. This is also abundantly clear from what participants in our leadership development programs tell us. When asked how many of them had received a thank you card (or e-mail, or voice mail) from a leader, most respond affirmatively. When asked further how many of them keep these cards for years, most will tell you that they do. But the story does not end there. When asked again how many of them go back to look at the cards when they are having a difficult time at work, a surprising number tell us that they do so—and seeing the card lifts them again.

The implications for leadership are clear: The smallest things that leaders choose to do (but do not have to) not only inspire followers, they re-inspire them again and again, sometimes years later, when their followers need it most, because how people are treated matters deeply to them. The smallest behaviors from their leaders convey the trust, respect, self-efficacy, and belongingness that employees seek, and they respond predictably when they experience these behaviors. Kivimäki and colleagues' research findings also remind us that choosing *not* to enact the small leadership behaviors that employees realize are well within the leader's reach, such as providing sufficient and consistent information, or offering praise when it was appropriate, can result in substantial health consequences.[33] Returning to the question asked in Chapter 6, as to how much leadership is necessary,[v] high-quality leadership is not simply dependent on huge investments in time and resources, but on remembering that people are remarkably sensitive to the smallest behaviors, and then choosing to act accordingly.

To conclude, the very best of leadership is not just about doing everything right, all the time, but about choosing to do the right thing at the right time. Organizational leaders have an incredible opportunity to change the way people see themselves, their future, and their work. Leaders need not be motivated to achieve the impossible to do so, but do need to ensure that they do the smallest things they can do, at the right time. The opportunity for leaders in doing so is to elevate those around them, enhance their well-being, and help them want to do what they can to see their organization thrive.

v. "How much of which leadership intervention offered by whom is most effective for which leaders with what type of challenge?"

SUGGESTED READING

Blanchard, K., & McBride, M. (2003). *The one minute apology: A powerful way to make things better*. New York: William Morrow.

Cohn, J., & Moran, J. (2011). *Why are we bad at picking good leaders?* San Francisco: Jossey-Bass.

Stengel, R. (2009). *Mandela's way: 15 lessons on life, love and courage*. New York: Crown Publishers.

Sutton, R.I. (2010). *Good boss, bad boss*. New York: Hachette Book Group.

NOTES

1. Cohn, J., & Moran, J. (2011). *Why are we bad at picking good leaders?* San Francisco: Jossey-Bass.
2. Vernon, P. E., & Parry, J. B. (1949). *Personnel psychology in the British Forces*. London: University of London Press.
3. Pfeffer, J. (1998). *The human equation*. Boston: Harvard Business School Press.
4. Pepitone, J. (2012, May 14). Yahoo confirms CEO is out after resume scandal. *CNN Money*. Retreived from http://money.cnn.com/2012/05/13/technology/yahoo-ceo-out/index.htm
5. Davidoff, S. M. (2012, July 24). When picking a C.E.O. is more random than wise. *New York Times Dealbook*. Retrieved from http://dealbook.nytimes.com/2012/07/24/when-picking-a-c-e-o-is-more-random-than-wise/
6. Silvester, J., & Dykes, C. (2007). Selecting political candidates: A longitudinal study of assessment centre performance and political success in the 2005 UK General Election. *Journal of Occupational and Organizational Psychology, 80*, 11–25.
7. Charan, R. (2005, February). Ending the CEO succession crisis. *Harvard Business Review, 83*, 72–81.
8. Grant, A. (2013). *Give and take: A revolutionary approach to success*. New York: Penguin.
9. Benson, G. S., Finegold, D., & Mohrman, S. A. (2004). You paid for the skills, now keep them: Tuition reimbursement and voluntary turnover. *Academy of Management Journal, 47*, 315–331.
10. Schumpeter. (2013, February 16). How to make a killing *The Economist*, 65.
11. Partridge, E. D. (1935). Leadership among adolescent boys. *Teachers College Record, 36*(5), 320–322.
12. Kazdin, A. E., & Blasé, S. L. (2011). Rebooting psychotherapy research practice to reduce the burden of mental illness. *Perspectives on Psychological Science, 6*, 21–37.
13. Kenwright, M., & Marks, I. M. (2004). Computer-aided self-help for phobia/panic via internet at home: A pilot study. *British Journal of Psychology, 184*, 448–449.
14. Osnos, E. (2011, January 10). Meet Dr. Freud: Does psychoanalysis have a future in an authoritarian state? *New Yorker*, 54–52.
15. Lawler, E. E. III (1994). *Motivation in work organizations*. San Francisco: Jossey-Bass.
16. Grant, A. M., Gino, F., & Hofmann, D. A. (2011). Reversing the extraverted leadership advantage: The role of employee proactivity. *Academy of Management Journal, 54*, 528–550.

17. Cain, S. (2012, September 15). Must great leaders be gregarious? *New York Times*. Retrieved from http://www.nytimes.com/2012/09/16/opinion/sunday/introverts-make-great-leaders-too.html

18. Katz, D., & Kahn, R. L. (1978). *The social psychology of organizations* (2nd ed.). New York: John Wiley & Sons.

19. Judge, T. A., & Cable, D. M. (2004). The effect of physical height on workplace success and income: Preliminary test of a theoretical model. *Journal of Applied Psychology, 89*, 428–441.

20. Judge, T. A., & Cable, D. M. (2011). When it comes to pay, do the thin win? The effect of weight on pay for men and women. *Journal of Applied Psychology, 96*, 95–112.

21. Deitch, E. A., Barsky, A., Butz, R. M., Chan, S., Brief, A. P., & Bradley, J. C. (2003). Subtle yet significant: The existence and impact of everyday racial discrimination in the workplace. *Human Relations, 56*, 1299–1234.

22. Berdahl, J. L., & Moore, C. (2006). Workplace harassment: Double jeopardy for minority women. *Journal of Applied Psychology, 91*, 426–436.

23. Ghumman, S., & Ryan, A. M. (2013). Not welcome here: Discrimination towards women who wear the Muslim headscarf. *Human Relations, 66*, 671–698.

24. Locke, E. A. (1983). The nature and causes of job satisfaction. In M. D. Dunnette (Ed.) *Handbook of industrial and organizational psychology* (pp. 1297–1349). New York: John Wiley & Sons.

25. Arvey, R. D., Bouchard, T. J., Segal, N. L., & Abraham, L. M. (1989). Job satisfaction: Environmental and genetic components. *Journal of Applied Psychology, 74*, 187–192.

26. Staw, B.M., & Ross, J. (1985). Stability in the midst of change: A dispositional approach to job attitudes. *Journal of Applied Psychology, 70*, 469–480.

27. Bass, B. M., & Riggio, R. E. (2006). *Transformational leadership* (2nd ed.). New York: Psychology Press.

28. Kelloway, E. K., & Barling, J. (2000). What we have learned about developing transformational leaders. *Leadership and Organization Development Journal, 21*, 355–362.

29. Roberts, A. (2008, June 26). Nelson Mandela is a hero, but not a saint. *The Guardian*. Retrieved from http://www.guardian.co.uk/commentisfree/2008/jun/26/nelsonmandela.zimbabwe

30. Tucker, S., Turner, N., Barling, J., Reid, E., & Elving, C. (2006). Apologies and transformational leadership. *Journal of Business Ethics, 63*, 195–207.

31. Byrne, A., Barling, J., & Dupré, K. E. (2013). Leader apologies and employee and leader well-being. *Journal of Business Ethics*. DOI: 10.1007/s10551-013-1685-3.

32. Grant, A. M., & Gino, F. (2010). A little thanks goes a long way: Explaining why gratitude expressions motivate prosocial behavior. *Journal of Personality and Social Psychology, 98*, 946–955.

33. Kivimäki, M., Ferrie, J. E., Brunner, E., Head, J., Shipley, M. J., Vahtera, J., & Marmot, M. G. (2005). Justice at work and reduced risk of coronary heart disease among employees: The Whitehall II Study. *Archives of Internal Medicine, 165*, 2245–2251.

INDEX

Abuse Supervision Scale, 117
abusive supervision, 238–41
    depression and, 240
    petty tyrants and, 238–39, 239t
    within QC Mart, 238
    "trickle-down" effect of, 239
Abusive Supervision Questionnaire, 240f
Academy of Management Journal, 97
achievement, as personality variable, 136
Adams, Nancy, 64
Adams, Scott, 238
adolescents, leadership development in
    coaches and, 133–34
    environmental factors for, 129
    parental influences on, 131
    self-reports for, 132
advantageous comparisons, 244
African Americans, stereotype threat and,
    211
African National Congress (ANC), 124, 228
aggression, in workplace, 252
Agho, Augustine, 270
Aherne, Michael, 40
Aktas, Nihat, 48
Alban-Metcalfe, Robert, 115
alcoholism, from destructive leadership,
    259–60
Alimo-Metcalfe, Beverly, 115
Allen, Natalie, 69
Ames, Daniel, 50, 251
Amin, Idi, 186
ANC. *See* African National Congress
Anderson, Roy, 124
anger, in leaders, 284–85
Antonakis, John, 165
apologies, from leaders, 285–86
Apple, after death of CEO, 51–52
Arnold, Kara, 35
Aronson, Joshua, 211

Arvey, Richard, 129, 135
Ashforth, Blake, 238
at-the-elbow strategy, 147
attitudes, of employees
    organizational commitment and, 32–33
    well-being and, 33–37
Atwater, Leanne, 18, 291
audience engagement, 48
Auerbach, Red, 195
augmentation hypothesis, 9
authentic leadership
    employee commitment and, 32
    internalized moral perspective in, 13
    positive psychology approach to, 12
    relational transparency in, 12–13
    self-awareness in, 12
    unbiased information processing in, 12
authentic self, 13
autocratic leadership, 214–15
Avanzi, Lorenzo, 77
Avolio, Bruce, 77, 83, 110, 132–33, 151

Babad, Elisha, 22
Bacharach, Sam, 259
Bad Bosses, 238
bad leaders, 139–41, 237. *See also* destruc-
    tive leadership
    parental influences on, 140
    self-control for, 140
Ballinger, Gary, 53–54
Balthazard, Pierre, 141
Bamberger, Peter, 259
Bandura, Albert, 64–65, 139–40
    on moral disengagement, 243–45
    social learning theory, 140
Barling, Julian, 18–19, 34, 36–37, 40–41,
    84, 98, 151, 161, 246–48, 252, 256,
    272
Bartol, Kathryn, 75

Bartone, Paul, 106
Bartz, Carol, 300
Baseball: The Biographical Encyclopedia, 49
Bass, Bernie, 5–6, 74, 130, 246
Bass Handbook of Leadership: Theory,
 Research, and Managerial Applications
 (Bass), 6
Bayazit, Mahmut, 177
Bearman, Lori, 229
Beauchamp, Mark, 34, 189–91
behaviors, of leadership
 under autocratic leadership, 214–15
 contingent rewards and, 217
 under democratic leadership, 214–16
 employees and, 37–42
 with ethical leadership, 19–20
 fight-or-flight response, 212–13
 followership as influence on, 289–91
 future approaches to, 307–10
 gender and, 212–18
 genetic factors for, 138–39
 interventions for, 166
 under laissez-faire leadership, 213,
  215–18
 management, 2
 outcome targets, 308
 patience and, 308
 social pressures as influence on, 213
 stress, 212–13
 under task-oriented leadership, 214–15
 tend and befriend, 212–13
 under transactional leadership, 215–18
 in transformational leadership, 2, 215–18
 undermining, as destructive, 262
belongingness, followership and, 286–87
Beng Chong Lim, 85
Benson, George, 301
Berdahl, Jennifer, 213
Berson, Yair, 82
Beyer, Janice, 64
bias, by gender
 contemporary examples of, 221–22
 towards female leaders, 209–12,
  221–22
 future approaches to, 304–6
 global studies for, 210–11
 motivation to lead and, 210–12
 project type as factor, 221
 stereotype threat and, 211
Blair, Tony, 185–86, 249
Blake, Robert, 250
blame attribution, 245
Bligh, Michelle, 183, 279

Boeker, Warren, 280
Bono, Joyce, 4, 34, 98, 282
booster sessions, 167
Borgadus, Emory, 127
Bouchard, Thomas, 135
Bowlby, John, 131, 288
Branson, Douglas, 229
Brass, Daniel, 261
Braun, Susanne, 217
Brazil. *See* BRIC countries
Bregman, Nat, 125
Brescoll, Tori, 109
BRIC countries, 101–2
Brockner, Joel, 242
Bronfenbrenner, Urie, 130–32
Bruning, Roger, 64–65
Burch, Giles, 47
Bush, George W., 5, 183, 185–86, 249
 followership and, 274–78
Byrne, Alyson, 309

Cable, Daniel, 305
Canada, labor union leadership in, 177
capital. *See* human capital, development of
Caprara, Gian-Vittorio, 245
Carless, Sally, 115
Carli, Linda, 213
Carlson, Dawn, 262
Carsten, Melissa, 271, 273, 292
Caspi, Avi, 142
CEOs. *See* chief executive officers
CFOs. *See* chief financial officers
Cha, Sandra, 74
Chamberlain, Neville, 183
Chance, Zoë, 23
charisma hunger, 47, 184
 followership and, 276
charismatic leadership
 of CEOs, 45–47
 development of, 9–10
 goals of, 11
 interventions for, 150
 negative uses of, 10
 organizational commitment and, 32
 personalized, 11
 persuasiveness as factor in, 46
 political leadership and, 181–84
 positive uses of, 10
 of presidents, U.S., 45, 182, 184
 socialized, 10–11
 subjective assessment of, 11
 transformational compared to, 11
 vision as part of, 11

Chatterjee, Arijit, 48
Chatuverdi, Sankalp, 139
Chee Chow, 43
Chen, Gilad, 70, 76
Chen, Julie, 213
Chen, Tina, 272
Chew, Irene, 72
chief executive officers (CEOs)
    behavioral integration under, 43
    charisma of, 45–47
    compensation of, factors of, 46–47
    CSR and, 44–45
    death of, company performance influ-
        enced by, 51–54
    decentralization of responsibility under,
        43
    female, gender bias against, 209–12
    high-performance work systems and, 72
    hubris of, 49–51
    idealized influences for, 42
    leader role emergence and, 209
    management encouraged by, 43
    narcissism of, 47–49
    ownership status of, 80–81
    of privately-owned companies, 80
    of publicly-traded companies, 80
    public perception of, 41–42
    risk propensity assessment by, 43
    self-assessments by, 16
    servant leadership of, 16, 45, 47
    transformational leadership of, 42–45
chief financial officers (CFOs), 16
children, leadership development in. See
        also adolescents, leadership develop-
        ment in
    parents as influence on, 129–33
    self-reports for, 132
China. See BRIC countries
Christie, Amy, 98, 151, 246, 248, 272
Churchill, Winston, 183, 186, 269, 276
citizenship behaviors, 68
Clinton, Bill, 5, 124
coaches, 133–34
cognitive dissonance, 148
Cohen, Fiorette, 277
Cohn, Jeffrey, 299
collective efficacy, 66
Comer, James, 38
command-and-control leadership
    interventions for, 150
    in military, 181
communities, under servant leadership,
    16–17

conceptual drift, 15
Conchie, Stacey, 36
Conger, Jay, 11
consideration structure, 4
    employee commitment and, 32
contingency punishment, 39
contingency theories, for leadership,
    99
contingent rewards, 8
    leadership behaviors and, 217
continuance commitment, 69
Cook, Alison, 210
Cook, Tim, 52
Cooper, Cary, 128
Cornelis, Ilse, 287
corporate entrepreneurship, 43
corporate social responsibility (CSR),
    44–45
Costa, Paul, 281
Cox, Charles, 128
Cranfield Index, 111
creativity, destructive leadership influenced
    by, 257
Crossan, Mary, 81
CSR. See corporate social responsibility
Curtis, Bill, 106, 192

Danylchuk, Karen, 193
David, James, 75
Davidson, Jonathan, 51
Davies, Paul, 222
Dawson, Erica, 109
Day, David, 159, 272
death of CEOs, company performance
        influenced by, 51–54
    expected versus sudden, 52–53
    governance boards and, 53
    LMX relationships and, 54
    personal characteristics of CEO and,
        52
    for stakeholders, 52
    transaction costs of, 53
decision-making, CEO narcissism as influ-
        ence on, 48
De Cremer, David, 287
De Hoogh, Annabel, 87
dehumanization, 245
Deitch, Elizabeth, 305
democratic leadership, 214–16
De Neve, Jan-Emmanuel, 137
depression, 161
    abusive supervision and, 240
Desiderio, Katie, 33

destructive leadership
    abusive supervision and, 238–41
    alcoholism as result of, 259–60
    consequences of, 252–62
    counterproductive behavior and,
        253–54
    creativity influenced by, 257
    employee payback for, 252–55
    gender influences on, 258
    interactional injustice and, 241–43
    interpersonal sensitivity as factor in,
        253, 255–56
    interventions for, 151
    "kick the dog" phenomenon and,
        261–62
    laissez-faire leadership compared to,
        250
    mental health under, 260–61
    moral disengagement and, 254
    organizational performance under,
        256–57
    organizational withdrawal from,
        255–56
    passive-avoidant leadership as, 249–50
    physical health consequences of, 257–61
    in popular media, 238
    pseudo-transformational leadership as,
        246–48
    psychological health consequences of,
        257–61
    quality of leadership as influence on,
        251–52
    sexual harassment and, 252
    "trickle-down" effect of, 261
    undermining behaviors in, 262
    unethical behavior in, 243–49
    unfairness and, 241–43
    in unions, 259
    workplace aggression and, 252
Diallo, Amadou, 275
Dilbert, 238
displacement of responsibility, 244–45
distortion of consequences, 245
distributive fairness, 241
diversity training, 223–24
    legislative initiative, 226–30
    self-efficacy beliefs in, 223
Djibo, Idriss, 33
Doherty, Alison, 193
Donald, Ian, 36
Dong Jung, 77
downward extension hypothesis, 129
Duflo, Esther, 229

Dukerich, Janet, 279
Dunedin Multidisciplinary Health and
    Development Study, 142
Dunlop, (Chainsaw) Al, 291
Dupré, Kate, 309
Dvir, Taly, 110, 149, 180
Dykes, Christina, 300

Eagly, Alice, 205, 212–13, 215, 220
eclectic leadership, 180
The Economist, 155, 211
Eden, Anthony, 185
Eden, Dov, 22, 110, 153–54
educational leadership
    attitudes for, 189
    idealized influences on, 190
    as transactional leadership, 189
    as transformational leadership, 188–91
    Transformational Teaching
        Questionnaire, 191t
EEGs. See electroencephalograms
effectiveness, of leadership
    followership compared to, 270–71
    for intervention, 149–57
    for males, 218–21
    of organizations, 3
    social role theory and, 218
    for women, 218–21
Ehrlich, Sanford, 279
Elder, Glen, 111, 128–29
    downward extension hypothesis, 129
electroencephalograms (EEGs), 141–42
Elizabeth II (Queen), 275
Elkins, Teri, 250
Elovainio, Marko, 258
Emerson, Ralph Waldo, 285
empathy, leadership and, 177
employee commitment, to organizations.
        See also destructive leadership
    authentic leadership and, 32
    charismatic leadership and, 32
    consideration structure and, 32
    continuance, 69
    healthy employees and, 33–35
    LMX theory and, 32
    as normative, 69
    transformational leadership and, 69
    work experiences and, 68–70
employees. See also destructive leadership;
        self-perceptions, of followers; work
        experiences, of followers
    healthy, 33–35
    leadership behaviors and, 37–42

management transactions with, 4
sales performance of, 38–41
under servant leadership, 16
work engagement of, 70–72
Employment and Unemployment: A Social Psychological Analysis (Jahoda), 67
empowerment
through leadership, 40
transformational leadership and, 70
work experiences of followers and, 70–72
entrepreneurship. *See* corporate entrepreneurship
environmental factors, for leadership, 126–34
for adolescent males, 129
downward extension hypothesis, 129
early adversity as, 127–29
gender and, 127
genetic compared to, 134–39
Great Depression as, 128
for Mandela, N., 124
nonparental influences as, 133–34
parental influences as, 129–33
post-traumatic growth, 127
reverse causality in, 134
environmental-specific transformational leadership, 41
environmental sustainability, 41
Erev, Ido, 84
Erez, Miriam, 161
Erhart, Mark, 287
Ernst, William, 238–41, 239*t*
ethical leadership. *See also* unethical behavior
assessment of, 19–20, 117
care as part of, 18–19
LMX theory and, 78–79
moral reasoning as part of, 17–18
questionnaire for, 20*t*
self-efficacy beliefs and, 65
transformational leadership as, 18
universal behaviors as part of, 19–20
Ethical Leadership Questionnaire, 117
ethics of care, 18–19, 248
euphemistic labeling, 244
Europe, leadership studies in, 101
extroversion, of leaders, 283–84

family-friendly initiatives, for gender-diversity, 224–25
in private-sector organizations, 224

family influences, on leadership, for Mandela, N., 124
Fanelli, Angelo, 46
feedback. *See* 360-degree feedback
Fehr, Ryan, 285
Feingold, David, 301
Felfe, Jörg, 289
Fenly, Marika, 165
Fieldman, George, 259
fight-or-flight response, 212–13
Fincham, Frank, 51
Finnish 10-Town Cohort study, 259–60
Fischthal, Allison, 291
Flynn, Francis, 50, 251
fMRI. *See* functional magnetic reasoning imagery
followership
apologies and, 285–86
belongingness and, 286–87
Bush and, 274–78
charisma hunger and, 276
conceptions about, 270–74
effective leadership compared to, 270–71
implicit theories of, 271–74
leader personality and, 281–82
leadership and, 303–4
leadership behaviors influenced by, 289–91
leadership style preferences and, 287–89
in media, 278
media influence on, 278
mortality salience and, 276–78
personality of followers and, 287–89
psychology of, 269
self-construal in, 285–86
strongman role and, 291
subjectivity of, 274–81
360-degree feedback, 280–81
Fonda, Henry, 22
formal power
of labor union leadership, 176
in management, 2
Fortune 500 companies, women in, 204, 204*f*
Fortune 1000 companies, women in, 204, 204*f*
Framingham Heart study, 137–38
Francis, Lori, 36
Franklin, Benjamin, 127
Frey, Dieter, 217

Frost, Peter, 150
Fullagar, Clive, 178
functional magnetic reasoning imagery
    (fMRI), 141–42

Gadla, Henry, 124–25
Galvin, Benjamin, 16, 45
Gamson, William, 194
Gelfand, Michelle, 285
gender. *See also* males, as leaders; women,
    as leaders
    bias, towards female leaders, 209–12
    destructive leadership influenced by,
        258
    environmental factors for leadership
        and, 127
    genetic factors for leadership by,
        136–37
    glass cliff phenomenon and, 206–8
    interventions for gender-diversity,
        222–30
    interventions for leadership influenced
        by, 156–57, 162
    leader preferences and, 203–12
    leader role emergence and, 203–12
    leadership behaviors, 212–18
    in leadership studies, 99–100, 108
    sexism and, 207
    sexual harassment and, 213–14
    social role theory and, 218
    stereotypes, 207
gender bias. *See* bias, by gender
gender-diversity interventions, 222–30
    family-friendly initiatives for, 224–25
    legislative, 226–30, 228f
    mentorship programs for, 225–26
    self-efficacy beliefs in, 223
    training in, 223–24
genetic factors, for leadership, 134–39,
        306–7
    by gender, 136–37
    leader role occupancy and, 136–39
    in Minnesota Study of Twins Reared
        Apart, 135–36
    prediction of behaviors, 138–39
    social potency and, 136
    for transactional leadership, 139
    for transformational leadership,
        138–39
George, Lloyd, 186
Gerras, Stephen, 37
Gerstner, Wolf-Christian, 48–49
Ghaemi, Nassir, 187

Ghandi, Mahatma, 123
Ghumman, Sonia, 305
Gilligan, Carol, 18–19
Gino, Francesco, 84, 283, 303, 310
Giuliani, Rudy, 8, 274–75, 277
Gladstone, William, 127
Glass, Christy, 210
glass ceiling, 206
glass cliff phenomenon, 111
    gender and, 206–8
    in political leadership, 207–8
globalization, leadership influenced by, 83
Global Leadership and Organizational
        Effectiveness (GLOBE) study,
        102
Global Transformation Leadership Scale,
        115
GLOBE study. *See* Global Leadership and
        Organizational Effectiveness study
goal commitment, 68
Gogli, Larry, 85
Golem effect, 22
    implicit followership theories and, 274
Goodnight, Jim, 80
Goodwin, Doris Kearns, 128
Gordijn, Ernestine, 183
Gore, Al, 21
Gough Adjective Check List, 48
Graen, George, 14
Graham, Katherine, 204
Grant, Adam, 39, 67–68, 84, 283, 303, 310
Great Depression, 128
Greenberg, Jerald, 252
Greenleaf, Robert, 15
Griffin, Mark, 65
Grusky, Oscar, 194, 196
The Guardian, 309

Hackman, Richard, 67
Hall-Merenda, Kathryn, 38, 83
Hambrick, Donald, 48–49, 187
Hammer, Tove, 177
Hani, Chris, 125
Harris, Jeff, 131–32
Hartman, Sandra, 131–32
Haslam, Alex, 111, 206
Hausknecht, John, 242
Haythorn, William, 282
Hayward, Mathew, 51
Heilman, Madeline, 213, 221
Hemphill, John, 82
Hendrickse, Allen, 125
Hershcovis, Sandy, 252, 256

Hetland, Hilde, 288
Heuse, Morten, 227
high-performance work systems, 72
Hiller, Nathan, 187
Hitler, Adolf, 123, 186
    pseudo-transformational leadership
        of, 246
Ho, Geoffrey, 221
Hock-Peng Sin, 272
Hofmann, David, 37, 85, 283, 303
Hofstede, Geert, 102
Hogan Development Survey, 48
honeymoon effect, 115–17
Hoobler, Jenny, 261
Hood, Jacqueline, 44
Hoon Song, 71
Hoption, Colette, 98, 272
Hough, David, 208
House, Robert, 10, 102
Howell, Jane, 10, 38, 76, 83, 150
hubris, of CEOs, 49–51
    as counterproductive, 50
    ownership status as influence on, 81
    situational characteristics of, 51
hubris personality syndrome, 186–87
human capital, development of, 43, 72
Hunter, Sam, 289
Huselid, Mark, 72
Hussey, Trevor, 259
Hwee Khoo, 47

idealized influences, 6, 20–21
    for CEOs, 42
    on educational leadership, 190
    on pseudo-transformational leadership,
        246–47
Ilies, Remus, 137
implicit followership theories, 271–74
    Golem effect and, 274
    labeling and, 272–73
    Pygmalion effect and, 273–74
    social traditions as influence on, 271
Inbar, Jacinto, 22
India. See also BRIC countries
    legislative initiatives for diversity in,
        229
individualized consideration, 7–8, 23–24
informal power, 2
initiating structures, 4
injustice
    employee theft as result of, 254f
    interactional, 241–43
    interpersonal, 242–43

Inness, Michelle, 36
In Sickness and in Power (Owen), 185
inspirational motivation, 7, 21–22, 247–48
intellectual stimulation, 7, 22–23
    pseudo-transformational leadership
        and, 247
    sales performance and, 39
intelligence, leadership and, 7
interpersonal injustice, 242–43
interpersonal sensitivity, 253, 255–56
interpersonal unfairness, 242
interventions, for leadership
    adult models for, 147
    assessment measures for, 148–49
    at-the-elbow strategy in, 147
    behavioral changes and, 166
    booster sessions in, 167
    for charismatic leadership, 150
    cognitive dissonance and, 148
    with command-and-control manage-
        ment styles, 150
    comparative, 160
    for destructive leadership, 151
    development initiatives for, 156–57
    diversity training as, 223–24
    dose-dependence in, 164–65
    effectiveness of, 149–57
    family-friendly initiatives as, 224–25
    field studies for, 151–53
    in for-profit organizations, 155
    future applications in, 167
    for gender-diversity, 222–30
    gender influences on, 156–57, 162
    laboratory studies for, 150–51
    leader position as influence on, 155
    mentorship programs as, 225–26
    motivation to learn as, 163
    nonspecific factors for, 161–63
    in not-for-profit organizations, 155
    by organization type, 154–56
    outcomes as influence on, 154
    participant benefits from, 163–64
    post-intervention research on, 166–67
    preselection of individuals for, 158–59
    preselection of organizations for,
        159–60
    presenter/participant relationship and,
        161–63
    psychological distress from, 158
    psychotherapy compared to, 157–58,
        161–63
    relapse prevention in, 165–66
    renewal of, 157–58

interventions, for leadership (*Cont.*)
   RODI and, 152–53, 165
   self-reported learning for, 149
   skill decay and, 150
   stereotype threat and, 222–23
   technological necessities for, 162
   theories for, 153–54, 160–61
   transfer of training in, 163
   for transformational leadership, 149, 155–56
   wait-list control groups for, 160
   workplace context and, 163
   workplace initiatives as, 222–26
intrinsic motivation, 68
investors, leader role emergence and, 208–10

Jackson, Timothy, 69
Jahoda, Marie, 67
James, Erika, 209
Javidan, Mansour, 45
Jianyun Tang, 81
Jiatao Li, 51, 81
Jiayan Liu, 104
Jobs, Steve, 51–52
job satisfaction, 306
Johannesen-Schmidt, Mary, 215
Johnsen, Tom, 288
Johnson, Andrew, 139
Johnson, Blair, 212
Johnson, Lyndon, 186
Johnson, Stefanie, 273
Journal of Applied Psychology, 97
Journal of Organizational Behavior, 97
Judge, Timothy, 4, 13, 47, 98, 112, 282, 305
Jung, Don, 43

Kahn, Robert, 305
Kahneman, Daniel, 161
Kalinoski, Zachary, 223
Kan Shi, 104
Kanter, Rosabeth Moss, 124
Kanungo, Rabindra, 11
Karau, Steven, 205
Kark, Ronit, 76
Katz, Daniel, 305
Kaunda, Kenneth, 125
Keller, Tiffany, 270
Kelley, R. E., 269
Kelloway, Kevin, 34, 36–37, 40, 84, 132
   goal-setting research, 161
   on transformational leadership, 177

Kennedy, John F., 5, 24, 185–86
Kerry, John, 277–78
Khama, Seretse, 125
"kick the dog" phenomenon, 261–62
Kiewitz, Christian, 140, 240
Kirkpatrick, Shelley, 107, 150
Kivimäki, Mika, 241, 258
Klandermans, Bert, 175
Klein, Katherine, 287
Klonsky, Bruce, 220
Koh, William, 189
Kohlberg, Lawrence, 17, 99
Kohles, Jeffrey, 183, 279
Koning, Ruud, 195
Kornhauser, Arthur, 260
Kotter, John, 2
Kouvonen, Anne, 259–60
Kroeck, Galen, 155
Kulich, Clara, 208

labeling, implicit followership and, 272–73
labor union leadership, 100–101, 175–79
   in Canada, 177
   as democratic organizations, 176
   as destructive, 259
   formal power of, 176
   positive attitudes toward, 178
   from sense of obligation, 176
   shop stewards, 176–78
   socialization of, 178–79
   among teachers, 177
laissez-faire leadership
   behaviors of, 213, 215–18
   destructive leadership compared to, 250
   pseudo-transformational leadership compared to, 247*t*
   sales performance under, 38
   transactional leadership and, 8–9
Lam, Simon, 74
Lange, Donald, 16, 45
Lay, Ken, 49
leader-member exchange (LMX) theory
   contingency theories in, 99
   death of CEOs as influence on, 54
   employee commitment and, 32
   ethical leadership and, 78–79
   leader-member exchanges, 14–15, 37
   in leadership studies, 99
   passive-avoidant leadership and, 250
   quality of relationships in, 14
   self-efficacy beliefs and, 65
   supervisor-subordinate dyads in, 78
leader-member relationships, 74–79

dyads in, 14–15, 37
trust in leader as part of, 75–76
value congruence of, 77–78
leader preferences, gender and, 203–12
leader role emergence
CEOs and, 209
field studies on, 205–6
gender and, 203–12
investors as influence on, 208–10
leader role occupancy, 136–39
family experiences as influence on, 137
leaders. *See also* bad leaders; chief executive
officers; followership
anger in, 284–85
apologies from, 285–86
extroversion of, 283–84
in organizations, 31–41
personality of, followership influenced
by, 281–82
pseudo-transformational, 151
selection criteria for, 299–301
trust in, as dynamic of relationship,
75–76
leadership. *See also* environmental factors,
for leadership; interventions, for
leadership; leadership studies; *specific
styles of leadership*
behaviors for, 2
CEO ownership status and, 80–81
characteristics of, 79–80
charisma as predictor for, 182
complexity of, 1
consideration structure in, 4
contingency theories for, 99
definitions of, 1–2
development of, 301–3
effectiveness of, 3, 218–21
effects of, length of time for, 87–88
empathy and, 177
employee behaviors and, 37–42
as empowering, 40
evidence-based management approach
to, 2
external environment as influence on,
86–87
followership and, 303–4
globalization as influence on, 83
informal power of, 2
initiating structure in, 4
intelligence and, 7
management compared to, 2
maximum performance contexts for, 85
mediators and, 63–64

military, 110
moderating factors for, 79–87
negative, 73
newer theories, 153
organizational context for, 82–86
organizational size as influence on, 79,
82–83
outcomes influenced by, 63–64
physical distance as influence on, 83–84
positive, 34
as process, 64*f*
psychotherapy and, 303
Pygmalion theories of, 153–54
quality of, 3
reluctant, 176
role emergence of, 2
romance of, 279–81
safety climate and, 85–86
theories in research, 5–6, 5*f*
traditional theories, 153
training for, 301–3
12 Angry Men as teaching tool, 22–23
in union, 100–101
Leadership (McGregor Burns), 5
*Leadership, Psychology and Organizational
Behavior* (Bass), 130
*Leadership and Performance Beyond
Expectations* (Bass), 6
leadership behaviors. *See* behaviors, of
leadership
Leadership Quarterly, 97
leadership studies
archival research for, 111–12
in BRIC countries, 101–2
cross-national studies in, 101–3
cross-sectional data for, 105–7
databases of, 97
EEGs in, 141–42
in Europe, 101
experimental research for, 107–11
field research for, 109–11
fMRIs in, 141–42
future applications of, 141–43
gender as factor in, 99–100, 108
for gender bias, 210–11
GLOBE, 102
laboratory experiments for, 107–8
on leader role emergence, 205–6
literature for, 97
LMX theory in, 99
longitudinal data for, 105–7
by management level, 100–101
measurement issues in, 114–17

leadership studies (*Cont.*)
   meta-analysis of, 112–13
   methodological challenges for, 106
   organizational context as factor
      in, 103
   presidential inaugural speeches in, 111
   qualitative research for, 113–14
   for SMEs, 103
   supervisors in, 100–101
   survey research for, 104–5
   theories in, 98–99
   training as influence on, 110
   unions in, 100–101
   in United Kingdom, 101
   vignette studies, 109
Leavitt, Harold, 179
Lee, Peggy, 209
Lee, Robert E., 127
Lehman, David, 53
Levinson, Harry, 260
Liden, Robert, 15–16
Liechti, Sue, 165
Lippitt, Ronald, 147
LMX theory. *See* leader-member exchange
   theory
Locke, Ed, 75, 107, 150
Loeb, Daniel, 300
Logan, Gina, 289
Loughlin, Catherine, 36
Lowe, Kevin, 155
Lule, Yusuf, 125
Luria, Gil, 84

Macazoma, Saki, 228
Machel, Graça, 309
MacKenzie, Scott, 9
Majchrzak, Ann, 84
Makhijani, Mona, 219
males, as leaders
   effectiveness of, 218–21
   physical attractiveness as influence on,
      217
   social role theory and, 218
   stress behaviors for, 212
   as task-oriented, 206
males, in middle management, 220
management
   behaviors, 2
   formal power for, 2
   leadership compared to, 2
   in leadership studies, by level, 100–101
   safety-specific training in, 37
   transactions with employees, 4

management-by-exception, 8
managers, transformational leadership of,
   2, 77
Mandela, Nelson, 24, 123–26, 309
   ANC and, 124
   environmental factors for, 124
   family influences on, 124
Mandela, Winnie, 21
Mann, Leon, 115
Marmot, Michael, 258
Maslow, Abraham, 6, 286
Mathieu, John, 40
Mawritz, Mary Bardes, 261
May, Douglas, 12
Mayer, Roger, 75
Mayo, Margarita, 280
Mbeki, Govan, 125
McCann, Stewart, 183
McCoy, Don, 178
McCrae, Robert, 281
McDermott, Rose, 185
McGregor Burns, James, 1, 5–6, 246
McNeilly, Kevin, 38
McNulty, Jim, 50
meaningfulness of work, 67–68
   transformational leadership and, 68
media
   destructive leadership in, 238
   followership in, 278
   stereotypes in, 211
mediators, leadership and, 63–64
Meindl, James, 183, 279
mental health, under destructive leadership, 260–61
mentorship programs, for gender-diversity,
   225–26
Meyer, John, 69
Meyer, Marissa, 300
Mhlaba, Raymond, 125
middle management level, in leadership
   studies, 100–101
   males at, 220
   women at, 220
military leadership, 110
   as command-and-control, 181
   domain research for, 180
   as eclectic, 180
   theories of, 179–80
Minnesota Study of Twins Reared Apart,
   135–36
Mio, Jeffery Scott, 111
Misangyi, Vilmos, 46
Mitterand, Francois, 185

MLQ. *See* Multifactor Leadership
　Questionnaire
Mogilner, Cassie, 23
Mohrman, Susan, 301–2
moral disengagement, 243–46
　advantageous comparisons in, 244
　Bandura and, 243–45
　blame attribution and, 245
　dehumanization and, 245
　destructive leadership and, 254
　displacement of responsibility and,
　　244–45
　distortion of consequences and, 245
　euphemistic labeling and, 244
moral justification, 244
moral perspective, in authentic leadership,
　13
moral reasoning
　in ethical leadership, 17–18
　as theory, 99
　unethical behavior and, 248
Moran, Jay, 299
Morton, Katie, 191
Motsepe, Patrice, 228
Mouton, Jane, 250
Mugabe, Robert, 125, 186
Mullen, Jane, 36–37
Multifactor Leadership Questionnaire
　(MLQ), 114–15, 248
Murnighan, Keith, 249
My Fair Lady, 22

Nader, Ralph, 7
narcissism, of CEOs, 47–49
　audience engagement and, 48
　decision-making influenced by, 48
　transformational leadership influenced
　　by, 48
Narcissistic Personality Inventory, 48
National Longitudinal Sample of
　Adolescent Health, 137
National Longitudinal Survey of Youth,
　129
need hierarchy theory, 6, 286
negative leadership, 73
　charismatic leadership as, 10
Nelson, Erland, 126
Neubert, Mitchell, 16
Neufeld, Derrick, 83
new-genre leadership theory, 4. *See also*
　specific leadership styles
Nielsen, Karina, 35
Nielsen, Sabina, 227

9/11 attacks, followership in U.S. after,
　274–78
Nixon, Richard, 185–86
normative commitment, 69
Northouse, Peter, 1
Norton, Michael, 23
not-for-profit organizations, 155
Nyberg, Anna, 255, 258–59
Nyere, Julius, 125

Oakland Growth Study, 111, 128
Obama, Barack, 183, 304
O'Brien, Conan, 253–56, 262
O'Connor, Jennifer, 10
Oi-Ling Siu, 104
Okimoto, Tyler, 221
Oldham, Greg, 67
On War (von Clausewitz), 249
organizational leadership
　development of, 3–4
　history of, 1
organizational size, leadership influenced
　by, 79, 82–83
organizations. *See also* communities; safety,
　within organizations
　authentic leadership within, commit-
　　ment attitudes affected by, 32
　charismatic leadership within, commit-
　　ment attitudes affected by, 32
　consideration structure and, commit-
　　ment attitudes affected by, 32
　effectiveness of, 3
　employee attitudes within, 32–33
　environmental sustainability within, 41
　interventions for leadership and,
　　159–60
　leaders in, 31–41
　LMX theory and, commitment attitudes
　　affected by, 32
　not-for-profit, 155
　transformational leadership within,
　　commitment attitudes affected by,
　　32
Osofsky, Michael, 244
Owen, David, 185–86, 249

parents
　bad leaders influenced by, 140
　leadership development influenced by,
　　129–33
Parr, Alissa, 289
Parsons, Talcott, 10
Partridge, DeAlton, 303

passive-avoidant leadership, 249–50
  LMX theory and, 250
Pastor, Juan Carlos, 280
Paul, Gordon, 157
payback, by employees, 252–55
personality, of leaders, 281–85
  achievement variable in, 136
  anger and, 284–85
  extroversion, 283–84
  hubris personality syndrome, 186–87
  Narcissistic Personality Inventory, 48
  in transformational leadership, 282
personalized charismatic leaders, 11
persuasiveness, in charismatic leadership, 46
Peterson, Suzanne, 16, 45
petty tyrants, 238–39, 239t
Peus, Claudia, 217
Phillips, James, 250
physical distance, leadership influenced by,
    83–84
Piaget, jean, 17
Piccolo, Ronald, 112
Pillai, Rajnandini, 182, 279
Pillutla, Madan, 249
Pliskin, Nava, 241
Ployhart, Robert, 85
Podsakoff, Phillip, 9, 83, 115
political leadership. See also presidents, U.S.
  charisma in, 181–84
  core self-evaluations for, 187
  gender-diversity interventions for,
    226–30, 228f
  glass cliff phenomenon in, 207–8
  hubris personality syndrome and,
    186–87
  in India, 229
  mental health of leaders, 184–88
  personal power in, 182
  physical health of leaders, 184–88
  in South Africa, 228
  as transformational, 181–84
  of U.S. presidents, 182
Pol Pot, 123, 186
Popper, Micha, 288
positive psychology, in authentic leader-
    ship, 12
Postmes, Tom, 207
post-traumatic growth, 127
Potts, Malcolm, 50
Powell, Michael, 275
power. See also formal power
  abuse of, 248–49
  informal, 2

preferences. See leader preferences
Presidential Leadership, Illness, and Decision
    Making (McDermott), 185
presidents, U.S. See also specific presidents
  charisma of, 45, 182, 184
  inaugural speeches of, in leadership
    studies, 111
  political leadership of, 182
Price, Norience, 33
procedural fairness, 241
Prottas, David, 257
pseudo-transformational leadership, 151
  core components of, 248
  as destructive leadership, 246–48
  Hitler problem of, 246
  idealized influence in, 246–47
  inspirational motivation in, 247–48
  intellectual stimulation and, 247
  laissez-faire leadership compared to,
    247t
  transactional leadership and, 248
  transformational leadership compared
    to, 247t
psychotherapy
  early exits from, 158
  leadership and, 303
  leadership interventions compared to,
    157–58, 161–63
  therapist/patient relationship in, 162
publicly-traded companies
  CEOs of, 80
  women as leaders in, 209
Pygmalion (Shaw), 22
Pygmalion effect
  implicit followership theories and,
    273–74
  in leadership, 153–54

QC Mart, abusive supervision within,
    238–41, 239t

Rafferty, Alannah, 65, 68
Ramaphosa, Cyril, 228
relapse prevention, in leadership interven-
    tions, 165–66
relational transparency, in authentic lead-
    ership, 12–13
reluctant leadership, 176
Resick, Christian, 44
resilience gene, 142
Restubog, Simon, 68
return on development investment (RODI),
    152–53, 165

Rich, Gregory, 9
Riley, Pat, 195
Roberson, Quinetta, 242
Roberts, Adam, 309
RODI. *See* return on development investment
Roll, Richard, 51
Romm, Celia, 241
Romney, Mitt, 21
Roosevelt, Eleanor, 124, 186–87
Roosevelt, Franklin D., 8, 124, 185–86
Roosevelt: Soldier of Freedom 1940-1945 (McGregor Burns), 5
Rosenthal, Robert, 22
Rost, Joseph, 1
Rotundo, Maria, 132
Roush, Paul, 291
Rowe, Glenn, 81
Russ, Frederick, 38
Russia. *See* BRIC countries
Ryan, Anne Marie, 305
Ryan, Michelle, 111, 206

Sackett, Paul, 85
safety, within organizations
  leadership and, 85–86
  management training for, 37
  transformational leadership and, 36
  for well-being of employees, 35–37
  work experiences of followers and, 73
safety-specific transformational leadership, 36–37, 73
Salanova, Marisa, 71
sales performance, of employees, 38–41
  contingent punishment for, 39
  intellectual stimulation and, 39
  under laissez-faire leadership, 38
  under transactional leadership, 38–40
  under transformational leadership, 38–40, 40*f*
Sandal, Gro, 288
Sandler, Marion O., 204
Schachter, Stanley, 213
Schaubroeck, John, 74
Schoel, Christiane, 288
schools. *See* educational leadership
Schoorman, David, 53, 75
Schyns, Birgit, 289
Scotch, Norman, 194
Sealy, Ruth, 227
self-actualization theory, 6, 286
self-awareness, in authentic leadership, 12

self-control, in bad leaders, 140
self-efficacy beliefs, 64–66
  as collective, 66
  development factors for, 65
  in diversity training, 223
  ethical leadership and, 65
  LMX theory and, 65
  transformational leadership and, 65
  visionary leadership and, 65
self-perceptions, of followers
  employee mood, 66–67
  through self-efficacy beliefs, 64–66
Seligman, Martin, 184
The Servant as Leader (Greenleaf), 15
servant leadership
  of CEOs, 16, 45, 47
  CFOs under, 16
  characteristics of, 15
  community health and, 16–17
  conceptual drift in, 15
  employee development under, 16
Servant Leadership: A Journey into the Nature of Legitimate Power and Greatness (Greenleaf), 15
sexism, gender and, 207
sexual harassment, 213–14
  destructive leadership and, 252
Sexwale, Tokyo, 228
Shah of Iran, 184
Shakespeare, William, 123
Shalit, Alon, 288
Shamir, Boas, 76, 110, 280
Shaw, George Bernard, 22
Shih, Margaret, 221
shop stewards, 176–78
  transformational leadership of, 177
Shull, Carla, 178
Sidelsky, Lazar, 125
Silvester, Jo, 300
Simola, Sheldene, 19
Simon, Linda, 278
Simonton, Dean Keith, 7
Singh, Val, 227
Sisulu, Walter, 125
Sivanathan, Niro, 249
Sivasubramaniam, Nagaraj, 155
skill decay, 150
Skinner, B. F., 123, 279
small and medium enterprises (SMEs), 44
  leadership studies for, 103
  survey research for, 104–5
SMEs. *See* small and medium enterprises

Smith, Ronald, 192
Smoll, Frank, 192
Snyder, Elise, 162
Sobukwe, Robert, 125
socialized charismatic leaders, 10–11
social learning theory, 140
social potency, 136
social role theory, 218
Song, Zhaoli, 129
South Africa. *See also* BRIC countries;
    Mandela, Nelson
    ANC in, 124, 228
    legislative initiatives for diversity, 228
Spangler, William, 72
Spears, Larry, 15
Spencer, Steven, 222
sports leadership
    changes in, as influence, 194–96
    departures of coaches and, 194–95
    through instruction, 193
    international influences on, 194–95
    passive, 193
    through punitive techniques, 193
    as transactional leadership, 193
    as transformational leadership, 192–94
sports performance, 192–94
Srivastava, Abhishek, 75
Stalin, Joseph, 123, 186
Stapel, Diederik, 183
Steele, Claude, 211, 222
Steers, Richard, 189
stereotypes
    by gender, 207
    in media, 211
stereotype threat, 211
    in workplace initiatives, 222–23
Strauss, Karoline, 65, 69
stress
    female behaviors under, 213
    male behaviors under, 212
Stride Rite Corporation, 224
strongman role, 291
Sturman, Michael, 242
supervisors, in leadership studies,
    100–101
Swimming with Sharks, 238
Sy, Thomas, 271, 273

Tambo, Oliver, 125
task-oriented leadership, 214–15
task performance, 68
Taylor, Scott, 40
Taylor, Shelley, 212

teachers, labor union leadership
    among, 177
teaching of leadership. *See* interventions,
    for leadership
tend and befriend behaviors,
    212–13
Tepper, Bennett, 238–41
Terborg, James, 189
Terjeson, Siri, 227
Terpstra, David, 148
Tetrick, Lois, 80
Thatcher, Margaret, 186
Thompson, Scott, 300
360-degree feedback, 280–81
Time Magazine, 275–76
TLI. *See* Transformational Leader Behavior
    Inventory
too-much-of-a-good-thing
    phenomenon, 71
top management level, in leadership stud-
    ies, 100–101
Tosi, Henry, 46, 87
Towler, Annette, 131
Townsend, Joellyn, 250
traditional leadership. *See* eclectic
    leadership
training
    for gender-diversity, 223–24
    for leadership, 301–3
    leadership studies influenced by,
    110
    safety-specific, for management,
    37
transaction
    costs of, 53
    between managers and employees, 4
transactional leadership
    augmentation hypothesis and, 9
    behaviors under, 215–18
    contingent reward in, 8
    educational leadership as, 189
    genetic factors for, 139
    laissez-faire behavior in, 8–9
    management-by-exception in, 8
    pseudo-transformational leadership
    and, 248
    sales performance under, 38–40
    sports leadership as, 193
    transformational compared to, 9
    transformational leadership and, 248
Transformational Leader Behavior
    Inventory (TLI), 115, 116*t*
transformational leadership

augmentation hypothesis and, 9
behaviors under, 2, 215–18
CEO narcissism as influence on, 48
of CEOs, 42–45
charismatic compared to, 11
CSR under, 44–45
cultural applications of, 20–24
educational leadership as, 188–91
employee commitment to organizations and, 69
empowerment and, 70
ethical leadership as, 18
future-orientation of, 8
Golem effect under, 22
group-focused, 76
human capital development under, 43
idealized influence in, 6, 20–21
individualized consideration in, 7–8, 23–24
inspirational motivation in, 7, 21–22, 247–48
intellectual stimulation and, 7, 22–23
intelligence and, 7
interventions for, 149, 155–56
of managers, 2, 77
meaningfulness of work and, 68
neuroscientific foundations for, 142
organizational commitment and, 32, 69
personality as influence on, 282
political leadership as, 181–84
prediction behaviors for, 138–39
pseudo-transformational, 151, 246–48, 247t
safety-specific, 36–37, 73
sales performance under, 38–40, 40f
self-efficacy beliefs and, 65
of shop stewards, 177
within SMEs, 44
sports leadership as, 192–94
sports performance and, 192–94
trait theories for, 7
transactional compared to, 9
transactional leadership and, 248
Transformational Teaching Questionnaire, 191t
Transformation Leadership Questionnaire, 115
"trickle-down" effect
of abusive supervision, 239
of destructive leadership, 261
Truman, Harry, 185–86
trust, in leaders, 75–76
Tucker, Sean, 133

Turner, Nick, 18–19, 151, 246, 248
Tutu, Desmond, 21, 309
Twelfth Night (Shakespeare), 123
12 Angry Men, 22–23

Uhl-Bien, Mary, 273
Uhlmann, Eric, 109
unethical behavior, 243–49
abuse of power and, 248–49
moral disengagement as, 243–46
moral reasoning and, 248
unfairness, in workplace, 241–43
interpersonal, 242
unions. See labor union leadership
United Kingdom, leadership studies in, 101

van Engen, Marloes, 215
van Hiel, Alain, 287
Van Kleef, Gerben, 284–85
van Zeist, Raymond, 177
Varella, Paul, 45
Vinkenburg, Claartje, 216
vision, in charismatic leadership, 11
visionary leadership, 65
von Clausewitz, Carl, 249

Wachner, Linda, 204
Wagar, Nadia, 259
Waldman, David, 45, 86
Wall Street Journal, 225
Walters, Daniel, 221
Walumbwa, Fred, 13, 78–79, 132
Wang, Frank, 69, 76
Washington, George, 127
Wazeter, David, 177
Wearing, Alexander, 115
Webb, Beatrice, 128
Weber, Max, 10
Weber, Tom, 40
Weichun Zhu, 72
well-being, of employees
under destructive leadership, 257–61
healthy employees and, 33–35
positive leadership and, 34
safety factors for, 35–37
Weng-Dong Li, 129
Westerlund, Hugo, 255
Whitely, Paul, 273
Why Are We Bad at Picking Good Leaders? (Cohn and Moran), 299
Willer, Robb, 278
Williams, Andy, 3
Williams, Ethlyn, 182

Williams, Joan, 222
Williams, Stanley, 179
Wilson, Woodrow, 127, 185–86
women, as leaders
    effectiveness of, 218–21
    in Fortune 500 companies, 204, 204f
    in Fortune 1000 companies, 204, 204f
    gender bias against, 209–12, 221–22
    glass cliff phenomenon for, 206–8
    on governance boards, 226–30
    in lower status positions, 204
    in middle management, 220
    physical attractiveness as influence on,
        217
    in publicly-traded companies, 209
    role models for, 229
    social role theory and, 218
    stereotype threat and, 211
    stereotypical characteristics of, 207
    stress behaviors for, 213
    under-representation in leadership
        positions, 204
work engagement, 70–72
    too-much-of-a-good-thing phenomenon
        and, 71

work experiences, of followers
    employee engagement as part of,
        70–72
    empowerment and, 70–72
    high-performance work systems, 72
    meaningfulness of work, 67–68
    organizational commitment and,
        68–70
    potency of, 74
    safety climate and, 73
    team cohesion and, 74
Wu, Anne, 43

Yi Tang, 51, 81
Ylipaavalniemi, Jaana, 260

Zacharatos, Anthea, 132
Zakay, Dan, 288
Zaki, Jamil, 141
Zedeck, Sheldon, 85
Zhen Zhang, 137
Zimbardo, Philip, 244
Zohar, Dov, 73, 84
Zsolnai, Laszio, 245
Zullow, Harold, 184